Transaction Accounting

Transaction Accounting
for NVQ Level 2 Units 1 and 2

Frank Wood
and
Sheila Robinson

NVQ U1013779 Recording and Accounting for Cash Transactions
NVQ U1019100 Recording and Accounting for Credit Transactions

FINANCIAL TIMES
PITMAN PUBLISHING

FINANCIAL TIMES
MANAGEMENT

LONDON · SAN FRANCISCO
KUALA LUMPUR · JOHANNESBURG

*Financial Times Management delivers the knowledge,
skills and understanding that enable students,
managers and organisations to achieve their ambitions,
whatever their needs, wherever they are.*

London Office:
128 Long Acre, London WC2E 9AN
Tel: +44 (0)171 447 2000
Fax: +44 (0)171 240 5771
Website: www.ftmanagement.com

A Division of Financial Times Professional Limited

First published in Great Britain in 1998

© Financial Times Professional Limited 1998

The right of Frank Wood and Sheila Robinson to be identified
as authors of this work has been asserted by them in accordance
with the Copyright, Designs and Patents Act 1988.

ISBN 0 273 61349 9

British Library Cataloguing in Publication Data
A CIP catalogue record for this book can be obtained from the British Library

10 9 8 7 6 5 4 3 2 1

Typeset by Land & Unwin (Data Sciences) Ltd, Northampton
Printed and bound in Great Britain by Bell and Bain Ltd, Glasgow

The Publishers' policy is to use paper manufactured from sustainable forests.

Contents

Part 4 OTHER CONSIDERATIONS AND SUPPORTING TOPICS

Part 5 PRACTICE ASSESSMENTS AND MULTIPLE-CHOICE QUESTIONS

Full contents

**Part 5 PRACTICE ASSESSMENTS AND
MULTIPLE-CHOICE QUESTIONS**

Preface

This textbook has been written with three main objectives.

First, to meet the requirements of the Lead Body for Accounting at NVQ Level 2 in transaction accounting. It is intended to provide students with the knowledge and understanding required in the following units:

- Unit 1: Recording and accounting for cash transactions;

- Unit 2: Recording and accounting for credit transactions.

The Association of Accounting Technicians (AAT) requires students to demonstrate competence in these units as part of their Foundation Certificate. Edexcel (formerly BTEC) also requires demonstration of competence in the two units as part of their Accounting qualification at NVQ Level 2.

Second, to provide knowledge and understanding for students undertaking the following courses:

- Association of Accounting Technicians (AAT): Diploma in Accounting (non-UK students only);

- Association of Chartered Certified Accountants (ACCA): Certified Accounting Technician (CAT).

Third, for other accounting courses where a basic knowledge and understanding of bookkeeping is required and for training staff where there is no requirement to gain a qualification. The book can also be used as a guide for people working in financial departments who are actually involved in accounting transactions.

The book centres on the requirements of the two NVQ units, mentioned above, in Parts 2 and 3. Other topics have been included since they are needed when undertaking accounting transactions: for example, double entry in Chapters 4 and 5.

The AAT education and training scheme requires that students undertake assessments, which they call 'Devolved Assessments', in certain topics at Foundation Level. The scheme also requires that students undertake a Central Assessment which embraces a number of units at this level.

As a consequence Part 3 includes a chapter on the basic law of contract while Part 4 includes a chapter on communicating for accounting. Students will need to study these additional topics, together with the business administration units, before undertaking the AAT Central Assessment. Part 4 also includes a chapter on payroll procedures.

Part 5 contains practice assessments which have been devised to simulate the AAT Central Assessment and the ACCA multi-choice assessments. Students attempting these will gain a valuable indication as to their competence and readiness for undertaking either the AAT or ACCA assessments.

Each chapter includes a list of new terms with a series of Student Activities which can be used by students to assess their progress.

Where examining bodies have given permission for past questions to be included this has been acknowledged. In other instances, questions have been devised to reflect the type of questions normally used by examining bodies.

Where a question has been marked with the suffix 'X', e.g. 3.2X, the answers to such questions will be found in a separate answer book *Transaction Accounting Lecturer's Guide* which will be supplied free to lecturers on request to the publishers.

Matrix of subjects covered and examining bodies

Chapters	Subjects covered	AAT Foundation NVQ 2	AAT Diploma in Accounting: Foundation	ACCA Certified Accounting Tech: Level A	BTEC GNVQ	IAB Foundation	LCCI First Level	Pitman Qualifications Levels 1 & 2
	PART 1 INTRODUCTION TO ACCOUNTING							
1–8	Double entry to trial balance	✓	✓	✓	✓	✓	✓	✓
9	Division of the ledgers	✓	✓	✓	×	✓	✓	✓
	PART 2 UNIT 1: RECORDING AND ACCOUNTING FOR CASH TRANSACTIONS							
10	Banking system	✓	✓	✓	✓	✓	✓	✓
11/24	Cash book	✓	✓	✓	✓	✓	✓	✓
12	Handling receipts of money	✓	✓	✓	✓	✓	✓	✓
13	Recording outgoing payments	✓	✓	✓	✓	✓	✓	✓
14	Bank reconciliation	✓	✓	✓	✓	✓	✓	✓
15	Petty cash	✓	✓	✓	✓	✓	✓	✓
	PART 3 UNIT 2: RECORDING AND ACCOUNTING FOR CREDIT TRANSACTIONS							
16	Law of contract							
17	Capital and revenue expenditure	✓	✓	✓	✓	✓	✓	✓
18	Documents used in buying and selling	✓	✓	✓	✓	✓	✓	✓
19/24	Sales day book/sales ledger	✓	✓	✓	✓	✓	✓	✓
20/24	Purchases day book/purchases ledger	✓	✓	✓	✓	✓	✓	✓
21/24	Returns day books	✓	✓	✓	✓	✓	✓	✓
22	Further considerations of sales and purchases	✓	✓	✓	✓	✓	✓	✓
23	Value added tax (sales tax)	✓	✓	✓	✓	✓	✓	✓
25	Control accounts	✓	✓	✓	×	×	✓	✓
26	Reconciling ledger accounts	✓	✓	✓	✓	✓	✓	✓
27	Journal	✓	✓	✓	×	✓	✓	✓
	PART 4 OTHER CONSIDERATIONS AND TOPICS							
28	Payroll procedures	✓	✓	✓	✓	✓	×	×
29	Communicating for Accounting	✓	✓	✓	✓	*	*	*
	PART 5 PRACTICE ASSESSMENTS AND MULTIPLE-CHOICE QUESTIONS							
30	Practice assessments – cash and credit transactions	✓	✓	✓	†	†	†	†
31	Multiple-choice questions	✓	✓	✓	†	†	†	†

* Topics marked thus are not a specific requirement of the particular examining body but Communicating for Accounting is a general competence desirable for all students.

† The assessment format is different for these examining bodies but attempting these practice assessments and multiple-choice questions can provide additional competence.

Note: As syllabuses do change from time to time, check that the above details still apply to your examinations.

Part

1

Introduction to accounting

1 How to use this book

The book covers the specific requirements of both Unit 1 and Unit 2 which are shown in the preceding section, Accounting Standards. The requirements are stated under the headings of Performance Criteria and Knowledge and Understanding. Candidates studying these two units with the aim of gaining unit accreditation will be doing so with the guidance of their employer and/or a college of further education. The bodies, such as AAT and Edexcel, which are approved to make awards may have slight differences in their assessment practices but the employer or the college will be aware of their methods. The AAT Education and Training Scheme uses devolved assessments and central assessments at Foundation Level as an assessment of students' competence.

The authors have used the knowledge gained from their teaching experiences to structure the book in a logical learning sequence. It has been designed to allow students to study any particular chapter as they find appropriate without it being necessary to work through the book from front to back. For instance, if a student was competent in the double-entry system and wanted to study credit transactions they could go directly to Part 3. As a result of this experience additional parts have been included to support the main aims of the book.

It is recommended that each chapter should be read at least twice and that worked examples are fully understood. New terms which have been introduced in a particular chapter are listed at the end of the chapter and these appear with a brief definition immediately before the Student Activities. It is important to memorise these since examining bodies could well ask for an explanation of such terms. The student activities should then be attempted. Do not rush them but make sure that the format used in the chapter is used in producing the answer and that the work is neat and fully legible. Accounting procedures have been established over many years and are used extensively by accounting practitioners. Students should not use 'short cuts' but should follow the accepted procedures. In this way, any mistakes which are made can quickly be traced by going back over the various stages.

Answers to most of the Student Activities are provided at the end of the book but do not refer to these until each activity has been completed. The answers to the activities with the suffix 'X', e.g. 3.2X, are given in a Lecturer's Guide and these will be provided by the lecturer/tutor.

Part 1 Introduction to accounting

This has been included for students who may lack sufficient knowledge and competence in this particular discipline. The double-entry system is fundamental to bookkeeping and accounts and it is considered that full understanding and competence of the system is vital. For those who are unsure as to their ability it is suggested that they attempt the first Student Activities to assess their level of competence. Should any difficulties be experienced it would be better to study the whole of Part 1 and attempt all the Student Activities.

Part 2 Unit 1: Recording and accounting for cash transactions

Part 3 Unit 2: Recording and accounting for credit transactions

These parts contain the two main sections of the book and deal with the performance criteria and knowledge and understanding for Unit 1 and Unit 2. Many worked examples have been included to aid understanding of the various topics. Part 3 also includes a chapter on the basic law of contract since knowledge of this is required to undertake the practice assessments in Part 5.

Part 4 Other considerations and supporting topics

Chapter 28 covering payroll procedures has been included to cover the RSA Stage 1 requirements and to give other students a basic understanding of payroll procedures. For students who wish to cover the requirements of Unit 3, Recording Payroll Transactions, they can do so by using the specific book *NVQ Level 2 Accounting – Unit 3 Recording Payroll Transactions* by Sheila Robinson (ISBN 0–273–61348–0, Financial Times Management).

Chapter 29 on communication for accounting should be studied by students to enable them to deal with the AAT central assessment, section 3. It will also be useful for students taking the examinations of other bodies.

Part 5 Practice assessments and multiple-choice questions

Chapter 30 provides two full practice assessments which are typical of the central assessments used by the AAT. They simulate activities which may be found in an accounting situation and cover the requirements of Unit 1 and Unit 2. The recommended approach is first to read through the information given fairly quickly to gain an initial appreciation of the various facts and then to read through it again more slowly. The tasks should be read very carefully to make sure that what is required is fully understood. The various blank documents that are to be used should be examined so that their relevance is clear. A note should be made of the various steps to be taken so that a methodical approach is maintained.

As progress is made in dealing with the tasks, calculations should be checked since errors that are made early on will follow through making it impossible to balance certain figures where this is required. An estimate should be made before starting work of the time each task is likely to take. This will help to ensure that progress is to plan. The AAT central assessment paper is divided into three sections and it provides guidance as to how long to spend in answering each section:

Section 1	Processing Exercise	60 minutes
Section 2	20 Short Answer Tasks	75 minutes
Section 3	Communicating Accounting Information	45 minutes

A tip here is to complete Section 2 first and then answer Section 1, the Processing Exercise, and finally answer Section 3, Communicating Accounting Information.

Simulations of the AAT Devolved Assessment have not been included since their content is usually lengthy. Copies of actual devolved assessments can be purchased direct from the AAT by their student members. It is strongly advised that these be obtained and attempted before undertaking the assessment proper.

The chapter also includes typical examples of the type of questions used by the ACCA in their multiple-choice papers at Technician Level. Each multiple-choice question has four suggested answers, lettered (A), (B), (C) or (D). It is important to read each question carefully and then decide which choice is best, either (A) or (B) or (C) or (D) and then write down the answer on a *separate* piece of paper rather than write the answer in the textbook. This enables the questions to be attempted again at a later stage of study.

2 What is accounting?

AIMS

- To provide a general overview of what accounting is and the business environment in which it operates.
- To distinguish between bookkeeping and accounting.
- To know the main users of accounting information.

2.1 What is accounting?

People and business

Accounting is something that affects people in their personal lives just as much as it affects very large businesses. We all use accounting ideas when we plan what we are going to do with our money. We have to plan how much of it we will spend and how much we will save. We may write down a plan, known as a **budget**, or we may simply keep it in our minds.

Recording accounting data

However, when people normally talk about accounting it means the type used by businesses and other organisations. They cannot keep all the details in their minds so they have to write it all down.

They will not only record cash received and paid out. They will also record goods bought and sold, items bought to use rather than to sell, and so on. This part of accounting is usually called the **recording of data**. Data means the financial information shown in monetary terms.

Classifying and summarising

Prior to the data being recorded, it has to be sorted into a form that is useful to the business and that follows accounting procedures. This is known as **classifying** and **summarising** data.

Following such classifications and summaries, it will be possible to work out how much profit or loss has been made by the business during a period of time. It will also be possible to show what resources are owned by the business, and what is owed by it, on the closing date of the period.

Communicating information

From the data, those who are skilled in accounting should be able to tell whether or not the business or organisation is performing well financially. They should be able to work out what are their strengths and weaknesses.

Finally, they should be able to tell or **communicate** their results to the owners of the business, the managers of the organisation or others allowed to receive this information.

2.2 What is bookkeeping?

The part of accounting that is concerned with recording data is often known as bookkeeping. Until about one hundred years ago all accounting data was recorded in books, hence the term bookkeeping.

People still refer to the 'books of a business' even though computers are widely used for recording and processing accounting data.

2.3 Users of accounting information

The possible users are as follows.

Business

- **Owner(s) of the business.** They want to be able to see whether or not the business is profitable. In addition they want to know the financial resources of the business.

- **A prospective buyer.** When the owner wants to sell their business the buyer will want to see financial details of the business.

- **The bank.** If the owner of the business wants to borrow money for use in the business, then the bank will need financial information.

- **Tax inspectors.** They need details of the final accounts of the business in order to assess any tax liability.

- **A prospective partner.** If the owner wants to share ownership with someone else, then the would-be partner will want financial information on the business.

- **Investors,** either existing investors or others wondering whether or not to invest their money in the business.

- **Employees and trade unions.** If some sort of profit-sharing or bonus payments are in use, then either employees or trade union representatives may want to see the accounts.

There could also be other users. It is a fact that without properly recorded accounting data a business would have many difficulties, as the needs of the users could not be served.

Other organisations

We can all think of many non-profit-making organisations which exist to provide a public service such as hospitals, the police, fire service and charitable organisations.

They still need to do bookkeeping and accounting. Without it they would be unable to ascertain their financial position and know what they could and could not afford and so on.

This means that the people in charge of all these organisations will spend a great deal of their time recording and reviewing accounting data to assist them in their decision making.

NEW TERMS

Accounting   The uses to which data recorded by bookkeeping can be put for various purposes.

Bookkeeping   The recording of accounting data.

3 The accounting equation and the balance sheet

AIMS

- To understand the accounting equation.

- To understand what is meant by assets, liabilities and capital.

- To be able to draw up balance sheets after different transactions have occurred.

- To understand the difference between 'horizontal' and 'vertical' style balance sheets.

3.1 The accounting equation

The whole of accounting is based upon a very simple idea. This is called the **accounting equation**, which sounds complicated but in fact it is easy to understand.

It can be explained by saying that if a firm is to set up and start trading then it needs resources. Let us assume that in the first place it is the owner of the business who has supplied all of the resources. This can be shown as:

> Resources in the business = Resources supplied by the owner

In accounting, terms are used to describe things. The amount of the resources supplied by the owner is called **capital**. The actual resources that are then in the business are called **assets**. This means that the accounting equation above, when the owner has supplied all of the resources, can be shown as:

> Assets = Capital

Usually, however, someone other than the owner has supplied some of the assets. **Liabilities** is the name given to the amount owing to this person for these assets. This equation has now changed to:

> Assets = Capital + Liabilities

It can be seen that the two sides of the equation will have the same totals. This is because we are dealing with the same thing from two different points of view. It is:

> Resources: what they are = Resources: who supplied them
> (Assets)   (Capital + Liabilities)

It is a fact that the totals of each side will always equal one another, and that this will always be true no matter how many transactions there may be. The actual assets, capital and liabilities may change, but the total of the assets will always equal the total of capital + liabilities.

Assets consist of property of all kinds, such as buildings, machinery, stocks of goods and motor vehicles. Also benefits such as debts owed by customers and the amount of money in the bank account are included.

Liabilities consist of money owing for goods supplied to the firm and for expenses. Also loans made to the firm are included.

Capital is often called the owner's **equity** or net worth.

Note: The dates used in the examples and student activities in this book are for the new millennium, the year 2000 and onwards.

3.2 The balance sheet – horizontal presentation

The accounting equation is shown in a statement called the **balance sheet**. It is not the first bookkeeping record to be made, but it is a good place to start to consider accounting.

The introduction of capital

On 1 May 2000 K Grant started in business and deposited £5,000 into a bank account opened specially for the business. The balance sheet would appear:

K Grant
Balance Sheet as at 1 May 2000

Assets	£		£
Cash at bank	5,000	Capital	5,000
	5,000		5,000

The purchase of an asset by cheque

On 3 May 2000 Grant buys a building for £3,000 paying by cheque. The effect of this transaction is that the cash at the bank is decreased and a new asset, i.e. buildings, appears:

K Grant
Balance Sheet as at 3 May 2000

Assets	£		£
Buildings	3,000	Capital	5,000
Cash at bank	2,000		
	5,000		5,000

The purchase of an asset and the incurring of a liability

On 6 May 2000 Grant buys some goods for £500 from D Smith, and agrees to pay for them some time within the next two weeks. The effect of this is that a new asset, **stock** of goods, is acquired, and a liability for the goods is created. A person to whom money is owed for goods is known in accounting language as a **creditor**.

K Grant

Balance Sheet as at 6 May 2000

Assets	£	Capital and liabilities	£
Buildings	3,000	Capital	5,000
Stock of goods	500	Creditor	500
Cash at bank	2,000		
	5,500		5,500

Sale of an asset on credit

On 10 May 2000 goods which had cost £100 were sold to J Brown for the same amount, the money to be paid later. The effect is a reduction in the stock of goods and the creation of a new asset. A person who owes the firm money is known in accounting language as a **debtor**. The balance sheet now appears:

K Grant

Balance Sheet as at 10 May 2000

Assets	£	Capital and liabilities	£
Buildings	3,000	Capital	5,000
Stock of goods	400	Creditor	500
Debtor	100		
Cash at bank	2,000		
	5,500		5,500

Sale of an asset for immediate payment

On 13 May 2000 goods which had cost £50 were sold to D Daley for the same amount, Daley paying for them immediately by cheque. Here one asset, stock of goods, is reduced, while another asset, bank, is increased. The balance sheet now appears:

K Grant

Balance Sheet as at 13 May 2000

Assets	£	Capital and liabilities	£
Buildings	3,000	Capital	5,000
Stock of goods	350	Creditor	500
Debtor	100		
Cash at bank	2,050		
	5,500		5,500

The payment of a liability

On 15 May 2000 Grant pays a cheque for £200 to D Smith in part payment of the amount owing. The asset of bank is therefore reduced, and the liability of the creditor is also reduced. The balance sheet now appears:

K Grant

Balance Sheet as at 15 May 2000

Assets	£	Capital and liabilities	£
Buildings	3,000	Capital	5,000
Stock of goods	350	Creditor	300
Debtor	100		
Cash at bank	1,850		
	5,300		5,300

Collection of an asset

J Brown, who owed Grant £100, makes a part payment of £75 by cheque on 31 May 2000. The effect is to reduce one asset, debtor, and to increase another asset, bank. This results in a balance sheet as follows:

K Grant
Balance Sheet as at 31 May 2000

Assets	£	Capital and liabilities	£
Buildings	3,000	Capital	5,000
Stock of goods	350	Creditor	300
Debtor	25		
Cash at bank	1,925		
	5,300		5,300

3.3 Equality of the accounting equation

It can be seen that every transaction has affected two items. Sometimes it has changed two assets by reducing one and increasing the other. Other times it has reacted differently. A summary of the effect of transactions upon assets, liabilities and capital is shown below.

	Example of transaction	Effect			
1	Buy goods on credit	↑	Increase asset (Stock of goods)	↑	Increase liability (Creditors)
2	Buy goods by cheque	↑	Increase asset (Stock of goods)	↓	Decrease asset (Bank)
3	Pay creditor by cheque	↓	Decrease asset (Bank)	↓	Decrease liability (Creditors)
4	Owner pays more capital into the bank	↑	Increase asset (Bank)	↑	Increase capital
5	Owner takes money out of the business bank account for his own use	↓	Decrease asset (Bank)	↓	Decrease capital
6	Owner pays creditor from private money outside the firm	↓	Decrease liability (Creditors)	↑	Increase capital

Each transaction has, therefore, maintained the same total for assets as that of capital + liabilities. This can be shown:

Number of transaction as above	Assets	Capital and liabilities	Effect on balance sheet totals
1	+	+	Each side added to equally
2	+ −		A **plus** and a **minus** both on the assets side **cancelling out** each other
3	−	−	Each side has equal deductions
4	+	+	Each side has equal additions
5	−	−	Each side has equal deductions
6		− +	A plus and a minus both on the liabilities side cancelling out each other

3.4 The balance sheet – vertical presentation

You will notice that in the previous section the balance sheet has been shown using the horizontal method of presentation. Nowadays, almost everyone uses the vertical method of presentation.

The vertical presentation of final accounts, which includes the trading and profit and loss account and the balance sheet, is a requirement of the Companies Acts of 1985 and 1989. An example of a balance sheet using the vertical method of presentation is shown below but since this topic is not covered by the accounting standards until NVQ Level 3 it will not be covered fully until that stage.

K Grant's balance as at 31 May 2000 – vertical presentation

The balance sheet of K Grant using the vertical method of presentation would appear as follows:

K Grant
Balance Sheet as at 31 May 2000

	£	£	£
Fixed assets			
Fixtures			3,000
Current assets			
Stock	350		
Debtors	25		
Cash at bank	1,925	2,300	
Less: Current liabilities			
Creditors	300	300	
Net current assets			2,000
			5,000
Financed by:			
Capital			5,000

You will have noticed the use of the terms 'fixed assets', 'current assets' and 'current liabilities'. While a simple explanation of these terms is shown below they will be dealt with more fully at NVQ Level 3.

- **Fixed assets** are assets to be kept as such for a few years at least, e.g. buildings, machinery, fixtures, motor vehicles.

- **Current assets** are assets which change from day to day, e.g. the value of stock in hand goes up and down as it is bought and sold. Similarly, the amount of money owing to us by debtors will change quickly as we sell more to them on credit and they pay their debts. The amount of money in the bank will also change as we receive and pay out money.

- **Current liabilities** are those liabilities which have to be paid within the near future, e.g. creditors for goods bought.

NEW TERMS

Assets Resources owned by the business.

Balance sheet A statement showing the assets, capital and liabilities of a business.

Capital The total of resources supplied to a business by its owner.

Creditor A person to whom money is owed for goods or services.

Debtor A person who owes money to the business for goods or services supplied.

Equity Another name for the capital of the owner.

Liabilities Total of money owed for assets supplied to the business.

Stock Unsold goods.

 ## STUDENT ACTIVITIES

Note: *Questions with the letter X shown after the question number do **not** have answers shown at the back of the book. Answers to the other questions are shown on p. 361 onwards.*

3.1 You are to complete the gaps in the following table:

	Assets	Liabilities	Capital
	£	£	£
(a)	?	5,750	20,000
(b)	?	10,520	62,300
(c)	38,400	3,420	?
(d)	55,300	6,700	?
(e)	92,500	?	80,000
(f)	152,320	?	121,700

3.2X You are to complete the gaps in the following table:

	Assets	Liabilities	Capital
	£	£	£
(a)	75,428	12,300	?
(b)	?	4,562	63,400
(c)	122,500	?	110,900
(d)	88,700	16,212	?
(e)	?	29,200	42,500
(f)	99,100	?	85,100

3.3 From the following list show which are assets and which are liabilities:

(a) Office machinery
(b) Loan from C Shirley
(c) Fixtures and fittings
(d) Motor vehicles
(e) We owe for goods
(f) Bank balance

3.4X Which of the following are assets and which are liabilities?

(a) Motor vehicles
(b) Premises
(c) Creditors for goods
(d) Stock of goods
(e) Debtors
(f) Owing to bank
(g) Cash in hand
(h) Loan from D Jones
(i) Machinery

3.5 State which of the following are shown under the wrong headings for J White's business:

Assets	*Liabilities*
Loan from C Smith	Stock of goods
Cash in hand	Debtors
Machinery	Money owing to bank
Creditors	
Premises	
Motor vehicles	

3.6X Which of the following are shown under the wrong headings:

Assets	*Liabilities*
Cash at bank	Loan from J Graham
Fixtures	Machinery
Creditors	Motor vehicles
Building	
Stock of goods	
Debtors	
Capital	

3.7 A Smart sets up a new business. Before he actually sells anything he has bought Motor vehicles £2,000, Premises £5,000, Stock of goods £1,000. He did not pay in full for his stock of goods and still owes £400 in respect of them. He had borrowed £3,000 from D Bevan. After the events just described, and before trading starts, he has £100 cash in hand and £700 cash at bank. You are required to calculate the amount of his capital.

3.8X T Charles starts a business. Before he actually starts to sell anything he has bought Fixtures £2,000, Motor vehicle £5,000 and a Stock of goods £3,500. Although he has paid in full for the fixtures and the motor vehicle, he still owes £1,400 for some of the goods. J Preston had lent him £3,000. Charles, after the above, has £2,800 in the business bank account and £100 cash in hand. You are required to calculate his capital.

3.9 Draw up T Lymer's balance sheet, using either the vertical or horizontal presentation methods, from the following information as at 31 December 2000.

	£
Capital	34,823
Delivery van	12,000
Debtors	10,892
Office furniture	8,640
Stock of goods	4,220
Cash at bank	11,722
Creditors	12,651

3.10X Draw up A Pennington's balance sheet as at 31 March 2001 from the following information:

	£
Premises	50,000
Plant and machinery	26,500
Debtors	28,790
Creditors	32,320
Bank overdraft	3,625
Stock	21,000
Cash in hand	35
Capital	90,380

3.11 Look at this list:

(a) We pay a creditor £70 in cash.
(b) Bought fixtures £200 paying by cheque.
(c) Bought goods on credit £275.
(d) The proprietor introduces another £500 cash into the firm.
(e) J Walker lends the firm £200 in cash.
(f) A debtor pays us £50 by cheque.
(g) We return goods costing £60 to a supplier whose bill we had not paid.
(h) Bought additional shop premises paying £5,000 by cheque.

For each item shown, you are to state how it changes assets, capital or liabilities.
For example, the answer to (*a*) will be:

(a) − Assets £70
     − Liabilities £70

3.12X Show how each item on the following list changes assets, capital and liabilities.

(a) Bought a motor van on credit £500.
(b) Repaid by cash a loan owed to P Smith £1,000.
(c) Bought goods for £150 paying by cheque.
(d) The owner puts a further £5,000 cash into the business.
(e) A debtor returns to us £80 goods. We agree to make an allowance for them.
(f) Bought goods on credit £220.
(g) The owner takes out £100 cash for his personal use.
(h) We pay a creditor £190 by cheque.

3.13 C Sangster has the following items in his balance sheet as on 30 April 2001: Capital £18,900; Loan from T Sharples £2,000; Creditors £1,600; Fixtures £3,500; Motor vehicle £4,200; Stock of goods £4,950; Debtors £3,280; Cash at bank £6,450; Cash in hand £120.

During the first week of May 2001 Sangster:
(a) Bought extra stock of goods £770 on credit.
(b) One of the debtors paid us £280 in cash.
(c) Bought extra fixtures by cheque £1,000.

You are to draw up a balance sheet as on 7 May 2001 after the above transactions have been completed.

3.14X H Charles has the following balance sheet as at 31 March 2000:

Balance Sheet as at 31 March 2000

Assets	£	Capital and liabilities	£
Buildings	6,000	Capital	14,400
Motor vehicle	4,000	Loan from W Young	2,000
Stock of goods	2,000	Creditors	1,600
Debtors	2,800		
Cash at bank	3,200		
	18,000		18,000

The following transactions occur:

  2 April   Paid a cheque of £500 to a creditor.
  8 April   A debtor paid H Charles £300 by cheque.
10 April   W Young is repaid £1,000 by cheque.

Write up a balance sheet on 10 April 2000 after the transactions have been completed.

4 The double-entry system for assets, liabilities and capital

AIMS

- To explain the recording and layout of financial transactions using the double-entry system.

- To explain the meaning of debit and credit in bookkeeping terms.

- To state the rules of the double-entry system and to provide worked examples to illustrate the use of these rules.

4.1 Nature of a transaction

In the last chapter we saw how various events had changed two items in the balance sheet. Events which do result in such changes are known as 'transactions'. This means that if the proprietor asks the price of some goods but does not buy them, then there is no transaction. If he later asks the price of some other goods and then buys them, then there would be a transaction, and two balance sheet items would then have to be altered.

4.2 The double-entry system

We have seen that every transaction affects two items. If we want to show the effect of every transaction when we are doing our bookkeeping, we will have to show the effect of a transaction on each of the two items. For each transaction this means that a bookkeeping entry will have to be made to show an increase or decrease of that item, and another entry to show the increase or decrease of the other item. From this you will probably be able to see that the term **double-entry system** of bookkeeping is a good one, as each entry is made twice.

In Chapter 3 we drew up a new balance sheet after each transaction. You could do this easily if you had only a few transactions per day, but if there were hundreds of transactions each day it would become impossible for you to draw up hundreds of different balance sheets. You simply would not have enough time.

The double-entry system has an **account** (meaning details of transactions relating to a particular item) for every asset, every liability and for capital. Thus there will be a buildings account (for transactions in buildings), a motor vans account (for transactions in motor vans) and so on for every asset, liability and for capital.

4.3 The accounts for double entry

An account show us the 'history of' a particular asset, liability, capital or indeed any business transaction. Each account is usually shown on a separate page which is divided into two halves. The left-hand side of each page is known as the **debit** side and is abbreviated **Dr**; the right-hand side is known as the **credit** side and is abbreviated **Cr**.

The words debit and credit in bookkeeping terms do not mean the same as in normal language and should be viewed differently from the start to avoid confusion. Students new to studying double entry may find it useful to use 'IN' and 'OUT' initially, in addition to debit and credit.

The name of each account is usually written across the centre and each account has a reference number, which is essential both in manual and computerised systems. An example of an account is shown below:

Name of Account – Reference No

Dr *Cr*

Date	Details	£	Date	Details	£
	Debit side			Credit side	

You will notice that the account looks rather like a letter 'T' and indeed accounts are often referred to as 'T accounts'.

Rules for double entry

Double entry is relatively easy to learn and understand if the following rules are learnt and understood:

1 Double entry means that every transaction affects two things and should, therefore, be entered twice:

   Once on the **debit** side
   and
   Once on the **credit** side

2 The order in which the items are entered does not matter.

3 To increase or decrease assets, liabilities or capital, as seen in Chapter 3, the double-entry rules are:

Accounts	To record	Entry in the account
Assets	an increase a decrease	Debit Credit
Liabilities	an increase a decrease	Credit Debit
Capital	an increase a decrease	Credit Debit

Let us now look at the accounting equation:

	Assets	**= Liabilities and Capital**	
To increase each item	Debit	Credit	Credit
To decrease each item	Credit	Debit	Debit

The double-entry rules for liabilities and capital are the same, but they are the opposite of those for assets. this is because assets are on the opposite side of the equation and, therefore, follow opposite rules. Looking at the accounts the rules will appear as:

Any asset account		Any liability account		Capital account	
Increases	Decreases	Decreases	Increases	Decreases	Increases
+	−	−	+	−	+

We have not enough space in this book to put each account on a separate page, so we will have to list the accounts under each other. In a real firm at least one full page would be taken for each account.

To help students having difficulty deciding on which side of each account the items should be entered, a useful hint is to think of the debit side being 'IN' to the account and the credit side being 'OUT' of the account. To give two examples of the use of this approach we will look at the following:

1 **Paid case £200 to buy machinery**. The double entry for this transaction would be as follows:

(a) Cash goes 'OUT' – a credit entry in the cash account.
(b) Machinery comes 'IN' – a debit entry in the machinery account.

2 **Took £500 out of the cash till of the business and paid it into the bank account of the business**. The double entry for this transaction would be as follows:

(a) Money comes 'IN' to the bank – a debit entry in the bank account.
(b) Cash goes 'OUT' of the cash till – a credit entry in the cash account.

4.4 Worked examples

The entry of a few transactions can now be attempted:

1 The proprietor starts the firm with £1,000 in cash on 1 August 2000.

Effect	Action
1 Increases the *asset* of cash 2 Increases the capital	Debit the cash account – Cash goes 'IN' Credit the capital account – Cash comes 'OUT' of the owner's money

These are entered:

Cash Account

Dr				Cr
2000		£		
Aug 1		1,000		

Capital Account

Dr			Cr
	2000		£
	Aug 1		1,000

The date of the transaction has already been entered. Now there remains the description which is to be entered alongside the amount. The double entry to the item in the cash account is completed by an entry in the capital account, therefore the word 'Capital' will appear in the cash account. Similarly, the double entry to the item in the capital account is completed by an entry in the cash account, therefore the word 'Cash' will appear in the capital account.

The finally completed accounts are therefore:

Cash Account

Dr				Cr
2000			£	
Aug 1	Capital		1,000	

Capital Account

Dr				Cr
	2000			£
	Aug 1	Cash		1,000

This method of entering transactions therefore fulfils the requirements of the double-entry rules as shown on p. 17. Now let us look at the entry of some more transactions.

2   A motor van is bought for £275 cash on 2 August 2000.

Effect	Action
1 Decreases the *asset* of cash	Credit the cash account – Cash goes 'OUT'
2 Increases the *asset* of motor van	Debit the motor van account – Motor van comes 'IN'

Cash Account

Dr				Cr
	2000			£
	Aug 2	Motor van		275

Motor Van Account

Dr				Cr
2000			£	
Aug	2	Cash	275	

3 Fixtures bought on credit from shop fitters for £115 on 3 August 2000.

Effect	Action
1 Increases the *asset* of Fixtures	Debit the Fixtures account – Fixtures go 'IN'
2 Increases the *liability* to Shop fitters	Credit the Shop fitters' account – Fixtures come 'OUT' of the supplier's account

Fixtures Account

Dr				Cr
2000			£	
Aug	3	Shop fitters	115	

Shop Fitter's Account

Dr				Cr
	2000			£
	Aug	3	Fixtures	115

4 Paid the amount owing in cash to shop fitters on 17 August 2000.

Effect	Action
1 Decreases the *asset* of Cash	Credit the cash account – Cash goes 'OUT'
2 Decreases the *liability* to Shop fitters	Debit the Shop fitters' account – Cash goes 'IN' to the Supplier's account

Cash Account

Dr				Cr
	2000			£
	Aug	17	Shop fitters	115

Shop Fitter's Account

Dr				Cr
2000			£	
Aug	17	Cash	115	

5 Transactions to date – taking the transactions numbered **1** to **4** above, the records will now appear:

Cash Account

Dr				Cr			
2000			£	2000			£
Aug	1	Capital	1,000	Aug	2	Motor van	275
				Aug	17	Shop fitters	115

Capital Account

Dr				Cr
	2000			£
	Aug	1	Cash	1,000

Motor Van Account

Dr				Cr
2000			£	
Aug	2	Cash	275	

Shop Fitter's Account

Dr				Cr
2000		£	2000	£
Aug	17	Cash	115	Aug	3	Fixtures	115

Fixtures Account

Dr				Cr
2000			£	
Aug	3	Shop fitters	115	

Before you read further you are required to work through Student Activities 4.1 and 4.2 on p. 24.

4.5 A further worked example

Now you have actually made some entries in accounts you are to go carefully through the following example. Make certain you can understand every entry.

Transactions	Effect	Action	IN/OUT
2000 May 1 Started an engineering business putting £1,000 into a business bank account.	Increases **asset** of bank.	Debit bank account.	IN
	Increases **capital** of owner.	Credit capital account.	OUT
May 3 Bought works machinery on credit from Unique Machines £275.	Increases **asset** of machinery.	Debit machinery account.	IN
	Increases **liability** to Unique Machines.	Credit Unique Machines account.	OUT
May 4 Withdrew £200 cash from the bank and placed it in the cash box.	Decreases **asset** of bank.	Credit bank account.	OUT
	Increases **asset** of cash.	Debit cash account.	IN
May 7 Bought a motor van paying in cash £180.	Decreases **asset** of cash.	Credit cash account.	OUT
	Increases **asset** of motor van	Debit motor van account.	IN
May 10 Sold some of the machinery for £15 on credit to B Barnes.	Decreases **asset** of machinery.	Credit machinery account.	OUT
	Increases **asset** of money owing from B Barnes.	Debit B Barnes account.	IN
May 21 Returned some of the machinery, value £27, to Unique Machines.	Decreases **asset** of machinery.	Credit machinery account.	OUT
	Decreases **liability** of Unique Machines.	Debit Unique Machines.	IN
May 28 B Barnes pays the firm the amount owing, £15, by cheque.	Increases **asset** of bank.	Debit bank account.	IN
	Decreases **asset** of money owing from B Barnes.	Credit B Barnes account.	OUT
May 30 Bought another motor van paying by cheque £420	Decreases **asset** of bank.	Credit bank account.	OUT
	Increases **asset** of motor vans.	Debit motor van account.	IN
May 31 Paid the amount of £248 to Unique Machines by cheque.	Decreases **asset** of bank.	Credit bank account.	OUT
	Decreases **liability** to Unique Machines.	Debit Unique Machines.	IN

In account form this is shown as:

Bank Account

Dr							Cr
2000			£	2000			£
May	1	Capital	1,000	May	4	Cash	200
May	28	B Barnes	15	May	30	Motor van	420
				May	30	Unique Machines	248

Cash Account

Dr							Cr
2000			£	2000			£
May	4	Bank	200	May	7	Motor van	180

Capital Account

Dr							Cr
				2000			£
				May	1	Bank	1,000

Machinery Account

Dr							Cr
2000			£	2000			£
May	3	Unique Machines	275	May	10	B Barnes	15
				May	21	Unique Machines	27

Motor Van Account

Dr				Cr
2000			£	
May	7	Cash	180	
May	30	Bank	420	

Unique Machines Account

Dr							Cr
2000			£	2000			£
May	21	Machinery	27	May	3	Machinery	275
May	31	Bank	248				

B Barnes Account

Dr							Cr
2000			£	2000			£
May	10	Machinery	15	May	28	Bank	15

4.6 Abbreviation of 'Limited'

In this book when we come across transactions with limited companies the letters 'Ltd' are used as the abbreviation for 'Limited Company'. So we will know that if we see the name of a firm as T Lee Ltd, then that firm will be a limited company. In our books the transactions with T Lee Ltd will be entered the same as for any other customer or supplier.

NEW TERMS

Account The place in a ledger where all the transactions relating to a particular asset, liability or capital, expenses for revenue item are recorded. Accounts are part of the double-entry bookkeeping system. They are sometimes referred to as 'T accounts' or ledger accounts.

Credit The right-hand side of the accounts in double entry.

Debit The left-hand side of the accounts in double entry.

Double-entry bookkeeping A system where each transaction is entered twice, once on the debit side and once on the credit side.

STUDENT ACTIVITIES

4.1 Complete the following table showing which accounts are to be debited and which are to be credited:

	Account to be debited	Account to be credited
(a) Bought motor van for cash		
(b) Bought office machinery on credit from J Grant & Son		
(c) Introduced capital in cash		
(d) A debtor, J Beach, pays us by cheque		
(e) Paid a creditor, A Barrett, in cash		

4.2 The following table is also to be completed, showing the accounts to be debited and credited:

	Account to be debited	Account to be credited
(a) Bought machinery on credit from A Jackson & Son		
(b) Returned machinery to A Jackson & Son		
(c) A debtor, J Brown, pays us in cash		
(d) J Smith lends us money, giving it to us by cheque		
(e) Sold office machinery for cash		

4.3X Complete the following table:

	Account to be debited	Account to be credited
(a) Bought office machinery on credit from D Isaacs Ltd		
(b) The proprietor paid a creditor, C Jones, from his private monies outside the firm		
(c) A debtor, N Fox, paid us in cash		
(d) Repaid part of loan from P Exeter by cheque		
(e) Returned some office machinery to D Isaacs Ltd		
(f) A debtor, N Lyn, pays us by cheque		
(g) Bought motor van by cash		

4.4X Complete the following table showing which accounts are to be debited and which to be credited:

	Account to be debited	Account to be credited
(a) Bought motor lorry for cash		
(b) Paid creditor, T Lake, by cheque		
(c) Repaid P Logan's loan by cash		
(d) Sold motor lorry for cash		
(e) Bought office machinery on credit from Ultra Ltd		
(f) A debtor, A Hill, pays us by cash		
(g) A debtor, J Cross, pays us by cheque		
(h) Proprietor puts a further amount into the business by cheque		
(i) A loan of £200 in cash is received from L Lowe		
(j) Paid a creditor, D Lord, by cash		

4.5 Write up the asset and liability accounts in the records of D Coy to record these transactions:

2001
May   1   Started business with £1,000 cash
May   3   Bought a motor lorry on credit from Speed & Sons for £698
May 14   Bought office machinery by cash for £60
May 31   Paid Speed & Sons the amount owing to them, £698, in cash

4.6 Write up the asset and liability and capital accounts to record the following transactions in the records of G Powell.

2001
July   1   Started business with £2,500 in the bank
July   2   Bought office furniture by cheque £150
July   3   Bought machinery £750 on credit from Planers Ltd
July   5   Bought a motor van paying by cheque £600
July   8   Sold some of the office furniture – not suitable for the firm – for £60 on credit to J Walker & Sons
July 15   Paid the amount owing to Planers Ltd £750 by cheque
July 23   Received the amount due from J Walker £60 in cash
July 31   Bought more machinery by cheque £280

4.7X You are required to open the assets, liability and capital accounts, and record the following transactions for June 2001 in the records of C Williams.

2001
June   1   Started business with £2,000 in cash
June   2   Paid £1,800 of the opening cash into a bank account for the business
June   5   Bought office furniture on credit from Betta-Built Ltd for £120
June   8   Bought a motor van paying by cheque £950
June 12   Bought works machinery from Evans & Sons on credit £560
June 18   Returned faulty office furniture costing £62 to Betta-Built Ltd
June 25   Sold some of the works machinery for £75 cash
June 26   Paid amount owing to Betta-Built Ltd £58 by cheque
June 28   Took £100 out of the bank and put it in the cash till
June 30   J Smith lent us £500 – giving us the money by cheque

4.8   Write up the asset, capital and liability accounts in the books of C Walsh to record the following transactions:

2000
June 1   Started business with £5,000 in the bank
June 2   Bought motor van paying by cheque £1,200
June 5   Bought office fixtures £400 on credit from Young Ltd
June 8   Bought motor van on credit from Super Motors £800
June 12   Took £100 out of the bank and put it into the cash till
June 15   Bought office fixtures paying by cash £60
June 19   Paid Super Motors a cheque for £800
June 21   A loan of £1,000 cash is received from J Jarvis
June 25   Paid £800 of the cash in hand into the bank account
June 30   Bought more office fixtures paying by cheque £300

4.9X   Write up the various accounts needed in the books of S Russell to record the following transactions:

2002
April 1   Opened business with £10,000 in the bank
April 3   Bought office equipment £700 on credit from J Saunders Ltd
April 6   Bought motor van paying by cheque £3,000
April 8   Borrowed £1,000 from H Thompson – he gave us the money by cheque
April 11   Russell put further capital into the firm in the form of cash £500
April 12   Paid £350 of the cash in hand into the bank account
April 15   Returned some of the office equipment costing £200 – it was faulty – to
           J Saunders Ltd
April 17   Bought more office equipment, paying by cash £50
April 19   Sold the motor van, as it has proved unsuitable, to R Jones for £3,000. R Jones
           will settle for this by three payments later this month
April 21   Received a loan in cash from J Hawkins £400
April 22   R Jones paid us a cheque for £1,000
April 23   Bought a suitable motor van £3,600 on credit from Phillips Garages Ltd
April 26   R Jones paid us a cheque for £1,800
April 28   Paid £2,000 by cheque to Phillips Garages Ltd
April 30   R Jones paid us cash £200

5 The double-entry system: the treatment of stock

AIMS

- To explain the various accounts used in recording the movement of stocks.

- To show how the purchase and sale of goods by both cash and credit are dealt with in the double-entry system.

- To show how the return of goods is recorded in the double-entry system.

5.1 Stock movements

The stock of goods in a business is constantly changing because some of it is bought, some of it is sold, some is returned to the suppliers and some is returned by the firm's customers.

To keep a check on the movement of stock, an account is opened for each type of dealing in goods. Thus we will have the following accounts:

Account	Reason
Purchases Account	For the purchase of goods
Sales Account	For the sale of goods
Returns Inwards Account	For goods returned to the firm by its customers
Returns Outwards Account	For goods returned by the firm to its suppliers

As stock is an asset, and these four accounts are all connected with this asset, the double-entry rules are those used for assets.

We shall now look at some entries in the following sections.

5.2 Purchase of stock on credit

On 1 August 2000 goods costing £165 are bought on credit from D Henry.

First, the twofold effect of the transaction must be considered so that the bookkeeping entries can be worked out.

1   **The asset of stock is increased**. An increase in an asset needs a debit entry in an account. Here the account is a stock account showing the particular movement of stock; in this case it is the 'purchases' movement so the account must be the purchases account.

2   **An increase in a liability**. This is the liability of the firm to D Henry because the goods bought have not yet been paid for. An increase in a liability needs a credit entry, so to enter this part of the transaction a credit entry is made in D Henry's account.

Here again we can use the idea of the debit side being 'IN' to the account, and the credit side being 'OUT' of the account. In this case Purchases have come 'IN' – thus a debit in the purchases account, while they have come 'OUT' of D Henry – needing a credit in the account of D Henry.

Purchases Account

Dr				Cr
2000		£		
Aug	1	D Henry	165	

D Henry Account

Dr				Cr
		2000		£
		Aug	1	Purchases	165

5.3 Purchases of stock for cash

On 2 August 2000 goods costing £22 are bought, cash being paid for them immediately.

1   The asset of stock is increased, so a debit entry will be needed. The movement of stock is that of a purchase, so it is the purchases account which needs debiting (purchases have come 'IN' – debit the account).

2   The asset of cash is decreased. To reduce an asset a credit entry is called for, and the asset is that of cash so the cash account needs crediting (cash has gone OUT – credit the account).

Cash Account

Dr				Cr
		2000		£
		Aug	2	Purchases	22

Purchases Account

Dr				Cr
2000		£		
Aug	2	Cash	22	

5.4 Sales of stock on credit

On 3 August 2000 sold goods on credit for £250 to K Leach.

1   The asset of stock is decreased. For this a credit entry to reduce an asset is needed. The movement of stock is that of 'Sales' so the account credited is the sales account (sales have gone 'OUT' – credit the sales account).

2 An asset account is increased. This is the account showing that K Leach is a debtor for the goods. The increase in the asset of debtors requires a debit and the debtor is K Leach, so the account concerned is that of K Leach (goods have gone 'IN' to K Leach – debit K Leach account).

Sales Account

Dr						Cr
		2000				£
		Aug	3	K Leach		250

K Leach Account

Dr					Cr
2000			£		
Aug	3	Sales	250		

5.5 Sales of stock for cash

On 4 August 2000 goods are sold for £55, the cash being received at once upon sale.

1 The asset of cash is increased. A debit in the cash account is needed to show this (cash has come 'IN' – debit the cash account).

2 The asset of stock is reduced. The reduction of an asset requires a credit and the movement of stock is represented by 'sales' so the entry needed is a credit in the sales account (sales have gone 'OUT' – credit the sales account).

Sales Account

Dr						Cr
		2000				£
		Aug	4	Cash		55

Cash Account

Dr					Cr
2000			£		
Aug	4	Sales	55		

5.6 Returns inwards

These represent goods sold which have now been returned. Just as the original sale was entered in a double-entry fashion, so also is the return of those goods.

On 5 August 2000 goods which had previously been sold to F Lowe for £29 are now returned by him.

1 The asset of stock is increased by the goods returned, so a debit representing an increase of an asset is needed, and this time the movement of stock is that of 'returns inwards'. The entry required therefore is a debit in the returns inwards account (the goods have come 'IN' – debit the returns inwards account).

2 A decrease in an asset. The debt of F Lowe to the firm is now reduced, and to record this a credit is needed in F Lowe's account (the goods have come 'OUT' from F Lowe – credit F Lowe's account).

Returns Inwards Account

Dr					Cr
2000			£		
Aug	5	F Lowe	29		

F Lowe Account

Dr						Cr
			2000			£
			Aug	5	Returns inwards	29

An alternative name for a returns inwards account is a sales returns account.

5.7 Returns outwards

These represent goods which were purchased and are now being returned to the supplier. As the original purchase was entered in a double-entry fashion, so also is the return to the supplier of those goods.

On 6 August 2000 goods previously bought for £96 are returned by the firm to K Howe.

1   The asset of stock is decreased by the goods sent out so a credit representing a reduction in an asset is needed, and the movement of stock is that of 'returns outwards' so the entry will be a credit in the returns outwards account (the returns have gone 'OUT' – credit the returns outwards account).

2   The liability of the firm to K Howe is decreased by the value of the goods returned to him. The decrease in a liability needs a debit, this time in K Howe's account (the returns have gone 'IN' to K Howe – debit K Howe's account).

Returns Outwards Account

Dr						Cr
			2000			£
			Aug	6	K Howe	96

K Howe Account

Dr					Cr
2000			£		
Aug	6	Returns outwards	96		

An alternative name for a returns outwards account is a purchases returns account.

5.8 A worked example

Enter the following transactions in suitable double-entry accounts:

2002
May   1   Bought goods on credit £68 from D Small
May   2   Bought goods on credit £77 from A Lyon & Son
May   5   Sold goods on credit to D Hughes for £60
May   6   Sold goods on credit to M Spencer for £45
May   10   Returned goods £15 to D Small

May   12   Goods bought for cash £100
May   19   M Spencer returned £16 goods to us
May   21   Goods sold for cash £150
May   22   Paid cash to D Small £53
May   30   D Hughes paid the amount owing by him £60 in cash
May   31   Bought goods on credit £64 from A Lyon & Son

The double-entry accounts can now be shown as:

Purchases Account

Dr				Cr
2002			£	
May	1	D Small	68	
May	2	A Lyon & Son	77	
May	12	Cash	100	
May	31	A Lyon & Son	64	

Sales Account

Dr				Cr
	2002			£
	May	5	D Hughes	60
	May	6	M Spencer	45
	May	21	Cash	150

Returns Outwards Account

Dr				Cr
	2002			£
	May	10	D Small	15

Returns Inwards Account

Dr				Cr
2002			£	
May	19	M Spencer	16	

D Small Account

Dr			£	2002			£
May	10	Returns outwards	15	May	1	Purchases	68
May	22	Cash	53				

A Lyon & Son Account

Dr				Cr
	2002			£
	May	2	Purchases	77
	May	31	Purchases	64

D Hughes Account

Dr			£	2002			£
2002			£	2002			£
May	5	Sales	60	May	30	Cash	60

M Spencer Account

Dr			£	Cr			£
2002				2002			
May	6	Sales	45	May	19	Returns inwards	16

Cash Account

Dr			£	Cr			£
2002				2002			
May	21	Sales	150	May	12	Purchases	100
May	30	D Hughes	60	May	22	D Small	53

5.9 Special meaning of 'purchases' and 'sales'

It must be emphasised that 'purchases' and 'sales' have a special meaning in accounting language.

'Purchases' in accounting means **the purchase of those goods which the firm buys with the prime intention of selling**. Sometimes the goods may be altered, added to or used in the manufacture of something else, but it is the element of **resale** that is important. To a firm that deals in typewriters, for instance, typewriters are purchases. If something else is bought, such as a motor van, such an item cannot be called purchases, even though in ordinary language it may be said that a motor van has been purchased. The prime intention of **buying** the motor van is for use by the company and not for resale.

Similarly, 'sales' means the **sale of those goods in which the firm normally deals and which were bought with the prime intention of resale**. The word 'sales' must never be given to the disposal of other items.

If we did not keep to these meanings, it would result in the different kinds of stock accounts containing something other than goods sold or for resale.

5.10 Comparison of cash and credit transactions for purchases and sales

The difference between the records needed for cash and credit transactions can now be seen.

The complete set of entries for purchases of goods where they are paid for immediately by cash would be:

1 Credit the cash account.

2 Debit the purchases account.

On the other hand the complete set of entries for the purchase of goods on credit can be broken down into two stages. First, the purchase of the goods and second, the payment for them.

The first part is:

1 Debit the purchases account.

2 Credit the supplier's account.

The second part is:

1 Credit the cash account.

2 Debit the supplier's account.

The difference can now be seen: with the cash purchase no record is kept of the supplier's account. This is because cash passes immediately and therefore there is no need to keep a check of indebtedness (money owing) to a supplier. On the other hand, in the credit purchase the records should show to whom money is owed until payment is made.

A study of cash sales and credit sales will reveal a similar difference.

Cash Sales	Credit Sales

Complete entry:
  Debit cash account
  Credit sales account
	First part:
	  Debit customer's account
	  Credit sales account
	Second part:
	  Debit cash account
	  Credit customer's account

NEW TERMS

Purchases Goods bought by the business for the purpose of selling them again.

Returns inwards Goods returned to the business by its customers.

Returns outwards Goods returned by the business to its suppliers.

Sales Goods sold by the business.

STUDENT ACTIVITIES

5.1 Complete the following table showing which accounts are to be debited and which are to be credited:

(a) Goods bought, cash being paid immediately
(b) Goods bought on credit from E Flynn
(c) Goods sold on credit to C Grant
(d) A motor van sold for cash
(e) Goods sold for cash

Account to be debited	Account to be credited

5.2X Similarly, complete this next table:

(a) Goods returned to H Flynn
(b) Goods bought on credit from P Franklin
(c) Goods sold on credit to S Mullings
(d) M Patterson returns goods to us
(e) Goods bought being paid for by cheque immediately

Account to be debited	Account to be credited

5.3 Complete the following table showing which accounts are to be debited and which are to be credited:

	Account to be debited	Account to be credited
(a) Goods bought on credit from J Reid		
(b) Goods sold on credit to B Perkins		
(c) Motor vans bought on credit from H Thomas		
(d) Goods sold, a cheque being received immediately		
(e) Goods sold for cash		
(f) Goods we returned to H Hardy		
(g) Machinery sold for cash		
(h) Goods returned to us by J Nelson		
(i) Goods bought on credit from D Simpson		
(j) Goods returned to H Forbes		

5.4X Complete the following table:

	Account to be debited	Account to be credited
(a) Goods bought on credit from T Morgan		
(b) Goods returned to us by J Thomas		
(c) Machinery returned to L Jones Ltd		
(d) Goods bought for cash		
(e) Motor van bought on credit from D Davies Ltd		
(f) Goods returned by us to I Prince		
(g) D Picton paid us his account by cheque		
(h) Goods bought by cheque		
(i) We paid creditor, B Henry, by cheque		
(j) Goods sold on credit to J Mullings		

5.5 You are to write up the following in the books:

2000
July 1 Started business with £500 cash
July 3 Bought goods for cash £85
July 7 Bought goods on credit £116 from E Morgan
July 10 Sold goods for cash £42
July 14 Returned goods to E Morgan £28
July 18 Bought goods on credit £98 from A Moses
July 21 Returned goods to A Moses £19
July 24 Sold goods to A Knight £55 on credit
July 25 Paid E Morgan's account by cash £88
July 31 A Knight paid us his account in cash £55

5.6 You are to enter the following in the accounts needed:

2001
Aug 1 Started business with £1,000 cash
Aug 2 Paid £900 of the opening cash into the bank
Aug 4 Bought goods on credit £78 from S Holmes
Aug 5 Bought a motor van by cheque £500
Aug 7 Bought goods for cash £55
Aug 10 Sold goods on credit £98 to D Moore

Aug 12 Returned goods to S Homes £18

Aug 19 Sold goods for cash £28

Aug 22 Bought fixtures on credit from Kingston Equipment Co £150

Aug 24 D Watson lent us £100 paying us the money by cheque

Aug 29 We paid S Holmes his account by cheque £60

Aug 31 We paid Kingston Equipment Co by cheque £150

5.7 Enter up the following transactions in the records of E Sangster:

2002

July 1 Started business with £10,000 in the bank

July 2 T Cooper lent us £400 in cash

July 3 Bought goods on credit from F Jones £840 and S Charles £3,600

July 4 Sold goods for cash £200

July 6 Took £250 of the cash and paid it into the bank

July 8 Sold goods on credit to C Moody £180

July 10 Sold goods on credit to J Newman £220

July 11 Bought goods on credit from F Jones £370

July 12 C Moody returned goods to us £40

July 14 Sold goods on credit to H Morgan £190 and J Peat £320

July 15 We returned goods to F Jones £140

July 17 Bought motor van on credit from Manchester Motors £2,600

July 18 Bought office furniture on credit from Faster Supplies Ltd £600

July 19 We returned goods to S Charles £110

July 20 Bought goods for cash £220

July 24 Goods sold for cash £70

July 25 Paid money owing to F Jones by cheque £1,070

July 26 Goods returned to us by H Morgan £30

July 27 Returned some office furniture costing £160 to Faster Supplies Ltd

July 28 E Sangster put a further £500 into the business in the form of cash

July 29 Paid Manchester Motors £2,600 by cheque

July 31 Bought office furniture for cash £100

5.8X Enter up the following transactions in the records:

2003

May 1 Started business with £2,000 in the bank

May 2 Bought goods on credit from C Shaw £900

May 3 Bought goods on credit from F Hughes £250

May 5 Sold goods for cash £180

May 6 We returned goods to C Shaw £40

May 8 Bought goods on credit from F Hughes £190

May 10 Sold goods on credit to G Wood £390

May 12 Sold goods for cash £210

May 18 Took £300 of the cash and paid it into the bank

May 21 Bought machinery by cheque £550

May 22 Sold goods on credit to L Moore £220

May 23 G Wood returned goods to us £140

May 25 L Moore returned goods to us £10

May 28 We returned goods to F Hughes £30

May 29 We paid Shaw by cheque £860

May 31 Bought machinery on credit from D Lee £270

5.9X You are to enter the following in the accounts needed:

2002

June	1	Started business with £1,000 cash
June	2	Paid £800 of the opening cash into a bank account for the firm
June	3	Bought goods on credit from H Grant £330
June	4	Bought goods on credit from D Clark £140
June	8	Sold goods on credit to B Miller £90
June	8	Bought office furniture on credit from Barrett's Ltd £400
June	10	Sold goods for cash £120
June	13	Bought goods for credit from H Grant £200
June	14	Bought goods for cash £60
June	15	Sold goods on credit to H Sharples £180
June	16	We returned goods £50 to H Grant
June	17	We returned some of the office furniture £30 to Barrett's Ltd
June	18	Sold goods on credit to B Miller £400
June	21	Paid H Grant's account by cheque £480
June	23	B Miller paid us the amount owing in cash £490
June	24	Sharples returned to us £50 goods
June	25	Goods sold for cash £150
June	28	Bought goods for cash £370
June	30	Bought motor van on credit from J Kelly £600

6 The effect of profit or loss on capital and the double-entry system for expenses and revenue

AIMS

- To understand the nature of profit and loss.

- To see the effect of profits and losses on capital.

- To show how expenses are recorded using the double-entry system.

- To understand the term 'revenues' and be able to record them in the double-entry system.

- To understand drawings, be able to record them and recognise the effect of drawings on capital.

6.1 The nature of profit or loss

To an accountant **profit** means the amount by which **revenues** are greater than **expenses** for a set of transactions. The term revenues means the sales value of goods and services that have been supplied to customers. The term expenses means the value of all the assets that have been used up to obtain those revenues.

If, therefore, we had supplied goods and services valued for sale at £100,000 to customers, and the expenses incurred by us to be able to supply those goods and services amounted to £70,000, then the result would be a profit calculated:

		£
Revenues:	goods and services supplied to our customers for the sum of	100,000
Less Expenses:	value of all the assets used up to enable us to supply	
	the above goods and services	70,000
Profit is therefore:		30,000

On the other hand, it could also be possible that our expenses may exceed our revenues for a set of transactions. In this case the result is a loss. For instance a loss would be incurred given the following details:

		£
Expenses:	value of all the assets used up to supply goods and	
	services to our customers	80,000
Less Revenues:	what we have charged to our customers in respect of all	
	the goods and services supplied to them	60,000
Loss is therefore:		20,000

6.2 The effect of profit and loss on capital

We can now look at the effect of profit upon capital by the use of an example.

On 1 January the assets and liabilities of a firm are:

Assets: Fixtures £10,000, Stock £7,000, Cash at the bank £3,000.
Liabilities: Creditors £2,000.

The capital is found by the formula:

> **Assets − Liabilities = Capital**

In this case capital works out at £10,000 + £7,000 + £3,000 − £2,000 = £18,000.

During January the whole of the £7,000 stock is sold for £11,000 cash. On 31 January the assets and liabilities have become:

Assets: Fixtures £10,000, Stock nil, Cash at the bank £14,000.
Liabilities: Creditors £2,000.

The capital can be calculated:

Assets £10,000 + £14,000 − Liabilities £2,000 = £22,000

It can be seen that capital has increased from £18,000 to £22,000, a £4,000 increase because the £7,000 stock was sold for £11,000, a profit of £4,000. Profit, therefore, increases capital:

> **Old capital + Profit = New capital**
> **£18,000 + £4,000 = £22,000**

On the other hand, a loss would reduce the capital so that it would become:

> **Old capital − Loss = New capital**

6.3 Profit or loss and sales

Profit will be made when goods or services are sold at more than cost price, while the opposite will mean a **loss**.

6.4 Profit or loss and expenses

While the firm is selling its goods there will be other **expenses** on top of the cost of the goods being sold. Every firm has other expenses such as rent, salaries, wages, telephone expenses, motor expenses and so on. Every extra £1 of expenses will mean £1 less profit.

It would be possible simply to have one account with the title 'Expenses Account'. However, rather than just know that the total expenses were £50,000 it would be more useful if we knew exactly how much of that figure was for rent, how much for motor expenses and so on. An expense account is, therefore, opened for each type of expense.

6.5 Debit or credit

We have to decide whether expense accounts are to be debited or credited with the costs involved. Assets involve expenditure by the firm and are shown as debit entries. Expenses also involve expenditure by the firm and therefore should also be debit entries.

An alternative explanation may also be used for expenses. Every expense results in a decrease in an asset or an increase in a liability, and because of the accounting equation this means that the capital is reduced by each expense. The decrease of capital needs a debit entry and therefore expense accounts contain debit entries for expenses.

6.6 Effect of transactions

A few illustrations will demonstrate the double entry required.

1   The rent of £20 is paid in cash.
    Here the twofold effect is:

    (a)   The asset of cash is decreased – money goes 'OUT'. This means crediting the cash account to show the decrease of the asset.
    (b)   The total of the expenses of rent is increased – the benefit goes 'IN'. As expense entries are shown as debits, and the expense is rent, so the action required is the debiting of the rent account.

    Summary: Credit the cash account with £20 – 'OUT'.
                  Debit the rent account with £20 – 'IN'.

2   Motor expenses are paid with a cheque for £55.
    The twofold effect is:

    (a)   The asset of money in the bank is decreased – money goes 'OUT'. This means crediting the bank account to show the decrease of the asset.
    (b)   The total of the motor expenses paid is increased – a benefit is received 'IN'. To increase an expenses account needs a debit, so the action required is to debit the motor expenses account.

    Summary: Credit the bank account with £55 – 'OUT'.
                  Debit the motor expenses account with £55 – 'IN'.

3   £60 cash is paid for telephone expenses.

    (a)   The asset of cash is decreased – money goes 'OUT'. This needs a credit in the cash account to decrease the asset.
    (b)   The total of telephone expenses is increased – a benefit is received goes 'IN'. Expenses are shown by a debit entry, therefore to increase the expense account in question the action required is to debit the telephone expenses account.

    Summary: Credit the cash account with £60 – 'OUT'.
                  Debit telephone expenses account with £60 – 'IN'.

It is now possible to study the effects of some more transactions showing the results in the form of a table:

	Increase	Action	Decrease	Action
2001 June 1 Paid for postage stamps by cash £5	Expense of postages	Debit postages account	Asset of cash	Credit cash account
2 Paid for advertising by cheque £29	Expense of advertising	Debit advertising account	Asset of bank	Credit bank account
3 Paid wages by cash £90	Expense of wages	Debit wages account	Asset of cash	Credit cash account
4 Paid insurance by cheque £42	Expense of insurance	Debit insurance account	Asset of bank	Credit bank account

The above four examples can now be shown in account form:

Cash Account

Dr						Cr
			2001			£
			June	1	Postages	5
			June	3	Wages	90

Bank Account

Dr						Cr
			2001			£
			June	2	Advertising	29
			June	4	Insurance	42

Advertising Account

Dr				Cr
2001			£	
June	2	Bank	29	

Insurance Account

Dr				Cr
2001			£	
June	4	Bank	42	

Postages Account

Dr				Cr
2001			£	
June	1	Cash	5	

Wages Account

Dr				Cr
2001			£	
June	3	Cash	90	

6.7 Revenues and double entry

For most firms the main revenue will be in the form of sales. There may well be other revenues, such as commission received, rent received and so on. As you have seen, expense accounts are debited for each item of expense. Revenue is the opposite of expenses, and therefore revenue accounts are credited with each item of revenue. This follows the same pattern as that for the main revenue of sales.

Two illustrations now show the double entry required.

1   Commission is received in cash £150.
    Here the twofold effect is:

    (a)   The asset of cash is increased – money comes 'IN'. This means debiting the cash account to show the increase of the asset.

    (b)   The total of the revenue of commission is increased – the benefit comes 'OUT' of commission, so the action required is the crediting of the commission account.

       Summary: Debit the cash account with £150 – 'IN'.
                         Credit the commission account with £150 – 'OUT'.

2   We have sublet part of our buildings. We receive rent of £250 by cheque.
    Here the twofold effect is:

    (a)   The asset of bank is increased – money comes 'IN'. This means debiting the bank account to show the increase of the asset.

    (b)   The total of the revenue of rent received is increased – the benefit comes 'OUT' of rent received so the action required is the crediting of the rent received account.

       Summary: Debit the bank account with £250 – 'IN'.
                         Credit the rent received account with £250 – 'OUT'.

6.8 Drawings

Sometimes the owner will want to take cash out of the business for his or her private use. These are known as **drawings**. Any money taken out as drawings will reduce capital.

The capital account is a very important account. To help to stop it getting full of small details, each item of drawings is not entered in the capital account. Instead a drawings account is opened, and the debits are entered there.

The following example illustrates the entries for drawings.

A worked example

25 August 2001: Proprietor takes £50 cash out of the business for his own use.

Effect	Action
1 Capital is decreased by £50	Debit the drawings account £50
2 Cash is decreased by £50	Credit the cash account £50

Cash Account

Dr					Cr
		2001			£
		Aug	25	Drawings	50

Drawings Account

Dr				Cr
2001			£	
Aug	25	Cash	50	

Sometimes goods are also taken for private use. These are also known as drawings. Entries for such transactions are shown below.

Goods for own use

A trader will often take items out of his or her business stocks for personal use, without paying for them. There is nothing wrong about this, but an entry should be made to record the event. This is done as follows:

1 Credit purchases account.

2 Debit drawings account.

Adjustments may also be needed for other private items. For instance, if a trader's private insurance had been incorrectly charged to the insurance account, then the correction would be:

1 Credit insurance account.

2 Debit drawings account.

 NEW TERMS

Drawings Cash or goods taken out of a business by the owner for his or her personal use.

Expenses Costs of operating the business.

Profit When goods are sold for more than they cost, the result is a **profit**; if they are sold for less than they cost then a **loss** would be incurred.

6.1 Complete the following table, showing the accounts to be debited and those to be credited:

(a) Paid rates by cheque
(b) Paid wages by cash
(c) Rent received by cheque
(d) Received by cheque refund of insurance previously paid
(e) Paid general expenses by cash

Account to be debited	Account to be credited

6.2 Complete the following table:

(a) Paid rent by cash
(b) Paid for goods by cash
(c) Received by cheque a refund of rates already paid
(d) Paid general expenses by cheque
(e) Received commissions in cash
(f) Goods returned by us to T Jones
(g) Goods sold for cash
(h) Bought office fixtures by cheque
(i) Paid wages in cash
(j) Took cash out of business for private use

Account to be debited	Account to be credited

6.3X Complete the following table, showing the accounts to be debited and those to be credited:

(a) Paid insurance by cheque
(b) Paid motor expenses by cash
(c) Rent received in cash
(d) Paid rates by cheque
(e) Received refund of rates by cheque
(f) Paid for stationery expenses by cash
(g) Paid wages by cash
(h) Sold surplus stationery receiving proceeds by cheque
(i) Received sales commission by cheque
(j) Bought motor van by cheque

Account to be debited	Account to be credited

6.4X The following table should be completed:

	Account to be debited	Account to be credited
(a) Sold surplus stationery, receiving proceeds in cash		
(b) Paid salaries by cheque		
(c) Rent received for premises sublet, by cheque		
(d) Goods returned to us by Royal Products		
(e) Commission received by us previously in error, we now refund this by cheque		
(f) Bought machinery by cheque		
(g) Paid lighting expenses in cash		
(h) Insurance rebate received by cheque		
(i) Buildings bought by cheque		
(j) Building repairs paid in cash		

6.5 Enter the following transactions in the necessary accounts in double entry:

2000
Jan 1 Started business with £200 in the bank
Jan 2 U Surer lent us £1,000 giving us the money by cheque
Jan 3 Bought goods on credit £296 from T Parkin
Jan 5 Bought motor van by cheque £250
Jan 6 Cash sales £105
Jan 7 Paid motor expenses in cash £15
Jan 8 Paid wages in cash £18
Jan 10 Bought goods on credit from C Moore £85
Jan 12 Paid insurance by cheque £22
Jan 25 Received commission in cash £15
Jan 31 Paid electricity bill by cheque £17

6.6 You are to enter the following transactions, completing double entry in the books for the month of May 2001.

2001
May 1 Started business with £2,000 in the bank
May 2 Purchased goods £175 on credit from M Mills
May 3 Bought fixtures and fittings £150 paying by cheque
May 5 Sold goods for cash £275
May 6 Bought goods on credit £114 from S Waites
May 10 Paid rent by cash £15
May 12 Bought stationery £27, paying by cash
May 18 Goods returned to M Mills £23
May 21 Let off part of the premises receiving rent by cheque £5
May 23 Sold goods on credit to U Henry for £77
May 24 Bought a motor van paying by cheque £300
May 30 Paid the month's wages by cash £117
May 31 The proprietor took cash for himself £44

6.7 Write up the following transactions in the books of L Thompson:

2002
Mar 1   Started business with cash £1,500
Mar 2   Bought goods on credit from A Hanson £296
Mar 3   Paid rent by cash £28
Mar 4   Paid £1,000 of the cash of the firm into a bank account
Mar 5   Sold goods on credit to E Linton £54
Mar 7   Bought stationery £15 paying by cheque
Mar 11 Cash sales £49
Mar 14 Goods returned by us to A Hanson £17
Mar 17 Sold goods on credit to S Morgan £29
Mar 20 Paid for repairs to the building by cash £18
Mar 22 E Linton returned goods to us £14
Mar 27 Paid Hanson by cheque £279
Mar 28 Cash purchases £125
Mar 29 Bought a motor van paying by cheque £395
Mar 30 Paid motor expenses in cash £15
Mar 31 Bought fixtures £120 on credit from A Webster

6.8X Enter the following transactions in double entry:

2003
July 1   Started business with £8,000 in the bank
July 2   Bought stationery by cheque £30
July 3   Bought goods on credit from I Walsh £900
July 4   Sold goods for cash £180
July 5   Paid insurance by cash £40
July 7   Bought machinery on credit from H Morgan £500
July 8   Paid for machinery expenses by cheque £50
July 10 Sold goods on credit to D Small £320
July 11 Returned goods to I Walsh £70
July 14 Paid wages by cash £70
July 17 Paid rent by cheque £100
July 20 Received cheque £200 from D Small
July 21 Paid H Morgan by cheque £500
July 23 Bought stationery on credit from Express Ltd £80
July 25 Sold goods on credit to N Thomas £230
July 28 Received rent £20 in cash for part of premises sublet
July 31 Paid Express Ltd by cheque £80

6.9X You are to enter the following transactions, completing double entry in the records of J Collins for the month of June 2000.

June	1	Started business with £10,000 in the bank and £300 cash
June	1	Bought goods on credit from: J Carby £400; F McIntyre £1,188; C Morrison £1,344
June	2	Bought shop fittings by cheque £240
June	3	Bought shop fittings on credit from M Johnson Ltd £575
June	5	Paid insurance by cash £88
June	6	Bought motor van paying by cheque £3,200
June	7	Sold goods for cash £140
June	7	Sold goods on credit to: W Graham & Co £450; F Phillips Ltd £246; D R Edwards £80
June	8	Bought office stationery £180 on credit from D Ball & Co
June	9	Paid rent by cheque £75
June	10	Paid rates by cheque £250
June	11	We returned goods to F McIntyre £168
June	12	Paid D Ball & Co £180 by cheque
June	13	Sold goods on credit to K P Prince & Co £220; F Phillips Ltd £154; Kay & Edwards Ltd £270
June	14	Goods returned to us by W Graham & Co £40
June	15	Paid wages by cash £120
June	16	Loan from D Clayton by cheque £500
June	17	W Graham & Co paid us the amount owing by cheque £410
June	18	Some of the stationery was bought unwisely. We sell it for cash £15
June	20	We had overpaid insurance. A refund of £8 received by cheque
June	21	Paid motor expenses by cash £55
June	23	Paid wages by cash £120
June	25	Cheques received from K P Prince & Co £220; F Phillips Ltd £100 (as part payment)
June	26	Some of the shop fittings were unsuitable and were returned to M Johnson Ltd £25
June	28	Paid F McIntyre £1,188, rent £75, both by cheque
June	30	J Collins took drawings by cheque £200

7 The double-entry system: closing balances

AIMS

- To demonstrate how to obtain the closing balances of personal accounts for both debtors and creditors.

- To show how to distinguish between a debit balance and a credit balance.

- To explain how to show personal ledger accounts in a three-column format instead of as 'T' accounts.

7.1 Accounts for debtors

Where debtors have paid their accounts

What you have been reading so far is the recording of transactions in the books by means of debit and credit entries. At the end of each period we will have to look at each account to see what is shown by the entries.

Probably the most obvious reason for this is to find out how much our customers owe us for goods we have sold to them. In most firms this is done at the end of each month. Let us look at the account of one of our customers, K Tandy, for transactions in August 2000.

K Tandy Account

Dr				Cr
2000		£	2000	£
Aug 1 Sales		144	Aug 22 Bank	144
Aug 19 Sales		300	Aug 28 Bank	300

This shows that during the month we sold a total of £444 goods to Tandy, and have been paid a total of £444 by him. At the close of business at the end of August he therefore owes us nothing. His account can be closed off on 31 August 2000 by inserting the totals on each side, as follows:

K Tandy Account

Dr				Cr
2000		£	2000	£
Aug 1 Sales		144	Aug 22 Bank	144
Aug 19 Sales		300	Aug 28 Bank	300
		444		444

Notice that totals in accounting are shown with a single line above them and a double line underneath. Totals on accounts at the end of a period are always shown on a level with one another, as shown in the following completed account for C Lee:

C Lee Account

Dr							Cr
2000			£	2000			£
Aug	11	Sales	177	Aug	30	Bank	480
Aug	19	Sales	203				
Aug	22	Sales	100				
			480				480

In this account, C Lee also owed us nothing at the end of August 2000, as he had paid us for all sales to him.

If an account contains only one entry on each side and they are equal, totals are unnecessary. For example:

K Wood Account

Dr							Cr
2000			£	2000			£
Aug	6	Sales	214	Aug	12	Bank	214

Where debtors still owe for goods

On the other hand, some of our customers will still owe us something at the end of the month. In these cases the totals of each side would not equal one another. Let us look at the account of D Knight for August 2000:

D Knight Account

Dr							Cr
2000			£	2000			£
Aug	1	Sales	158	Aug	28	Bank	158
Aug	15	Sales	206				
Aug	30	Sales	118				

If you add the figures you will see that the debit side adds up to £482 and the credit side adds up to £158. You should be able to see what the difference of £324 (i.e. £482 – £158) represents. It consists of sales of £206 and £118 not paid for and therefore owing to us on 31 August 2000.

In double entry we only enter figures as totals if the totals on both sides of the account agree. We do, however, want to close off the account for August, but showing that Knight owes us £324. If he owes £324 at close of business on 31 August 2000 then he will still owe us that same figure when the business opens on 1 September 2000.

We show this by **balancing the account**. This is done in five stages:

1   Add up both sides to find out their totals. Do not write anything in the account at this stage.

2   Deduct the smaller total from the larger total to find the balance.

3   Now enter the balance on the side with the smallest total. This now means the totals will be equal.

4 Enter totals on a level with each other.

5 Now enter the balance on the line below the totals. The balance below the totals should be on the opposite side to the balance shown above the totals.

Against the balance above the totals, complete the date column by showing the last day of that period. Below the totals show the first day of the next period against the balance. The balance above the totals is described as balance **carried down**. The balance below the total is described as balance **brought down**.

Knight's account when 'balanced off' will appear as follows:

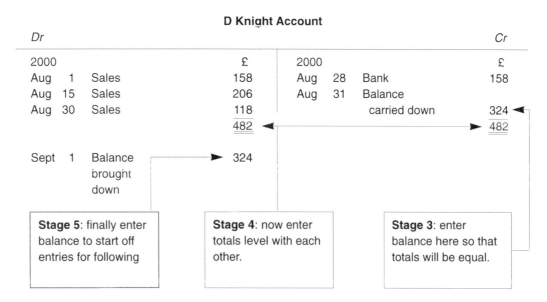

D Knight Account

Dr						Cr
2000			£	2000		£
Aug	1	Sales	158	Aug 28	Bank	158
Aug	15	Sales	206	Aug 31	Balance	
Aug	30	Sales	118		carried down	324
			482			482
Sept	1	Balance brought down	324			

Stage 5: finally enter balance to start off entries for following

Stage 4: now enter totals level with each other.

Stage 3: enter balance here so that totals will be equal.

We can now look at another account prior to balancing:

H Henry Account

Dr						Cr
2000			£	2000		£
Aug	5	Sales	300	Aug 24	Returns inwards	50
Aug	28	Sales	540	Aug 29	Bank	250

We will abbreviate 'carried down' to 'c/d' and 'brought down' to 'b/d' from now on.

H Henry Account

Dr						Cr
2000			£	2000		£
Aug	5	Sales	300	Aug 24	Returns inwards	50
Aug	28	Sales	540	Aug 29	Bank	250
				Aug 31	Balance c/d	540
			840			840
Sept	1	Balance b/d	540			

Notes:

- The date given to balance c/d is the last day of the period which is finishing and balance b/d is given the opening date of the next period.
- As the total of the debit side originally exceeded the total of the credit side, the balance is said to be a debit balance. This being a personal account (for a person), the person concerned is said to be a debtor – the accounting term for anyone who owes money to the firm. The use of the term debtor for a person whose account has a debit balance can again thus be seen.

If accounts contain only one entry it is unnecessary to enter the total. A double line ruled under the entry will mean that the entry is its own total. For example:

B Walters Account

Dr			£				Cr
2000				2000			£
Aug	18	Sales	51	Aug	31	Balance c/d	51
Sept	1	Balance b/d	51				

7.2 Accounts for creditors

Exactly the same principles will apply when the balances are carried down to the credit side. We can look at two accounts of our suppliers which are to be balanced off:

E Williams Account

Dr			£				Cr
2000				2000			£
Aug	21	Bank	100	Aug	2	Purchases	248
				Aug	18	Purchases	116

K Patterson Account

Dr			£				Cr
2000				2000			£
Aug	14	Returns outwards	20	Aug	8	Purchases	620
Aug	28	Bank	600	Aug	15	Purchases	200

We now add up the totals and find the balance, i.e. stages 1 and 2.

When balanced these will appear as:

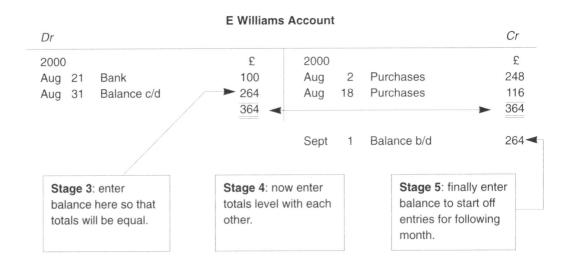

E Williams Account

Dr			£				Cr
2000				2000			£
Aug	21	Bank	100	Aug	2	Purchases	248
Aug	31	Balance c/d	264	Aug	18	Purchases	116
			364				364
				Sept	1	Balance b/d	264

Stage 3: enter balance here so that totals will be equal.

Stage 4: now enter totals level with each other.

Stage 5: finally enter balance to start off entries for following month.

K Patterson Account

Dr				Cr		
2000		£	2000			£
Aug 14	Returns outwards	20	Aug 8	Purchases		620
Aug 28	Bank	600	Aug 15	Purchases		200
Aug 31	Balance c/d	200				
		820				820
			Sept 1	Balance b/d		200

Before you read further attempt Student Activities 7.1, 7.2 and 7.3 on p 53.

7.3 Computers and accounts

Through the main part of this book the type of account used shows the left-hand side of the account as the debit side, and the right-hand side as the credit side. However, when most computers are used the style of the ledger account is different. It appears as three columns of figures, there being one column for debit entries, another column for credit entries, and the last column for the balance. If you have a current account at a bank your bank statements will normally be shown using this method.

The accounts used in this chapter will now be redrafted to show the ledger accounts drawn up in this way.

K Tandy Account

	Debit	Credit	Balance (and whether debit or credit)	
2000	£	£	£	
Aug 1 Sales	144		144	Dr
Aug 19 Sales	300		444	Dr
Aug 22 Bank		144	300	Dr
Aug 28 Bank		300	0	

C Lee Account

	Debit	Credit	Balance	
2000	£	£	£	
Aug 11 Sales	177		177	Dr
Aug 19 Sales	203		380	Dr
Aug 22 Sales	100		480	Dr
Aug 30 Bank		480	0	

K Wood Account

	Debit	Credit	Balance	
2000	£	£	£	
Aug 6 Sales	214		214	Dr
Aug 12 Bank		214	0	

D Knight Account

	Debit	Credit	Balance	
2000	£	£	£	
Aug 1 Sales	158		158	Dr
Aug 15 Sales	206		364	Dr
Aug 28 Cash		158	206	Dr
Aug 31 Sales	118		324	Dr

H Henry Account

	Debit	Credit	Balance	
2000	£	£	£	
Aug 5 Sales	300		300	Dr
Aug 24 Returns		50	250	Dr
Aug 28 Sales	540		790	Dr
Aug 29 Bank		250	540	Dr

B Walters Account

	Debit	Credit	Balance	
2000	£	£	£	
Aug 18 Sales	51		51	Dr

E Williams Account

	Debit	Credit	Balance	
2000	£	£	£	
Aug 2 Purchases		248	248	Cr
Aug 18 Purchases		116	364	Cr
Aug 21 Bank	100		264	Cr

K Patterson Account

	Debit	Credit	Balance	
2000	£	£	£	
Aug 8 Purchases		620	620	Cr
Aug 14 Returns	20		600	Cr
Aug 15 Purchases		200	800	Cr
Aug 28 Bank	600		200	Cr

It will be noticed that the balance is calculated again after every entry. This can be done quite simply when using a computer because it is the machine which calculates the new balance.

However, when manual methods are being used it is often too much work to have to calculate a new balance after each entry. It also means that the greater the number of calculations the greater the possibility of errors. For these reasons it is usual for students to use two-sided accounts. However, it is important to note that there is no difference in principle, the final balances are the same using either method.

NEW TERM

Balancing the account Finding and entering the difference between the two sides of an account.

STUDENT ACTIVITIES

7.1 Enter the following items in the necessary debtors and creditors accounts only; do **not** write up other accounts. Then balance down each personal account at the end of the month. (Keep your answer – it will be used as a basis for question activity 7.3.)

2001
May 1 Sales on credit to H Harvey £690, N Morgan £153, J Lindo £420
May 4 Sales on credit to L Masters £418, H Harvey £66
May 10 Returns inwards from H Harvey £40, J Lindo £20
May 18 N Morgan paid us by cheque £153
May 20 J Lindo paid us £400 by cheque
May 24 H Harvey paid us £300 by cash
May 31 Sales on credit to L Masters £203

7.2 Enter the following in the personal accounts only. Do **not** write up the other accounts. Then balance down each personal account at the end of the month. (Keep your answer – it will be used as the basis of activity 7.4X.)

2002
June 1 Purchases on credit from J Young £458, L Williams £120, G Norman £708
June 3 Purchases on credit from L Williams £77, T Harris £880
June 10 We returned goods to G Norman £22, J Young £55
June 15 Purchases on credit from J Young £80
June 19 We paid T Harris by cheque £880
June 28 We paid J Young by cash £250
June 30 We returned goods to L Williams £17

7.3 Redraft each of the accounts given in your answer to 7.1 in three-column ledger-style accounts.

7.4X Redraft each of the accounts given in your answer to 7.2 in three-column ledger-style accounts.

7.5 Enter the following in the personal accounts only, do **not** write up the other accounts. Balance down each personal account at the end of the month. After completing this, state which of the balances represent debtors and those which are creditors.

2001
Sept 1 Sales on credit to D Williams £458, J Moore £235, G Grant £98
Sept 2 Purchases on credit A White £77, H Samuels £231, P Owen £65
Sept 8 Sales on credit to J Moore £444, F Franklin £249
Sept 10 Purchases on credit from H Samuels £12, O Oliver £222
Sept 12 Returns inwards from G Grant £9, J Moore £26
Sept 17 We returned goods to H Samuels £24, O Oliver £12
Sept 20 We paid A White by cheque £77
Sept 24 D Williams paid us by cheque £300
Sept 26 We paid O Oliver by cash £210
Sept 28 D Williams paid us by cash £100
Sept 30 F Franklin pays us by cheque £249

7.6X Enter the following in the necessary personal accounts. Do *not* write up the other accounts. Balance each personal account at the end of the month. (Keep your answer – it will be used as the basis of question 7.8X.)

2003

Aug 1 Sales on credit to L Sterling £445, L Lindo £480, R Spencer £221
Aug 4 Goods returned to us by L Sterling £15, R Spencer £33
Aug 8 Sales on credit to L Lindo £66, R Spencer £129, L Banks £465
Aug 9 We received a cheque for £430 from L Sterling
Aug 12 Sales on credit to R Spencer £235, L Banks £777
Aug 19 Goods returned to us by L Banks £21, R Spencer £25
Aug 22 We received cheques as follows: R Spencer £300, L Lindo £414
Aug 31 Sales on credit to L Lindo £887, L Banks £442

7.7X Enter the following, personal accounts only. Bring down balances at end of the month. After completing this state which of the balances represent debtors and those which are creditors.

2001

May 1 Credit sale B Flynn £241, R Kelly £29, J Long £887, T Fryer £124
May 2 Credit purchases from S Wood £148, T DuQuesnay £27, R Johnson £77, G Henriques £108
May 8 Credit sales to R Kelly £74, J Long £132
May 9 Credit purchases from T DuQuesnay £142, G Henriques £44
May 10 Goods returned to us by J Long £17, T Fryer £44
May 12 Cash paid to us by T Fryer £80
May 15 We returned goods to S Wood £8, G Henriques £18
May 19 We received cheques from J Long £500, B Flynn £241
May 21 We sold goods on credit to B Flynn £44, R Kelly £280
May 28 We paid by cheque the following: S Wood £140, G Henriques £50, R Johnson £60
May 31 We returned goods to G Henriques £4

7.8X Redraft each of the accounts given in your answer to 7.6X in three-column style accounts.

8 The trial balance

AIMS

- To explain why trial balance totals should equal one another.

- To demonstrate how to draw up a trial balance from a given set of figures.

- To understand that when some kinds of errors are made the trial balance totals can still equal one another.

8.1 Total debit entries = total credit entries

You have already seen that the method of bookkeeping in use is that of the double-entry method. This means:

- for each debit entry there is a credit entry;

- for each credit entry there is a debit entry.

All the items recorded in all the accounts on the debit side should equal in **total** all the items recorded on the credit side of the books. We need to check that for each debit entry there is also a credit entry. To see if the two totals are equal, usually known as seeing if the two sides of the books 'balance', a **trial balance** may be drawn up at the end of a period.

A form of trial balance could be drawn up by listing all the accounts and adding together all the debit entries, at the same time adding together all the credit entries. Using the worked exercise on pages 56–58 such a trial balance would appear as below. Note that it could not be drawn up until after all the entries had been made. It will therefore be dated as on 31 May 2002.

Trial Balance as on 31 May 2002		
	Dr £	Cr £
Purchases	309	
Sales		255
Returns outwards		15
Returns inwards	16	
D Small	68	68
A Lyon & Son		141
D Hughes	60	60
M Spencer	45	16
Cash	210	153
	708	708

8.2 Total debit balances = total credit balances

Section 8.1 is not the normal method of drawing up a trial balance, but it is the easiest to understand at first. Usually, a trial balance is a list of balances only, arranged according to whether they are debit balances or credit balances. If the trial balance on p. 55 had been drawn up using the normal balances method it would appear as below:

Trial Balance as on 31 May 2002		
	Dr	Cr
	£	£
Purchases	309	
Sales		255
Returns outwards		15
Returns inwards	16	
A Lyon & Son		141
M Spencer	29	
Cash	57	
	411	411

Here the two sides also 'balance'. The sums of £68 in D Small's account, £60 in D Hughes' account, £16 in M Spencer's account and £153 in the cash account have, however, been cancelled out from each side of these accounts by taking only the **balances** instead of **totals**. As equal amounts have been cancelled from each side, £297 in all, the new totals should still equal one another, as in fact they do at £411.

This form of trial balance is the easiest to extract when there are more than a few transactions during the period. Also the balances are either used later when the profits are being calculated or else appear in a balance sheet. Trial balances, therefore, are not just done to find errors.

8.3 A worked example

The following accounts, for K Potter, have been entered up for May 2001 and balanced off

K Potter's Books Bank Account

Dr								Cr
2001			£	2001				£
May	1	Capital	9,000	May	21	Machinery		550
May	30	T Monk	300	May	29	T Wood		860
				May	31	Balance c/d		7,890
			9,300					9,300
June	1	Balance b/d	7,890					

Cash Account

Dr								Cr
2001			£	2001				£
May	5	Sales	180	May	30	K Young		170
May	12	Sales	210	May	31	Balance c/d		220
			390					390
June	1	Balance b/d	220					

T Wood Account

Dr					Cr				
2001			£		2001				£
May	6	Returns outwards	40		May	2	Purchases		900
May	29	Bank	860						
			900						900

K Young Account

Dr					Cr				
2001			£		2001				£
May	28	Returns outwards	80		May	3	Purchases		250
May	30	Cash	170		May	18	Purchases		190
May	31	Balance c/d	190						
			440						440
					June	1	Balance b/d		190

T Monk Account

Dr					Cr				
2001			£		2001				£
May	10	Sales	590		May	23	Returns inwards		140
					May	30	Bank		300
					May	31	Balance c/d		150
			590						590
June	1	Balance b/d	150						

C Howe Account

Dr					Cr				
2001			£		2001				£
May	22	Sales	220		May	25	Returns inwards		10
					May	31	Balance c/d		210
			220						220
June	1	Balance b/d	210						

AB Ltd Account

Dr					Cr				
					2001				£
					May	31	Machinery		2,700

Capital Account

Dr					Cr				
					2001				£
					May	1	Bank		9,000

Purchases Account

Dr					Cr				
2001			£		2001				£
May	2	T Wood	900		May	31	Balance c/d		1340
May	3	K Young	250						
May	18	K Young	190						
			1,340						1,340
June	1	Balance b/d	1,340						

Sales Account

Dr			£	Cr			£
2001				2001			
May	31	Balance c/d	1,200	May	5	Cash	180
				May	10	T Monk	590
				May	12	Cash	210
				May	22	C Howe	220
			1,200				1,200
				June	1	Balance b/d	1,200

Returns Inwards Account

Dr			£	Cr			£
2001				2001			
May	23	T Monk	140	May	31	Balance c/d	150
May	25	C Howe	10				
			150				150
June	1	Balance b/d	150				

Returns Outwards Account

Dr			£	Cr			£
2001				2001			
May	31	Balance c/d	120	May	6	T Wood	40
				May	28	K Young	80
			120				120
				June	1	Balance b/d	120

Machinery Account

Dr			£	Cr			£
2001				2001			
May	21	Bank	550	May	31	Balance c/d	3,250
May	31	AB Ltd	2,700				
			3,250				3,250
June	1	Balance b/d	3,250				

The trial balance would appear as follows:

K Potter Trial Balance as on 31 May 2001		
	Dr £	Cr £
Bank	7,890	
Cash	220	
K Young		190
T Monk	150	
C Howe	210	
AB Ltd		2,700
Capital		9,000
Purchases	1,340	
Sales		1,200
Returns inwards	150	
Returns outwards		120
Machinery	3,250	
	13,210	13,210

8.4 Trial balances and errors

It may at first sight appear that the balancing of a trial balance proves that the books are correct. This, however, is quite wrong. It means that certain types of error have not been made, but there are several types of error that will not affect the balancing of a trial balance, such as omitting a transaction altogether. Examples of the errors which would be revealed, provided there are no compensating errors which cancel them out, are errors in additions, using one figure for the debit entry and another figure for the credit entry, entering only one aspect of a transaction, and so on. We shall consider these in greater detail in later chapters.

Skeleton trial balance

Some examining bodies provide a list of balances from which a trial balance must be drawn up, while other questions involve the correction of a trial balance. It is essential to understand the basic principles of double entry to carry out this task, i.e. a debit balance is always an asset, expense or loss and a credit balance is capital, a liability or income.

A skeleton trial balance is shown below which will act as a guide enabling you to answer such questions. Later in your studies you will come across other items, but we will keep it fairly simple at this stage.

Skeleton Trial Balance as at 31 May 2001

	Dr	Cr
All **debit** balances will include:		
Assets	Stock (1 June 2000) Cash Bank Machinery Motor vans Fittings Debtors Premises	
Expenses and losses	Purchases Carriage in and out Wages and salaries Advertising Rent and rates Stationery Bad debts written off Light and heat	
Others	Drawings	
All **credit** balances will include:		
Capital and liabilities		Capital Creditors Loans *from* others
Income, profits and gains		Sales Commissions received Rents received

Note: Closing stock appears as a note.

NEW TERM

Trial balance: A list of all the balances in the books at a particular point in time. The balances are shown in debit and credit columns. These columns should balance provided no errors have occurred.

STUDENT ACTIVITIES

8.1 You are to enter up the necessary amounts for the month of May from the following details, and then balance off the accounts and extract a trial balance as at 31 May 2002.

2002

May	1	Started firm with capital in cash of £250
May	2	Bought goods on credit from the following persons: D Ellis £54; C Mendez £87; K Gibson £25; D Booth £76; L Lowe £64
May	4	Sold goods on credit to: C Bailey £43; B Hughes £62; H Spencer £176
May	6	Paid rent by cash £12
May	9	Bailey paid us his account by cheque £43
May	10	H Spencer paid us £150 by cheque
May	12	We paid the following by cheque: K Gibson £25; D Ellis £54
May	15	Paid carriage by cash £23
May	18	Bought goods on credit from C Mendez £43; D Booth £110
May	21	Sold goods on credit to B Hughes £67
May	31	Paid rent by cheque £18

8.2 Enter up the books from the following details for the month of March and extract a trial balance as at 31 March 2003.

2003

March	1	Started business with £800 in the bank
March	2	Bought goods on credit from the following persons: K Henriques £76; M Hyatt £27; T Braham £56
March	5	Cash sales £87
March	6	Paid wages in cash £14
March	7	Sold goods on credit to: H Elliott £35; L Lane £42; J Carlton £72
March	9	Bought goods for cash £46
March	10	Bought goods on credit from: M Hyatt £57; T Braham £98
March	12	Paid wages in cash £14
March	13	Sold goods on credit to: L Lane £32; J Carlton £23
March	15	Bought shop fixtures on credit from Betta Ltd £50
March	17	Paid M Hyatt by cheque £84
March	18	We returned goods to T Braham £20
March	21	Paid Betta Ltd a cheque for £50
March	24	J Carlton paid us his account by cheque £95
March	27	We returned goods to K Henriques £24
March	30	J King lent us £60 by cash
March	31	Bought a motor van paying by cheque £400

8.3 The following transactions are to be entered up in the books for June, and accounts balanced off and a trial balance extracted as at 30 June 2005.

2005

June	1	Started business with £600 in the bank and £50 cash in hand
June	2	Bought £500 goods on credit from C Jones
June	3	Credit sales: H Henry £66; N Neita £25; P Potter £43
June	4	Goods bought for cash £23
June	5	Bought motor van paying by cheque £256
June	7	Paid motor expenses by cheque £12
June	9	Credit sales: B Barnes £24; K Lyn £26; M Moore £65
June	11	Goods bought on credit: C Jones £240; N Moss £62; O Hughes £46
June	13	Goods returned by us to C Jones £25
June	15	Paid motor expenses by cash £5
June	19	Goods returned to us by N Neita £11
June	20	Cash taken for own use (drawings) £10
June	21	We paid the following by cheque: N Moss £62; O Hughes £46
June	23	H Henry paid us in cash £66
June	25	P Potter paid us by cheque £43
June	26	Cash sales £34
June	27	Cash taken for own use £24
June	28	Goods returned by us to C Jones £42
June	29	Paid for postage stamps by cash £4
June	30	Credit sales: N Neita £43; M Edgar £67; K Lyn £45

8.4X Record the following transactions of D Chatsworth for the month of May 2002, balance off all the accounts and then extract a trial balance as on 31 May 2002.

2002

May	1	D Chatsworth started business with £8,000 cash
May	2	Put £7,500 of the cash into a bank account
May	2	Bought goods on credit from: Burton Brothers £180; Lyew & Co £560; P McDonald £380; K Black Ltd £410
May	3	Bought office fixtures by cheque £185
May	4	Bought goods for cash £190
May	5	Cash sales £110
May	6	Goods sold on credit: J Gayle & Son £190; P Gentles £340; T Sutherland £110; T Brown Ltd £300
May	7	Paid rent by cheque £100
May	8	Paid wages by cash £70
May	10	Bought goods on credit from: Lyew & Co £340; C Rose £160
May	11	Goods returned to us by J Gayle & Son £60
May	13	Goods sold on credit to: N Mattis £44; J Gayle & Son £300
May	14	Bought office fixtures on credit from Tru-kits Ltd £178
May	15	Bought office stationery for cash £90
May	16	Paid cheques to the following: Tru-kits Ltd £178; Burton Brothers £180
May	17	Paid wages by cash £90
May	18	D Chatsworth takes £100 drawings in cash
May	20	We returned goods to P McDonald £60; K Black Ltd £44
May	22	Bought office stationery £220 on credit from EP & Co
May	24	Received cheques from N Mattis £44; T Brown Ltd £180
May	26	Cash sales £140
May	29	D Chatsworth took cash drawings £150
May	31	Paid sundry expenses by cash £5

8.5X Record the following details for the month of November 2000 and extract a trial balance as at 30 November 2000.

2000

Nov	1	Started with £5,000 in the bank
Nov	3	Bought goods on credit from: T Henriques £160; J Smith £230; W Rogers £400; P Boone £310
Nov	5	Cash sales £240
Nov	6	Paid rent by cheque £20
Nov	7	Paid rates by cheque £190
Nov	11	Sold goods on credit to: L Matthews £48; K Allen £32; R Hall £1,170
Nov	17	Paid wages by cash £40
Nov	18	We returned goods to: T Henriques £14; P Boone £20
Nov	19	Bought goods on credit from: P Boone £80; W Rogers £270; D Diaz £130
Nov	20	Goods were returned to us by K Allen £2; L Matthews £4
Nov	21	Bought motor van on credit from UZ Motors £500
Nov	23	We paid the following by cheque: T Henriques £146; J Smith £230; W Rogers £300
Nov	25	Bought another motor van, paying by cheque immediately £700
Nov	26	Received a loan of £400 cash from A Williams
Nov	28	Received cheques from: L Matthews £44; K Allen £30
Nov	30	Proprietor brings a further £300 into the business, by a payment into the business bank account

8.6X Record the following for the month of January, balance off all the accounts and then extract a trial balance as at 31 January 2002.

2002

Jan	1	Started business with £3,500 cash
Jan	2	Put £2,800 of the cash into a bank account
Jan	3	Bought goods for cash £150
Jan	4	Bought goods on credit from: L Coke £360; M Burton £490; T Hill £110; C Small £340
Jan	5	Bought stationery on credit from: Swift Ltd £170
Jan	6	Sold goods on credit to: S Walters £90; T Binns £150; C Howard £190; P Peart £160
Jan	8	Paid rent by cheque £55
Jan	10	Bought fixtures on credit from Matalon Ltd £480
Jan	11	Paid salaries in cash £120
Jan	14	Returned goods to M Burton £40; T Hill £60
Jan	15	Bought motor van by cheque £700
Jan	16	Received loan from J Henry by cheque £600
Jan	18	Goods returned to us by: S Walters £20; C Howard £40
Jan	21	Cash sales £90
Jan	24	Sold goods on credit to: T Binns £100; P Peart £340; J Smart £115
Jan	26	We paid the following by cheque: M Burton £450; T Hill £50
Jan	29	Received cheques from: J Smart £115; T Binns £250
Jan	30	Received a further loan from J Henry by cash £200
Jan	30	Received £500 cash from P Peart

8.7 Correct and balance the following trial balance:

Trial Balance of P Brown as at 31 May 2003

	Dr £	Cr £
Capital		20,000
Drawings	7,000	
General expenses		500
Sales	38,500	
Purchases		29,000
Debtors		6,800
Creditors	9,000	
Bank balance (Dr)	15,100	
Cash		200
Plant and equipment		5,000
Heating and lighting		1,500
Rent	2,400	

8.8 Reconstruct the trial balance after making the necessary corrections.

Trial Balance of S Higton as at 30 June 2004

	Dr £	Cr £
Capital	23,820	
Sales		119,439
Stationery	1,200	
General expenses	2,745	
Motor expenses		4,476
Cash at bank	1,950	
Wages and salaries		9,492
Rent and rates	10,500	
Office equipment	6,000	
Purchases	89,421	
Heating and lighting		2,208
Debtors	10,353	
Drawings		4,200
Creditors		10,230
Motor vehicle	7,500	
Insurance		3,444
	153,489	153,489

8.9 From the following list of balances prepare a trial balance as at 31 December 2003 for Ms Anita Hall:

	£
Plant and machinery	21,450
Motor vehicles	26,000
Premises	80,000
Wages	42,840
Purchases	119,856
Sales	185,944
Telephone, printing and stationery	3,600
Creditors	27,200
Debtors	30,440
Cash at bank	624
Capital	131,250
Drawings	10,680
General expenses	3,584
Lighting and heating	2,960
Motor expenses	2,360

9 Division of the ledgers: books of original entry

AIMS

- To introduce the reader to the various types of books of original entry and to the way in which they are used.

- To explain the different types of accounts, i.e. personal and impersonal.

9.1 Introduction

While a business or organisation is very small, all the double-entry accounts can be kept in one book, which we would call the ledger. In a larger business or organisation it would be impossible to use one book as the large number of pages needed for the numerous transactions would mean that the book would be too big to handle. Also, if there were several bookkeepers, they could not all do their work properly if there was only one ledger.

The answer to this problem is for us to use more books. When we do this we put similar types of transactions together and have a book for that type. In each book we will not mix together transactions which are different from one another.

9.2 Books of original entry

These are books in which we record transactions first of all. We have a separate book for each different kind of transaction. The nature of the transaction affects which book it is entered into. Sales will be entered in one book, purchases in another book, cash in another book, and so on. We enter the transactions in these books giving the following details:

- date: the transactions should be shown in date order;

- details column completed;

- folio column for cross-referencing purposes;

- money column completed.

The types of books of original entry are:

- **Sales day book** – for credit sales (Chapter 19).

- **Purchases day book** – for credit purchases (Chapter 20).

- **Returns inwards day book** – for returns inwards (Chapter 21).

- **Returns outwards day-book** – for returns outwards (Chapter 21).

- **Cash books** – for receipts and payments of cash (Chapter 11).

- **General journal** – for other items (Chapter 27).

9.3 Types of ledger

Although we have now made lists of transactions in the books of original entry, we still have more work to do. We have got to show the effect of the transactions by putting them into double-entry accounts. Instead of keeping all the double-entry accounts in one ledger, we have several ledgers. This again makes it easier to divide the work between different bookkeepers.

The different types of ledger we use are:

- **Sales ledger**. This is the record of customers' personal accounts.

- **Purchases ledger**. This is the record of suppliers' personal accounts.

- **General ledger.** This contains the remaining double-entry accounts such as expenses, fixed assets, capital, etc.

9.4 Description of books used

In the next few chapters we will look at the books used in more detail, except for the general journal which will be dealt with at a later stage. An overview of the books used is given in Exhibit 9.1.

Exhibit 9.1 Diagram of books used

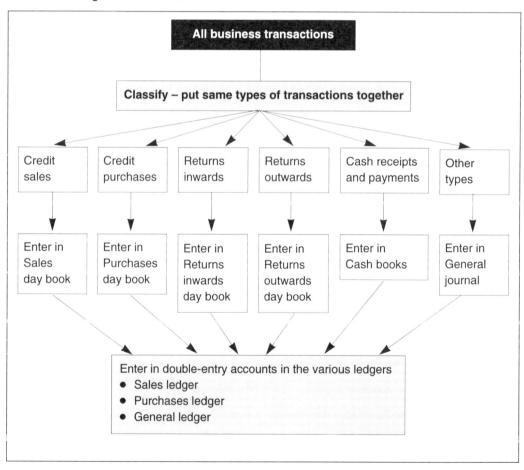

9.5 Types of accounts

Some people describe all accounts as **personal** accounts or as **impersonal** accounts.

- **Personal accounts** – these are for debtors and creditors.

- **Impersonal accounts** – divided between real accounts and nominal accounts.

- **Real accounts** – accounts in which property is recorded. Examples are buildings, machinery, fixtures and stock.

- **Nominal accounts** – accounts in which expenses, income and capital are recorded.

Exhibit 9.2 may make this clearer.

Exhibit 9.2 Types of accounts

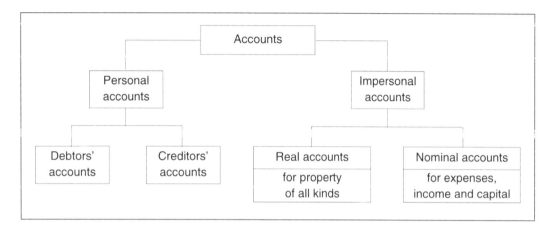

9.6 Nominal and private ledgers

The ledger in which the impersonal accounts are kept is known as the **nominal** (or general) **ledger**. Very often, to ensure privacy for the proprietor(s), the capital and drawing accounts and similar accounts are kept in a **private ledger**. By doing this office staff cannot see details of items which the proprietors want to keep a secret.

9.7 The use of computers in accounting

So far it has been assumed that all bookkeeping procedures are carried out using manual systems, but nowadays many businesses use computer systems especially when dealing with large numbers of transactions. Computers are used for recording information in the same ways as manual systems, therefore throughout the book the accounting terms of 'book' or 'journal' will be referred to for their use in either system.

NEW TERMS

Books of original entry Books where the first entry of a transaction is made.

Cash book Book of original entry for cash and bank receipts and payments.

General journal Book of original entry for all items other than those for cash or goods.

General ledger All accounts other than those for customers and suppliers.

Impersonal accounts All accounts other than debtors' and creditors' accounts.

Nominal accounts Accounts in which expenses, revenue and capital are recorded.

Nominal ledger Ledger for impersonal accounts (also called general ledger).

Personal accounts Accounts for both creditors and debtors.

Private ledger Ledger for capital and drawings accounts.

Purchases day book Book of original entry for credit purchases.

Purchases ledger A ledger for suppliers' personal accounts.

Real accounts Accounts in which property of all kinds is recorded.

Returns inwards day book Book of original entry for goods returned by customers.

Returns outwards day book Book of original entry for goods returned to suppliers.

Sales day book Book of original entry for credit sales.

Sales ledger A ledger for customers' personal accounts.

Unit 1: Recording and accounting for cash transactions

10 The banking system

AIMS

- To show the difference between current accounts and deposit accounts.

- To demonstrate how to make out cheques and paying-in slips.

- To explain how payments can be made by:
  - (a) bank giro credits/credit transfer;
  - (b) Bankers' Automated Clearing Service (BACS).

- To show how standing orders and direct debits can be used.

- To explain some of the problems related to cheques, namely:
  - (a) stopped cheques;
  - (b) post-dated cheques;
  - (c) out-of-date cheques;
  - (d) dishonoured cheques.

- To explain the relationship between banks and their customers and its importance.

- To provide information on the service provided by banks:
  - (a) loan/overdraft accounts;
  - (b) mortgage facilities;
  - (c) insurance services;
  - (d) financial advice.

10.1 Introduction

This chapter gives details of the banking system and bank accounts. It also explains the procedure for making payments into and out of these accounts.

10.2 Types of account

There are two main types of bank account:

- **Current accounts** are used for regular payments into and out of a bank account. A **cheque book** will be given by the bank to the holder of the account, who will use it to make payments to people to whom they owe money. Payment may also be made by standing order or direct debit. The holder will be given a paying-in book to enable money to be paid into their current account.

- **Deposit or business reserve accounts** are for holding money that is not needed for making payments in the foreseeable future. Interest is given by the bank on money kept in such accounts. Current accounts do not usually earn interest.

10.3 Cheques

When a current account is opened the bank will ask the account holder for a specimen signature before issuing a cheque book. This allows them to prove that the cheques have, in fact, been signed by the holder and have not been forged. The account must have sufficient money in it to cover the amounts being paid. If it is envisaged that more money is to be paid out than previously banked then the bank's permission will be needed to allow the account to be 'overdrawn'. This is known as arranging a **bank overdraft**. The bank will stipulate the amount that they will allow the account to be overdrawn which will depend on the holder's financial standing.

The person writing the cheque and using it for payment is known as the **drawer**. The person to whom the cheque is paid is known as the **payee** and the **drawee** is the bank.

Exhibit 10.1 Blank cheque form

```
 _____ 20 __     Cheshire Bank Ltd  _____ 20 __         09-07-99

 PAYEE _____          Stockport Branch
                        324 Low Road, Stockport, Cheshire SK6 8AP

 _____        PAY _____

 _____                                    ┌──────────────┐
                                                     │ £            │
 _____                                     └──────────────┘
                                                     J WOODSTOCK
 ┌───────────┐
 │ £         │          _____
 └───────────┘
   914234              ⑈914234⑈ 09⑈0799 ⑊ 058899⑈

 This part is
 the counterfoil
```

On the face of the cheque are various sets of numbers. These are:

914234   Every cheque printed for the Cheshire Bank will be given a different number, so that individual items can be traced.

09-07-99 Each branch of every bank in the United Kingdom has a different number given to it. Thus this branch has a 'code' number 09-07-99.

058899   Each account with the bank is given a different number. This particular number is kept only for the account of J Woodstock at the Stockport branch.

Once the cheque has been filled in the details are copied on the counterfoil which is then kept for our own records.

The completion of a cheque can now be shown. Assume that £72.85 is being paid to K Marsh on 22 May 2002. Exhibit 10.2 shows the completed cheque, for which the **drawer** is J Woodstock and the **payee** is K Marsh.

Exhibit 10.2 Completed cheque form

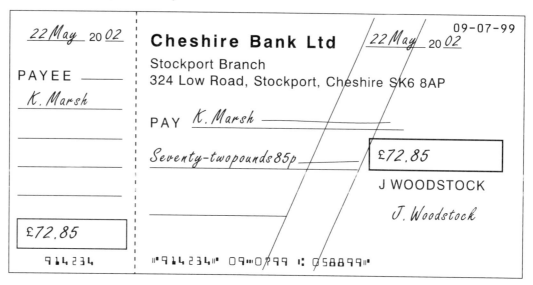

The two parallel lines across the face of the cheque are drawn as a safeguard. If this had not been done the cheque would have been an 'uncrossed cheque'. If someone had stolen a signed uncrossed cheque it could have been cashed at the Stockport branch of the Cheshire Bank. When the cheque is crossed it means it **must** be paid into a bank account, Post Office Giro bank or Savings Bank. Virtually all cheques today are pre-printed crossed, as 'Account payee'.

Notice that the writing of the name of the payee (K Marsh) leaves no room for it to be altered fraudulently which is why the rest of the PAY space is struck through with a line. When writing the amount of the cheque in both figures and in words no space should be left between the figures or the letters so that no insertions can be made.

10.4 Cheque crossing

Cheques can be further safeguarded by using a specific crossing, i.e. writing a form of instruction within the crossing on the cheques as shown in Exhibit 10.3.

Exhibit 10.3 Specific crossings

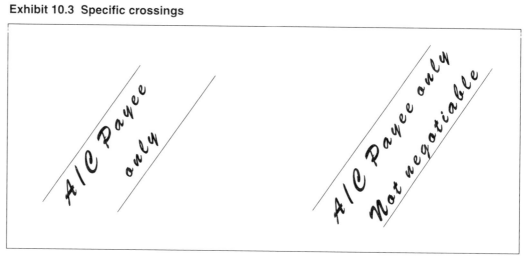

These are specific instructions to the banks about the use of the cheque. The use of 'A/c payee only' means the cheques should be paid only into the account of the payee named. If cheques are lost or stolen the drawer must advise his bank immediately and confirm by letter. These cheques will be 'stopped', i.e. payment will not be made on these cheques, provided they act swiftly. The safest crossing is that of 'A/c payee only. Not negotiable'. If the cheque is lost or stolen it will be of no use to the thief or finder. This is because it is impossible for this cheque to be paid into any bank account other than that of the named payee. Cheques are now often printed with the 'Account payee' crossing on them as a result of the Cheques Act 1992.

Banks have a general agreement only to issue cheque books crossed with 'Account payee' to combat fraudulent transactions. This policy also virtually eliminates the practice of endorsing cheques. Endorsing a cheque involved signing the back of the cheque together with the words 'Pay ————— or order' and then passing it on to the person named as payment of a debt.

10.5 Paying-in slips

To enable money, either cash or cheques, to be paid into a current account, a paying-in slip is used as shown in Exhibit 10.4 relating to the following items banked by J Woodstock on 22 May 2002:

Four	£5 notes
Three	£1 coins
One	50p coin
Other silver	30p
Bronze coins	12p

Cheques received from:

E Kane & Son	£184.15	Sort Code: 02–58–76
J Gale	£ 65.44	Sort Code: 05–77–85

10.6 Bank giro credits/credit transfer

Another way of paying creditors, wages and salaries, etc. is by **bank giro credits**, also known as credit transfer. Here the business prepares payments in the usual way but in addition prepares a list and bank giro credit slips detailing each person's or organisation's name, account number, bank code number, bank name and branch title and lastly the amount of the payment. The list and slips are then sent to the bank with one cheque to cover all the payments and the payments are automatically credited to the various bank accounts via the banking system.

One distinct advantage is that only one cheque has to be made out and signed. The disadvantage is the preparation of the bank giro credit list and slips. However, this method is very outdated and very few organisations use this method of payment.

10.7 Payment by BACS

Many businesses are changing over from payment via bank giro credit to payment by **Bankers' Automated Clearing Service**, known as **BACS**. BACS is a company owned by the Bank of England, the high street banks and some building societies, which offers a computerised payment transfer system that organisations may use to pay not only wages and salaries but also creditors, dividends, grants, pensions, etc.

Exhibit 10.4 Paying-in slip

Face of paying-in slip

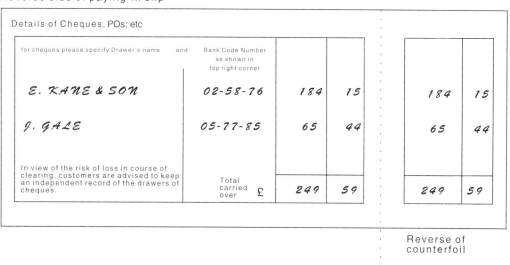

Counterfoil retained by Woodstock : Paying-in slip and cash and cheques handed in to bank

Reverse side of paying-in slip

Reverse of counterfoil

If an employer decides to use this method for paying creditors, wages and/or salaries, then they need to send to BACS a disk or magnetic tape giving the following details of each employee or organisation:

- person's or organisation's name;
- bank name and branch title;
- bank sort code number;
- person's or organisation's bank account number.

The above information is sent prior to the payment and held permanently on computer file by BACS Processing Computer Centre at Edgware in London.

As the payment is prepared periodically on the business's own computer, a magnetic tape or disk containing details of the payment is prepared at the same time and the data is then sent by courier or telephone link to BACS which automatically processes the data, crediting each person's or organisation's bank or building society account and debiting the business's account. Processing the transfers is a three-day cycle; the information is received on the first day, processed on the second day and then sent for checking by the employers prior to the transfers being made on the third day.

Sometimes a business may not have the computer facilities to enable payment to be made in this way. In these circumstances they may wish to use the services of a computer bureau or bank, which, on receipt of a list of payments, will process the data to BACS via magnetic tape or disk.

10.8 Standing orders and direct debits

A person may make a regular payment from their bank account, or receive a regular amount into their account, by standing order or direct debit.

Standing order

This is a straightforward method of making regular fixed payments over which the payer has full control. The steps necessary to make payments by a standing order are as follows:

1   Payer instructs the bank in writing to pay a certain amount, on a particular day to a specific organisation.

2   Bank makes payment via the computer banking system.

Payer can instruct the bank to cease or amend the payment at any time by giving written notification.

Direct debit

This is becoming a more common method of paying both fixed and variable amounts of money. The system of operation is as follows:

1   The proposed receiver (**payee**) of the money sends a mandate to the payer.

2   **Payer** completes the mandate and returns it to the payee.

3   Payee sends the mandate to the payer's bank who will arrange to send the money to the payee's bank via the computer banking system.

The amounts that the payer has authorised to be withdrawn from their own account can vary as the payee makes changes. Typical examples of variations are usually increases in insurance premiums, business rates and loan repayments. It is normal for the payee to advise the payer of such increases.

Payees prefer this method of regular payments since they have control over them and should the payer wish to cancel a direct debit they have to do so through the payee. While this method of payment is convenient for both parties, the payer should exercise great care in giving permission for the setting up of direct debits.

10.9 Stopped cheques

On occasions a cheque may be issued which the drawer later decides should not be paid. To stop the payment the drawer must act quickly, and before, the payee presents the cheque to the drawer's bank. This instruction to the bank by the drawer to stop payment results in a 'stopped cheque'.

The reasons for this action may be as follows:

- The drawer has reason to believe that someone has stolen the cheque in transit to the payee.

- A dispute has arisen between the drawer and the payee of the cheque, leading to the drawer wanting to stop payment.

- The drawer realises that the cheque has been incorrectly made out for too large an amount.

The drawer cannot stop a cheque which has been issued using a cheque guarantee card.

10.10 Postdated cheques

When a cheque is issued with a date later than the issuing date it is known as a 'postdated' cheque. If it is then presented before the date on the cheque the drawer's bank should refuse to pay it. To issue this form of cheque, or to accept one, is not good practice since it can cause problems with the bank and the recipient.

10.11 Out-of-date cheques

Usually, banks look on cheques which have been dated more than **six** months previously to be 'out-of-date'. The bank will normally return such cheques to the person banking them and will not treat them as being paid into the account. These are often known as 'stale' cheques.

10.12 Dishonoured cheques

When a cheque is received from a customer and paid into the bank, it is recorded on the debit side of the cash book. It is also shown on the bank statement as a banking by the bank. However, at a later date it may be found that the customer's bank will not honour it. They will not let it go through the customer's account. It is called a **dishonoured cheque**.

There are several possible reasons for this. Let us suppose that K King gave us a cheque for £5,000 on 20 May 2003. We bank it, but a few days later our bank returns the cheque to us. Typical reasons are:

1   King had put £5,000 in figures on the cheque, but had written it in words as five thousand five hundred pounds. You will have to give the cheque back to King for amendment.

2   Normally cheques are considered **stale** six months after the date on the cheque; in other words the banks will not pay cheques over six months old. If King had put the year 2002 on the cheque instead of 2003, then the cheque would be returned to us by our bank.

3   King simply did not have sufficient funds in his bank account. Suppose he had previously only got a £2,000 balance and yet he has given us a cheque for £5,000. His bank has not allowed him to have an overdraft.

   In such a case the cheque would be dishonoured. The bank would write on the cheque **refer to drawer**, and we would have to get in touch with King to see what he was going to do about it.

In all of these cases the bank would show the original banking as being cancelled, by showing the cheque paid out off our bank account. As soon as this happens they will notify us. We will then also show the cheque being cancelled by a credit in the cash book. We will then debit that amount to King's account.

When King originally paid his account our records would appear as:

K King Account

Dr							Cr
2003			£	2003			£
May	1	Balance b/d	5,000	May	20	Bank	5,000

Bank Account

Dr					Cr
2003			£		
May	20	K King	5,000		

After our recording the dishonour, the records will appear as:

K King Account

Dr							Cr
2003			£	2003			£
May	1	Balance b/d	5,000	May	20	Bank	5,000
May	25	Bank: cheque					
		dishonoured	5,000				

Bank Account

Dr							Cr
2003			£	2003			£
May	20	K King	5,000	May	25	K King: cheque	
						dishonoured	5,000

In other words King is once again shown as owing us £5,000.

10.13 The relationship between banks and their customers

There is a legal relationship between a bank and its customers (but not everyone who goes into a bank and uses its services in some way is legally a customer of that bank – *see* below). The fact that there is such a relationship between banker and customer becomes very important when something goes wrong. Both banker and customer have duties and rights under the law.

A banker is someone whose duties include:

- depositing cash and cheques received from, or for, a customer into an account for them;
- enabling a customer's cheques or orders to be paid when there is sufficient money in the account;
- sending statements of the account to the customer.

A customer is someone who may be covered by one of the following descriptions:

- opens a current account at the bank to enable cheque transactions to be carried out;
- opens a deposit account at the bank – money placed in this type of account will earn interest from the bank;
- opens an account at the bank to obtain some type of loan;
- uses the investment services of the bank.

There are other circumstances where dealings with a bank do not form a banker/customer relationship. These could include:

- asking the bank to change a £50 note for five £10 notes which you then receive;
- cashing travellers' cheques at the bank;
- paying money into another customer's account at the bank;
- use of a credit card to obtain cash from another bank.

10.14 The importance of the banker/customer relationship

The relationship is important because a bank owes many legal duties to its customers, but both the bank and its customers have certain rights as well. If a bank does not adequately perform its legal duties for a customer, then that customer may sue the bank and take the case to court. Obviously this would not be for trivial matters such as the bank making a small arithmetical error which it corrects as soon as it is found.

Suppose that a customer quite correctly pays a supplier by cheque, but while there is enough money in the account to cover the cheque, the bank fails to pay it. This could have serious consequences for the customer. Much of business life depends on the confidence in others of the customer being able to meet his or her commitments as they fall due. In this case it could lead to the supplier refusing to carry on supplying goods on credit and such news could spread to other suppliers. There have been many cases of businesses becoming bankrupt because of a loss of business confidence. In such a case the customer could sue the bank for damages, since the bank was the cause of the lack of business confidence even though this was unjustified.

Customers also have duties to the bank, and these include ensuring that there is always money in the account unless a prior agreement has been made with the bank for a loan or overdraft facilities. They must also ensure the security of their bank documents, for instance making certain that cheques are properly made out so that other people cannot use them for fraudulent purposes. If the customer fails in his or her duties, then the bank has a legal right to sue the customer in court to recover any money lost by the bank.

10.15 Loan accounts

An overdraft is a facility provided by the bank where they will continue to make payments from a current account even though there are insufficient funds to cover the payment. This is a short-term loan, on which the bank charges interest on a day-to-day basis. The bank, however, is confident that, due to the prior arrangement, the account will soon be back in credit.

A bank will also make long-term loans over a period of years for large items of expenditure such as new buildings or expensive machinery. The rate of interest to be paid on the loan will be agreed initially.

10.16 Mortgage accounts

The bank may lend money to an organisation on a long-term basis to help it to buy the property and land it needs. These are commercial mortgages whereas a loan to an individual to buy a house is known as a private mortgage. In these cases the bank is known as the mortgagee while the borrower is the mortgagor.

10.17 Banks as insurance agents/investment advisers

Banks will often act to arrange insurances for its customers. In such cases the bank is known as the agent, the customer is the principal. The same relationship exists where the customer uses the services of a bank for investment advice and to buy shares or government investments.

10.18 Banks as a safe deposit

Banks have safe deposit facilities where customers may store valuable items such as important documents or expensive jewellery in a secure environment.

10.19 Cheque clearings

It is important to understand how cheques paid from one person's bank account pass into another person's bank account. How this process is carried out is detailed below with reference to the cheque in Exhibit 10.2.

2002

May 22 — Woodstock, in Stockport, sends the cheque to K Marsh who lives in Leeds. Woodstock enters the payment in his cash book.

May 23 — Cheque received by Marsh. He banks it the same day in his bank account at Barclays Bank in Leeds. Marsh shows the cheque in his cash book as being received and banked on 23 May.

May 24 — Barclays in London receive the cheque. They exchange it with the head office of the Cheshire Bank in London.
The Cheshire Bank send the cheque to their Stockport branch.

May 25 — The Stockport branch of the Cheshire Bank examine the cheque.
If there is nothing wrong with it, the cheque can now be debited by the bank to J Woodstock's account.

Note: The entry is made into Woodstock's cash book on 22 May but it is not entered by the bank into Woodstock's account until 25 May.

Organisations regularly reconcile their cash book with the bank statement. This procedure is known as a bank reconciliation and is dealt with in Chapter 14.

NEW TERMS

Agent   Where a bank acts for a customer to obtain insurance or to deal in investments etc.

Bank giro credits   Method used by businesses to pay creditors, wages and/or salaries. A bank giro credit list and slips containing information about each person or organisation to be paid and the amount payable are sent to the bank, together with one cheque to cover all the payments. The bank then automatically transfers the funds from the business's account to the accounts of each of the respective people or organisations.

Bank overdraft   An overdraft is a facility provided by the bank where they will continue to make payments from a current account even though there are insufficient funds to cover the payment. This is a short-term loan, on which the bank charges interest on a day-to-day basis.

Bankers' Automated Clearing Service (BACS)   Computerised payment transfer system which is a very popular way of paying creditors, wages and salaries.

Cheque book   Book containing forms (cheques) used to pay money out of a current account.

Current account   Bank account used for regular payments in and out of the bank.

Deposit or business reserve account   Bank account for money to be kept in for a long time. Interest is given on money deposited.

Direct debit   Payment made out of payer's bank, direct to payee's bank, on **payee's** instructions.

Dishonoured cheque   When a bank dishonours a cheque it will not pay up on the cheque because there are insufficient funds in the **drawer's** account.

Drawee   The bank or organisation on which a payment is drawn.

Drawer   The person making out a cheque and using it for payment.

Loan accounts   Long-term borrowing by a customer of a fixed amount of money.

Mortgage   Money lent to a customer by a bank or building society to enable them to buy property or land.

Mortgagee   The person who makes the loan (i.e. bank or building society).

Mortgagor   A person or business who borrows money by mortgaging their property as security.

Out-of-date cheques   Where the cheque bears a date more than (usually) six months previously.

Payee   The person to whom a cheque is paid.

Paying-in-slip   Form used for paying money into a bank account.

Postdated cheque   One which is dated for payment at some future date.

Principal   The customer for whom the bank is acting as an agent.

Standing order   Payment made out of payer's bank, direct to payee's bank, on **payer's** instructions.

Stopped cheques   Where a customer has sent a cheque to someone, but has requested that payment be stopped by the bank.

STUDENT ACTIVITIES

10.1 Explain the difference between a current account and a deposit account. Which account would be best suited for making regular savings?

10.2X Briefly explain the effect of the crossing on the cheque shown in Exhibit 10.5.

Exhibit 10.5

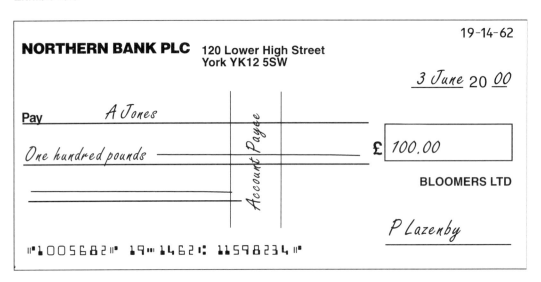

(AAT (part of Central Assessment))

10.3X Referring to the cheque shown in Exhibit 10.5, give the name of:

(a) the drawer
(b) the drawee
(c) the payee.

(AAT (part of Central Assessment))

10.4 MMS Textiles Ltd banks at the Moxley branch of the Norwest Bank, sort code no. 36-24-41 and account number 479836806.

Fill in the paying-in slip and counterfoil given in Exhibit 10.6 to bank the cash takings on 1 December 2002 which are as follows:

Four	£50 notes
Twenty-three	£20 notes
Thirty-two	£10 notes
Seven	£5 notes
Eight	50 pence coins
Twelve	10 pence coins

(AAT (part of Central Assessment))

10.5 Organisations today pay many of their creditors and staff salaries using BACS. Explain fully how the system operates and its main advantage.

10.6X Bloomers has agreed to make regular monthly payments to Apollo Communications plc. The amount of the payment varies from month to month. Which service provided by the banks would appear to be most appropriate for these payments?

(AAT (part of Central Assessment))

10.7 What is a postdated cheque?

(AAT (part of Central Assessment))

Exhibit 10.6

Date _____	Date _____
Credit _____	

bank giro credit

Cashier's stamp
and initials

Code No   — —

Bank _____

Branch _____

Credit _____

Account no _____

Number of
cheques

Paid in by _____

Left slip:

£50 Notes		
£20 Notes		
£10 notes		
£5 Notes		
£1		
50p		
20p		
10, 5p		
Bronze		
Total cash		
Cheques etc. *see over*		
£		

Right slip:

£50 Notes		
£20 Notes		
£10 notes		
£5 Notes		
£1		
50p		
20p		
10, 5p		
Bronze		
Total cash		
Cheques etc. *see over*		
£		

11 Writing up the cash book

AIMS

- **To be able to enter data into cash books and balance off.**

- **To understand and be able to use folio columns for cross referencing purposes.**

- **To understand and complete entries for discounts allowed and discounts received.**

- **To be able to enter contra items in the cash book.**

11.1 Introduction

The cash book consists of the cash account and the bank account put together in one book. We used to show these two accounts on different pages of the ledger. Now it is easier to put the two sets of account columns together. This means that we can record all money received and paid out on a particular date on the same page.

In the cash book the debit column for cash is put next to the debit column for bank. The credit column for cash is put next to the credit column for bank.

11.2 Drawing up a cash book

In Exhibit 11.1 we can now see a cash account and a bank account as they would appear if they were kept separately. In Exhibit 11.2 they are shown as if the transactions were instead kept in a cash book.

The bank column contains details of the payments made by cheque and of the money received and paid into the bank account. The bank will have a copy of the account in its own books.

The bank will send a copy of the account in its books to the firm, this copy usually being known as the **bank statement**. When the firm receives the bank statement, it will check it against the bank column in its own cash book to ensure that there are no errors.

Exhibit 11.1

Cash Account

Dr			£	Cr			£
2005				2005			
Aug	2	T Moore	33	Aug	8	Rent	20
Aug	5	K Charles	25	Aug	12	C Potts	19
Aug	15	F Hughes	37	Aug	28	Wages	25
Aug	30	H Howe	18	Aug	31	Balance c/d	49
			113				113
Sept	1	Balance b/d	49				

Bank Account

Dr			£	Cr			£
2005				2005			
Aug	1	Capital	1,000	Aug	7	Rates	105
Aug	3	W P Ltd	244	Aug	12	F Small Ltd	95
Aug	16	K Noone	408	Aug	26	K French	268
Aug	30	H Sanders	20	Aug	31	Balance c/d	1,204
			1,672				1,672
Sept	1	Balance b/d	1,204				

Exhibit 11.2

Dr			Cash	Bank	Cr			Cash	Bank
			Cash Book						
			£	£				£	£
2005					2005				
Aug	1	Capital		1,000	Aug	7	Rates		105
Aug	2	T Moore	33		Aug	8	Rent	20	
Aug	3	W P Ltd		244	Aug	12	C Potts	19	
Aug	5	K Charles	25		Aug	12	F Small Ltd		95
Aug	15	F Hughes	37		Aug	26	K French		268
Aug	16	K Noone		408	Aug	28	Wages	25	
Aug	30	H Sanders		20	Aug	31	Balances c/d	49	1,204
Aug	30	H Howe	18						
			113	1,672				113	1,672
Sept	1	Balances b/d	49	1,204					

11.3 Cash paid into the bank

In Exhibit 11.2 the payments into the bank have been cheques received by the firm which have been banked immediately. We must now consider cash being paid into the bank.

1 Let us look at the position when a customer pays his account in cash, and later a part of this cash is paid into the bank. The receipt of the cash is debited to the cash column on the date received, the credit entry being in the customer's personal account. The cash banked has the following effect needing action as shown:

Effect		Action
1	Asset of cash is decreased	Credit the asset account, i.e. the cash account which is represented by the cash column in the cash book.
2	Asset of bank is increased	Debit the asset account, i.e. the bank account which is represented by the bank column in the cash book.

A cash receipt of £100 from M Davies on 1 August 2005, later followed by the banking on 3 August of £80 of this amount, would appear in the cash book as follows:

Dr		Cash Book			Cr
	Cash £	Bank £		Cash £	Bank £
2005 Aug 1 M Davies	100		2005 Aug 3 Bank	80	
Aug 3 Cash		80			

The details column shows entries against each item stating the name of the account in which the completion of double entry has taken place. Against the cash payment of £80 appears the word 'bank', meaning that the debit £80 is to be found in the bank column, and the opposite applies.

2 Where the whole of the cash received is banked immediately the receipt can be treated in exactly the same manner as a cheque received, i.e. it can be entered directly in the bank column.

3 If the firm requires cash it may withdraw cash from the bank. This is done by making out a cheque to pay itself a certain amount in cash. The bank will give cash in exchange for the cheque over the counter.

The twofold effect and the action required is as follows:

Effect		Action
1	Asset of bank is decreased	Credit the asset account, i.e. the bank column in the cash book.
2	Asset of cash is increased	Debit the asset account, i.e. the cash column in the cash book.

A withdrawal of £75 cash on 1 June 2005 from the bank would appear in the cash book thus:

Dr		Cash Book			Cr
	Cash £	Bank £		Cash £	Bank £
2005 June 1 Bank	75		2005 June 1 Cash		75

Both the debit and credit entries for this item are in the same book. When this happens it is known as a **contra** item.

11.4 The use of folio columns

As you have already seen, the details column in an account contains the name of the other account in which double entry has been completed. Anyone looking through the books would therefore be able to find where the other half of the double entry had been entered.

However, when many books are being used, just to mention the name of the other account would not be enough information to find the other account quickly. More information is needed, and this is given by using **folio columns**.

In each account and in each book being used, a folio column is added, always shown on the left of the money columns. In this column the name of the other book, in abbreviated form, and the number of the page in the other book where the double entry is completed, is stated against each and every entry in the books.

An entry of receipt of cash from C Kelly whose account was on page 45 of the sales ledger, and the cash recorded on page 37 of the cash book, would use the folio column thus:

● In the cash book: in the folio column would appear SL 45.

● In the sales ledger: in the folio column would appear CB 37.

By this method a full cross-reference would be given. Each of the contra items, being shown on the same page of the cash book, would use the letter 'C' in the folio column.

The act of using one book as a means of entering the transaction to the other account so as to complete the double entry is known as '**posting**' the items.

11.5 Advantages of folio columns

These are:

● As described in section 11.4 it speeds up reference to the other book where the double entry for the item is completed.

● The folio column is filled in when the double entry has been completed. If it has not been filled in, double entry will not have been made.

Looking through the folio columns to ensure they have all been filled in will help us to detect such errors.

11.6 Example of a cash book with folio columns

The following transactions are written up in the form of a cash book. The folio columns are filled in as though double entry had been completed to other accounts.

2005			£
Sept	1	Proprietor puts capital into a bank account for the business	940
Sept	2	Received cheque from M Boon	115
Sept	4	Cash sales	102
Sept	6	Paid rent by cash	35
Sept	7	Banked £50 of the cash held by the firm	50
Sept	15	Cash sales paid direct into the bank	40
Sept	23	Paid cheque to S Wills	277
Sept	29	Withdrew cash from bank for business use	120
Sept	30	Paid wages in cash	118

		Folio	Cash	Bank			Folio	Cash	Bank
Dr					**Cash Book**			page 1 Cr	
			£	£				£	£
2005					2005				
Sept 1	Capital	GL 1		940	Sept 6	Rent	GL 65	35	
Sept 2	M Boon	SL 98		115	Sept 7	Bank	C	50	
Sept 4	Sales	GL 87	102		Sept 23	S Wills	PL 23		277
Sept 7	Cash	C		50	Sept 29	Cash	C		120
Sept 15	Sales	GL 87		40	Sept 30	Wages	GL 39	118	
Sept 29	Bank	C	120		Sept 30	Balances	c/d	19	748
			222	1,145				222	1,145
Oct 1	Balances	b/d	19	748					

The abbreviations used in the folio column are as follows:

GL = General Ledger; SL = Sales Ledger; C = Contra; PL = Purchases Ledger.

Note: Before you read further you are recommended to attempt Student Activities 11.1 and 11.2 on p. 95.

11.7 Cash discounts

It is better if customers pay their accounts quickly. A firm may accept a smaller sum in full settlement if payment is made within a certain period of time. The amount of the reduction of the sum to be paid is known as a **cash discount**. The term 'cash discount' thus refers to the allowance given for quick payment. It is still called cash discount even if the account is paid by cheque.

The rate of cash discount is usually stated as a percentage. Full details of the percentage allowed and the period within which payment is to be made are quoted on all sales documents by the selling company. A typical period during which discount may be allowed is one month from the date of the original transaction.

11.8 Discounts allowed and discounts received

A firm may have two types of cash discounts in its books. These are:

1 **Discounts allowed** – cash discounts allowed by a firm to its customers when they pay their accounts quickly.

2 **Discounts received** – cash discounts received by a firm from its suppliers when it pays their accounts quickly.

We can now see the effect of discounts by looking at two examples.

Example 1

W Clarke owed us £100. He pays on 2 September 2005 by cash within the time limit laid down, and the firm allows him 5 per cent cash discount. So he will pay £100 – £5 = £95 in full settlement of his account.

Effect	Action
1 Of cash: Cash is increased by £95. Asset of debtors is decreased by £95.	Debit cash account, i.e. enter £95 in debit column of cash book. Credit W Clark £95.
2 Of discounts: Asset of debtors is decreased by £5. (After the cash was paid the balance of £5 still appeared. As the account has been paid this asset must now be cancelled.) Expenses of discounts allowed increased	Credit W Clark £5. Debit discounts allowed account £5.

Example 2

The firm owed S Small £400. It pays him on 3 September 2005 by cheque within the time limit laid down by him and he allows 2½ per cent cash discount. Thus the firm will pay £400 – £10 = £390 in full settlement of the account.

Effect	Action
1 Of cheque: Asset of bank is reduced by £390. Liability of creditors is reduced by £390.	Credit bank, i.e. enter in credit bank column £390. Debit S Small's account £390.
2 Of discounts: Liability of creditors is reduced by £10. (After the cheque was paid the balance of £10 remained. As the account has been paid the liability must now be cancelled.) Revenues of discounts received increased	Debit S Small's account £10. Credit discounts received account £10.

The accounts in the firm's books would appear:

				Cash Book				page 32
Dr								Cr
	Folio	Cash	Bank		Folio	Cash	Bank
2005		£	£	2005		£	£
Sept 2 W Clarke	SL 12	95		Sept 3 S Small	PL 75		390

Discounts Received Account   (General Ledger *page 18*)

			Dr			Cr
			2005		Folio	£
			Sept 2 S Small		PL 75	10

Discounts Allowed Account   (General Ledger *page 17*)

Dr					Cr

		Folio	£		
2005					
Sept	2	W Clarke	SL 12	5	

W Clarke Account   (Sales Ledger *page 12*)

Dr								Cr

			Folio	£			Folio	£
2005					2005			
Sept	1	Balance	b/d	100	Sept	2	Cash	CB 32	95
					Sept	2	Discount	GL 17	5
				100					100

S Small Account   (Purchases Ledger *page 75*)

Dr								Cr

			Folio	£			Folio	£
2005					2005			
Sept	3	Bank	CB 32	390	Sept	1	Balance	b/d	400
Sept	3	Discount	GL 18	10					
				400					400

It is the accounting custom to enter the word 'Discount' in the personal accounts, not stating whether it is a discount received or a discount allowed.

11.9 Discount columns in the cash book

The discounts allowed account and the discounts received account are in the general ledger along with all the other revenue and expense accounts. It has already been stated that every effort should be made to avoid too much reference to the general ledger.

In the case of discounts this is done by adding an extra column on each side of the cash book in which the amounts of discounts are entered. Discounts received are entered in the discounts column on the credit side of the cash book, and discounts allowed in the discounts column on the debit side of the cash book.

The cash book, if completed for the two examples so far dealt with, would appear:

Dr							Cash Book					Cr
			Folio	Discount	Cash	Bank				Folio	Discount	Cash	Bank
				£	£	£					£	£	£
2005							2005						
Sept	2	W Clarke	SL 12	5	95		Sept	3	S Small	PL 75	10		390

There is no alteration to the method of showing discounts in the personal accounts.

To make entries in the discount accounts

Total of discounts column on receipts side of cash book } Enter on debit side of discounts allowed account

Total of discounts column on payments side of cash book } Enter on credit side of discounts received account

11.10 A worked example

2005		£
May 1	Balances brought down from April:	
	Cash balance	29
	Bank balance	654
	Debtors accounts:	
	B King	120
	N Crank	280
	D Shand	40
	Creditors accounts:	
	U Barrow	60
	A Allen	440
	R Long	100
May 2	B King pays us by cheque, having deducted 2 ½ per cent cash discount £3	117
May 8	We pay R Long his account by cheque, deducting 5 per cent cash discount £5	95
May 11	We withdrew £100 cash from the bank for business use	100
May 16	N Crank pays us his account by cheque, deducting 2½ per cent discount £7	273
May 25	We paid wages in cash	92
May 28	D Shand pays us in cash after having deducted 5 per cent cash discount.	38
May 29	We pay U Barrow by cheque less 5 per cent cash discount £3	57
May 30	We pay A Allen by cheque less 2½ per cent cash discount £11	429

Cash Book									*page 64*
Dr									*Cr*
		Folio	Discount	Cash	Bank		Folio	Discount	Cash	Bank

			Folio	Discount	Cash	Bank				Folio	Discount	Cash	Bank
				£	£	£					£	£	£
2005							2005						
May	1	Balances	b/d		29	654	May	8	R Long	PL 58	5		95
May	2	B King	SL 13	3		117	May	11	Cash	C			100
May	11	Bank	C		100		May	25	Wages	GL 77		92	
May	16	N Crank	SL 84	7		273	May	29	U Barrow	PL 15	3		57
May	28	D Shand	SL 91	2	38		May	30	A Allen	PL 98	11		429
							May	31	Balances	c/d		75	363
				12	167	1,044					19	167	1,044
June	1	Balances	b/d		75	363							

We have included folio numbers to make the example more realistic.

Sales Ledger
B King Account
(page 13)

Dr   Cr

2005			Folio	£	2005			Folio	£
May	1	Balance	b/d	120	May	2	Bank	CB 64	117
					May	2	Discount	CB 64	3
				120					120

N Crank Account
(page 84)

Dr   Cr

2005			Folio	£	2005			Folio	£
May	1	Balance	b/d	280	May	16	Bank	CB 64	273
					May	16	Discount	CB 64	7
				280					280

D Shand Account
(page 91)

Dr   Cr

2005			Folio	£	2005			Folio	£
May	1	Balance	b/d	40	May	28	Bank	CB 64	38
					May	28	Discount	CB 64	2
				40					40

Purchases Ledger
U Barrow Account
(page 15)

Dr   Cr

2005			Folio	£	2005			Folio	£
May	29	Bank	CB 64	57	May	1	Balance	b/d	60
May	29	Discount	CB 64	3					
				60					60

R Long Account
(page 58)

Dr   Cr

2005			Folio	£	2005			Folio	£
May	8	Bank	CB 64	95	May	1	Balance	b/d	100
May	8	Discount	CB 64	5					
				100					100

A Allen Account
(page 98)

Dr   Cr

2005			Folio	£	2005			Folio	£
May	30	Bank	CB 64	429	May	1	Balance	b/d	440
May	30	Discount	CB 64	11					
				440					440

General Ledger
Wages Account
(page 77)

Dr   Cr

2005			Folio	£					
May	25	Cash	CB 64	92					

Discounts Received Account (page 88)

Dr | | | | | Cr

		2005		Folio	£
		May 31 Total for the month		CB 64	19

Discounts Allowed Account (page 89)

Dr | | | | Cr

2005		Folio	£	
May 31 Total for the month		CB 64	12	

Is the above method of entering discounts correct?

You can easily check. See the following:

Discounts in ledger accounts	Debits		Credits	
		£		
Discounts received	U Barrow	3	Discounts	
	R Long	5	received	
	A Allen	11	account	£19
		19		
				£
Discounts allowed	Discounts		B King	3
	allowed		N Crank	7
	account	£12	D Shand	2
				12

You can see that proper double entry has been carried out. Equal amounts, in total, have been entered on each side of the accounts.

11.11 Bank overdrafts

A firm may borrow money from a bank by means of a bank overdraft. This means that the firm is allowed to pay more out of the bank account, by paying out cheques, than the total amount which is placed in the account.

Up to this point the bank balances have all been money at the bank, so they have all been assets, i.e. debit balances. When the account is overdrawn the firm owes money to the bank, so the account is a liability and the balance becomes a credit one.

Taking the cash book last shown, suppose that the amount payable to A Allen was £1,429 instead of £429. Thus the amount in the bank account, £1,044, is exceeded by the amount withdrawn. We will take the discount for Allen as being £11. The cash book would appear as follows:

			Cash Book					page 64	
Dr									Cr

			Discount	Cash	Bank				Discount	Cash	Bank
2005			£	£	£	2005			£	£	£
May	1	Balances b/d		29	654	May	8	R Long	5		95
May	2	B King	3		117	May	11	Cash			100
May	11	Bank		100		May	25	Wages		92	
May	16	N Crank	7		273	May	29	U Barrow	3		57
May	28	D Shand	2	38		May	30	A Allen	11		1,429
May	31	Balance c/d			637	May	31	Balance c/d		75	
			12	167	1,681				19	167	1,681
June	1	Balance b/d		75		June	1	Balance b/d			637

On a balance sheet a bank overdraft will be shown as an item included under the heading current liabilities.

11.12 Bank cash books

In the United Kingdom, except for very small organisations, three-column cash books will not usually be found. All receipts, whether of cash or cheques, will be banked daily. A petty cash book will be used for payments of cash. This means that there will not be a need for cash columns in the cash book itself. This is described on p. 140.

This would certainly not be true in many other countries in the world, especially where banking systems are not as developed as in the UK. Three-column cash books will be much more widely used in these countries.

Note: Analytical cash books will be covered in Chapter 24 on columnar sales and purchases day books and analytical cash books, after value added tax has been dealt with in Chapter 23.

NEW TERMS

Bank statement   Copy of our current account given to us by our bank.

Contra   A contra, for cash book items, is where both the debit and credit entries are shown in the cash book.

Discounts allowed   A reduction given to customers who pay their accounts within the time allowed.

Discounts received   A reduction given to us by a supplier when we pay their account before the time allowed has elapsed.

Folio columns   Columns used for entering reference numbers.

Posting   The act of using one book as a means of entering the transactions to another account.

STUDENT ACTIVITIES

11.1 Write up a two-column cash book from the following details, and balance off as at the end of the month:

2002

May	1	Started business with capital in cash £100
May	2	Paid rent by cash £10
May	3	F Lake lent us £500, paying by cheque
May	4	We paid B McKenzie by cheque £65
May	5	Cash sales £98
May	7	N Miller paid us by cheque £62
May	9	We paid B Burton in cash £22
May	11	Cash sales paid direct into the bank £53
May	15	G Moores paid us in cash £65
May	16	We took £50 our of the cash till and paid it into the bank account
May	19	We repaid F Lake £100 by cheque
May	22	Cash sales paid direct into the bank £66
May	26	Paid motor expenses by cheque £12
May	30	Withdrew £100 cash from the bank for business use
May	31	Paid wages in cash £97

11.2 Write up a two-column cash book from the following details, and balance off as at the end of the month:

2003

Mar	1	Balances brought down from last month: Cash in hand £56: Cash in bank £2,356
Mar	2	Paid rates by cheque £156
Mar	3	Paid for postage stamps in cash £5
Mar	5	Cash sales £74
Mar	7	Cash paid into bank £60
May	8	We paid T Lee by cheque £75; we paid C Brooks in cash £2
Mar	12	J Moores pays us £150, £50 being in cash and £100 by cheque
Mar	17	Cash drawings by proprietor £20
Mar	20	P Jones pays us by cheque £79
Mar	22	Withdrew £200 from the bank for business use
Mar	24	Bought a new motor van for £195 cash
Mar	28	Paid rent by cheque £40
Mar	31	Cash sales paid direct into the bank £105

11.3X A two-column cash book is to be written up from the following, carrying the balances down to the following month:

2001

Jan	1	Started business with £4,000 in the bank
Jan	2	Paid for fixtures by cheque £660
Jan	4	Cash sales £225: Paid rent by cash £140
Jan	6	T Thomas paid us by cheque £188
Jan	8	Cash sales paid direct into the bank £308
Jan	10	J King paid us in cash £300
Jan	12	Paid wages in cash £275
Jan	14	J Walters lent us £500 paying by cheque
Jan	15	Withdrew £200 from the bank for business use
Jan	20	Bought stationery paying by cash £60
Jan	22	We paid J French by cheque £166
Jan	28	Cash drawings £100
Jan	30	J Scott paid us by cheque £277
Jan	31	Cash sales £66

11.4X Write up a two-column cash book from the following:

2000
Nov 1 Balance brought forward from last month: Cash £105, Bank £2,164
Nov 2 Cash sales £605
Nov 3 Took £500 out of the cash till and paid it into the bank
Nov 4 J Matthews paid us by cheque £217
Nov 5 We paid for postage stamps in cash £60
Nov 6 Bought office equipment by cheque £189
Nov 7 We paid J Lucas by cheque £50
Nov 9 Received rates refund by cheque £72
Nov 11 Withdrew £250 from the bank for business use
Nov 12 Paid wages in cash £239
Nov 14 Paid motor expenses by cheque £57
Nov 16 L Levy lent us £200 in cash
Nov 20 R Norman paid us by cheque £112
Nov 28 We paid general expenses in cash £22
Nov 30 Paid insurance by cheque £74

11.5 Enter up a three-column cash book from the details following. Balance off at the end of the month, and show the relevant discount accounts as they would appear in the general ledger.

2002
May 1 Started business with £6,000 in the bank
May 1 Bought fixtures paying by cheque £950
May 2 Bought goods paying by cheque £1,240
May 3 Cash sales £407
May 4 Paid rent in cash £200
May 5 N Morgan paid us his account of £220 by a cheque for £210, we allowed him £10 discount
May 7 Paid S Thompson & Co £80 owing to them by means of a cheque £76, they allowed us £4 discount
May 9 We received a cheque for £380 from S Cooper, discount having been allowed £20
May 12 Paid rates by cheque £410
May 14 L Curtis pays us a cheque for £115
May 16 Paid M Monroe his account of £120 by cash £114, having deducted £6 cash discount
May 20 P Exeter pays us a cheque for £78, having deducted £2 cash discount
May 31 Cash sales paid direct into the bank £88.

11.6 A three-column cash book is to be written up from the following details, balanced off and the relevant discount accounts in the general ledger shown.

2004
Mar 1 Balances brought forward: Cash £230; Bank £4,756
Mar 2 The following paid their accounts by cheque, in each case deducting 5 per cent cash discounts. Accounts: R Burton £140; E Taylor £220; R Harris £300
Mar 4 Paid rent by cheque £120
Mar 6 J Cotton lent us £1,000 paying by cheque
Mar 8 We paid the following accounts by cheque, in each case deducting a 2½ per cent cash discount: N Black £360; P Towers £480; C Rowse £800
Mar 10 Paid motor expenses in cash £44
Mar 12 H Hankins pays his account of £77 by cheque £74, deducting £3 cash discount
Mar 15 Paid wages in cash £160
Mar 18 The following paid their accounts by cheque, in each case deducting 5 per cent cash discount. Accounts: C Winston £260; R Wilson & Son £340; H Winter £460
Mar 21 Cash withdrawn from the bank £350 for business use
Mar 24 Cash drawings £120

Mar 25 Paid T Briers his account of £140 by cash £133, having deducted £7 cash discount

Mar 29 Bought fixtures paying by cheque £650

Mar 31 Received commission by cheque £88

11.7X Enter the following in a three-column cash book. Balance off the cash book at the end of the month and show the discount accounts in the general ledger.

2006

June 1 Balances brought forward: Cash £97; Bank £2,186

June 2 The following paid us by cheque in each case deducting a 5 per cent cash discount: R Harris £1,000; C White £280; P Peers £180; O Hardy £600

June 3 Cash sales paid direct into the bank £134

June 5 Paid rent by cash £88

June 6 We paid the following accounts by cheque, in each case deducting 2½ per cent cash discount: J Charlton £400; H Sobers £640; D Shallcross £200

June 8 Withdrew cash from the bank for business use £250

June 10 Cash sales £206

June 12 D Deeds paid us their account of £89 by cheque less £2 cash discount

June 14 Paid wages by cash £250

June 16 We paid the following accounts by cheque: L Lucas £117 less cash discount £6; D Fisher £206 less cash discount £8

June 20 Bought fixtures by cheque £8,000

June 24 Bought motor lorry paying by cheque £7,166

June 29 Received £169 cheque from D Steel

June 30 Cash sales £116

June 30 Bought stationery paying by cash £60

11.8X You are to write up a three-column cash book for M Pinero from the details which follow. Then balance off at the end of the month and show the discount accounts in the general ledger.

2001

May 1 Balances brought forward:
        Cash in hand £58
        Bank overdraft £1,470

May 2 M Pinero pays further capital into the bank £1,000

May 3 Bought office fixtures by cheque £780

May 4 Cash sales £220

May 5 Banked cash £200

May 6 We paid the following by cheque, in each case deducting 2½ per cent cash discount: B Barnes £80; T Horton £240; T Jacklin £400

May 8 Cash sales £500

May 12 Paid motor expenses in cash £77

May 15 Cash withdrawn from the bank £400

May 16 Cash drawings £120

May 18 The following firms paid us their accounts by cheque, in each case deducting a 5 per cent discount: L Graham £80; B Crenshaw £140; H Green £220

May 20 Salaries paid in cash £210

May 22 T Weiskopf paid us his account in cash £204

May 26 Paid insurance by cheque £150

May 28 We banked all the cash in our possession except for £20 in the cash till

May 31 Bought motor van, paying by cheque £4,920

12 Handling receipts of money

AIMS

- To show how receipts of cash and cheques are processed and the importance of cash control and security.

- To provide information on bank and building society cards:
  - cheque guarantee cards
  - credit cards
  - debit cards.

- To explain payments made by banker's draft.

- To understand the Electronic Funds Transfer at Point of Sale (EFTPOS) system of making a payment.

12.1 Money received

This can be received by the business or organisation in a number of different ways:

- cash

- cheques

- credit cards

- debit cards

- direct into the bank by inter-bank transfers

- bank drafts

- building society cheques.

12.2 Cash received

Cash is still used extensively in both the United Kingdom and overseas, especially in the retail business. However, for customers making purchases involving large amounts of money paying by cash is not feasible these days, for not only is the cash bulky to carry but it is at risk from loss or theft. The business or organisation receiving the cash would also find it is a disadvantage for again it is a security problem and would involve additional work such as counting the cash and ensuring it is stored safely and banked with the minimum of risk. Another security problem these days are forged bank notes and organisations need to be vigilant when receiving large amounts of notes. To guard against this problem special machines may be used to detect forgeries, but again this imposes additional costs.

12.3 The importance of cash control

Large amounts of cash, which may have been received from the sale of goods or perhaps drawn from the bank to pay employees' wages, should be carefully controlled and handled as follows:

- Cash must be checked to ensure that it corresponds with any documentation showing the amount to be received.

- Where appropriate, correct change must be given.

- There should be adequate internal checks to ensure that the persons handling cash do not steal any of it.

- Cash must be kept in as secure a place as possible before it is banked or paid out.

- Cash must be banked as soon as possible.

These points will now be examined in more detail.

12.4 The receipt of payments in cash

Cash may be received by organisations in respect of the following:

- **Settlement of debtors' accounts.** In such cases the amount received should be checked thoroughly against any remittance advice or similar documentation given by the customer. When receiving cash from either a debtor or cash customer, notes should be checked for forgery and coins examined to exclude any foreign coins. A receipt should always be given to credit customers for cash payments received and a copy kept on file. Exhibit 12.1 shows an example of such a receipt.

Exhibit 12.1 Receipt for cash payment

Receipt No. 586/02	Date *15 May 2002*
Received from	*A. Rawsthorn*
the sum of	*Fifty pounds 40p*
in respect of	*Settlement of account*
Signed	*J. Hall*
on behalf of Johnson & Longden Ltd	

- **Cash sales.** With cash sales there is no need to keep a note of the payer's identity. There is, therefore, no legal need to issue a receipt. However, where cash tills are in use, the modern cash till will automatically issue a receipt for the cash when it is operated.

The larger retail stores in the UK all use electronic cash tills which issue receipts automatically. The receipts are kept by customers, not only as proof of payment to ensure that they cannot be accused of having stolen the goods, but as evidence of the purchase should the goods have to be returned as faulty or unsuitable. An example of such a receipt is shown in Exhibit 12.2.

Exhibit 12.2 Receipt for a cash sale

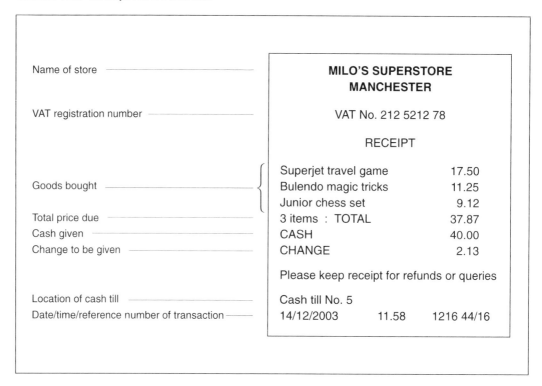

In this case the customer may have handed the cashier 2 × £20 notes = £40. This is recorded on the cash till which automatically calculates that the required change is £2.13.

For customers shopping at a retail store the VAT (value added tax) number is not required. However, if a business or organisation purchases goods for use in the business and they are VAT registered this information is required. Chapter 23 on value added tax covers this topic more fully.

12.5 Tills and cash floats

At the end of a day's transactions the takings received are totalled up, balanced and banked as soon as possible. However, not all of the takings are banked since many businesses like to keep a certain amount of money back to provide change in each till at the start of the next day's trading.

The store will know from past experience how much change will be needed. For instance, a store may want to start each day with £100 cash in each till made up as follows:

	£
6 × £10 notes	60.00
6 × £5 notes	30.00
12 × 50p coins	6.00
10 × 20p coins	2.00
15 × 10p coins	1.50
50p in copper coins	0.50
	£100.00

This amount of money is known as the 'cash float'. A typical day's cash activity at one of these tills may be as follows:

	£
Cash float at start of each day	100.00
Add Cash received from sales during the day	
(per list on till roll)	1,845.60
Total in till at end of day	1,945.60
Less Cash float for starting tomorrow	100.00
Amount to be banked or held securely	1,845.60

Where the cash in the till does not equal the float plus the list of sales from the till roll then an investigation will be needed. Minor errors in giving change will inevitably occur. Large discrepancies will need a greater scrutiny.

12.6 Cash: security measures

Any business or organisation that deals with large amounts of cash is responsible for ensuring that security measures are well defined and adhered to. Some of the risks might include the following:

- **Theft by staff.** This is a risk that has to be taken by any business, therefore, it is important that proper procedures are carried out when recruiting staff by ensuring that references are obtained and thoroughly checked. With modern cash tills it is easier these days to check the cashier's shift takings since they use their own individual key to log on and off the cash till at the start and end of their working period. At the end of the shift the till will provide a total of the amount of cash received by the cashier which can then be checked with the cash. The business may conduct further checks at irregular intervals without warning staff, and in this way can keep a check on the cashier's honesty.

- **Theft by others.** Cash tills should be kept locked when not in use and operated only by authorised personnel. Tills should be emptied at intervals throughout the day to prevent too great an accumulation of cash. It should then be moved to a safe or strongroom. Caution should be observed when taking cash to a bank. The timing of the bankings should be varied, different routes to the bank should be taken, and there should always be more than one person accompanying the money. Where cash takings are very large it is usual to employ security personnel or the services of a specialist security company to transport the cash.

- **Safes and strongboxes.** Safes must be kept out of view of customers. The use of safe keys must be limited to a few authorised personnel. Some safes have a chute mechanism which allows money to be put into the safe without opening the door. Certain cash tills have strongboxes connected to them. When money in the till reaches a given amount excess banknotes are put into the strongbox by means of a chute or slot. The strongbox is then emptied at the close of business when no customers are present.

12.7 Receipt of payments by cheque from customers with credit accounts

Most customers who have received goods and services pay for them by cheque. This is both a safe and more convenient method of making a payment than by cash. In Chapter

10 on the banking system the types of cheques and their use were covered and consideration will now be given to the receipt of cheques by businesses and organisations.

Cheques received from well-established credit account customers should be carefully examined for the following:

1 that the cheque is drawn payable to the receiver;

2 that the correct amount is stated both in words and in figures;

3 that the cheque is dated and is not out of date or postdated;

4 that the cheque has been properly signed.

If any of these factors are not in order the cheque will have to be returned to the drawer for amendment or for a new cheque to be issued. Cheques sent by post will not be accompanied by bank guarantee cards. It is not a legal requirement to issue a receipt for payment by cheque since the cheque is evidence of such payment. In spite of this many businesses do issue receipts.

12.8 Bank and building society cards

Banks and many building societies issue plastic cards that can be used by their customers for various purposes, such as:

- guaranteeing that a cheque is valid and that payment will be met by the bank on presentation – this is known as a **cheque guarantee card**;

- enabling a customer to buy goods or services on credit – this is known as a **credit card**;

- allowing customers to buy goods or services without paying cash or making out a cheque but instead the money is transferred from the customer's bank account to the supplier's bank account within a very short time – this is known as a **debit card**;

- allowing customers to obtain cash from cash dispensing machines – customers can also usually obtain an up-to-date balance on their account and a bank statement from these machines.

Very often these cards fulfil at least two, and sometimes all, of the functions just described.

The use of bank and building society cards is covered in more detail in 12.9 to 12.12.

12.9 Cheques received from cash customers

It would not be normal to accept a cheque in payment of goods or services unless the customer supported the cheque with a valid bank guarantee card.

An example of one of these cards is shown as Exhibit 12.3. The design of the cards varies slightly between the various banks and building societies but they are all the same size.

Key to details shown on Exhibit 12.3:
(a) Name of the bank issuing the card.

(b) Reference number.

(c) Period during which card may be used, i.e. 1 February 2001 to 31 January 2003.

(d) Name of cardholder.

Exhibit 12.3 Cheque guarantee card (see text for key)

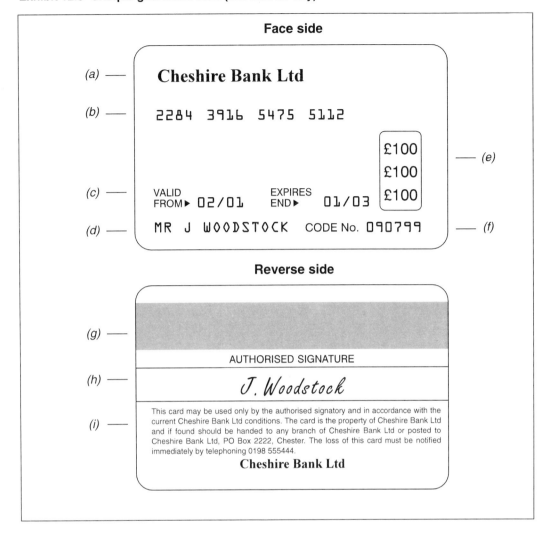

(e) In the rectangle shown is a hologram. This is a three-dimensional image which needs complicated machinery to produce, thus making it more difficult for forgeries to be made. In this case the last four numbers of the reference number are shown, as well as the amount of the limit of the guarantee card, i.e. in this case £100. All cheque guarantee cards will not necessarily have the limit shown in this position.

(f) The code number of the bank. This should be the same as the code number on the cheque being used.

(g) A black magnetic strip which holds all the information shown on the card. This can be read by a computer.

(h) The signature of the holder of the card.

(i) Instructions concerning the use, or loss, of the card.

Cheque guarantee cards are issued by banks to encourage the use of cheques instead of cash. The card will state the limit up to which the guarantee is effective, e.g. £50, £100 or £200. Provided the following conditions are carried out the bank will guarantee that the business will be paid the amount concerned.

1 The signature on the cheque must be scrutinised to ensure that it corresponds with the signature on the cheque guarantee card. The cheque must be signed in full view of the cashier to help limit forgeries.

2 The code number on the guarantee card should be the same as that printed on the cheque.

3   The expiry date must be later than the date on the cheque.

4   For UK cheque guarantee cards the cheques are guaranteed only if they are paid in the United Kingdom, the Channel Islands or the Isle of Man.

5   The card number must be written on the back of the cheque by the payee.

6   The card must not have been defaced or altered in any way.

7   The amount of the cheque must not exceed the guarantee limit on the card. If the cost of an item exceeds the limit, customers should not make out an extra cheque for the difference. The guarantee covers only one cheque per transaction. If the guarantee limit is £50, it is not allowable for two cheques, one for £50 and another for £26, to be used to buy an item costing £76.

In addition the items already outlined in section 12.6 of this chapter should also be observed.

12.10 Credit cards: a description

Credit cards are a way for customers to buy goods without making out a cheque or paying by cash. The credit card company will send a bill to the customer, usually monthly, for all the credit card purchases made in that month. A credit limit is established for each customer. If the customer pays the credit card company within a stated time limit, then no interest will be charged to them. Amounts outstanding past the stated date will attract quite a heavy rate of interest, which the customer will eventually have to pay.

The main credit companies in the UK are **Visa, Mastercard** and **American Express**.

Exhibit 12.4 shows an example of a credit card – in this instance a Visa card.

Exhibit 12.4 Visa card: face side

As you can see, the card is almost identical to the cheque guarantee card shown as Exhibit 12.3, the main difference being the Visa sign shown. The reverse side of the card is also almost identical with Exhibit 12.3. Both are made out of plastic.

All the time improvements are being made to credit cards so that they are more difficult to forge or to use fraudulently. Increasingly a photo of the cardholder is shown on the card. In addition the magnetic strip will in the future bear more information on it to deter the card's fraudulent use.

Some credit cards are given free to the public, while others incur a fixed charge per year. Apart from any interest these are the only costs borne by customers.

The businesses which sell goods or services and allow payment by credit card have to pay the credit card company a percentage commission based on the value of sales. The actual rate of commission will depend largely on the amount of business transacted. A large retailer with many branches will pay a lower rate of commission than a small retail shop.

12.11 Credit cards in use

On being handed a credit card as payment for goods or services, businesses should carry out the following procedures:

- **Larger businesses or organisations.** Larger businesses will have a special attachment to their cash tills. The card is passed through a slot in this machine (known as swiping the card) and the machine will automatically record the details of the card from its magnetic strip. This will electronically pass a message back along the telephone cables to the credit card company where the information is fed into a computer. The computer will then authorise the sale or reject it. Rejection could take place for several reasons:

  - The cardholder may have exceeded his or her credit limit on the card.
  - The card may have been reported stolen or lost by its lawful owner – in this case a message to this effect will be passed back to the suplier of the goods or services and possibly the thief may be caught (there is a reward from the credit card company for stolen cards recovered).
  - Unusual patterns of spending on the card may provoke the card company into suspending any more dealings until the queries are settled.

  When approved the cash till will automatically print out a credit card voucher with the details of the card and the amount involved. The customer will then be asked to sign the voucher.

- **Smaller businesses.** Smaller businesses may have cash tills which automatically produce credit card vouchers but are not connected to the credit card company's computer, or alternatively they may use a non-automatic machine into which the card is inserted together with a special voucher (*see* below). These businesses will be given a limit as to the size of a sale that can be passed without reference to the credit card company. If the sale is greater than the limit for the business, then it must telephone the credit card company for permission to proceed. When the voucher has been completed the customer will then be asked to sign it.

- **Security checks.** The following security checks must be made:

  - **Signature.** Ensure that you retain the credit card while the customer is signing the voucher. This makes forgery more difficult. Examine the signatures on the card and on the voucher – they should be sufficiently similar for you to feel that they have been written by the same person.
  - **Signature panel.** Rubbing your finger along this panel on the card should indicate whether or not it has been tampered with. The touch should feel smooth.
  - **Dates of use.** Check that the card is being used before its 'expiry date'.
  - **Limits.** Where limits on the amount spent are placed upon businesses, it should be ensured that such limits are not exceeded.
  - **Stolen cards.** Where there is no automatic access to the credit card company's computers, check the card number against a list of stolen or lost cards issued by the credit card company.

When all the security checks have been carried out to your satisfaction, then the credit card and the copy credit voucher can be handed to the customer with their purchases.

When printed automatically by an electronic till a completed credit card voucher may appear as in Exhibit 12.5. In such cases each business will have its own design for the voucher.

Exhibit 12.5 Electronically produced credit card voucher

When a hand-held imprinter machine is used the credit card is first placed on the machine, then the machine's mechanism is used to get an imprint of the card on to a credit card voucher. A completed voucher may appear as in Exhibit 12.6.

Exhibit 12.6 Credit card voucher from a hand-held machine

Key to details shown in Exhibit 12.6:

(a), (b) and (c) Imprinted from the raised letters and figures on the credit card, being the number of the card, the valid dates and the name of the cardholder.

(d) Imprinted from the machine giving the reference number and name of the business.

(e) The cardholder should sign this while the card is still in the possession of the cashier to help prevent forgeries.

(f) The type of credit card being used for payment – in this case it is a Visa card.

(g) Date and reference numbers for the use of the business.

(h) Details of goods sold.

(i) Authorisation number where sale is in excess of the limit granted (obtained by telephoning the credit card company) and the total value of the sale. In this case the first two spaces provided for the pounds figures have not been used. They should be struck through, as shown, to prevent a fraudulent person inserting extra figures. Customers should also ensure that the blank spaces are struck through for their own protection.

When goods are paid for by a credit card and a refund is later made for the return of the goods because of faults etc., the business will not usually refund by cash or cheque. It will issue a special form so that the refund is credited to the cardholder's account. This is partly to deter people buying goods by credit card who have no intention of keeping them but want to get refunds in cash when the goods are returned.

12.12 Debit cards

These are the same shape and size as credit cards but are for people who want their bank account charged with the cost of sales as soon as possible. People using credit cards such as Visa, Mastercard, American Express, etc. get quite a few weeks' credit before payment has to be made by them. Debit cards do not have this credit element built into them. Examples of debit cards are 'Switch' and 'Delta' cards.

The seller of the goods processes them in the same manner as credit cards but the funds are deducted directly from the customer's bank account.

12.13 EFTPOS (Electronic Funds Transfer at Point of Sale)

Most larger businesses with electronic cash registers have this system attached to them. When the debit card or credit card is swiped through the special attachment it automatically reads the magnetic strip on the back.

When the transaction is approved via the credit card's computer, or by the bank's computer for debit cards, the following happens:

- **Credit cards.** The amount involved will automatically be charged to the customer's credit card account.

- **Debit cards.** The amount involved will be transferred immediately from the customer's account at the bank to the credit of the bank account of the business, even though different banks may be involved.

This means that the business does not have to send the copy vouchers to the bank in respect of debit cards before payment can be received. Smaller businesses with nonelectronic tills will not be able to use this system and will have to take the vouchers to the bank before payment can be made.

12.14 Direct payment into the bank by inter-bank transfers

In respect of credit customers the money owing may be paid direct into the bank account of their suppliers:

- **by BACS** – this is the Bankers' Automated Clearing Service as described on p. 74;
- **by bank giro credits** – *see* p. 74;
- **by direct debit or standing orders** – *see* p. 76.

12.15 Banker's drafts

These are cheques issued by the bank itself, not drawn by the person making the payment. The bank is both the drawer (the one drawing up the cheque) and also the drawee (the one who is going to have to pay the cheque). This means that the cheque (the draft) is just as good as cash as it cannot be dishonoured in the way that may happen to normal cheques. They may be used either where the sum involved is a large one or the business which is owed the money is not certain as to the financial standing of its creditor.

12.16 Building society cheques

These have exactly the same effect as banker's drafts, in that both the drawer and drawee are the building society. Again these cheques cannot be dishonoured.

Both building society cheques and banker's drafts may have to be ordered in advance and a charge may be made for the service. The amount of the draft or building society cheque is taken from the customer's account.

12.17 Postal orders

These are bought from the post office and are mainly used for payment by people who do not possess bank cheque accounts.

12.18 EFTPOS and the banking of transactions

Where plastic cards have been used by customers, and the business is using the EFTPOS system (*see* section 12.13), then the banks and credit card companies will automatically pay the amounts due direct into the business bank account, usually within a fairly short time. Our business will indicate where the funds have come from, e.g. Visa, Mastercard, Switch, Delta, American Express, etc.

The business will keep a summary each day of the amounts received from sales via each type of plastic card. It will then be checked against the bank statement to ensure that the correct amounts have been received from the credit and debit card companies.

12.19 Banking other payments by plastic cards

Where manual imprinted machines are in use then the vouchers issued, e.g. Exhibit 12.6, will be listed by the business and paid into its bank account. The bank will then claim the money from the card-issuing company. Thus, in effect, the card company pays the bank and the bank pays their customer.

NEW TERMS

Banker's draft Cheques issued by the bank itself whereby the bank acts as both drawer and drawee which means that the cheque (or draft) is as good as cash and cannot be dishonoured.

Cash float An amount of money held by businesses to provide change in the cash till at the start of a day's trading. The amount held may vary from one business to another but usually it ranges from £50 to £100.

Cash till Machine which records the business's takings, issues receipts for the customer and provides a safe place in which to keep the takings during trading.

Cheque guarantee card A card issued to customers by banks or building societies which guarantees that a cheque is valid and will be paid when it is banked.

Credit card A card issued to customers by banks or building societies which enables them to buy goods or services without making out a cheque or paying by cash. The customer is sent a monthly bill by the credit company which has to be paid in a short specified period otherwise interest may be charged.

Debit card A card issued to customers of banks or building societies which enables the purchase of goods or services to be made, but when the transaction is processed by the seller the customer's bank account is charged almost immediately.

Electronic Funds Transfer at Point of Sale (EFTPOS) A system used by most large retail businesses which involves the use of electronic cash registers. This automatically transfers payments from the purchaser's account to the seller's bank account.

Postal order Often used by people who do not have a bank account to enable them to send money safely to another party and are purchased from post offices for the amount required.

Receipt Document issued by the seller which acknowledges the purchase of goods or services by the customer. This is a most important document because it must be produced if the goods are faulty and need to be changed or a refund given.

STUDENT ACTIVITIES

12.1 Organisations mainly receive payment from their suppliers by cheque. However, some people still prefer to pay their accounts in cash. Discuss some of the implications that receiving large amounts of cash might create for suppliers.

12.2 (a) What is the purpose of issuing a receipt?
 (b) Why is it important that customers retain receipts received when making a purchase in a large retail store?
 (c) If a debtor pays his supplier by cheque would a receipt normally be given? Discuss.

12.3X A cashier at the local stationers made the following sales during their shift:

Customer	Amount of sale	Amount tendered
	£	
1	5.99	£10 note
2	8.91	£20 note
3	1.49	2 × £1 coins
4	23.45	1 × £20 note, 1 x £5 note
5	0.54	£20 note
6	17.50	3 × £5 notes, 3 × £1 coins
7	11.22	1 × £20 note, 1 × 20p coin, 2 × 1p coins
8	7.34	£10 note
9	14.50	2 × £10 notes
10	3.10	1 × £5 note

(a) Calculate the amount of change to be given to each customer.

(b) Total the amount of sales made during the shift.

(c) Assuming the cash till opened with a float of £50.00 how much money would be in the till at the end of the shift?

12.4 (a) When payment for goods or services is made by cheque and accompanied by a cheque guarantee card what checks should the supplier make to ensure that payment is honoured by the bank?

(b) If you received the cheques and accompanying cheque guarantee cards from two customers as shown in Exhibit 12.7 would you accept them in payment of goods supplied? Discuss.

12.5X (a) A cheque guarantee card is presented in support of a payment by cheque. Other types of cards can be used when purchasing goods. Explain briefly why the following would be used:

(i) a credit card

(ii) a debit card.

(b) You have today received a cheque for £799 from a debtor. However, you notice that the cheque is undated. Is it acceptable for you to insert today's date?

(AAT (part of Central Assessment))

12.6 Janet and Sam Bennett are in partnership and run a small café in one of the Peak District's villages. Although business is steady during the week, trade increases at the weekend, especially in the summer. There has recently been an outbreak of petty crime in the area and Sam is getting increasingly concerned about the takings which are mainly in cash. He takes them home every evening prior to banking them the following day or on a Monday for the weekend takings.

Suggest what measures Sam might take to limit the possibility of the cash being stolen.

12.7X (a) What is a banker's draft and when might it be used?

(b) What does EFTPOS stand for?

(c) List three advantages of a large retail store using EFTPOS.

12.8X Keith Warrington is a full-time student at the local college where he is taking an HND business and finance course. To supplement his grant he has a part-time job at Smithy Garage where his duties include the following:

● taking receipts of money and cheques from the sale of petrol for which a till receipt is given, calculating and handing out correct change to customers;

Note: The garage does not accept payment by credit card

● receiving cheques and cash in payment of customers' car repair invoices, for which a receipt must be issued;

● completing a 'Payments Received Analysis Sheet' for customers paying their car repair accounts and buying petrol;

Exhibit 12.7 Details of cheques and cheque guarantee cards

Customer No 1

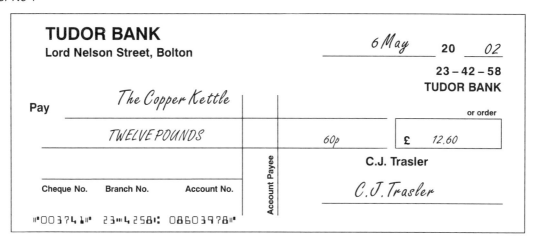

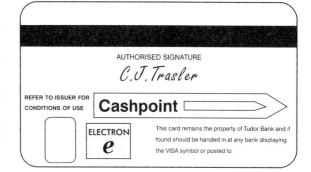

Customer No 2

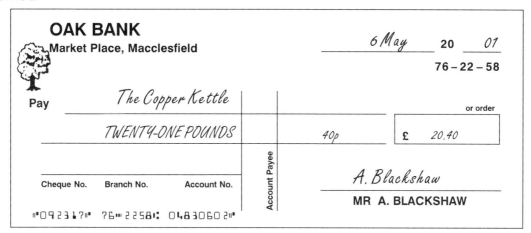

- completing a 'Takings Summary Form' at the end of a shift by:
  - balancing total receipts from petrol sales and customer account receipts;
  - ensuring that the cash/cheques takings are correct.

Required:

(a) The following receipts were received on Saturday 4 April 2001 from customers paying their repair accounts. Make out a receipt for each and record the payment on the Payments Received Analysis Sheet – *see* blank forms in Exhibits 12.8 and 12.9.

			Invoice number
Mr Michael Dickinson	Cheque	£87.50	A 231
Mr Owen Riley	Cheque	£123.10	A 173
Mr P J Durose	Cash	£52.70	A 203
Forge Services	Cheque	£75.10	A 71
Dr J B Hirst	Cash	£92.00	A 174

The next receipt number to use is H 3021.

(b) The 'float' in the till on Saturday morning 4 April 2001 was £50. During the day you received the following amounts from petrol sales.

You are required to calculate the amount of change to be given to each customer.

Customer	Amount tendered	Amount of sale (£)
1	£20 note	17.30
2	£10 note	8.53
3	£10 note, 50p coin, 2p coin	6.52
4	2 × £20 notes, 5p coin, 2p coin	29.17
5	£5 note, 10p coin	3.60
6	Cheque	12.10
7	Cheque	16.58
8	£20 note	9.63

In addition, total the petrol takings for the day. You may use the workings section in Exhibit 12.10 for your answer.

(c) At the end of the shift all cash/cheque receipts from both the sale of petrol and customer repair accounts must be entered on to the attached blank Takings Summary Form (Exhibit 12.10).

This should then be completed, balanced off and the correct amount of float, £50, carried forward to the next shift.

Carry out this task.

Exhibit 12.8

No _____	No _____	*SMITHY GARAGE*	*20* _____
_____ *20* _____	Received from _____		
from _____	the sum of _____		pounds
_____	_____		pence
_____		Cheque/Cash	
£ _____	£ _____	Signature _____	
			for SMITHY GARAGE

No _____	No _____	*SMITHY GARAGE*	*20* _____
_____ *20* _____	Received from _____		
from _____	the sum of _____		pounds
_____	_____		pence
_____		Cheque/Cash	
£ _____	£ _____	Signature _____	
			for SMITHY GARAGE

No _____	No _____	*SMITHY GARAGE*	*20* _____
_____ *20* _____	Received from _____		
from _____	the sum of _____		pounds
_____	_____		pence
_____		Cheque/Cash	
£ _____	£ _____	Signature _____	
			for SMITHY GARAGE

No _____	No _____	*SMITHY GARAGE*	*20* _____
_____ *20* _____	Received from _____		
from _____	the sum of _____		pounds
_____	_____		pence
_____		Cheque/Cash	
£ _____	£ _____	Signature _____	
			for SMITHY GARAGE

No _____	No _____	*SMITHY GARAGE*	*20* _____
_____ *20* _____	Received from _____		
from _____	the sum of _____		pounds
_____	_____		pence
_____		Cheque/Cash	
£ _____	£ _____	Signature _____	
			for SMITHY GARAGE

Exhibit 12.9

PAYMENTS RECEIVED ANALYSIS SHEET		Date _____		
Customer	Total amount received £	By cash £	By cheque £	Invoice No
Totals	£	£	£	

Exhibit 12.10

TAKINGS SUMMARY FORM

ASSISTANT'S NAME _____ **DATE** _____

1	**Opening Float**	£
2	**Total of Payments Rec'd Analysis Sheet** (re: Customers' Accounts)	
3	**Total of Cash/Cheque Petrol Receipts**	
	TOTAL	£
4	**Deduct Opening Float**	
	TOTAL AMOUNT TAKEN	£

ANALYSIS OF CASH/CHEQUES

Cheques Total

Cash Total

£

DISCREPANCIES (if any)

Workings

13 Making and recording outgoing payments

- To understand the importance of controlling payments.

- To consider the various methods available for making payments.

- To understand that payments must be correctly authorised.

- To understand the procedures for making payments supported by the correct documentation.

- To consider the necessary safety and security measures when making payments.

13.1 The importance of control of payments

All payments should be made and recorded in accordance with the organisation's policies, regulations, procedures and timescales. What these are will depend very much on the nature and size of the organisation or business. No one would suggest that a small business employing three people should organise payments in the same way as a business employing 30,000 people. In a small business the owner can see more or less everything that is going on, whereas management in the larger company is more remote and will need tighter and more elaborate systems.

Basically a payments system should ensure the following:

- All payments are made on time, neither before nor later than specified in the procedures. If payment is made late valuable cash discounts may be lost and the goodwill of the business may suffer.

    If payment is made too early then the cash/bank resources are unnecessarily depleted. Should the business have a bank overdraft it will suffer extra unnecessary interest on the overdraft. Lack of cash/bank resources may mean the business is unable to carry out activities which would have been profitable simply because it lacked the money to finance them.

- Regulations and procedures must exist to ensure that payments are made to the correct organisations, that they are of the correct amounts and that they are for the proper value of goods or services which have been received. Many frauds have occurred by payments being made to fictitious people for goods or services which have never been received or where prices have been inflated above what they should have been. The advent of computers has made sophisticated fraud more possible.

- The policies laid down by management should determine what regulations, procedures and timetables are needed to fulfil them.

The remainder of the chapter will consider the above in greater detail.

13.2 Paying trade suppliers

Depending on the policies and procedures laid down by the business or organisation, the following should occur:

- Payment should take place neither earlier nor later than has been set down in the procedures.

- The documents relating to the transaction (these will be examined in more detail in Chapters 18, 20 and 21) should be checked against each other. These would consist of the purchase order, delivery or goods received note and the invoice. All totals, calculations and balances should be checked on the documents.

- Checks should be made to ensure that the goods were received in good order and are not being returned because of any faults.

- If goods have been or are being returned, the appropriate credit note should have been received from the supplier.

- All discounts such as cash discounts and trade discounts *(see* section 19.8) have been correctly calculated, allowed and deducted before calculating final payment.

- Payment should only be made when it has been given the necessary final authorisation. The power to authorise payments should be given to as senior a person in the organisation as possible.

- Limits may be set above which the approval of another senior person is also required. For instance, cheques under £1,000 may be paid out without such extra permission, but over that amount further authorisation would be needed. The bank could be instructed that such high value cheques require two signatures from approved signatories instead of just one.

Each document received, whether invoice, credit note and so on, will probably be stamped with a rubber stamp, and the person or persons responsible for checking it will add their initials and the date to it.

13.3 Time for payment

This will depend on the business's or organisation's policies and procedures. It will also depend on arrangements made with suppliers. Some may give a period of seven days for payment, others one month, two months and so on. The following are, therefore, general statements:

- Unless cash discounts are involved, the usual procedure is for payment to be made monthly following the receipt of the monthly statement.

- Payments should be made on the due date stated on the invoice. This is especially true if cash discounts are involved.

With monthly statements most payments will be made on the same day of each month. This makes it easier to use the bank's BACS system *(see* section 10.7) instead of sending separate cheques by post. A small business will probably issue individual cheques.

13.4 **Remittance advices**

A remittance advice should be used for all payments by cheque and for payments via BACS. Otherwise the business receiving the money may not know exactly who had made the payment and for which item it had been paid.

- **Paying by cheque.** The remittance advice should be attached to each cheque being paid. This should identify all the particulars of the payment, so that the items paid for can easily be traced by the receiver. Exhibit 13.1 is an example of such a remittance advice.

  Notice that in the payment column £12.90 is shown in brackets. This means it is to be deducted from the other figures.

Exhibit 13.1 Cheque remittance advice

<table>
<tr><td colspan="5" align="center">REMITTANCE ADVICE</td></tr>
<tr><td colspan="5" align="center">ANGLER'S SUPPLY LTD
28 Barnsfold Road
Upper Chilworth
Warwickshire RG1 2PN
Tel: 0128 596432</td></tr>
<tr><td colspan="2">Jerry's Fishing Supplies
75 Lower Throgmorton
Kendal
Cumbria WN7 2P</td><td colspan="3">Date   31 May 2001
Account   2738
Cheque No. 156492</td></tr>
<tr><td>Date</td><td>Invoice or
Credit note no.</td><td>Invoices</td><td>Credit
notes</td><td>Payment</td></tr>
<tr><td>10.04.01
19.04.01
24.04.01
27.04.01</td><td>63982
65121
CR1586
66118</td><td>54.50
171.75

220.00</td><td>

12.90</td><td>54.50
171.75
(12.90)
220.00</td></tr>
<tr><td colspan="4" align="right">Cheque total</td><td>£433.35</td></tr>
</table>

- **Payment by BACS.** In section 10.7 we have already described how this system operates. However, we must also send the supplier a remittance advice. Failing this the supplier will not know that the payment has been made until they receive their bank statement. They may also have difficulty in tracing the identity of the business paying the amount. It is not unknown for action to be taken to chase a debt when in fact it has already been paid via BACS. The remittance advice may resemble that in Exhibit 13.1 except that it must be clearly stated, preferably in fairly large print, that the BACS system has been used.

- **Paying by bank giro credits.** This system has been described in section 10.6. It is now mainly used by smaller businesses as the large concerns will use BACS. An example of a cheque payment to J Black Ltd for £128.70 is shown in Exhibit 13.2. The person filling in the bank giro credit will need to know the following details concerning the creditor's account:

- code number of the creditor's bank

- name of that bank

- name of the branch of the bank

- title of the supplier's bank account

- account number of the creditor.

Unless these are known the bank giro credit form cannot be completed.

Exhibit 13.2 A completed bank giro credit form

13.5 Methods of payment

No two businesses or organisations will use exactly the same methods of payments in respect of all outgoings. A small business may use cash to pay its wages, while a larger business may use the BACS system. Another business may pay rates by direct debit while another may pay by cheque. This chapter therefore considers the general principles involved. Typical examples may be as follows:

- Payments by cheque:

  - for expensive items such as machinery and motor lorries;

  - employees for major items of expense.

- Paying by other methods through the bank account:

  - suppliers for goods and services received on credit by the BACS system;

  - wages by the BACS system;

  - rates and water charges – by direct debit;

  - mortgage repayments – by standing order.

- Cash payments (through the petty cash system – *see* Chapter 15):

  - casual labour;

  - postages;

  - small items of expense such as coffee and tea for the office.

13.6 Cheque requisition forms

Normally there will be evidence to back up the need to make a payment. For instance, the need for payment may be evidenced by purchases invoices and the supplier's statement. Payments for expenses, e.g. electricity charges, will have a bill from the electricity company as evidence for the need for payment.

There will be cases where payments need to be made without having the supporting evidence for it. An instance might be the hiring of a room at a conference centre for a meeting of the sales force. The hire charge may well have to be paid in advance.

In this case the sales manager will have to fill in a cheque requisition form and get the authorisation of the marketing director. An example of such a requisition form is shown in Exhibit 13.3.

Exhibit 13.3 Cheque requisition form

Manley Lamps Ltd	No. 1785

CHEQUE REQUISITION FORM

Date:	*16 May 2003*
Cheque required:	
PAYABLE TO:	*Swinley Hotels Ltd*
AMOUNT:	*£750*
PURPOSE:	*To hire rooms for annual conference of sales staff*
TO BE SENT TO:	*Swinley Hotels Ltd PO Box 7899, Harlow, Essex CM20 2JE*
LEDGER REFERENCE:	*60/549*
INVOICE:	*Not yet received*
OTHER EVIDENCE:	*Copy letter from Swinley Hotels — attached*
AUTHORISED BY:	*Charles Stone, Marketing Director*

13.7 Other methods of payment

These methods have been looked at in Chapter 12, but from the viewpoint of the receiving business. In each case, when a business uses any method of payment proper documentation and control should be used.

- **Credit cards.** Some of the staff may be given business credit cards. When used the charge will be made to the business, not to the individual who has used the card. Limits, which must not be exceeded, should be laid down. The copy credit card vouchers, and any other form of receipt, must be handed in on a regular basis by the employee. These will be checked and recorded by the cashier, with queries or discrepancies being referred to a senior member of staff.

- **Standing orders.** The business may pay various organisations by standing orders via the bank, e.g. to an insurance company, to the council for rates and so on. All standing orders must be authorised by a responsible member of staff and should be fully documented.

- **Bank drafts.** These are likely to be for large amounts where the certainty of the draft means that payment is guaranteed. This is very often found in the purchase of land or buildings.

- **Telegraphic transfers.** Payments can be made by instructing the bank to transfer an amount by electronic funds transfer. This will transfer funds from the account of the business direct to the account of the supplier. They are usually used only for large payments and where the supplier has specifically asked for it.

13.8 Safety and security measures

Just as cash and other forms of money received must be kept in safes and strongboxes, so also must items connected with payments.

Cheques:

- Cheque books must be kept locked away except when in use.

- Cheques must be properly made out, supported by documentation and signed only by the person(s) authorised to do so.

- Cheques must be crossed 'Account payee only' except in specially authorised cases.

- A proper system for sending cheques by post must be observed to help ensure that they do not fall into the wrong hands.

- Items showing that payment has been made should be examined, e.g. receipts, customers' statements.

Cash:

- Payment by cash should only be used when there is not a sensible alternative.

- Receipts must be obtained for all cash payments.

- Payment limits for cash must be adhered to by the employee handling the cash.

- Should a larger amount of cash above the limit be needed, a senior member of staff with the proper powers must authorise it.

- Cash should be kept in safes or strongboxes and should not be allowed to reach excessive amounts.

 NEW TERMS

Bank draft A cheque issued and drawn on a bank for a customer where the certainty of the draft means that payment is guaranteed.

Cheque requisition form Internal form used to request payment by cheque, often used for a one-off specific purpose.

Remittance advice A document which accompanies payment by cheque or via BACS and gives details of the payment.

Telegraphic transfer Payments made by instructing the bank to transfer funds by electronic funds transfer from one bank account to another. Usually used for large amounts of money or if specifically requested by the supplier.

STUDENT ACTIVITIES

13.1 As accounts assistant for a medium sized printing company one of your responsibilities is to ensure purchase invoices are properly checked and authorised for payment prior to the payment being processed.

(a) Discuss the essential features of a payment system.

(b) Describe the steps you would take to check and verify an invoice received from a supplier before passing it for payment.

13.2 Describe how the following documents are used in business:

(a) remittance advice

(b) cheque requisition.

13.3 Fir Foods Ltd supply animal feed and sundry farm accessories and equipment. They purchase the majority of their goods on a weekly credit basis from several animal food manufacturers. There is a quick turnround and it is important that suppliers are paid promptly, otherwise supplies could be affected.

You have been employed as Junior Accounts Assistant to help Ms Linda Howson, the company's accountant, with many of the routine tasks.

Task:

The date is Friday, 14 June 2002. Ms Howson requires help in the preparation of this week's cheque payments and asks you to make out cheques for the following creditors.

Name of creditor	Amount
Trent Farm Feeds plc	£754.20
Baldwins	£32.75
Derbyshire Animal Foods Ltd	£2,512.13
Ratcliffs (Mfrs)Ltd	£74.03
Grove Farm Supplies	£132.40
Websters Animal Feeds Ltd	£521.32

Blank cheques are available for this task – *see* Exhibit 13.4.

On completion hand the cheques to Ms Howson who will arrange for them to be signed by herself and the company secretary.

13.4 Your employer, Hart Motors Ltd, asks you to make the following payment to one of your main suppliers of new vehicles:

Date	–	12 May 2002
Supplier	–	Davies Distribution Service Ltd
Amount	–	£89,570.00
Bank details		
Name	–	Oak Bank plc
Branch	–	Derby
Sort code	–	07-44-83
Supplier account no.	–	01793856

You are required to complete the bank giro credit slip shown in Exhibit 13.5.

13.5 Organisations can make payments to their suppliers of goods and services using various methods. Describe briefly four methods of payment which they may use.

13.6 It is important that satisfactory safety and security procedures are complied with when organisations make payments to their suppliers.

Describe fully the procedures you would consider essential when making both cash and cheque payments.

Exhibit 13.4

Date _____

Payee _____

_____

_____

Amount £

007722

OAK BANK

High Street, Ripon

20 ____

33 - 57 - 02

Pay _____

or order

£

FIR FOODS LTD

Cheque No.   Branch No.   Account No.

Account Payee

⑈007722⑈ 33⑈ 5702⑈ 06041758⑈

Date _____

Payee _____

_____

_____

Amount £

007723

OAK BANK

High Street, Ripon

20 ____

33 - 57 - 02

Pay _____

or order

£

FIR FOODS LTD

Cheque No.   Branch No.   Account No.

Account Payee

⑈007723⑈ 33⑈ 5702⑈ 06041758⑈

Date _____

Payee _____

_____

_____

Amount £

007724

OAK BANK

High Street, Ripon

20 ____

33 - 57 - 02

Pay _____

or order

£

FIR FOODS LTD

Cheque No.   Branch No.   Account No.

Account Payee

⑈007724⑈ 33⑈ 5702⑈ 06041758⑈

Exhibit 13.4 *(continued)*

| Date _____ | | **OAK BANK** | | 20 ___ |
| Payee _____ | | **High Street, Ripon** | | 33 – 57 – 02 |

Pay _____ or order

£ _____

FIR FOODS LTD

Amount £ _____

Cheque No.   Branch No.   Account No.   Account Payee

007725

॥‟007725॥‟ 33॥‟ 5702॥: 06041758 ॥‟

| Date _____ | | **OAK BANK** | | 20 ___ |
| Payee _____ | | **High Street, Ripon** | | 33 – 57 – 02 |

Pay _____ or order

£ _____

FIR FOODS LTD

Amount £ _____

Cheque No.   Branch No.   Account No.   Account Payee

007726

॥‟007726॥‟ 33॥‟ 5702॥: 06041758 ॥‟

| Date _____ | | **OAK BANK** | | 20 ___ |
| Payee _____ | | **High Street, Ripon** | | 33 – 57 – 02 |

Pay _____ or order

£ _____

FIR FOODS LTD

Amount £ _____

Cheque No.   Branch No.   Account No.   Account Payee

007727

॥‟007727॥‟ 33॥‟ 5702॥: 06041758 ॥‟

Exhibit 13.5

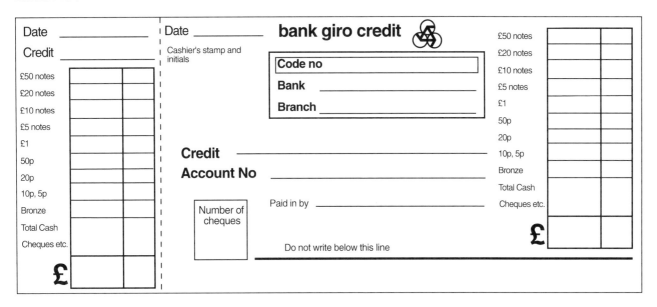

13.7 The invoice shown in Exhibit 13.6 relating to the redecoration of a retail property has been received by JLW Ltd.

Exhibit 13.6

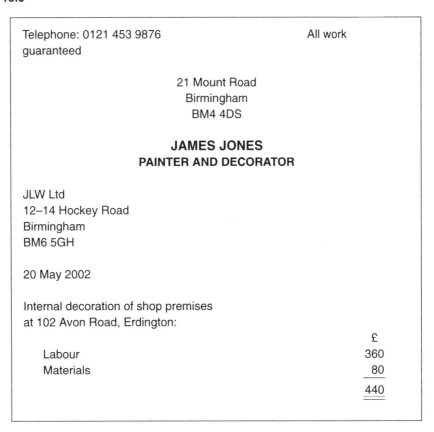

Prepare the cheque provided in Exhibit 13.7 to pay the invoice.

Exhibit 13.7

49-27-42

NORTHLAND 34 MARKET STREET HANDSWORTH
WEST MIDLANDS BM7 9AH
TEL 0121 564 2398

____________ 20______

PAY ______________________ A/C PAYEE ______________________

£ [ ]

JLW Ltd

⑈180098 ⑈ 49⑉ 27421⑆ 12344567 ⑈

(AAT (part of Central Assessment))

14 Bank reconciliation statements

AIMS

- To be able to reconcile cash book balances with bank statement balances.
- To understand how bank overdrafts affect the reconciliation process.

14.1 The need for bank reconciliation statements

At the end of each period the cash book will be balanced off. About the same time the firm will receive a bank statement. When the closing balance in the cash book is compared with the balance on that date on the bank statement, the two balances will usually be found to be different.

At this point a **bank reconciliation statement** should be prepared. This will either show:

1 that the reasons for the difference between the two balances are valid ones, showing that it has not been as a result of errors made by us or the bank, or

2 that there is not a good reason for the difference between the balances.

In the case of **2** we will have to find out exactly what the errors are and then they can be corrected.

14.2 An example of a bank reconciliation statement

Let us assume that we have just written up our cash book. We call at the bank on 30 June 2002 and get from the bank manager a copy of our bank statement. On our return we tick off in our cash book and on the bank statement the items that are similar. A copy of our cash book (bank columns only) and of our bank statement are now shown as Exhibit 14.1.

Exhibit 14.1

Cash Book

Dr				£						Cr
				(bank columns only)						
2002				£	2002					£
June	1	Balance b/f	✓	80	June	27	I Gordon		✓	35
June	28	D Jones	✓	100	June	29	B Tyrell			40
					June	30	Balance c/d			105
				180						180
July	1	Balance b/d		105						

Bank Statement

				Dr	Cr	Balance
2002				£	£	£
June	26	Balance b/f	✓			80 Cr
June	28	Banking	✓		100	180 Cr
June	30	I Gordon	✓	35		145 Cr

By comparing the cash book and the bank statement, it can be seen that the only item that was not in both of these was the cheque payment to B Tyrell £40 in the cash book.

The reason this was in the cash book but not on the bank statement is simply one of timing. The cheque had been posted to B Tyrell on 29 June, but there had not been time for it to be banked by Tyrell and passed through the banking system. Such a cheque is called an **unpresented cheque** because it has not yet been presented at the drawer's bank.

To prove that although they are different figures the balances are not different because of errors, a bank reconciliation statement is drawn up. This is as follows:

Bank Reconciliation Statement as at 30 June 2002

	£
Balance in hand as per cash book	105
Add Unpresented cheque: Tyrell	40
Balance in hand as per bank statement	145

It would have been possible for the bank reconciliation statement to have started with the bank statement balance:

Bank Reconciliation Statement as at 30 June 2002

	£
Balance in hand as per bank statement	145
Less Unpresented cheque: Tyrell	40
Balance in hand as per cash book	105

You should notice that the bank account is shown as a debit balance in the firm's cash book because to the firm it is an asset. In the bank's books the bank account is shown as a credit balance because this is a liability of the bank to the firm.

14.3 Some reasons for differences in balances

We can now look at a more complicated example in Exhibit 14.2. Similar items in both cash book and bank statement are shown ticked.

Exhibit 14.2

Cash Book

Dr				£	Cr				£
2004					2004				
Dec	27	Total b/f		2,000	Dec	17	Total b/f		1,600
Dec	29	J Potter	✓	60	Dec	28	J Jacobs	✓	105
Dec	31	M Johnson **(B)**		220	Dec	30	M Chatwood **(A)**		15
					Dec	31	Balance c/d		560
				2,280					2,280
2005									
Jan	1	Balance b/d		560					

Bank Statement

				Dr	Cr	Balance
				£	£	£
2004						
Dec	27	Balance b/f				400 CR
Dec	29	Cheque	✓		60	460 CR
Dec	30	J Jacobs	✓	105		355 CR
Dec	30	Credit transfers: L Shaw **(C)**			70	425 CR
Dec	30	Bank charges **(D)**		20		405 CR

The balance brought forward in the bank statement £400 is the same figure as that in the cash book, i.e. totals b/f £2,000 – £1,600 = £400. However, items (A) and (B) are in the cash book only, and (C) and (D) are on the bank statement only. We can now examine these in detail:

(A) This is a cheque recently sent by us to Mr Chatwood. It has not yet passed through the banking system and been presented to our bank, and is therefore an 'unpresented cheque'.

(B) This is a cheque banked by us on our visit to the bank when we collected the copy of our bank statement. As we handed this banking over the counter at the same time as the bank clerk gave us our bank statement, naturally it has not yet been entered on the statement.

(C) A customer, L Shaw, has paid his account by instructing his bank to pay us direct through the banking system instead of paying by cheque. Such a transaction is usually called a **credit transfer**.

(D) The bank has charged us for the services given in keeping a bank account for us. It did not send us a bill: it simply takes the money from our account by debiting it and reducing the amount of our balance.

We can show these differences in the form of a table. This is followed by bank reconciliation statements drawn up both ways. This is for illustration only; we do not have to draw up a table or prepare two bank reconciliation statements. All we need in practice is one bank reconciliation statement, drawn up whichever way we prefer.

			Adjustment required to one balance to reconcile it with the other	
Items not in both sets of books	Effect on Cash Book balance	Effect on Bank Statement	To Cash Book balance	To Bank Statement balance
1 Payment M Chatswood £15	reduced by £15	none – not yet entered	add £15	deduct £15
2 Banking M Johnson £220	increased by £220	none – not yet entered	deduct £220	add £220
3 Bank Commission £20	none – not yet entered	reduced by £20	deduct £20	add £20
4 Credit Transfers £70	none – not yet entered	increased by £70	add £70	deduct £70

Bank Reconciliation Statement as on 31 December 2004

	£	£
Balance in hand as per cash book		560
Add Unpresented cheque – M Chatwood	15	
Credit transfers	70	
		85
		645
Less Bank commission	20	
Bank lodgement not yet entered on bank statement	220	
		240
Balance in hand as per bank statement		405

Bank Reconciliation Statement as on 31 December 2004

	£	£
Balance in hand as per bank statement		405
Add Bank commission	20	
Bank lodgement not yet entered on bank statement	220	
		240
		645
Less Unpresented cheque M Chatwood	15	
Traders credit transfers	70	
		85
Balance in hand as per bank statement		560

Other reasons for the differences in balances between the cash book and the bank statement may arise where the bank has paid a standing order or direct debit out of the customer's account at the bank but the customer has not entered the payment in the firm's cash book. In these circumstances the cash book will require updating before preparation of the bank reconciliation statement.

Both standing orders and direct debits have been dealt with previously in Chapter 10, section 10.8.

14.4 Writing up the cash book before attempting a reconciliation

The easiest way to do a reconciliation is to complete the cash book first. All items on the bank statement will then be in the cash book. This means that the only differences will be items in the cash book but not on the bank statement. In an examination it is possible that the examiner will ask you not to do it this way.

If in Exhibit 14.2 the cash book had been written up before the bank reconciliation statement had been drawn up, then the cash book and reconciliation statement would have appeared as follows in Exhibit 14.3.

Exhibit 14.3

Cash Book

Dr			£				Cr
2004			£	2004			£
Dec	27	Total b/fwd	2,000	Dec	27	Total b/fwd	1,600
Dec	29	J Potter	60	Dec	28	J Jacobs	105
Dec	31	M Johnson	220	Dec	30	M Chatwood	15
Dec	31	Credit transfers:		Dec	31	Bank commission	20
		L Shaw	70	Dec	31	Balance c/d	610
			2,350				2,350
2005							
Jan	1	Balance b/d	610				

Bank Reconciliation Statement as on 31 December 2004

	£
Balance in hand as per cash book	610
Add Unpresented cheque – M Chatwood	15
	625
Less Bank lodgement not yet entered on bank statement	220
Balance in hand as per bank statement	405

14.5 Bank overdrafts

When there is a bank overdraft the adjustments needed for reconciliation work are opposite to those needed for a balance.

Exhibit 14.4 presents a cash book and a bank statement showing an overdraft.

Note: On a bank statement an overdraft is often shown with the letters O/D following the amount or else shown as a debit balance, indicated by the letters DR after the amount.

Only the cheque for G Cumberbatch (A) £106 and the cheque paid to J Kelly (B) £63 need adjusting. Work through the reconciliation statement in Exhibit 14.4 and then compare the reconciliation statements in Exhibits 14.3 and 14.4.

Exhibit 14.4

Cash Book
(bank columns only)

Dr			£				Cr
2001			£	2001			£
Dec	5	I Howe	308	Dec	1	Balance b/f	709
Dec	24	L Mason	120	Dec	9	P Davies	140
Dec	29	K King	124	Dec	27	J Kelly (B)	63
Dec	31	G Cumberbatch (A)	106	Dec	29	United Trust	77
Dec	31	Balance c/f	380	Dec	31	Bank Charges	49
			1,038				1,038
				2002			
				Jan	1	Balance b/f	380

Exhibit 14.4 *(continued)*

Bank Statement			
	Dr	*Cr*	*Balance*
2001	£	£	£
Dec 1 Balance b/f			709 O/D
Dec 5 Cheque		308	401 O/D
Dec 14 P Davies	140		541 O/D
Dec 24 Cheque		120	421 O/D
Dec 29 K King: Credit transfer		124	297 O/D
Dec 29 United Trust: Standing Order	77		374 O/D
Dec 31 Bank Charges	49		423 O/D

Bank Reconciliation Statement as on 31 December 2001

	£
Overdraft as per cash book	380
Add Bank lodgements not on bank statement	106
	486
Less Unpresented cheque	63
Overdraft per bank statement	423

This shows:

	Exhibit 14.3	Exhibit 14.4
	Balances	*Overdrafts*
Balance/Overdraft per cash book	XXXX	XXXX
Adjustments		
Unpresented cheque	PLUS	LESS
Banking not entered	LESS	PLUS
Balance/Overdraft per bank statement	XXXX	XXXX

Adjustments are, therefore, made in the opposite way when there is an overdraft.

14.6 Dishonoured cheques

This is a cheque which the bank will not honour because there are insufficient funds in the drawer's account. This is more fully explained in Chapter 10, section 10.12.

NEW TERMS

Bank reconciliation statement A calculation comparing the cash book balance with the bank statement balance.

Unpresented cheque A cheque which has been sent but has not yet gone through the receiver's bank account.

STUDENT ACTIVITIES

14.1 From the following draw up a bank reconciliation statement from details as on 31 December 2005.

	£
Cash at bank as per bank column of the cash book	678
Unpresented cheques	256
Cheques received and paid into the bank, but not yet entered on the bank statement	115
Credit transfers entered as banked on the bank statement but not entered in the cash book	56
Cash at bank as per bank statement	875

14.2X On 30 September 2003 George Snow's statement of account from his bank showed a credit balance in his favour of £1,024.66. On comparing the statement with his cash book he found the following entries in the cash book did not appear on the statement:

Cheques paid in 30 Sept	£342.51
Cheques drawn on 30 Sept	£297.82

The following entries on the statement did not appear in his cash book:

Bank charges to 30 Sept 2003	£15.48
Payment direct to the bank by one of his debtors	£230.17

Prepare a bank reconciliation statement to show the bank balance in his cash book on 30 September 2003.

(Pitman Qualifications)

14.3X Cunningham & Co is an old-established firm of accountants in Huddersfield. You have been employed as bookkeeper to the company to assist the senior partner, Mr Cunningham, with the accounting records and day-to-day routine duties.

The company's policies when dealing with both payments and receipts is extremely strict. All cash and cheques received are to be banked immediately. Any payments over £10 must be made by cheque. Small cash payments are all paid by the petty cash system.

One of your tasks is to enter (make the entries in) the company's cash book and reconcile this with the bank statement. This task must be carried out on a weekly basis.

Required

(a) Having obtained the company's cheque book and paying-in book (Exhibits 14.5 and 14.6), enter up the cash book (bank column only) for the period commencing 3 November 2004. Unfortunately, on that date the company was overdrawn by £2,356.00.

(b) Balance up the cash book at the end of the week and bring the balance down.

(c) From the bank statement (Exhibit 14.7) you are required to prepare:

    (i) the corrected cash book balance as at 10 November 2004;

    (ii) a bank reconciliation statement as at 10 November 2004.

(NVQ Level 2)

Exhibit 14.5 Details of cheque book stubs: Cunningham & Co

Date _3 Nov 2004_ Payee _Post Office_ _Stamps_ **Amount £ 146.50** 001763	Date _3 Nov 2004_ Payee _The Law_ _Society_ **Amount £ 121.80** 001764	Date _4 Nov 2004_ Payee _Bayleys_ _Office Supplies_ **Amount £ 94.10** 001765
Date _5 Nov 2004_ Payee _Lower Bents_ _Garage_ _(Petrol A/c – Sept)_ **Amount £ 450.15** 001766	Date _6 Nov 2004_ Payee _Wages_ **Amount £ 489.20** 001767	Date _10 Nov 2004_ Payee _Petty Cashier_ _(Restoring_ _Imprest)_ **Amount £ 46.00** 001768

Exhibit 14.6 Details from paying-in book: Cunningham & Co

Date _3 Nov 2004_ A/c _Cunningham & Co_ Cash Cheques _Mrs Stoddard £540.00_ £ 540.00	Date _5 Nov 2004_ A/c _Cunningham & Co_ Cash _Bent Garage £221.00_ _P Ralphs £ 53.00_ Cheques _Gardeners £1500.000_ £ 1774.00	Date _6 Nov 2004_ A/c _Cunningham & Co_ Cash _Mr Prince £130.50_ Cheques _Stephens & Smith £523.10_ £ 653.60

Date _7 Nov 2004_ A/c _Cunningham & Co_ Cash Cheques _Rileys (Printers) & Co £759.00_ £ 759.00	Date _7 Nov 2004_ A/c _Cunningham & Co_ Cash _Brindle Bros £165.50_ Cheques _Robert Andrews Ltd £325.00_ £ 490.50

Exhibit 14.7 Bank statement: Cunningham & Co

TUDOR BANK		CONFIDENTIAL	

High Street
Huddersfield

Account: Cunningham & Co
Chestergate
Huddersfield

Account No: 0012770123

Sheet No: 67
Date: 8 November 2004

2004				Dr	Cr	Balance
Nov	3	Balance b/f				2,356.00 O/D
	4	Cheque	001763	146.50		2,502.50 O/D
	3	Deposit			540.00	1,962.50 O/D
	5	Deposit			1,774.00	188.50 O/D
	6	S/O Noble Insurance		62.00		250.50 O/D
	6	Cheque	001767	489.20		739.70 O/D
	6	Deposit			653.60	86.10 O/D
	7	Deposit			759.00	672.90
	7	Bank charges		22.45		650.45
	7	Cheque	001765	94.10		556.35

14.4X William Kay's cash book on 28 February 2001 showed a balance at the bank of £456.48. On attempting a reconciliation with his bank statement the following matters were discovered:

(a) A payment from B Green to W Kay of £40 by direct bank transfer had not been recorded in the cash book.

(b) Cheques drawn but not presented to the bank were: A Roe £21.62; C Mills £36.55.

(c) A paying-in slip dated 27 February 2001 totalling £372.31 was not credited by the bank until 1 March 2001.

(d) A standing order for £21.58 payable on 20 February 2001 for fire insurance had been paid by the bank but not entered in the cash book.

(e) Bank charges £15 had not been entered in the cash book.

    (i) Open the cash book and make such additional entries as you consider necessary;

    (ii) Prepare a statement reconciling your **revised** cash book balance with the balance shown by the bank statement.

(RSA)

14.5 Mitchell's cash book showed a balance of £2,200 as at 31 December and his bank statement showed a balance of £2,245. A comparison of the two records showed the following outstanding items:

- non-presented cheques £250;
- payments made by the bank out of his account under a standing order but not yet recorded in the cash book £40;
- credit transfer from customer paid directly to bank account but not yet entered in cash book £175;
- bank charges not in cash book £40;
- takings deposited in night-safe on 31 December £300, but not recorded on bank statement.

Reconcile the two balances.

(Pitman Qualifications)

14.6 Finnikin Trading Co is situated on the outskirts of Uttoxeter and is a busy general supplier to the local traders and farming community.

As office trainee, one of your duties is to keep an eye on the firm's bank balance, as the owner, Joe Finnikin, never likes it to go into an overdraft situation.

You are given the following details of the firm's cash book (Exhibit 14.8) for July and a copy of their most recent bank statement (Exhibit 14.9).

Required

(a) You are to prepare:
   (i) the corrected cash book balance as at 31 July;
   (ii) a bank reconciliation statement as at 31 July.

(b) Explain briefly to Janice, one of the shop assistants, the difference between a standing order and a direct debit. Unfortunately Janice has only just opened her first bank account and is unfamiliar with some of the bank's terms.

(c) The firm's storekeeper asks you, in strict confidence, what position the firm is in financially. In particular he is interested to learn of the present bank position. What would be your reaction to this request?

(NVQ Level 2)

Exhibit 14.8

				Finnikin Trading Co				
				Cash Book (bank column only)				
Dr								*Cr*
Date	Details	Folio	Bank	Date	Details	Folio	Bank
2003				2003			
Jul 1	Balance b/d		2,310.20	Jul 1	D. Oultram Supplies	00236	54.00
3	F. Oakden		332.70	3	Electricity	00237	236.33
4	H. Mellor & Sons		110.00	4	Swindels & Co	00238	219.18
7	J. Mayer (Mfr) Co		249.00	6	Wages	00239	321.40
10	Geoff Burgess		180.20	9	A. & A. Parker	00240	7.42
17	Sales		522.66	10	Green Lane Garage	00241	450.25
20	G. Biscoe Ltd		52.30	12	Drawings	00242	125.00
21	Johnson's		42.60	17	Wages	00243	336.10
23	Bentley & Bradley		152.00	21	Hudson Supplies Co	00244	1,427.30
27	Sales		629.30	24	Mace Stationers	00245	51.90
30	Alcock's		34.10	25	Wages	00246	316.50
				31	Balance c/d		1,069.68
			4,615.06				4,615.06
Aug 1	Balance b/d		1,069.68				

Exhibit 14.9

		Oak Bank			
		Market Square, Uttoxeter			

STATEMENT OF ACCOUNT

Account Name: Finnikin Trading Co
Nunn Lane
Uttoxeter

Account No: 00639972 Sheet No: 41

Date	Code	Reference	Debit	Credit	Balance
2003					
July 1		Brought forward			2,310.20
3	DEP			332.70	2,642.90
6	CHQ	0239	321.40		
		0237	236.33		
7	DD	United Insurance	35.00		2,050.17
	DEP			359.00	2,409.17
9	SO	Uttoxeter CC	76.00		
	CHQ	0240	7.42		
17	CHQ	0243	336.10		1,989.65
17	DEP			702.86	2,692.51
18	BC	Charges	24.40		2,668.11
23	DEP			246.90	2,915.01
	CHQ	0238	219.18		
25	CHQ	0246	316.50		2,379.33
	BGC	Wheeldons		217.00	
28	DEP			629.30	3,225.63

Note	BC	= Bank Charges	BGC	= Bank Giro Credit	
	CHQ	= Cheque	DD	= Direct Debit	
	DEP	= Deposit	SO	= Standing Order	

14.7X On 31 October 2005 the cash book of N Orange showed a balance at the bank of £570. An examination of his records located the following errors:

1 Orange paid to R Jones £175 by cheque on 15 October. This cheque was entered in the cash book as £195.

2 Bank charges not recorded in the cash book amounted to £25.

3 A cheque dated 19 October, value £150, payable to T Jack was not paid by the bank until 5 November.

4 Orange on 23 October received from W Green a cheque, value £125. This cheque was dishonoured on 29 October. No entry for the dishonour has been made in the cash book.

5 On 31 October a cheque, value £200, received from F Brown was banked; however, the bank statement was not credited until 1 November.

You are required to:

(a) Make the necessary entries in the cash book in order to show the revised cash book balance at 31 October 2005.

(b) Prepare a statement reconciling the corrected cash book balance with the bank statement at 31 October 2005.

(c) State the balance at bank at 31 October 2005 as shown by the bank statements.

(RSA)

14.8X From the following cash book and bank statement draw up a statement reconciling the two balances.

Dr	Cash Book (bank columns only)					Cr
		£				£
April 1	Balance b/f	600.00	April 8	Rates		110.00
April 6	Cash paid in	75.20	April 15	Wages		40.00
April 12	Cheque from A	64.80	April 15	Electricity		60.42
April 18	Cheque from B	72.40	April 15	Paid X		72.15
April 28	Cash paid in	85.00	April 26	Rent		30.00
April 30	Cheque from C	54.62	April 26	Wages		40.00
			April 27	Paid Y		64.10
			April 30	Paid Z		24.10
			April 30	Balance c/f		511.25
		952.02				952.02
May 1	Balance b/f	511.25				

Bank statement

		Dr	Cr	Balance
April 1	Balance			600.00
April 6	Cash		75.20	675.20
April 12	A		64.80	740.00
April 12	Rates	110.00		630.00
April 15	Wages	40.00		590.00
April 18	B		72.40	662.40
April 19	Electricity	60.42		601.98
April 20	X	72.15		529.83
April 26	Wages	40.00		489.83
April 28	Cash		85.00	574.83

(Pitman Qualifications)

14.9 Give three reasons for the differences between the balance in a firm's cash book and the balance on the bank statement.

14.10 Would a bank interest charge of £411 shown in the cash book appear as a debit entry or a credit entry on the bank statement?

(AAT (part of Central Assessment))

14.11X J Pearce makes all payments over £15 by cheque and pays all receipts into the bank at the end of each day. On 1 October the bank cash book showed a balance of £3,960 in hand.

The following information is available for October:

Bank lodgements:

2 October	Cash sales		£275.00
10 October	Cheques	N Islam	£60.40
		H Briggs	£93.00
		K Tobin	£72.82
18 October	Cash sales		£365.00
	Cheques	L Smith	£600.00
		J Stevens	£275.00 (in settlement of account of £285.00)
27 October	AB Supplies		£100.00

Cheques drawn:

3 October	A Wright (creditor), £350.00	Cheque No 1515
11 October	Purchases of stock, £550.00	Cheque No 1516
13 October	Petty cash, £100.00; J Pearce's drawings, £50.00	Cheque No 1517
17 October	Electricity, £175.00	Cheque No 1518
20 October	Motor expenses, £80.00	Cheque No 1519
25 October	C Gauntlett, £1,000.00 (loan repayment)	Cheque No 1520

On 3 November you receive the bank statement shown in Exhibit 14.10.

Exhibit 14.10

Loanshire Bank A/c No 11379022					
Date	Details		Debit	Credit	Balance
1 Oct	Brought forward				3,960.00
3 Oct	Bank charges		30.00		3,930.00
5 Oct	Cash			275.00	4,205.00
6 Oct		1515	350.00		3,855.00
13 Oct	Cash and cheques			226.22	4,081.22
14 Oct		1517	150.00		3,931.22
20 Oct		1518	175.00		3,756.22
22 Oct	Cash and cheques			1,240.00	4,996.22
23 Oct	XY insurance (s/o)		100.00		4,896.22
26 Oct		1519	80.00		4,816.22
27 Oct	CDF Ass (credit transfer)			60.00	4,876.22

You are required to:

(a) Write up and balance the cash book for October after receipt of the bank statement.

(b) Prepare a bank reconciliation statement as at 31 October.

(RSA)

15 The analytical petty cash book and the imprest system

AIMS

- To be able to write up an analytical petty cash book.

- To understand the imprest system.

- To be able to post the petty cash items to ledger accounts.

15.1 Division of the cash book

With the growth of the firm it has been seen that it becomes necessary to have several books instead of just one ledger.

These ideas can be extended to the cash book. It is obvious that in almost any firm there will be many small cash payments to be made. It would be an advantage if the records of these payments could be kept separate from the main cash book. Where a separate book is kept it is known as a **petty cash book**.

The advantages of such an action can be summarised:

- The task of handling and recording the small cash payments could be given by the cashier to a junior member of staff who would then be known as the petty cashier. The cashier, who is a higher paid member of staff, would be saved from routine work. This would then be done by the petty cashier who is a junior and lower paid member of staff.

- If small cash payments were entered into the main cash book, these items would then need posting one by one to the ledgers. If travelling expenses were paid to staff on a daily basis this could mean over 250 postings to the staff travelling expenses account during the year, i.e. 5 days per week × 50 working weeks per year. However, if a special form of a petty cash book is kept, it would only be the monthly totals for each period that would need posting to the general ledger. If this was done, only 12 entries would be needed in the staff travelling expenses account instead of over 250.

When the petty cashier makes a payment to someone, then that person will have to fill in a voucher showing exactly what the payment was for. He or she may have to attach bills – e.g. bills for petrol – to the petty cash voucher. An example of a petty cash voucher is shown in Exhibit 15.1. The recipient would sign the voucher to certify that the expenses had been paid by the petty cashier.

Exhibit 15.1

15.2 The petty cash imprest system

The **imprest system** is where the cashier gives the petty cashier enough cash to meet the needs for the following period. At the end of the period the cashier finds out the amounts spent by the petty cashier, and gives back an amount equal to that spent. The petty cash in hand should then be equal to the **original** amount with which the period was started. Exhibit 15.2 shows an example of this method.

Exhibit 15.2

		£
Period 1	The cashier gives the petty cashier	100
	The petty cashier pays out in the period	78
	Petty cash now in hand	22
	The cashier now gives the petty cashier the amount spent	78
	Petty cash in hand at the end of period 1	100
Period 2	The petty cashier pays out in the period	84
	Petty cash now in hand	16
	The cashier now gives the petty cashier the amount spent	84
	Petty cash in hand end of period 2	100

It may be necessary to increase the fixed sum, often called the cash 'float', to be held at the start of each period. In the above case, if we had wanted to increase the 'float' at the end of the second period to £120, then the cashier would have given the petty cashier an extra £20, i.e. £84 + £20 = £104.

15.3 Illustration of an analytical petty cash book

An analytical petty cash book is often used. One of these is shown as Exhibit 15.3 for the following items:

	2003		£
	Sept 1	The cashier gives £50 as float to the petty cashier	
		Payments out of petty cash during September:	
	Sept 2	Petrol	6
	Sept 3	J Green – travelling expenses	3
	Sept 3	Postages	2
	Sept 4	D Davies – travelling expenses	2
	Sept 7	Cleaning expenses	1
	Sept 9	Petrol	1
	Sept 12	K Jones – travelling expenses	3
	Sept 14	Petrol	3
	Sept 15	L Black – travelling expenses	5
	Sept 16	Cleaning expenses	1
	Sept 18	Petrol	2
	Sept 20	Postages	2
	Sept 22	Cleaning expenses	1
	Sept 24	G Wood – travelling expenses	7
	Sept 27	Settlement of C Brown's account in the Purchases Ledger	3
	Sept 29	Postages	2
	Sept 30	The cashier reimburses the petty cashier the amount spent in the month	

Exhibit 15.3

Petty Cash Book   *Page 31*

Receipts	Folio	Date		Details	Voucher No	Total	Motor expenses	Staff travelling expenses	Postages	Cleaning	Ledger folio	Ledger accounts
£		2003				£	£	£	£	£		£
50	CB 19	Sept	1	Cash								
		"	2	Petrol	1	6	6					
		"	3	J Green	2	3		3				
		"	3	Postages	3	2			2			
		"	4	D Davies	4	2		2				
		"	7	Cleaning	5	1				1		
		"	9	Petrol	6	1	1					
		"	12	K Jones	7	3		3				
		"	14	Petrol	8	3	3					
		"	15	L Black	9	5		5				
		"	16	Cleaning	10	1				1		
		"	18	Petrol	11	2	2					
		"	20	Postages	12	2			2			
		"	22	Cleaning	13	1				1		
		"	24	G Wood	14	7		7				
		"	27	C Brown	15	3					PL 18	3
		"	29	Postages	16	2			2			
						44	12	20	6	3		3
							GL 17	GL 29	GL 44	GL 64		PL 18
		Sept	30	Balance	c/d	6						
50						50						
6		Oct	1	Balance	b/d							
44	CB 22	"	1	Cash								

The receipts column is the debit side of the petty cash book. On giving £50 to the petty cashier on 1 September the credit entry is made in the cash book while the debit entry is made in the petty cash book. A similar entry is made on 30 September for the £44 paid by the chief cashier to the petty cashier. This amount covers all expenses paid by the petty cashier.

On the credit side:

1 Enter the date and details of each payment. Put the amount in the total column.

2 For **1** also put the amount in the column for the type of expense.

3 At the end of each period, add up the totals column.

4 Now add up each of the expense columns. The total of **3** should equal the total of all the expense columns. In Exhibit 15.3 this is £44.

To complete double entry for petty cash expenses paid:

1 The total of each expense column is debited to the expense account in the general ledger.

2 Enter the folio number of each general ledger page under each of the expense columns in the petty cash book.

3 The last column in the petty cash book is a ledger column. In this column items paid out of petty cash which need posting to a ledger other than the general ledger are shown. This would happen if a purchases ledger account was settled out of petty cash, or if a refund was made out of the petty cash to a customer who had overpaid his account.

The double entry for all the items in Exhibit 15.3 appears as Exhibit 15.4.

Exhibit 15.4

	Cash Book			Page 19
Dr				Cr
	2003			£
	Sept 1	Petty cash	PCB 31	50
	Sept 30	Petty cash	PCB 31	44

General Ledger
Motor Expenses Account Page 17

Dr					Cr
2003				£	
Sept 30	Petty cash	PCB 31	12		

Staff Travelling Expenses Account Page 29

Dr					Cr
2003				£	
Sept 30	Petty cash	PCB 31	20		

Postages Account Page 44

Dr					Cr
2003				£	
Sept 30	Petty cash	PCB 31	6		

Cleaning Account Page 64

Dr					Cr
2003				£	
Sept 30	Petty cash	PCB 31	3		

Purchases Ledger
C Brown Account Page 18

Dr				£	2003			£
2003								
Sept 30	Petty cash	PCB 31	3		Sept 1	Balance b/d		3

15.4 Bank cash book

In a firm with both a cash book and a petty cash book, the cash book is often known as a bank cash book. This means that **all** cash payments are entered in the petty cash book and the bank cash book will contain **only** bank columns and discount columns. In this type of firm any cash sales will be paid direct into the bank.

In such a cash book, as in fact could happen in an ordinary cash book, an extra column could be added. In this would be shown the details of the cheques banked, just the total of the banking being shown in the total column.

Exhibit 15.5 shows the receipts side of the bank cash book. The totals of the banking made on the three days were £192, £381 and £1,218. How the bankings are made up is shown in the details column.

Exhibit 15.5

Dr	Bank Cash Book	(receipts side)		
Date	Details		Items	Total banked
2003			£	£
May 14	G Archer		95	
May 14	P Watts		57	
May 14	C King		40	192
May 20	K Dooley		114	
May 20	Cash Sales		55	
May 20	R Jones		60	
May 20	P Mackie		152	381
May 31	J Young		19	
May 31	T Broome		950	
May 31	Cash Sales		116	
May 31	H Tiller		133	1,218

NEW TERMS

Imprest system A system used for controlling expenditure of small cash items which are recorded in the petty cash book. A cash 'float' of a fixed amount is provided initially to the person responsible for operating the petty cash system. Any cash paid out during a particular period, i.e. a week, is reimbursed to the petty cashier so restoring the 'float' to its original sum.

Petty cash book A cash book used for making small (petty) payments. Payments are usually analysed and the totals of each column later posted to the various accounts in the general ledger. The source document used for entry into the petty cash book is a petty cash voucher.

Petty cash voucher The form used by anyone requesting payment for a small item of expenditure incurred on behalf of the business. The form gives details of the expense and should be signed and duly authorised.

STUDENT ACTIVITIES

15.1 The following is a summary of the petty cash transactions of Jockfield Ltd for May 2002.

May   1   Received from Cashier £300 as petty cash float

			£
May	2	Postages	18
May	3	Travelling	12
May	4	Cleaning	15
May	7	Petrol for delivery van	22
May	8	Travelling	25
May	9	Stationery	17
May	11	Cleaning	18
May	14	Postage	5
May	15	Travelling	8
May	18	Stationery	9
May	18	Cleaning	23
May	20	Postage	13
May	24	Delivery van 5,000 mile service	43
May	26	Petrol	18
May	27	Cleaning	21
May	29	Postage	5
May	30	Petrol	14

Required

(a) Rule up a suitable petty cash book with analysis columns for expenditure on cleaning, motor expenses, postage, stationery, travelling.

(b) Enter the month's transactions.

(c) Enter the receipt of the amount necessary to restore the imprest and carry down the balance for the commencement of the following month.

(d) State how the double entry for the expenditure is completed.

(Association of Accounting Technicians)

15.2X O Zone, a sole trader, uses an analysed petty cash book with columns for travelling, postage and stationery, motor expenses, cleaning, ledger accounts.

The petty cash system is based on an imprest of £100 which Zone replenishes on the Monday following the period of expenditure. O Zone supplies the following information for the month of August.

2004			£
Aug	1	Petrol	4.00
Aug	3	Postage stamps	1.50
Aug	4	One ream of typing paper	3.00
Aug	6	H Wise – settlement of account	15.00
Aug	7	Office cleaning materials	2.00
Aug	8	Taxis	4.00
Aug	10	Refund of clerk's bus fares	2.00
Aug	14	Car polish	3.00
Aug	16	Petrol and oil	7.00
Aug	18	Registered mail	2.00
Aug	20	Office carpet shampoo	1.00
Aug	21	Petrol	7.00
Aug	25	Petrol	7.00
Aug	27	J Brown – settlement of account	25.00
Aug	28	W Smith – settlement of account	6.00
Aug	29	Carbon paper (one packet)	4.00

Required

(a) Enter the above transactions into a suitably ruled Petty Cash Book.

(b) Replenish the imprest on Monday, 3 September.

(RSA)

15.3 You work for S Dickinson (Estate Agents) as receptionist, but some of your duties include administration tasks and dealing with the firm's petty cash, which is operated using the imprest system. A 'float' of £120 is used by the firm for petty cash and this is given to you on 1 March 2004.

Required

(a) From the petty cash vouchers in Exhibit 15.6 you are required to enter details in the petty cash book, using analysis columns as you think appropriate. Balance off at the end of the month and obtain cash to restore the imprest from Ms Dickinson.

(b) Post the petty cash expense columns to the accounts in the general ledger and enter the cash obtained to restore the imprest in the cash book.

(c) What are the advantages to using the imprest system? Draft a short memo outlining these to Ms Dickinson.

(NVQ Level 2)

Exhibit 15.6

No. 1
Petty Cash Voucher
Date 2/3/2004

For what required	Amount £	p
Postage Stamps	6	50
	6	50

Signature A. Bond
Passed by SMD

No. 2
Petty Cash Voucher
Date 3rd March 2004

For what required	Amount £	p
Second-class rail fare to Stourbridge	23	—
	23	—

Signature G. Jones
Passed by SMD

No. 3
Petty Cash Voucher
Date 7th March 2004

For what required	Amount £	p
Parcel Post to London	4	—
	4	—

Signature A. Bond
Passed by SMD

No. 4
Petty Cash Voucher
Date 9th March 2004

For what required	Amount £	p
Window cleaning	8	—
	8	—

Signature C. Cotton
Passed by SMD

Exhibit 15.6 (continued)

No. 5	
Petty Cash Voucher	
Date 12th March 2004	

For what required	Amount £	p
Envelopes	2	64
VAT		46
	3	10

Signature _A. Bond_
Passed by _SMD_

No. 6	
Petty Cash Voucher	
Date 14th March 2004	

For what required	Amount £	p
Tea etc. (Hospitality)	6	40
	6	40

Signature _A. Bond_
Passed by _SMD_

No. 7	
Petty Cash Voucher	
Date 16th March 2004	

For what required	Amount £	p
Petrol (including VAT)	10	—
	10	—

Signature _G. Jones_
Passed by _SMD_

No. 8	
Petty Cash Voucher	
Date 19th March 2004	

For what required	Amount £	p
3 1/4" Computer Disks	11	06
VAT @ 17.5%	1	94
	13	—

Signature _S. Dickinson_
Passed by _SMD_

No. 9	
Petty Cash Voucher	
Date 20/3/2004	

For what required	Amount £	p
Dusters & Polish	1	47
17.5% VAT		26
	1	73

Signature _J. Pratt_
Passed by _SMD_

No. 10	
Petty Cash Voucher	
Date 23 March 2004	

For what required	Amount £	p
Postage Stamps	2	40
	2	40

Signature _A. Bond_
Passed by _SMD_

No. 11	
Petty Cash Voucher	
Date 27th March 2004	

For what required	Amount £	p
Payment of creditors: J. Cheetham (Ac No C44)	7	30
	7	30

Signature _S. Dickinson_
Passed by _SMD_

No. 12	
Petty Cash Voucher	
Date 31st March 2004	

For what required	Amount £	p
Magazines, Newspapers etc. (for reception)	6	40
	6	40

Signature _A. Bond_
Passed by _SMD_

15.4X You are employed as junior accountant's assistant of Morridge Products Ltd and one of your main tasks is that of petty cashier. The company uses an analytical petty cash book with columns for travelling expenses, postages, stationery, cleaning, sundry expenses and VAT and they operate the imprest system.

Required:

(a) On 1 January 2001 the company's accountant, Mr Brammer, restores the petty cash float to £100 and gives you the petty cash vouchers in Exhibit 15.7. You are required to enter them in the petty cash book, balance off the book at the end of January and obtain reimbursement from Mr Brammer to restore the imprest.

(b) Mr Brammer is anxious for you to become involved with all the financial aspects of the business and would like you to complete the bookkeeping entries by posting the totals of the 'petty cash analysis columns' to the relevant accounts in the general ledger.

(c) Unfortunately you have to go in hospital for a few days and will probably be absent from work for a couple of weeks. Mr Brammer asks you to write out a set of instructions in note form on the operation of the petty cash book as Jenny Cadwaller, his secretary, will be taking over in your absence. Ensure the instructions are clear, concise and easy to follow.

(NVQ Level 2)

Exhibit 15.7

No. 1		
Petty Cash Voucher		
Date 1st Jan 2001		
For what required	Amount £	p
Travelling Expenses to Crewe	5	36
	5	36
Signature Jim Steadman		
Passed by G. Brammer		

No. 2		
Petty Cash Voucher		
Date 5 Jan 2001		
For what required	Amount £	p
Office Cleaning	10	—
	10	—
Signature A. Duffy		
Passed by G. Brammer		

No. 3		
Petty Cash Voucher		
Date 9 Jan 2001		
For what required	Amount £	p
Parcel to Northampton	1	98
	1	98
Signature Tom Finikin		
Passed by G. Brammer		

No. 4		
Petty Cash Voucher		
Date 10 Jan 2001		
For what required	Amount £	p
Milk & Coffee for Office	6	50
	6	50
Signature J. Cadwaller		
Passed by G. Brammer		

Exhibit 15.7 *(continued)*

No.	5

Petty Cash Voucher

Date *12 Jan 2001*

For what required	Amount £	p
Air-mail Stationery	7	15
VAT	1	25
	8	40

Signature *J. Cadwaller*

Passed by *G. Brammer*

No.	6

Petty Cash Voucher

Date *15 Jan 2001*

For what required	Amount £	p
Light Bulbs & 3 plugs	3	64
VAT		64
	4	28

Signature *Tom Finikin*

Passed by *G. Brammer*

No.	7

Petty Cash Voucher

Date *21 Jan 2001*

For what required	Amount £	p
Office cleaning (2 weeks)	20	—
	20	—

Signature *A. Duffy*

Passed by *G. Brammer*

No.	8

Petty Cash Voucher

Date *22 Jan 2001*

For what required	Amount £	p
1 Ream Copier Paper + VAT	4	30
		75
	5	05

Signature *J. Cadwaller*

Passed by *G. Brammer*

No.	9

Petty Cash Voucher

Date *24 Jan 2001*

For what required	Amount £	p
Car Allowance: Manchester – Visiting Customer 60 miles x 25p	15	—
	15	—

Signature *J. Steadman*

Passed by *G. Brammer*

No.	10

Petty Cash Voucher

Date *24 Jan 2001*

For what required	Amount £	p
Financial Times & Economist for Reception	2	10
	2	10

Signature *J. Cadwaller*

Passed by *G. Brammer*

No.	11

Petty Cash Voucher

Date *30 Jan 2001*

For what required	Amount £	p
Milk	1	50
	1	50

Signature *G. Brammer*

Passed by *G. Brammer*

No.	12

Petty Cash Voucher

Date *31 Jan 2001*

For what required	Amount £	p
First class stamps	4	80
	4	80

Signature *J. Cadwaller*

Passed by *G. Brammer*

15.5 As junior clerk for Edwards Manufacturing Co, you are required to look after the petty cash as part of your duties. On 1st June 2003 there was £9.25 left in the petty cash box from the previous month, the Accountant Miss Bennett, gave you £140.75 to restore the imprest to its original float of £150.00.

Required

Record the balance brought down and cash receipt restoring the imprest then enter the following petty cash vouchers for June, balance off at the end of the month and obtain reimbursement from Miss Bennett.

Use analysis columns you feel appropriate and ensure that petty cash vouchers have been authorised for payment by Mr George Edwards, Company Secretary.

Exhibit 15.8

No. 21		
Petty Cash Voucher		
Date 1 June 2003		
For what required	Amount £	p
Paper for Photo-copying machine (incl. VAT)	18	30
	18	30
Signature S. Thorn		
Passed by G. Edwards		

No. 22		
Petty Cash Voucher		
Date 3 June 2003		
For what required	Amount £	p
Coffee, sugar, tea & milk for office visitors	6	27
	6	27
Signature P. Thomas		
Passed by G. Edwards		

No. 23		
Petty Cash Voucher		
Date 4 June 2003		
For what required	Amount £	p
A4 Folders & Plastic Folders (inc. VAT)	16	70
	16	70
Signature Robert Bradley		
Passed by G. Edwards		

No. 24		
Petty Cash Voucher		
Date 8 June 2003		
For what required	Amount £	p
Postage stamps	2	40
	2	40
Signature P.J. Jones		
Passed by G. Edwards		

No. 25		
Petty Cash Voucher		
Date 11 June 2003		
For what required	Amount £	p
Bus fare to Stoke taking documents to Bank	4	35
	4	35
Signature S. Hammond		
Passed by G. Edwards		

No. 26		
Petty Cash Voucher		
Date 12 June 2003		
For what required	Amount £	p
Nails, Screws & Welding rods VAT	36	30
	6	35
	42	65
Signature P. Thomas		
Passed by G. Edwards		

Exhibit 15.8 *(continued)*

No.	28

Petty Cash Voucher

Date *16 June 2003*

For what required	Amount	
	£	p
Correction fluid (incl. VAT)	2	20
	2	20

Signature *P. Thomas*

Passed by *G. Edwards*

No.	27

Petty Cash Voucher

Date *20 June 2003*

For what required	Amount	
	£	p
Cleaning Windows in Workshop & Office	12	50
	12	50

Signature *M. Robinson*

Passed by *G. Edwards*

No.	29

Petty Cash Voucher

Date *21 June 2003*

For what required	Amount	
	£	p
Light Bulbs	2	10
VAT		37
	2	47

Signature *P. Thomas*

Passed by *G. Edwards*

No.	30

Petty Cash Voucher

Date *23 June 2003*

For what required	Amount	
	£	p
Parcel Postage	3	52
	3	52

Signature *S. Hammond*

Passed by *G. Edwards*

No.	31

Petty Cash Voucher

Date *27 June 2003*

For what required	Amount	
	£	p
Plasters, etc., for first aid box	4	20
	4	20

Signature *S. Thorn*

Passed by *G. Edwards*

No.	32

Petty Cash Voucher

Date *30 June 2003*

For what required	Amount	
	£	p
Travelling Expenses to Birmingham	29	50
	29	50

Signature *S. Hammond*

Passed by *G. Edwards*

Unit 2: Recording and accounting for credit transactions

16 Basic law of contract

AIMS

- To provide an introduction to the law of contract covering the essentials of a contract, counter-offers, termination, intention to create legal relations, and terms and conditions.

- To appreciate the Sale of Goods Acts 1893 and 1979 in relation to goods of satisfactory quality.

- To appreciate that contracts for the supply of services is covered by the Supply of Goods and Services Act 1982.

16.1 Introduction

In a business we are constantly buying goods or services from suppliers, and also selling goods or services to our customers. Each time an agreement is made between ourselves and suppliers, or between customers and ourselves, then a contract is made. This will mean, depending on the size of the business, that we will have hundreds, thousands or possibly millions of contracts each year.

Most UK contract law has been created by case law. When in one case a senior judge makes a rule of contract law other judges, in later cases, must apply that rule. A few areas of contract law have been created by statutes (laws passed by Parliament).

Most Commonwealth countries have based their laws on those of the United Kingdom. Students outside the United Kingdom should therefore check how far their laws are different. However, if they are sitting a UK examination then the contents of this book are applicable for such an examination.

When statute law is referred to, it will be in such words as: Sale of Goods Act 1979, Supply of Goods and Services Act 1982, and so on. Case law is distinguished by the names of the two parties in the case being shown, e.g. *Fisher* v *Bell*. (The 'v' is an abbreviation for versus, meaning against.)

16.2 Importance of the law of contract

Each and every contract is a legally binding agreement. Contracts do not necessarily have to be in writing. They could be by word of mouth, or even inferred from the conduct of the parties involved such as someone shaking hands in agreement, or any combination of these acts.

If one of the parties to the contract does not keep to the agreement they can be taken to court and sued. The usual remedy is for the party breaking the agreement to be forced to pay damages to the other party. Exceptionally, however, the court will make the party who broke the contract carry out the agreed promise.

Anyone being sued and subsequently losing their case can find it very costly indeed. The legal costs of court action can be quite high in addition to the damages awarded.

It is therefore important for anyone in business, or in any other kind of organisation, to understand the law of contract. They will then know what their rights and duties are under the contract.

You must not think that contracts only cover the buying or selling of goods and services, although this aspect is what we are concerned with in this book. There are also contracts of employment, loans, etc.

16.3 Essential elements of a contract

There are three basic elements in a contract

- **Agreement** – the parties involved must have reached an agreement, or else have been deemed to have reached it.

- **Intention** – the parties must have intended to create a legal relationship, or be deemed to do so.

- **Consideration** – each of the parties to the contract gives consideration (a value of some kind) to the other. One of the parties usually gives money.

The following sections deal with each of these elements in more details.

16.4 Nature of an agreement

For an agreement to be made, there must be an offer and an acceptance.

- **The offer.** The offer must be clear, it must be complete and it must be final. It can be made to a single party, to a group of people, or be open to anyone in the world.

An obvious example is that you see a car advertised in a showroom for £10,000. You then go into the showroom office and say that you will buy the car for £10,000. Your offer is therefore clear, complete and final.

- **The acceptance.** The offer must be accepted before there is a contract. The acceptance must also be clear, must be unconditional and must conform exactly to the terms of the offer.

In the case of buying the car, if the salesman says that he agrees, or signs a form or note to that effect or similar, then there will have been a valid offer on your part and an acceptance from him on behalf of the car showroom. Thus a clear, valid and legally enforceable contract has been made. Contrast the situation given in Exhibit 16.1.

Exhibit 16.1

Walters offers some goods to Jones at a price of £1,000. Jones says he will accept the offer if he can get his partner to agree to the price.

Question: Has Walters now got a valid contract?

Answer : No, because it was not a clear and unconditional acceptance.

16.5 Invitation to treat

An offer must not be confused with an invitation to treat. This is where a person is invited to make an offer.

For instance, your local store may have goods displayed on its shelves with prices marked on them. This is an invitation to treat, whereby you take the goods to the cash till and offer to buy them at the price shown. You do not necessarily have to speak. Handing the goods to the cashier with the cash needed is the offer. If the cashier puts the cash in the till and lets you take the goods, then this is the acceptance. There is a valid contract, yet no one may have spoken or signed anything. Again contrast the situation in Exhibit 16.2.

Exhibit 16.2

You have gone into Buddy's Electrical Store and see a music centre on display. The price is shown as £45. You realise this is a fantastic bargain. You take it to the cashier and hand it to him plus £45 cash. He says sorry, the price should be £450.

Question: Can you make him sell it to you for £45?

Answer: No. You have made an offer, but he has not accepted it. Therefore there is no legally enforceable contract.

It would be ridiculous for it to be otherwise. Imagine a car showroom where a luxury car is being displayed for sale. The selling price is really £200,000 but the salesman has put on a price of £20 and forgotten to add the remaining figures 0,000. When you offer to buy the car for £20 then they will obviously refuse to accept your offer. Were it not so, all errors in pricing goods could bring terrible consequences to the businesses involved.

16.6 Bilateral and unilateral contracts

A 'bilateral' contract is one where an offer is made and accepted, of the type already described in this chapter. These constitute the vast majority of contracts.

There are also 'unilateral' contracts, which could be described as 'if' contracts. The person making the offer (the offeror) is legally bound by a contract 'if' the offeree (person receiving the offer) performs whatever act is needed of them according to the terms of the offer.

'Reward' offers come under this heading, for instance an advertisement saying that you will give anyone £50 for the return to you of a lost dog. This constitutes an offer. If someone delivers the dog to you, there will then be a valid contract as this constitutes the acceptance and you will have to pay the £50 reward.

As you can see, in a unilateral contract, the offeror does not know when he makes the offer exactly who will perform the act described. Consider Exhibit 16.3.

Exhibit 16.3

You are the owner of a business dealing in medical preparations. One of these is 'The Carbolic Smoke Ball'. You advertise that you will pay £100 to anyone who gets influenza after using these smoke balls in the way described. A lady called Mrs Carlill buys one of the smoke balls, uses it in the required manner but still gets influenza.

Question: If you refuse to pay £100 to Mrs Carlill, can she sue you in court?

Answer: She certainly can and she would win. She has performed the acts as stated in the advertisement, and therefore this constitutes the acceptance of the offer by your business.

These were indeed the facts in the well known law case of *Carlill* v *Carbolic Smoke Ball Company*.

16.7 Communication of an offer

There are no limits as to how an offer may be communicated. It may be expressed in words, either in writing or orally, but it may also be implied from conduct, e.g. shaking hands with the other party, putting your hand up (for instance, in an auction), etc. It may also be partly expressed and partly implied.

Until it is communicated to the offeree (the other party) the offer does not bind either party; it is only when the offeree knows about the offer that the offer can possibly become part of a legal contract.

When the offer stipulates the means of acceptance, e.g. by post, by fax, by Internet, etc., then that method of acceptance must be used.

Special rules govern the time of an acceptance by post. The letter containing the acceptance must be correctly addressed, bearing the correct amount of postage stamps and must actually be posted. If that is so the acceptance is deemed to take place when the letter is posted – not when it is received. Consider Exhibit 16.4.

Exhibit 16.4

Brady has offered you some goods for £500 and asks you to accept by post. You post a letter of acceptance on 31 May, correctly addressed and bearing the correct amount of postage stamps. There is an unofficial postal strike starting on 1 June, and the letter does not reach Brady until 10 June. He says he rejects your attempt at acceptance as he has already sold the goods on 9 June.

Question: What is your legal position? Have you got a legal contract?

Answer: You have a legal contract and could sue him if you wished. The date of your acceptance was 31 May, which was the date the letter was correctly posted. The fact that there was a strike by postmen does not alter the contract.

Note that 'postal rules' cover acceptances only, not offers.

16.8 The termination of an offer

Just because someone has made an offer, it does not mean that the offer must remain open for acceptance. The following instances show when an offer is terminated.

- The person making the offer may withdraw it.

- Where a time limit has been put on the offer, and that time has now elapsed.

- If no time limit has been stated then the offer will lapse after a 'reasonable period of time'. In a court case often the court will decide what a 'reasonable period of time' is, but common sense must prevail.

- Where someone makes a counter-offer. For instance, if you offer a computer for sale at £500 and someone instead offers you £450, then that is a counter-offer and the first offer has lapsed. If you then do not accept the counter-offer of £450 the offeror cannot force you to sell it at £500 as your original offer has lapsed.

- By the offer being accepted or rejected. Consider Exhibit 16.5.

Exhibit 16.5

You are a jeweller and have an antique watch for sale at £2,000. Larkins enters your shop and offers you £1,600 for it. You refuse this offer. In the meantime Trotter enters the shop, listens to the discussion and says he will give you £1,900 instead. You say that that is a deal and shake hands with Trotter. Larkins now says he will give you £2,000 for the watch. You tell Trotter that you are sorry, but you are going to accept the £2,000 offer from Larkins.

Question: What action, if any, can Trotter now take?

Answer: If Trotter wished he could insist on your selling him the watch for £1,900. The original offer of £1,600 from Larkins was not accepted. When Trotter offered you £1,900 you accepted – and therefore a valid contract existed. You have therefore sold the watch to Trotter who can take the watch as soon as he pays for it.

16.9 Intention to create legal relations

In any contract there must be an intention that an agreement, which involves consideration, is to be legally binding. This means that the parties expect that there could be a legal remedy if the contract is broken. Consequently there is a difference between:

- commercial agreements which are intended to be legally binding; and

- social or domestic promises which are not intended to be legally binding.

Thus if you buy some goods for your business then there is a legally binding contract and you can take the matter to court if there is a dispute. On the other hand, if you promise to take a friend to a football match and you do not turn up to take them, then the friend can hardly expect to be able to take you to court for not carrying out your promise.

16.10 Consideration

First of all a contract must have the elements of offer and acceptance with the intention that it should be legally enforceable. Finally, there must be consideration – without this a contract cannot exist.

In the normal course of events:

- A supplier will agree to deliver the goods or services as promised.

- The buyer will agree to pay for the goods or services.

This appears to be simple enough, but there are some other factors involved as follows:

- The consideration given must have value, even though many people would think that the value was inadequate. A payment of £10 for a car that your friends thought was worth £1,000 is still consideration. On the other hand, to supply someone with goods because 'they like you' and do not ask for payment does not constitute consideration, and there will be no legally binding contract.

- The consideration must be in return for the promise. If it is for some other reason it cannot be treated as consideration.

- The person who is promised the goods or services must be the one who agrees that the price will be paid.

- Consideration must not be past. Where one party has performed an act before the other party's promise, then that promise is not binding. If you perform a service for someone with no promise of consideration, then if the other party says one week later that they will give you £100 for the service, you cannot take legal action if they do not pay it. Consider Exhibit 16.6.

Exhibit 16.6

A friend of yours asks you if you would let him mend your car free of charge. You agree and are pleased with his work, and give him £50. The next week the car bursts into flames, the cause being faulty work by your friend.

Question: Can you sue him for breach of contract?

Answer: No there was no legally enforceable contract as the consideration was past. The friend might, however, be liable for the tort of negligence.

16.11 Terms of contract

The purchase of goods and services may be made by a telephoned order or by seeing the supplier and ordering the goods verbally. In most larger concerns a purchases order will be made out and sent. Whichever method is used in placing the order, the goods will be sent or services supplied, usually accompanied by a delivery note. This will then be followed by an invoice. Very rarely would a formal contract be drawn up, except for expensive items or where there needs to be special instructions of a complicated sort.

When the order is received the supplier may send a list of its 'Terms and Conditions', either separately or else they may be printed somewhere on any quotation sent to the prospective buyer. If the buyer does not object to these terms and conditions, or ask for them to be altered in some way, then the terms and conditions will normally be treated as being part of the contract.

It is therefore essential for the prospective buyer to check any such terms and conditions before proceeding. Silence on the buyer's part will be taken as agreeing to the terms and conditions. They usually cover such things as specifications, prices, actions needed if goods are damaged or needed to be returned, when payment has to be made, and so on.

Quite separate from a list of terms and conditions, the parties may have specifically agreed to certain express statements. Both these and the lists are known as 'express terms'.

There are also 'implied terms'. These come either from an Act of Parliament (statute law) or from the courts who try to give effect to what seems to be the presumed intentions of the parties to the contract.

16.12 Sale of Goods Act 1979

The Act of Parliament concerning implied terms in contracts is that of the Sale of Goods Act 1979. Such implied terms will apply unless a properly valid exclusion clause has been agreed between the parties.

The Act says that the buyer of goods from a business is entitled to expect the following:

- **That the goods are of satisfactory quality.** Basically this means that, given the description of the goods and the price involved, the goods must be of a standard that a reasonable person would expect. Obviously, if goods are described as being luxury goods and a high price is paid, the buyer should not expect to receive cheap rubbishy goods.

  However, if any defects are notified to the buyer and they still buy the goods, they cannot then take legal action because of the defects. Legal action also cannot be taken if the buyer inspects the goods and misses a defect that the examination should have revealed.

- **That the goods are 'fit for the purpose' of the buyer.** They must do what they are supposed to do – for instance a radio or television must function satisfactorily, a hot water bottle must not leak.

  In addition, where the buyer makes known to the seller the particular purpose for which the goods are being bought, then the goods must be reasonably fit for such a purpose. For instance, if you buy a car which you say is to pull a caravan of a certain size, then the car should be capable of doing just that.

- **That if goods are sold by description then they should be what they are said to be.** Thus cotton shirts must be made of cotton, steel bars must be made of steel.

- **That where the sale is made 'by sample' the bulk of the goods should correspond to the sample.**

If the conditions are not met then the buyer is entitled to take legal action, should they so wish.

For many students, the place where they will be able to demonstrate their knowledge on contracts is when you visit a store to buy goods. Signs in a store which say 'No Refunds' or 'Goods Not Refundable' are made ineffective by the Unfair Contract Terms Act 1977.

- A buyer is entitled to a refund of his cash if the conditions are not met, but can instead accept a replacement.

- A buyer does not have to accept a credit note to use against other possible purchases from the store.

Some of the larger stores in the UK will give you a refund for goods returned simply because on getting them home you have realised you did not want them. This is not a legal obligation, simply a goodwill gesture by the store.

Exhibit 16.7 illustrates these points further.

Exhibit 16.7

You have bought the following items from local stores:

(a) A microwave oven. When you try to cook a very large turkey in it at a festive season, the turkey will not fit into the oven. Can you return the oven because of this fact?

(b) A milk-pan. When you put the pan on an electric stove to boil milk, the pan handle gets so hot you cannot get hold of it. Can you return the milk pan because of this fact?

(c) You walk into a store, pick up an electric drill and pay for it without speaking. You want to be able to drill holes in 20 mm thick steel plates, but it will not drill plates thicker than 10 mm. Can you return the drill for a refund of your money?

Answers:

(a) Only if you specified to the store exactly what you wanted to do with the oven and stated the size of turkey to be cooked.

(b) Yes – a full refund should be given. You are entitled to assume that you can pick up the pan by the handle when in proper use on an electric stove. The milk pan is obviously not of 'satisfactory quality'.

(c) The answer depends on whether or not the drill itself, or a container in which it was sold, stated exactly what the drill could be used for. If it was printed that the drill could bore holes in steel plates, or similar, 20 mm thick or more, then a full refund should be made, as the drill does not comply to its description. If no such information is shown, and you did not indicate the exact use to which it was to be put, then no refund need be given.

16.13 Contracts for the supply of services

The Supply of Goods and Services Act 1982 covers such contracts in the United Kingdom. Basically the implied terms can be set down as follows:

- **Care and skill**. Someone supplying services as a business must exercise reasonable care and skill in providing such services.

- **Time of performance**. If this is not agreed to previously, the services must be performed within a 'reasonable time'.

- **Consideration**. When not previously agreed the charge for the service must be reasonable and not excessive for such type of service.

Exhibit 16.8 provides an example.

Exhibit 16.8

You employ an electrician to carry out some electrical wiring in your store. In carrying out the work he accidentally drills through a water tank, resulting in a flood of water which ruins a lot of your stock-in-trade. He does not want to pay compensation.

Question: What action can you take?

Answer: Sue him for damages. He has not exercised the care and skill expected of an electrician.

16.14 Legal action as the last resort

You must not think that every time a contract is broken that legal action will take place. For small amounts of money legal action would not be worth it. Similarly, suppose that your best customer to whom you sell over £100,000 of goods a year on which you make £25,000 profit has a dispute with you about goods costing you £50. Would you sue him and possibly lose him as a customer? Common sense – we hope – would make you come to an amicable arrangement with the customer and avoid legal action.

Business considerations must therefore be taken into account before even thinking of legal action. There obviously cannot be any hard and fast rule about such matters.

 ## NEW TERMS

Acceptance Where the party selling the goods or services agrees to accept an offer. Acceptance may be expressed in words or by action, or inferred by contract.

Bilateral contract Normal form of contract between two parties.

Case law Where a case decided in court can affect decisions in similar cases in the future.

Communication The ways by which an offer may be made known to the recipient.

Consideration The value passing between the parties to a contract.

Contract A legally binding agreement between two parties.

Counter-offer Where an original offer is rejected by the introduction of a new offer, this is known as a 'counter-offer'.

Intention Where both parties to a contract intend to create legal relations.

Invitation to treat Where items are on display inviting people to make offers for them.

Offer A definite promise by a prospective purchaser that they wish to enter into and be bound by the specific terms of a contract.

Postal rules The rules governing the acceptance of a contract by post.

Statute law Laws made and governed by Acts of Parliament.

Termination The cessation of an offer.

Terms and conditions A business or organisation's list of specific terms and conditions of trade which relate to a contract under offer.

Unilateral contracts Where an offer may be made to anyone for the performance of something to again acceptance.

 ## STUDENT ACTIVITIES

16.1 Describe the difference between case law and statute law.

16.2 What are the three essential elements without which a contract cannot exist?

16.3 Jones is offered a second-hand television set for £100. He agrees to the price but says that first of all he will have to see if the set can fit into a cabinet he has bought. He finds that the cabinet will accommodate the set but refuses to buy it. Can he be sued for a breach of contract?

16.4X You have bought a luxury waterproof watch that says it will remain waterproof until it is immersed 20 metres under water. You go on holiday to Barbados and wear it while swimming, not going more than a few metres under the surface. Water enters the watch and ruins it. The seller of the watch says he is not liable because you were swimming in warm seas and since the watch was bought in the UK, where the seas are relatively cold, he is not responsible. What is your legal position?

16.5 Elgin sees some paving slabs described as marble slabs. The salesman tells him that in fact they are made of a special type of imitation composition. Elgin buys the slabs and receives a receipt which states 'marble slabs' on it. When he arrives home his wife refuses to let him lay the slabs as she wants genuine marble. He says that the store should return his money or give him genuine marble slabs instead especially as the receipt states that is what they were. What is the legal position of the store?

16.6X You purchase a computer from a store for £300, which was the price shown on the computer. The sales assistant says the price is wrong, it should be £500, but to save bother he says you can have it for £300. Later that day the store telephones you and asks you to pay another £200 as the salesman had no authority to reduce the price. What can you do about it?

16.7 Jenkins offers you some goods for £500 and asks you to accept by fax. On 9 January you try to send a fax to Jenkins but a severe storm has blown down power lines and so the fax cannot be sent. Instead you post a letter on that same date, correctly addressed, containing the offer and a cheque correctly made out. Jenkins receives the letter on 10 January but sells the goods to someone else on 11 January. What legal action is open to you?

16.8X During a party at your house a water pipe is damaged. A plumber friend of yours at the party mends it with some material that he brings in from out of his own car. During the following day the pipe bursts open and causes £20,000 of damage to your house. The repair had been carried out using the wrong kind of material. Under what circumstances would you be allowed to sue your friend?

16.9 You enter a store and see a compact disc player with a £150 price ticket on it. You tell the storekeeper that you are prepared to pay £110 but no more. He refuses your offer. You then say that you will pay the full price of £150, but he refuses to sell it to you saying that he objected to you complaining that he had overpriced the item. You insist on him selling you the item for £150. Can the storekeeper be forced to sell it to you?

16.10X You see an offer in a magazine advertising a razor that it guarantees will never need new blades providing you shave with it every day. You buy the razor and after six months give it to your brother. The razor is used every day but after three years the blades need replacing. You send the razor back to the seller, explaining all the details, and ask for your money back. Are you entitled to this, or is there some other remedy?

16.11 Jackson has had his car repaired at a garage. The back axle had needed attention, during the course of which the back wheels had been taken off. Jackson collected his car and after a few miles one of the back wheels came off and as a result the car hit a tree. The garage denies responsibility. It was paid for repairing the back axle, a job which had been properly done. The garage insisted that Jackson should have checked his rear wheels before commencing to drive. Advise Jackson.

16.12X You see an old speedboat which needs attention and decide to buy it when a friend tells you that he will help you repair it as you are not mechanically minded. If he had not said this you would not have bought the boat. You then buy £1,000 of spares for the necessary repairs, but your friend refuses to help because he is going to help someone else instead. What legal remedies have you got against him?

16.13X Wendy Roberts, one of Comart Supplies Ltd's sales staff, offers to sell a secondhand printer to Robert Ford for £175. Robert wants time to think about it and Wendy tells him that she will leave the offer open until the end of the day. At 2.00 p.m. Robert calls back to say that he is willing to buy the printer for £160. At 3.00 p.m. Wendy sells the printer to Caroline Brown for £175 and arranges delivery for the following day. At 4.30 p.m. Robert returns and tells Wendy that he is now willing to buy the printer £175.

(a) Can Robert claim that he has a contract with the company and insist that the printer is sold to him?

(b) Briefly explain the reason for your answer.

(AAT (part of Central Assessment))

16.14X   Bloomers Ltd has been asked to give a quotation for supplying flowers for an international conference, which is to be organised by CMP plc. The quotation was sent by post on 22 May 2002 and received by CMP plc the next day. CMP plc posted a letter accepting Bloomer's quotation on 29 May 2002. This letter was received by Bloomers on 30 May 2002.

(a) On which date was the contract made?
  (i) 23 May 2002
  (ii) 29 May 2002
  (iii) 30 May 2002

(b) Explain briefly the reason for your answer.

(AAT (part of Central Assessment))

16.15X   The receptionist at Centro Steelstock Limited purchased a radio/cassette player from Concord Electrical Limited. However, the following day it was discovered that although the radio worked, the cassette did not. When it was returned to Concord Electrical the assistant stated that the company was unable to offer a refund or replacement as the fault lay with the manufacturer, whom the customer should contact direct.

(a) Was the assistant's advice legally correct?

(b) Briefly explain your answer.

(AAT (part of Central Assessment))

16.16X   Mariam Saleem has promised to make a set of curtains free of charge for a regular customer, Jane Walker. After three months the curtains have not been made and Jane has phoned Mariam and demanded that the curtains be made as promised.

(a) Can Jane legally insist that the curtains are made as promised?

(b) Briefly explain the reason for your answer.

(AAT (part of Central Assessment))

17 Capital and revenue expenditures

AIMS

- To be able to distinguish between different types of expenditure, namely capital expenditure and revenue expenditure.

- Be able to deal with transactions that involve both capital and revenue expenditures.

- To understand the effects of the final accounts of the business or organisation if items of expenditure are wrongly classified.

17.1 Expenditure

All organisations incur expenditure as a normal part of their day-to-day trading activities. Expenditure is the payment, or promise to make a payment, for benefits received which may be either assets or services. The expenditure is classified into either **capital expenditure** or **revenue expenditure**.

17.2 Capital expenditure

This is expenditure on the purchase of fixed assets or buying additions to existing fixed assets. Fixed assets are those assets which have an expected life of greater than one year and are used in the business to enable it to generate income and ultimately profit. Examples include:

- land and buildings;

- plant and equipment;

- office and computer equipment;

- furniture and fittings.

Additions to existing fixed assets are also classified as **capital expenditure**. Examples include:

- purchasing a printer for the computer;

- adding extra storage capacity to a mainframe computer;

- expenses incurred in updating machinery to increase production;

- additional shelving and fittings in a retail store.

It is important to include the following items of expenditure as capital expenditure when fixed assets are purchased:

- the cost of acquiring the fixed assets;
- the cost of delivery to the firm;
- legal costs of buying land and buildings;
- carriage inwards on machinery purchases;
- any other cost required to get the fixed asset ready for use;
- installation costs;
- architects' fees for building plans and for supervising the construction of buildings;
- demolition costs to remove obsolete buildings before new work can begin.

17.3 Revenue expenditure

Expenditure which does not increase the value of fixed assets but is incurred in the day-to-day running expenses of the business is known as **revenue expenditure**.

The difference can be seen when considering the cost of running a motor vehicle for a business. The expenditure incurred in acquiring the motor vehicle is classed as **capital expenditure** while the cost of the petrol used to run the vehicle is **revenue expenditure**. This is because the revenue expenditure is used up in a few days and does not add to the value of the fixed asset.

17.4 Difference between capital and revenue expenditure

The difference between capital and revenue expenditure can be seen in Exhibit 17.1. Revenue expenditure is a day-to-day running expense of the business and as such is chargeable to the trading and profit and loss account, whereas capital expenditure results in an increase in the fixed assets which is shown in the balance sheet.

Exhibit 17.1

Capital expenditure	Revenue expenditure
Premises purchased	Rent of premises
Legal charges for conveyancing	Legal charges for debt collection
New machinery	Repairs to machinery
Installation of machinery	Electricity costs of using machinery
Additions to assets	Maintenance of assets
Motor vehicles	Current Road Fund Tax
Delivery charges on new assets	Carriage on purchases and sales
Extension costs of new offices	Redecorating existing offices
Cost of adding air-conditioning to room	Interest on loan to purchase air-conditioning

17.5 Joint expenditure

In certain cases one item of expenditure will need dividing between capital and revenue expenditure.

Suppose a builder was engaged to tackle some work on your premises, the total bill being for £3,000. If one-third of this was for repair work and two-thirds for improvements, £1,000 should be charged in the profit and loss account as revenue expenditure, and £2,000 identified as capital expenditure and, therefore, added to the value of premises and shown as such in the balance sheet.

17.6 Incorrect treatment of expenditure

If one of the following occurs:

1   capital expenditure is incorrectly treated as revenue expenditure, or

2   revenue expenditure is incorrectly treated as capital expenditure

then both the balance sheet figures and trading and profit and loss account figures will be incorrect.

This means that the net profit figure will also be incorrect. For example, if a motor vehicle is posted to the motor expenses account instead of the motor vehicle account, then:

> **Net profit** would be understated
> *and*
> **Balance sheet** values would not include the value of the asset.

If revenue expenditure is incorrectly posted to capital expenditure, for example if stationery is posted to the office equipment instead of the stationery account, then:

> **Net profit** would be overstated
> *and*
> **Balance sheet** values would be over-valued.

If the expenditure affects items in the trading account, then the **gross profit** figure will also be incorrect.

17.7 Treatment of loan interest

If money is borrowed to finance the purchase of a fixed asset then interest will have to be paid on the loan. The loan interest, however, is **not** a cost of acquiring the asset, but is simply a cost of financing it. This means that loan interest is revenue expenditure and **not** capital expenditure.

17.8 Capital and revenue receipts

When an item of capital expenditure is sold, the receipt is called a capital receipt. Suppose a motor van is bought for £8,000, and sold five years later for £1,750. The £8,000 was treated as capital expenditure. The £1,750 received is treated as a capital receipt.

Revenue receipts are sales or other revenue items, such as rent receivable or commissions receivable.

NEW TERMS

Capital expenditure When a firm spends money to buy or add value to a fixed asset.

Revenue expenditure Expenses needed for the day-to-day running of the business.

STUDENT ACTIVITIES

17.1   For the business of K Thorne, wholesale chemist, classify the following between 'capital' and 'revenue' expenditure:

(a)   Purchase of an extra motor van.
(b)   Cost of rebuilding a warehouse wall which had fallen down.
(c)   Building extension to the warehouse.
(d)   Painting extension to warehouse when it is first built.
(e)   Repainting extension to warehouse three years later than that done in (d).
(f)   Carriage costs on bricks for new warehouse extension.
(g)   Carriage costs on purchases.
(h)   Carriage costs on sales.
(i)   Legal costs of collecting debts.
(j)   Legal charges on acquiring new premises for office.
(k)   Fire insurance premium.
(l)   Costs of erecting new machine.

17.2X   For the business of H Ward, a foodstore, classify the following between 'capital' and 'revenue' expenditure:

(a)   Repairs to meat slicer.
(b)   New tyre for van.
(c)   Additional shop counter.
(d)   Renewing signwriting on store.
(e)   Fitting partitions in store.
(f)   Roof repairs.
(g)   Installing thief detection equipment.
(h)   Wages of store assistant.
(i)   Carriage on returns outwards.
(j)   New cash register.
(k)   Repairs to office safe.
(l)   Installing extra toilet.

17.3   Explain clearly the difference between capital expenditure and revenue expenditure. State which of the following you would classify as capital expenditure, giving your reasons:

(a)   Cost of building extension to factory.
(b)   Purchases of filing cabinets for sales office.
(c)   Cost of repairs to accounting machine.
(d)   Cost of installing reconditioned engine in delivery van.
(e)   Legal fees paid in connection with factory extension.

17.4 The following data was extracted from books of account of H E Worth, a building contractor, on 31 March 2000, his financial year end:

		£
(a)	Wages (including wages of two of Worth's employees who worked on improvements to Worth's premises, amount involved £4,500)	18,000
(b)	Light and heat (including new wiring £1,000, part of premises improvement)	4,000
(c)	Purchase of extra cement mixer (includes £200 for repair of old dumper)	2,500
(d)	Rent	1,400
(e)	Carriage (includes £100 carriage on new cement mixer)	800
(f)	Purchases of new lathe (extra)	4,000

You are required to:

Allocate each of the items listed above to either capital or revenue expenditure.

(RSA)

17.5X Geoff worked for many years as a commercial banker but at the recent reorganisation of the staff he decided to take early retirement. One of his and his wife's ambitions has been to own and run a small hotel in the Lake District catering for walkers and climbers. Geoff and Anne are both keen walkers and have been members of walking clubs for many years.

Holly Dale Hotel is situated near Grasmere in its own grounds of approximately one and a half acres. All its six bedrooms are en-suite and amongst its facilities are a dining-room, lounge and two other rooms which can be used for storing climbing and walking equipment and a drying room.

Structurally the hotel is sound and the previous owners have kept up with the maintenance and some refurbishment.

Geoff and Anne have now moved into the private flat situated at the rear of the hotel. They have decided to proceed cautiously with the upgrading of certain parts of the hotel and have produced a budget for the first year's expenditure.

Required

(a) From the attached list classify the following items as either capital or revenue expenditure prior to the books, papers, etc. being forwarded to Geoff and Anne's accountant.

Holly Dale Hotel Grasmere
Items of expenditure
One double and two single beds
10 feather pillows (purchased as a special offer at £5.00 each including a free pillow case)
Bathroom suites
Labour to plumb in bathroom suites
Curtains
Carpeting
Table linen
Cutlery
Vase and dried flower arrangement
Reception desk
Stationery
Portable typewriter
6 waste-paper bins
Towels
Toilet rolls and tissues
Soap and bubble bath
Road tax on estate car
Garage repair account re: estate car
Estate car (second-hand)
2 boxes pansies and wallflowers
6 rose bushes
2 five-litre tins emulsion paint ⎫ Geoff is going to do
20 rolls of wallpaper and paste ⎭ his own decorating

2 storage heaters for drying room

Coat and shoe racks for drying room

(local joiner to provide materials and labour for making and fitting)

(b) Although Geoff has years of banking experience he is not too familiar with some of the terms used by the accountancy profession. He drops you a line requesting the following explanation:

Could you please explain to me the difference between 'capital' and 'revenue expenditure' and why it is so important to make the distinction before I enter the invoices into the books of account.

Draft a suitable reply to Geoff.

(NVQ Level 2)

17.6X You are required to distinguish the following items between capital and revenue expenditure, giving reasons for your answer:

(a) Purchase of a new car for the sales representative.

(b) Fuel for the vehicle.

(c) Fitting a new mobile telephone in the vehicle.

(d) Insurance for the vehicle.

(e) Fitting new tyres to the company's other vehicle.

17.7X Business Data Systems specialises in providing computer services to small commercial businesses.

You are required to state whether the following transactions should be classified as capital or revenue expenditure, giving reasons for your choice.

(a) Salaries of the computer operators.

(b) Purchase of new computer for use in the office.

(c) Purchase of computer printout paper.

(d) Insurance of all the company's computer hardware.

(e) Cost of adding additional storage capacity to a mainframe computer to be used by the company.

(f) Cost of providing additional security to the company's offices.

17.8 Comart Supplies Ltd has recently purchased five ITC computers. Would the purchase be regarded as capital expenditure or revenue expenditure if:

(a) The computers are to be used for data processing by the company?

(b) The computers are to be held as stock for sale to customers?

(AAT (part of Central Assessment))

17.9 Summit Glazing Ltd are planning to purchase a new van. Would the following be items of capital or revenue expenditure?

(a) The purchase price of the van.

(b) Modification work to the side of the van to allow the external carriage of sheets of glass.

(c) Motor insurance of the van.

(AAT (part of Central Assessment))

17.10 If capital expenditure is treated as revenue expenditure, then:

(a) How would the total expenses and the net profit for the profit for the period be affected?

(b) What effect would the error have on the value of the fixed assets in the balance sheet?

(AAT (part of Central Assessment))

17.11 JLW Ltd has recently bought a machine costing £16,000 to produce a range of gold chains. Would the following items be capital or revenue expenditure?

(a) The purchase price of the machine.

(b) The cost of initial training for staff to operate the machine. (This cost is significant.)

(c) The cost of an annual maintenance contract with the manufacturer of the machine.

(AAT (part of Central Assessment))

17.12X Various costs have recently been incurred in building an extension to the showroom and offices. In each case indicate whether the expenditure was capital or revenue.

(a) Architect's fees for drawing up the plans.

(b) Charge by contractor for clearing the site in preparation for building.

(c) Payment to the builder for carrying out the extension work.

(AAT (part of Central Assessment))

18 Documents used in buying and selling

AIMS

- To cover the documentation used in the trading activity of buying and selling goods and/or services including: quotation, purchase order, advice note, delivery note, goods received note, invoice, pro-forma invoice, returns note, credit note, statement of account and remittance advice.

18.1 Introduction

All businesses and organisations are involved in trading, i.e. the buying and selling of goods and/or services in order to make a profit. The financial transaction of buying and selling involves some very important documents which are used by both the buyer and the seller. The documents have been in general use for many years and are part of an established procedure. Their proper use enables trading to proceed smoothly and in the event of a dispute between a buyer and a seller, the matter can normally be settled quickly. Since both parties use the same documents they will be dealt with in the sequence normally found in the trading activity.

A diagram of the flow of documents is shown in Exhibit 18.1.

Exhibit 18.1 The trading activity

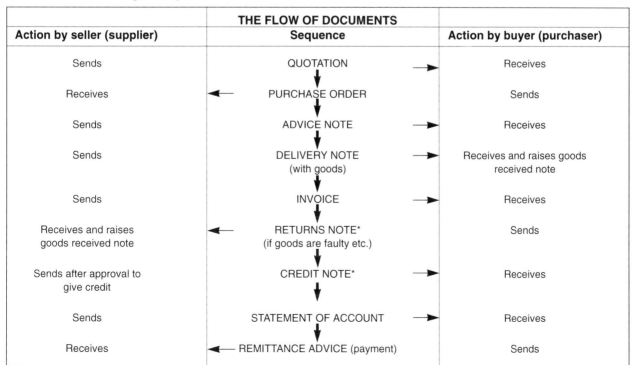

Action by seller (supplier)	THE FLOW OF DOCUMENTS	Action by buyer (purchaser)
	Sequence	
Sends	QUOTATION →	Receives
Receives	← PURCHASE ORDER	Sends
Sends	ADVICE NOTE →	Receives
Sends	DELIVERY NOTE (with goods) →	Receives and raises goods received note
Sends	INVOICE →	Receives
Receives and raises goods received note	← RETURNS NOTE* (if goods are faulty etc.)	Sends
Sends after approval to give credit	CREDIT NOTE* →	Receives
Sends	STATEMENT OF ACCOUNT →	Receives
Receives	← REMITTANCE ADVICE (payment)	Sends

* Both the returns note and the credit note would only be used if there was some problem with the goods supplied.

18.2 Quotation

At the request of a prospective purchaser a company will issue a quotation (an offer to supply goods or services). The quotation will normally be in the form of a formal document detailing what is to be supplied, when, where and the price. It will also state the terms, usually known as the conditions of sale, under which it is prepared to supply the goods or services. When the purchaser requires an urgent quotation a fax may be sent by the supplier. Some suppliers may have a standard range of products to offer and choose to issue a catalogue as the quotation from which purchasers may order goods.

The quotation is a very important document since it could well be the starting point for a contract between the supplier and the purchaser. On receiving the quotation the purchaser should check it to ensure it meets their full requirements. Only then should the purchaser consider raising a purchase order.

An example of a quotation is shown in Exhibit 18.2.

Exhibit 18.2 Quotation

Morridge Products Ltd
Moor Top Lane
Leek

Telephone: 01538 703101
Fax: 01538 703203
VAT Reg No: 761 9849 16

QUOTATION

Stoke Engineering Co Ltd   Date: 4 March 2000
Blythe End Works   Our Ref: 2432
Stoke-on-Trent

Thank you for your enquiry of 24 Feb 2000. We are pleased to quote for the supply of the following:

Quantity	Description	Part No	Price each
120	Suspension Arm	B402	£38.50
60	Axle Shaft	B424	£27.65
120	Backplate	B432	£43.20

Delivery: 6 weeks from receipt of your order.
Terms: Strictly net with payment within 30 days from date of invoice.
VAT: Prices quoted are exclusive of VAT.
Prices: Include delivery to your works in one consignment.

Signed   *P T Thompson*
          Sales Manager

18.3 Purchase order

When a business or organisation decides to buy goods or engage the services of another company it usually issues a purchase order.

This document contains the following information:

- name and address of supplier

- purchase order number

- date of order

- details of the goods or services ordered including part numbers or catalogue references

- quantity required

- delivery date

- authorised signature of a senior member of the company such as the buyer.

It is normally raised by the customer's purchasing office and then sent to the supplier. Once it has been accepted by the supplier a formal contract will exist between the two parties.

An example of a purchase order is shown in Exhibit 18.3.

Exhibit 18.3 Purchase order

PURCHASE ORDER

Stoke Engineering Co Ltd
Blythe End Works
Stoke-on-Trent

Telephone:	01782 923116	Order No:	ST 6032
Fax:	01782 923431	Date:	12 March 2000
VAT Reg No:	964 7688 21		

Morridge Products Ltd
Moor Top Lane
Leek

Please supply the following:

120 off	Suspension arm	Part No B402	£38.50 each
60 off	Axle Shaft	Part No B424	£27.65 each
120 off	Backplate	Part No B432	£43.20 each

Delivery required: by end April 2000 to our works.

If there are any queries regarding this order please contact the undersigned immediately.

Signed *A Barton*
Buyer

18.4 Advice note

This will be sent to the customer before the goods are despatched. This means that the customer will know that the goods are on the way and when they should arrive. If the goods do not arrive within a reasonable time then the customer will notify the supplier so that enquiries may be made with the carrier to establish what has happened to the goods.

The advice note is usually raised as part of a pack of documents including the delivery note and the invoice since the information on each document is essentially the same. Only the invoice will have the price details and total amount due. The delivery note is explained in section 18.5 and the invoice in section 18.6.

An advice note is shown in Exhibit 18.4.

Exhibit 18.4 Advice note

Morridge Products Ltd
Moor Top Lane
Leek

Telephone: 01538 703101
Fax: 01538 703203
VAT Reg No: 761 9849 16

Stoke Engineering Co Ltd   Date: 2 May 2000
Blythe End Works   Our Ref: 2432
Stoke-on-Trent

Your Order No: ST 6032

ADVICE NOTE

We have today despatched the items shown below by *Coopers Transport*

Quantity	Description	Part No
120	Suspension arm	B402
60	Axle shaft	B424
120	Backplate	B432

Please advise us if the goods have not been received within *3 days*.

18.5 Delivery note

When the company supplying the goods is ready to despatch them to the purchaser they prepare a delivery note (sometimes called a despatch note). As we mentioned in section 18.4 this document is normally prepared at the same time as the invoice, usually by using a suitable computer accounting package. The document contains the following information:

- name and address of purchaser;

- date and number of customer's purchase order;

- details of goods despatched including their description and part number or catalogue reference;

- quantity being supplied;
- delivery address and any relevant instructions, i.e. must be delivered between 8 a.m. and 6 p.m.

Price details are not shown on this document. When a supplier uses their own transport or the services of a carrier a copy of the delivery note will be signed by the receiving company and this note will be returned to the supplier. This copy will be safely filed as it may be needed as 'proof of delivery' of the goods should a dispute arise as to their safe receipt.

Exhibit 18.5 shows a delivery note.

Exhibit 18.5 Delivery note

Morridge Products Ltd
Moor Top Lane
Leek

Telephone: 01538 703101
Fax: 01538 703203
VAT Reg No: 761 9849 16

Stoke Engineering Co Ltd   Date: 2 May 2000
Blythe End Works   Our Ref: 2432
Stoke-on-Trent

Your Order No: ST 6032

DELIVERY NOTE

Please receive the following:

Quantity	Description	Part No
120	Suspension arm	B402
60	Axle shaft	B424
120	Backplate	B432

Would you please acknowledge receipt of the goods by signing this note and pass accompanying copy to the driver making the delivery.

Received by: *M Jordan*   Date: 4 May 2000

18.6 Invoice

An invoice is a document prepared by the seller whenever they sell goods or provide services on credit. The invoice is usually numbered for easy identification and for filing in a suitable storage system. It contains the following information:

- seller's name and address;
- seller's VAT registration number;
- purchaser's name and address;
- purchaser's order number and date;
- date of delivery;
- description of goods and services supplied including part number and catalogue reference;

- quantity;

- price per item;

- VAT payable;

- total amount due;

- terms and conditions of sale.

From a bookkeeper's point of view the invoice is one of the most important documents since details of the transaction need to be entered in the books of account of both the seller and the buyer. The following Chapters 19 and 20 deal with the entry of invoices.

Exhibit 18.6 shows an invoice.

Exhibit 18.6 Invoice

INVOICE

Morridge Products Ltd
Moor Top Lane
Leek

Telephone: 01538 703101
Fax: 01538 703203
VAT Reg No: 761 9849 16

Invoice to

Stoke Engineering Co Ltd		Invoice No:	5/232	
Blythe End Works		Advice Note:	2432	
Stoke-on-Trent				

Your Order No: ST 6032   Date/Tax point: 2 May 2000

Quantity	Description	Part No	Price each £	Amount £
120	Suspension arm	B402	38.50	4,620.00
60	Axle shaft	B424	27.65	1,659.00
120	Backplate	B432	43.20	5,184.00

	Total		11,463.00
	VAT at 17½%		2,006.03
	Amount due		13,469.03

Terms: Strictly net within 1 month
E & OE

18.7 Pro-forma invoice

In certain circumstances this type of invoice is raised and sent to the purchaser who will then make payment before any goods or services are supplied. A supplier might take this action if a purchaser is unknown to the supplier, has not yet established creditworthiness or is known to the supplier as a late or inconsistent payer.

18.8 Returns note

In certain circumstances a purchaser needs to return goods to the supplier because they are damaged, faulty or perhaps not to the specification ordered. The goods will be returned to the supplier accompanied by a returns note which gives details of the goods being returned and the reason together with the details of the order number, date, etc. On receiving the returns note and goods the supplier will raise a goods received note which tells the departments concerned of the return of these goods. A senior member of staff will then have to decide whether or not it is appropriate to give credit for the returned goods.

Exhibit 18.7 shows a returns note.

Exhibit 18.7 Returns note

RETURNS NOTE	
Stoke Engineering Co Ltd **Blyth End Works** **Stoke-on-Trent**	**Return Note No**: 1186
Telephone: 01782 923116 Fax: 01782 923431 Vat Reg No: 964 7688 21	**Date:** 13 May 2000

Morridge Products Ltd
Moor Top Lane
Leek

We have today returned the following goods:

23 off Axle Shaft, Part No B424

Returned as agreed between our Mr J Barton and your Mr A Lowe due to 50 mm diameter being oversize.

J Barton   Inspection Department

18.9 Credit note

Once the supplier has decided to give credit then a credit note will be raised for the value of the returned goods including the applicable amount of VAT. The note will then be sent to the customer.

A credit note is usually printed in red to distinguish it from an invoice and while it contains similar information to that found in an invoice some details will differ. For instance, the customer may only have returned a part of a consignment and this will need to be clearly identified on the credit note.

Again credit notes are important documents which need to be entered in the books of account as the amount owed by the buyer will be reduced by the amount of the credit note. Chapter 21 deals with the entry of credit notes.

Exhibit 18.8 illustrates a credit note which, as mentioned above, is usually printed in red.

Exhibit 18.8 Credit note

CREDIT NOTE

Morridge Products Ltd
Moor Top Lane
Leek

Telephone: 01538 703101
Fax: 01538 703203
VAT Reg No: 761 9849 16

Stoke Engineering Co Ltd   Credit Note No: 532/00
Blythe End Works   Our Invoice No: 5/232
Stoke-on-Trent   Your Reference: 1186

Your Order No: ST 6032   Date/Tax point: 20 May 2000

Quantity	Description	Part No	Price each	Amount
23	Axle shaft	B 424	£27.65	£635.95

Total	£635.95
VAT at 17½%	£111.29
Amount credited	£747.24

Note: Credit notes are usually printed in 'red'.

18.10 Statement of account

At the end of each month businesses send out a document known as a statement of account.

This statement contains details of all the customer's transactions during the previous month, starting off with the opening balance outstanding from the previous month plus the amounts owing from the current month's invoices. Any amounts that are paid are deducted together with any credit note allowances. This gives the total amount outstanding which is then due for payment at the end of the month.

On receipt of the statement of account the customer should check the details with their own records to ensure that they agree with the statement. Provided the invoices listed on the statement have been approved for payment then arrangements will be made to pay the account. Chapter 22 and 26 also cover the preparation of statements of account.

Exhibit 18.9 shows a statement of account.

Exhibit 18.9 Statement of account

STATEMENT OF ACCOUNT					

Morridge Products Ltd
Moor Top Lane
Leek

Telephone: 01538 703101
Fax: 01538 703203
VAT Reg No: 761 9849 16

Stoke Engineering Co Ltd
Blythe End Works
Stoke-on-Trent

Statement date: 31 May 2000
Account number: 2432
Page number: 1

Date	Reference	Debit	Credit	Balance
		£	£	£
30/4/00	Balance from previous statement			931.28
2/5/00	Invoice No 5/232	13,469.03		14,400.31
7/5/00	Payment received		931.28	13,469.03
20/5/00	Credit note No 532/00		747.24	12,721.79
	Total outstanding			12,721.79

Terms: Strictly net 30 days from date of invoice
Payment due 30/6/00

E & OE

18.11 Remittance advice

When payment is made from one business to another it is important that the recipient of the money has details of the payment so that the money may be correctly allocated. Therefore, the business making the payment usually includes a remittance advice. This document is rather like a statement, and may in fact be prepared at the same time, in that it shows details of the business's most recent transactions and final balance outstanding which is represented by the accompanying cheque or advice if the payment is made by BACS (*see* Chapter 10).

If any invoice has not been paid for any reason it will be left outstanding and can then be queried. A remittance advice is shown in Exhibit 18.10.

See also Chapter 13, section 13.4, and Exhibit 13.1 for further example of a remittance advice.

Exhibit 18.10 Remittance advice

<table>
<tr><td colspan="6" align="center">**REMITTANCE ADVICE**</td></tr>
<tr>
<td colspan="3">Stoke Engineering Co Ltd
Blythe End Works
Stoke-on-Trent

Telephone: 01782 923116
Fax: 01782 923431
VAT Reg No: 964 7688 21</td>
<td colspan="3">Remittance advice: 6/962
Cheque No:

Date: 28 June 2000</td>
</tr>
<tr>
<td colspan="3">Morridge Products Ltd
Moor Top Lane
Leek</td>
<td colspan="3">Account No: 2432</td>
</tr>
<tr>
<td>*Date*</td><td>*Invoice or credit note No*</td><td>*Invoice*</td><td>*Credit note*</td><td colspan="2">*Payment*</td>
</tr>
<tr>
<td>2/5/00
20/5/00</td><td>5/232
532/00</td><td>13,469.03</td><td>
747.24</td><td colspan="2">13,469.03
(747.24)</td>
</tr>
<tr>
<td colspan="3"></td><td colspan="2" align="right">TOTAL PAYMENT</td><td>12,721.79</td>
</tr>
</table>

18.12 Goods received note (GRN)

When goods are received the purchaser will raise a goods received note (GRN) which details exactly what goods have been received. This note is raised as part of the purchaser's internal procedure and is used to advise various departments of their arrival. These departments will include:

- buying office – so that the progress of orders can be monitored;

- materials office – stock records can be updated;

- accounts department – the invoice from the supplier will be checked with the GRN as proof of delivery before payment is authorised.

It is important to both the supplier and the purchaser that details on the purchase order, invoice and goods received note are correct so as to avoid possible disputes which could result in delayed payment and the loss of goodwill.

If the supplier receives faulty goods back from the purchaser then they will also raise a GRN to inform all the departments concerned of the return of the goods.

A goods received note is shown as Exhibit 18.11.

Exhibit 18.11 Goods received note

Stoke Engineering Co Ltd			GRN No _____

Goods Received Note

Copies Accounts Dept ——— White
Purchasing Dept ——— Pink
O/No _____   Material control ——— Green
Inspection ———— Blue
Supplier Ref _____   With Goods ———— Yellow

Description	Part No	Quantity	Remarks

Received by (signature) _____   Date _____

Carrier _____

18.13 Abbreviations

Business documents frequently contain abbreviations and terms of trade the most common of which are as follows:

Carriage paid Another word for carriage is transport costs. Thus carriage paid indicates that the cost of transport has been included in the cost of the goods.

COD This abbreviation stands for 'cash on delivery' and means that the goods must be paid for on delivery.

E & OE On some invoices and other documents you will see the initials 'E & OE' printed at the bottom of the invoice. This abbreviation stands for 'errors and omissions excepted'. Basically, this is a warning that there may possibly be errors or omissions which could mean that the figures shown could be incorrect, and that the recipient should check the figures carefully before taking any action concerning them.

Ex works This means that the price of the goods does not include delivery costs.

Net monthly This phrase frequently appears at the foot of an invoice and means that the full amount of the invoice is due for payment within one month of the date of the invoice.

NEW TERMS

Advice note   Document sent by the supplier to inform the purchaser that the goods have been despatched on a particular date.

Carriage paid   *See* p. 183.

COD   *See* p. 183.

Credit note   This document is raised by the supplier when goods have been returned by the purchaser due to them being damaged, faulty or to the wrong specification, or when an overcharge has been made on an invoice. The amount owed by the customer (the debtor) will be reduced by the amount of a credit note.

Delivery note   This accompanies the goods when they are delivered to the purchaser and provides details of what exactly is being delivered. It does not include price information. The purchaser should sign the note to acknowledge receipt of the goods and this is returned to the supplier.

E & OE   *See* p. 183.

Ex works   *See* p. 183.

Goods received note (GRN)   Following the receipt of goods the purchaser will check the consignment and a GRN will be raised which will show the exact details of what has been received. Copies of the GRN usually go to the buying office, materials control dept, accounts dept and the inspection dept.

Invoice   This is a document prepared by the seller whenever goods or services are provided on credit. It tells the business receiving the goods or services that they now owe money to the supplier.

Net monthly   *See* p. 183.

Pro-forma invoice   This type of invoice is raised and sent to the purchaser who will then make payment before any goods or services are supplied. A supplier usually takes this course of action to safeguard themselves if there is any uncertainty of receiving payment were goods to be supplied on credit.

Purchase order   This document is prepared by the purchaser and it contains details of the goods or services required by the purchaser. The details will normally coincide with those contained in a quotation previously provided by a supplier or may have been taken from a catalogue issued by a supplier.

Quotation   A formal document prepared by a supplier which is an offer to supply goods or services. It is usually prepared in response to an enquiry from a prospective purchaser or it could consist of a catalogue offering a standard range of goods or services from which a prospective purchaser can make a selection.

Remittance advice   A document which accompanies payment by cheque or via BACS and gives details of the payment.

Returns note   Should a purchaser need to return goods to a supplier, a returns note will be raised by the purchaser detailing exactly what is being returned and the reasons for their return.

Statement of account   This is normally sent to purchasers at the end of each month and it states the amount owing to the supplier at the end of that particular month.

Trading activity   The process of buying and selling of goods and/or services.

STUDENT ACTIVITIES

18.1 As accounts administrator for Mellor's Business Systems Co, you have just received the letter shown in Exhibit 18.12 from one of the company's established customers.

Exhibit 18.12

HALSHAW PRINTING CO LTD
Unit 7, Barnfield Business Park, Leicester LE4 7TY

Miss M Mellor
Mellor's Business Systems Co
Dean House
High Street
Nottingham NH4 8NY   7 March 2001

Dear Miss Mellor

Due to increased trade the company is in urgent need of two additional photocopiers. On looking through your recent catalogue the following model would suit our immediate needs:

     Super Zoom Photocopier Z-90   Retail Price £600.00 each

As an established customer you normally allow us a Trade Discount of 20% on goods purchased.

Could you please let us have a quotation for the above machines and indicate the earliest delivery date.

Yours sincerely

James Halshaw
Secretary

Task:

Referring to the company's customer details you ascertain that Halshaw Printing Co is entitled to receive 20 per cent trade discount and that the earliest date the photocopiers could be despatched is 14 March 2001.

Draw up a suitable form and make out the quotation to be sent to Halshaw Printing Co. (Ignore VAT.)

18.2 Roberts Suppliers Co sells hardware, tools, lawnmowers and sundry garden tools to both cash and credit customers. Sales invoices are prepared on a weekly basis and are made out from the order details.

From the following purchase orders (Exhibit 18.13) you are required to prepare invoices for week ending 7 October 2002 (ignore VAT). Blank invoices are provided for completion of this task (Exhibit 18.14).

Exhibit 18.13

PURCHASE ORDER   Order No 1079

BURGESS & SON
27 Frith Street
Birkenhead B21 3RZ

Tel: (01601) 41732   VAT Reg No 632 117381

Roberts Suppliers Co   Date: 3rd Sept 2002
Liverpool Road
Liverpool

Quantity	Cat No	Description	Price
2	LM713	Easi-ride mowers complete with collection boxes Delivery included	£1,527.30 each

---

PURCHASE ORDER   Order No KT27

RUDKINS SUPERSTORES
Market Place, Runcorn

Tel: (01631) 233152

Roberts Suppliers Co
Liverpool Road
Liverpool   27th August 2002

Please supply: Price
                                                          £

    6 Garden Forks (Aluminium)   22.30 each
    10 Wheelbarrows   67.95 each
    2 x 24″ Quickmow Machines
     (Electric) with cable   324.00 each

Will collect, please advise

Exhibit 18.14

Invoice form

ROBERTS SUPPLIERS CO				**Invoice No S. 9270**
Liverpool Road				
Liverpool				
Telephone:	0151-307128			
Fax:	0151-307824			
VAT Reg No.	224 36658			Date/Tax point

Customer:				Your Order No

Product code	Description	Quantity	Unit price £ p	Total amount £ p

Comments:		**Net Total**	
		Total	

Registered office Park Avenue, Liverpool	Registered No: 263120

Invoice form

ROBERTS SUPPLIERS CO				**Invoice No S. 9271**
Liverpool Road				
Liverpool				
Telephone:	0151-307128			
Fax:	0151-307824			
VAT Reg No.	224 36658			Date/Tax point

Customer				Your Order No

Product code	Description	Quantity	Unit price £ p	Total amount £ p

Comments:		**Net Total**	
		Total	

Registered office Park Avenue, Liverpool	Registered No: 263120

18.3X The account of Window Box Ltd, a customer of MMS Textiles Ltd, is overdue for payment. A copy of the current Window Box Ltd statement of account, which was sent out on 31 October 2002, is given in Exhibit 18.15. MMS Textiles gives its credit customers 30 days credit from the date of supply. This is clearly stated on all MMS Textiles' invoices.

Exhibit 18.15

STATEMENT OF ACCOUNT

MMS Textiles Ltd	Tel: (01922) 211311
Unit 34 Brooklands Estate	Fax: (01922) 231461
Walsall	VAT Reg No 465 765811
WA3 7ZX	

Window Box Ltd
12/13 Market Street
West Bromwich
WE2 24LK   31 October 2002

Date	Reference	Debit £ p	Credit £ p	Balance £ p
2002				
Oct 1	*Balance brought forward*			*274 50*
Oct 4	*Invoice No 19861*	*435 75*		*710 25*
Oct 9	*Invoice No 20129*	*235 00*		*945 25*
Amount now due				*1,930.00*

Registered Office: Unit 34 Brooklands Estate, Walsall WA3 7ZX
Registered Number 6516428

Task:

Draw up a suitable letterhead and draft a letter to James Sinclair at Window Box Ltd pointing out that their account is overdue and requesting immediate payment of the outstanding balance. A copy of the statement is to be enclosed with the letter.

(AAT (part of Central Assessment))

18.4X *(a)* What is the purpose of a pro-forma invoice?
(b) What does it mean if goods are sold COD?
(c) What does 'terms net' on an invoice mean?
(d) What does the term 'ex works' mean?
(e) What does E&OE on an invoice mean?

18.5 Describe the function of the following documents:

(a) remittance advice
(b) goods received note (GRN)
(c) credit note.

18.6X Complete the following sentences:

(a) JWL Ltd sends out a .... to a credit customer to correct an overcharge on an invoice.
(b) JWL Ltd sends a .... to a supplier to order goods.
(c) JWL Ltd sends a .... with a payment to a supplier to indicate which invoices are being paid.

(AAT (part of Central Assessment))

18.7 Complete the following sentences:

(a) An .... is sent to the buyer before the goods are delivered to inform that the goods will be despatched shortly.

(b) A .... is packed with the goods so that the buyer can check that all the items listed have been received.

(c) An .... is sent by the seller to the buyer of goods to advise how much is owed for the goods supplied.

(AAT (part of Central Assessment))

19 The sales day book and the sales ledger

AIMS

- To be able to draw up a sales invoice.
- Be able to enter up a sales day book and post to the sales ledger.
- To understand how trade discount differs from cash discount.
- To appreciate the need for credit control.

19.1 Introduction

Chapter 9, 'Divisions of the ledgers: books of original entry' showed the division of the ledger into a set of day books, journals and ledgers. This chapter explains sales day books and sales ledgers.

19.2 Cash sales

When goods are purchased by a customer who pays for them immediately by cash then there is no necessity to enter the sale of these goods into the sales day book or the sales ledger since the customer is not in debt to the business. Keeping details of these customers' names and addresses is, therefore, not needed.

19.3 Credit sales

In many businesses most of the sales will be made on credit rather than for cash. In fact, the sales of some businessess or organisations will consist entirely of credit sales.

For each credit sale the supplier will send a document to the buyer showing details and prices of the goods sold. This document is known as a sales invoice to the supplier and a purchase invoice to the buyer. Section 18.6 in the previous chapter describes fully the function of an invoice and shows an example; a further example is shown in Exhibit 19.1.

Exhibit 19.1

```
                              INVOICE

        J BLAKE FOODS, UNIT 7, OVERLEA INDUSTRIAL ESTATE,
                      LEICESTER LE1 2AP

  To:    D Poole                           Invoice No 16554
         Deansgate Restaurant
         45 Charles Street                 Account No 3482
         Manchester M1 5ZN                 Date: 1 September 2000


  Your Purchase Order 10/A/980


         Quantity                      Per unit        Total

                                          £              £
      21 cases Cape Glory Pears           20            420
      5 cartons Kay's Flour                4             20
      6 cases Marson's Vinegar            20            120
                                                        ───
                                                        560
                                                        ═══


  Terms: 1¼% cash discount if paid within one month
```

Most businesses have individually designed invoices but inevitably they follow a generally accepted accounting format. All invoices will be numbered and contain the names and addresses of both the supplier and the customer. In Exhibit 19.1 the supplier is J Blake Foods and the customer is D Poole.

19.4 Copies of sales invoices

Once the goods have been despatched to the buyer a **sales invoice** is made out by the supplier. The top copy of the sales invoice is sent to the buyer and further copies are retained by the supplier for use within the organisation. For example, one copy is usually sent to the accounts department to enable the sale of goods on credit to be recorded in the sales day book and sales ledger, another copy may be passed to the sales department and so on.

19.5 Entering credit sales into the sales day book

As mentioned above, a copy of the sales invoice is passed to the accounts department where the supplier enters this into the sales day book. This book is merely a list, showing the following:

- date of sale;
- name of customer to whom the goods have been sold;
- invoice number;
- final amount of invoice.

There is no need to show details of the goods sold in the sales day book. This can be found by looking at copy invoices.

Exhibit 19.2 shows a **sales day book**, which illustrates how the invoices are entered starting with the entry of the invoice shown in Exhibit 19.1. Assume that the entries are on page 26 of the day book.

Exhibit 19.2

Sales Day Book			
		Invoice No	(page 26)
2000			£
Sept 1	D Poole	16554	560
8	T Cockburn	16555	1,640
28	C Carter	16556	220
30	D Stevens & Co	16557	1,100
			3,520

19.6 Posting credit sales to the sales ledger

Instead of having one ledger for all accounts, a sales ledger is used for recording credit sale transactions.

1 The credit sales are now posted, one by one, to the **debit** side of each customer's account in the sales ledger.

2 At the end of each period the total of the credit sales is posted to the **credit** side of the sales account in the general ledger.

It may be easier to use 'IN' and 'OUT', as shown in Chapter 5, to post these transactions, i.e. the goods sold go 'into' each individual customer's account and they come 'out' of the sales account.

This is illustrated in Exhibit 19.3.

Exhibit 19.3 Posting credit sales

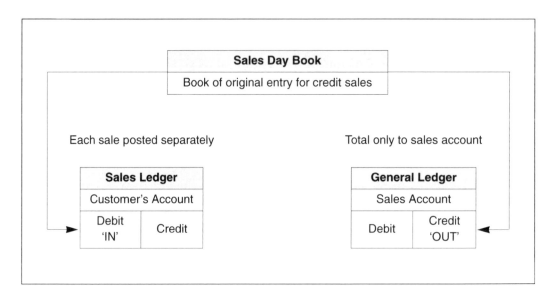

19.7 An example of posting credit sales

The sales day book in Exhibit 19.2 is now shown again. This time posting is made to the sales ledger and the general ledger. Notice the completion of the folio columns with the reference numbers.

Sales Day Book				
		Invoice No	Folio	(page 26)
2000				£
Sept 1	D Poole	16554	SL 12	560
8	T Cockburn	16555	SL 39	1,640
28	C Carter	16556	SL 125	220
30	D Stevens & Co	16557	SL 249	1,100
	Transferred to Sales Account		GL 44	3,520

Sales Ledger
D Poole Account
Dr   (page 12)
                                                                              Cr

2000			£	
Sept 1	Sales	SDB 26	560	

T Cockburn Account
Dr   (page 39)
                                                                              Cr

2000			£	
Sept 8	Sales	SDB 26	1,640	

C Carter Account
Dr   (page 125)
                                                                              Cr

2000			£	
Sept 28	Sales	SDB 26	220	

D Stevens & Co Account
Dr   (page 249)
                                                                              Cr

2000			£	
Sept 30	Sales	SDB 26	1,100	

General Ledger
Sales Account
Dr   (page 44)
                                                                              Cr

				2000			£
				Sept 30	Credit sales for the month	SDB 26	3,520

Alternative names for the sales day book are sales book and sales journal.

It is recommended that student activity 19.1 be attempted at this point.

19.8 Trade discounts

Suppose you are the proprietor of a business. You are selling to three different kinds of customers:

1   Traders who buy a lot of goods from you.

2   Traders who buy only a few items from you.

3   Direct to the general public.

The traders themselves have to sell the goods to the general public in their own areas. They have to make a profit, so they will want to pay you less than the retail price.

The traders who buy in large quantities will not want to pay as much as traders who buy in small quantities. You want to attract large customers, and so you are happy to sell to them at a lower price.

This means that your selling prices are at three levels: **1** to traders buying large quantities, **2** to traders buying small quantities, and **3** to the general public.

So that your staff do not need three different price lists, all goods are shown on your price lists at the same price. However, a reduction (discount), called a **trade discount** is given to traders **1** and **2**. An example illustrating this is shown in Exhibit 19.4.

Exhibit 19.4

You are selling a particular make of food mixing machine. The retail price is £200. Traders **1** are given 25 per cent trade discount, traders **2**, 20 per cent and the general public who pay the full retail price. The prices paid by each type of customer would be:

		Trader 1		Trader 2	General public 3
		£		£	£
Retail price		200		200	200
Less Trade discount	(25%)	50	(20%)	40	nil
Price to be paid by customer		150		160	200

Exhibit 19.5 is an invoice for goods supplied by R Grant (Catering Supplies) to D Poole. The items supplied by R Grant (Catering Supplies) are the same as supplied by J Blake Foods – *see* Exhibit 19.1; however, you will notice that R Grant (Catering Supplies) uses **trade discounts** to encourage customers to buy from him.

By comparing Exhibits 19.1 and 19.5 you can see that the prices paid by D Poole were the same. It is simply the method of calculating the price that is different.

Exhibit 19.5

INVOICE

R GRANT (CATERING SUPPLIES)
HIGHER SIDE PRESTON PR1 2NL

Telephone: (01703) 33122
Fax: (01703) 22331

D Poole
Deansgate Restaurant
45 Charles Street
Manchester M1 5ZN

Invoice No 30756
Account No P/4298
Date: 1 September 2000

Your Purchase Order 11/A/G80

Quantity	Per unit	Total
	£	£
21 cases Cape Glory Pears	25	525
5 cartons Kay's Flour	5	25
6 cases Marson's Vinegar	25	150
		700
Less 20% Trade Discount		140
		560

19.9 No double entry for trade discounts

As trade discount is simply a way of calculating sales prices, no entry for trade discount should be made in the double entry records nor in the sales day book. The recording of Exhibit 19.5 in R Grant's (Catering Supplies) sales day book and D Poole's personal account will appear:

Sales Day Book			
	Invoice No	Folio	(page 87)
2000			
Sept 2 D Poole	30756	SL 32	560

Sales Ledger (page 32)
D Poole Account

Dr					Cr
2000			£		
Sept 2 Sales	SDB 87	560			

To compare with cash discounts:

- Trade discounts: not shown in double entry accounts.

- Cash discounts: are shown in double entry accounts (refer to section 11.7).

19.10 Credit control

Any organisation which sells goods on credit should keep a close check to ensure that debtors pay their accounts on time. If this is not done properly, the amount of debtors can grow to an amount that will damage the business.

The following procedures should be carried out:

1 For each debtor a limit should be set and the debtor should not be allowed to owe more than this limit. The limit will depend upon particular circumstances and this will include the size of the customer's organisation and the amount of trade between the two parties, its credit rating and its record of past payments.

2 As soon as the payment date has been reached a system should be in place which highlights unpaid accounts. If there is no legitimate reason for withholding payment then the supplier may decide to withhold further supplies of goods to a customer.

3 If payment is not received after a reasonable time has elapsed and there is no obvious reason why the customer has withheld payment then legal action may be taken to recover the debt.

4 It is important that the customer is aware of what will happen if they do not pay their account by the due date.

NEW TERMS

Sales invoice   A document which is prepared when a business sells goods on credit to a customer. It gives details of the supplier and the customer, the goods sold and the price of those goods.

Trade discount   A reduction given by the supplier to a customer when calculating the selling price of goods to enable the customer to make a profit.

STUDENT ACTIVITIES

19.1 You are to enter up the sales day book from the following details. Post the items to the relevant accounts in the sales ledger and then show the transfer to the sales account in the general ledger.

Mar	1	Credit sales to J Gordon	£187
Mar	3	Credit sales to G Abrahams	£166
Mar	6	Credit sales to V White	£12
Mar	10	Credit sales to J Gordon	£55
Mar	17	Credit sales to F Williams	£289
Mar	19	Credit sales to U Richards	£66
Mar	27	Credit sales to V Wood	£28
Mar	31	Credit sales to L Simes	£78

19.2X Enter up the sales day book from the following, then post the items to the relevant accounts in the sales ledger. Then show the transfer to the sales account in the general ledger.

May	1	Credit sales to J Johnson	£305
May	3	Credit sales to T Royes	£164
May	5	Credit sales to B Howe	£45
May	7	Credit sales to M Lee	£100
May	16	Credit sales to J Jakes	£308
May	23	Credit sales to A Vinden	£212
May	30	Credit sales to J Samuels	£1,296

19.3 F Benjamin of 10 Lower Street, Plymouth, is selling the following items, the recommended retail prices being: white tape £10 per roll, green baize at £4 per metre, blue cotton at £6 per sheet, black silk at £20 per dress length. He makes the following sales:

May 1   To F Gray, 3 Keswick Road, Portsmouth: 3 rolls white tape, 5 sheets blue cotton, 1 dress length black silk. Less 25 per cent trade discount.

May 4   To A Gray, 1 Shilton Road, Preston: 6 rolls white tape, 30 metres green baize. Less 33⅓ per cent trade discount.

May 8   To E Hines, 1 High Road, Malton: 1 dress length black silk. No trade discount.

May 20   To M Allen, 1 Knott Road, Southport: 10 rolls white tape, 6 sheets blue cotton, 3 dress lengths black silk, 11 metres green baize. Less 25 per cent trade discount.

May 31   To B Cooper, 1 Tops Lane, St Andrews: 12 rolls white tape, 14 sheets blue cotton, 9 metres green baize. Less 33⅓ per cent trade discount.

You are to *(a)* draw up a sales invoice for each of the above sales, *(b)* enter them up in the sales day book and post to the personal accounts, *(c)* transfer the total to the sales account in the general ledger.

19.4 Morton's Garage is situated on the outskirts of Macclesfield and sells petrol and accessories in addition to carrying out repairs and maintenance on vehicles. At 1 January 2003 Morton's sales ledger showed the following balances on their customers' accounts:

	£	
C Crawford	1,078	Dr
S Brocklehurst	563	Dr
L Price & Partners	321	Dr
D Woolham & Co	146	Dr

During January 2002 the garage issued the following invoices in respect of credit sales of petrol, accessories and repairs.

2003	Invoice no	Name	Amount
			£
2 Jan	37542	D Woolham & Co	230
6 Jan	37543	C Crawford	345
7 Jan	37544	S Brocklehurst	1,980
9 Jan	37545	L Price & Partners	523
13 Jan	37546	D Woolham & Co	56
18 Jan	37547	L Price & Partners	200
21 Jan	37548	C Crawford	340
24 Jan	37549	C Crawford	45
29 Jan	37550	S Brocklehurst	845
31 Jan	37551	L Price & Partners	721

On 31 January 2003 the garage proprietor, Mr Morton, received cheques from the following customers, who settled their account for the previous month:

Customer	Amount of cheque
	£
C Crawford	1,078
L Price & Partners	321
D Woolham & Co	146

Required:

(a) Draw up a sales day book and enter the above invoices into the day book and total it for the month of January 2003.

(b) Open an account for each customer and enter the balances as at 1 January 2003. Post the sales from the day book to each account and the amounts received.

(c) Balance the customers' accounts at 1 January 2003 and bring down the balances.

(d) Post the total sales to the sales account in the general ledger.

19.5X During April 2004 the following credit sales were made by Dabell's Stationery Supplies Ltd:

Date	Debtor	Invoice No	Amount £
1 April	Fisher & Co	6265	1,459
3 April	Elder (Office Supplies)	6266	73
5 April	Haigh (Mfr) Ltd	6267	56
11 April	Ardern & Co (Solicitors)	6268	1,598
15 April	I Rafiq	6269	540
20 April	Royle's Business Systems	6270	2,456
22 April	Fisher & Co	6271	23
22 April	Ardern & Co (Solicitors)	6272	345
25 April	Elder (Office Supplies)	6273	71
27 April	Haigh (Mfr) Ltd	6274	176

Tasks:

(a) Draw up a sales day book and enter the above invoices into the day book for the month of April 2004.

(b) The sales ledger showed the following balances at 1 April 2004:

Customer	Amount outstanding £
Ardern & Co (Solicitors)	472
Elder (Office Supplies)	75
Fisher & Co	231
Haigh (Mfr) Ltd	1,267
I Rafiq	330
Royle's Business Systems	750

Open an account for each of the firm's customers in the sales ledger and enter the balances outstanding on 1 April 2004.

(c) Post the sales invoices for the month of April to the appropriate ledger account in the sales ledger.

(d) During April the firm received cheques from Fisher & Co for £231, I Rafiq for £330 and £1,000 on account from Haigh (Mfr) Ltd. Post the cheques to the customers' accounts in the sales ledger.

(e) Balance each account off at the end of April and draw up a list of outstanding debtors.

19.6X Morridge Products Ltd is a small manufacturing company which makes parts for tractors, farm equipment and general machine parts. In addition to manufacturing, the company also carries out repairs.

As accounts assistant, one of your tasks is to prepare sales invoices and enter the details into the books of account. This involves entering them initially in the sales day book then posting each individual item to the respective debtors accounts in the sales ledger. Finally, at the end of the month, you post the totals in the day book to the respective accounts in the general ledger.

Required

(a) From the following details prepare invoices, use the blank form provided (Exhibit 19.6) and photocopy further blank invoices to complete this task.

The date is 3 December 2001 and the next invoice No is 0932.

Invoice details

	Name/address	Details of order	Price £	Order No
1	Price, Barlow & Co Hulme End Derbyshire	1 Fork for Fordson tractor	240.00	PB 323

Exhibit 19.6 Invoice form

MORRIDGE PRODUCTS LTD Moor Top Lane Leek Telephone: 0538 703101 Fax: 0538 703203 VAT Reg No: 761 9849 16	**INVOICE**	Invoice No: Account No: Date/Tax point:

Product code	Description	Quantity	Unit price £ p	Total amount £ p
Comments:				
		Total		

Registered office: 16 Brook Lane, Manchester   Registered No: 384 1758

2	Rowley Farmers Dove End Farm Bakewell Derbyshire	Repairs to muckspreader Parts Labour	 73.50 38.00	Via telephone

3	Stoke Engineering Co Ltd
	Blythe End Works
	Stoke-on-Trent
		Machine parts
		  to your specification
		  as per quotation
			
			347.30
				
				64394

4	Peak Manufacturing Co Town End Buxton Derbyshire	6 tractor back boxes as per your drawing Price as quoted (each)	 234.70	K 2314

5	Robinson (Plant Hire)
	Leek
	Staffs
		Repair to JCB arm
		  Parts
		  Labour
			
			125.70
			210.00
				
				R945

6	Bennetts Farm Machinery
	c/o Holly Bank Farm
	Monyash
	Derbyshire
		Baler modified
		  as per our telephone
		  conversation
		As agreed
			
			220.00
				Per
				telephone

(b) Enter the sales invoices in the day book and post to the various customer accounts in the sales ledger and finally post the day book totals to the accounts in the general ledger.

(NVQ Level 2)

20 The purchases day book and the purchases ledger

AIMS

- To be able to enter purchase invoices into the purchases day book.

- To be able to post the purchases day book to the purchases ledger and general ledger.

20.1 Purchase invoices

When organisations purchase goods or services from suppliers on credit they are sent a purchase invoice detailing the goods or services and their price.

In the previous chapter, Exhibit 19.1 showed an invoice raised by J Blake Foods, the supplier, and sent to D Poole, the buyer. This invoice is common to both parties since it details the goods supplied and the amount outstanding.

1 In the books of D Poole it is a **purchases invoice**.

2 In the books of J Blake Foods: it is a **sales invoice**.

20.2 Entering credit purchases into the purchases day book

Upon receipt of the purchase invoice for goods and services supplied on credit, the purchaser enters the details in his purchases day book. This book is merely a list showing the following:

- date of purchase;

- name of supplier from whom the goods were purchased;

- the reference number of the invoice;

- final amount of the invoice.

There is no need to show details of the goods bought in the purchases day book. This can be found by looking at the invoices themselves. Exhibit 20.1 is an example of a purchases day book.

Exhibit 20.1

Purchases Day Book				
		Invoice No.	Folio	(page 49)
2000				£
Sept	2 R Simpson	9/101		670
	8 B Hamilton	9/102		1,380
	19 C Brown	9/103		120
	30 K Gabriel	9/104		510
				2,680

20.3 Posting credit purchases to the purchases ledger

A separate purchases ledger is used to record credit purchase transactions. The double entry is as follows:

1 The credit purchases are posted one by one to the **credit** side of each supplier's account in the purchases ledger.

2 At the end of each period the total of the credit purchases is posted to the **debit** side of the purchases account in the general ledger.

Again, you may find it easier to use 'IN' and 'OUT' as shown in Chapter 5, to post these transactions, i.e. the goods purchased come from each supplier, therefore their account is entered on the 'OUT' side. The total purchases for the period are then entered on the 'IN' side of the purchases account since the goods are coming 'IN' to the business. This is illustrated in Exhibit 20.2.

Exhibit 20.2 Posting credit purchases

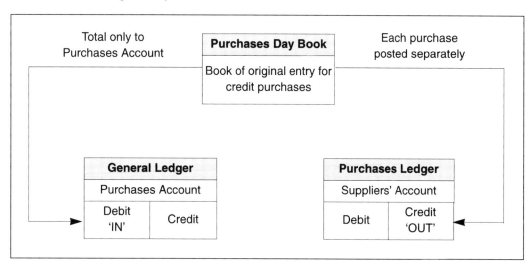

20.4 An example of posting credit purchases

The purchases day book in Exhibit 20.1 is now shown again. This time posting is made to the purchases ledger and the general ledger. Notice the completion of the folio columns.

Purchases Day Book				
		Invoice No	Folio	(page 49)
2000				£
Sept 2	R Simpson	9/101	PL 16	670
8	B Hamilton	9/102	PL 29	1,380
19	C Brown	9/103	PL 55	120
30	K Gabriel	9/104	PL 89	510
Transferred to purchases account			GL 63	2,680

Purchases Ledger
R Simpson Account   (page 16)

Dr | Cr

				£
	2000			
	Sept 2	Purchases	PJ 49	670

B Hamilton Account   (page 29)

Dr | Cr

				£
	2000			
	Sept 8	Purchases	PJ 49	1,380

C Brown Account   (page 55)

Dr | Cr

				£
	2000			
	Sept 19	Purchases	PJ 49	120

K Gabriel Account   (page 89)

Dr | Cr

				£
	2000			
	Sept 30	Purchases	PJ 49	510

General Ledger
Purchases Account   (page 63)

Dr | Cr

2000			£	
Sept 30	Credit purchases			
	for the month	PJ 49	2,680	

The purchases day book is often known also as the purchases book or the purchases journal.

NEW TERM

Purchase invoice A document prepared by the seller and sent to the purchaser whenever a business buys goods or services on credit. It gives details of the supplier and the customer, the goods purchased and their price.

STUDENT ACTIVITIES

20.1 B Mann has the following purchases for the month of May 2000:

2000

May	1	From K King: 4 radios at £30 each, 3 music centres at £160 each. Less 25 per cent trade discount.
May	3	From A Bell: 2 washing machines at £200 each, 5 vacuum cleaners at £60 each, 2 dish dryers at £150 each. Less 20 per cent trade discount.
May	15	From J Kelly: 1 music centre at £300 each, 2 washing machines at £250 each. Less 25 per cent trade discount.
May	20	From B Powell: 6 radios at £70 each, less 33⅓ per cent trade discount.
May	30	From B Lewis: 4 dish dryers at £200 each, less 20 per cent trade discount.

Required

(a) Enter up the purchases day book for the month.

(b) Post the transactions to the suppliers' accounts.

(c) Transfer the total to the purchases account.

20.2X A Rowland has the following purchases for the month of June 2003:

2003

June	2	From C Lee: 2 sets golf clubs at £250 each, 5 footballs at £20 each. Less 25 per cent trade discount.
June	11	From M Elliott: 6 cricket bats at £20 each, 6 ice skates at £30 each, 4 rugby balls at £25 each. Less 25 per cent trade discount.
June	18	From B Wood: 6 sets golf trophies at £100 each, 4 sets golf clubs at £300 each. Less 33⅓ per cent trade discount.
June	25	From B Parkinson: 5 cricket bats at £40 each. Less 25 per cent trade discount.
June	30	From N Francis: 8 goal post at £70 each. Less 25 per cent trade discount.

Required

(a) Enter up the purchases day book for the month.

(b) Post the items to the suppliers' accounts.

(c) Transfer the total to the purchases account.

20.3 C Phillips, a sole trader, has the following purchases and sales for March 2003:

2003

Mar	1	Bought from Smith Stores: silk £40, cotton £80, all less 25 per cent trade discount.
Mar	8	Sold to A Grantley: linen goods £28, woollen items £44. No trade discount.
Mar	15	Sold to A Henry: silk £36, linen £144, cotton goods £120. All less 20 per cent trade discount.
Mar	23	Bought from C Kelly: cotton £88, linen £52. All less 25 per cent trade discount.
Mar	24	Sold to D Sangster: linen goods £42, cotton £48. Less 10 per cent trade discount.
Mar	31	Bought from J Hamilton: linen goods £270 less 33⅓ per cent trade discount.

Required

(a) Prepare the purchases and sales day books of C Phillips from the above.

(b) Post the items to the personal accounts.

(c) Post the totals of the day books to the sales and purchases accounts.

20.4 G Bath, a retailer, purchased two items for resale in his shop, one of Product A and one of Product B. The following figures relate to these two items.

	Product A	Product B
Manufacturers' recommended retail price	£1,500	£4,000
Trade discount allowed to retailers	20%	25%

It is G Bath's intention to sell these two products at the recommended retail price.

You are required to:
(a) calculate the price which G Bath will pay for each product;
(b) calculate how much the gross profit will be on each product, if the products are sold at the recommended retail price;
(c) calculate the gross profit as a percentage of cost price for each product.
(Ignore VAT)

(RSA)

20.5X (a) You work in the purchases department of a manufacturing firm with responsibility for the approval of invoices prior to settlement by monthly cheque. List **five** steps which you would take in the processing of an invoice for approval.

(b) Your firm has received an invoice which shows the catalogue price of a small machine to be £360, subject to a trade discount of 25 per cent and a further 5 per cent cash discount if the invoice is settled within 14 days.

Your firm has purchased three of these machines and pays within seven days of receipt of the invoice. What is the total amount the firm should pay?
(Ignore VAT)

(RSA)

20.6 You are employed as sales assistant for a small company, Wilshaws Ltd, who sell farm supplies. As the company employs the minimum administrative staff, one of your duties is to look after the purchases ledger. This task involves entering the invoices received from suppliers into the day book and posting to the relevant creditors' accounts in the ledger.

Wilshaws's purchase invoices received for November 2004 are as follows:

Date		Supplier	Our Inv No	Total £
2004				
Nov	1	Bould & Co	SR 2103	104.26
Nov	3	Hambleton's	SR 2104	140.57
Nov	7	Farm Supplies Co	SR 2105	448.12
Nov	10	Worthington's Ltd	SR 2106	169.91
Nov	12	Sigley Bros	SR 2107	47.00
Nov	15	Hambleton's	SR 2108	259.09
Nov	20	Harlow's Mfr	SR 2109	84.96
Nov	20	Bould & Co	SR 2110	29.14
Nov	25	Clark & Robinson	SR 2111	61.63
Nov	30	T Adams Ltd	SR 2112	233.83

Required:
(a) Draw up a purchases day book, enter the invoices and total up at the end of the month.
(b) Open accounts for each of the suppliers, use your own folio numbers and post the invoices to the suppliers' accounts in the purchases ledger.
(c) Post the totals to the purchases account in the general ledger.

21 The returns day books

AIMS

- To be able to enter credit notes in the returns inwards day book.
- To be able to enter debit notes in the returns outwards day book.
- To be able to post the day book entries to the sales and purchases ledgers.

21.1 Returns inwards and credit notes

Customers may return goods to the supplier if they are faulty, damaged or not suitable for their requirements, where the consignment is incomplete when compared to the delivery note or where an overcharge has been made. When this happens the supplier will make an allowance to correct the situation. Occasionally a customer may decide to keep the goods but will expect a reduction in price as compensation.

Since customers will have been sent an invoice at the same time as the goods were delivered, they will be in debt to the supplier for the value of the goods. When a supplier makes an allowance for goods which have been returned or a reduction in price has been agreed, the supplier will issue a **credit note** to the customer. It is called a credit note since the customer's account will be credited with the amount of the allowance thereby showing a reduction in the amount owed by the customer. This procedure involving credit notes is necessary so that the various books of account which are maintained by the supplier and customer do, in fact, reflect the correct amount owed.

Exhibit 21.1 shows an example of a credit note – *see also* Chapter 18, section 18.8, which states that credit notes are usually printed in red to distinguish them from invoices.

21.2 Returns inwards day book

The credit notes are listed in a returns inwards day book. This is then used for posting the items, as follows:

1 **Sales ledger.** Credit the amount of credit notes, one by one, to the accounts of the customers in the sales ledger.

2 **General ledger.** At the end of the period the total of the returns inwards day book is posted to the debit of the returns inwards account.

Again, you may find it easier to use 'IN' and 'OUT' as discussed previously, i.e. goods returned to us are entered on the 'IN' side of the returns inwards account since the goods are coming 'IN' to us, and on the 'OUT' side of the individual customers' accounts.

Exhibit 21.1

```
                        CREDIT NOTE

              R GRANT (CATERING SUPPLIES)
              HIGHER SIDE PRESTON PR1 2NL

                                    Telephone: (01703) 33122
                                    Fax:       (01703) 22331

  D Poole
  Deansgate Restaurant              Credit Note No    0/37
  45 Charles Street                 Account No        P/4298
  Manchester M1 5ZN                 Date:  8 September 2000
```

Quantity	Per unit	Total
	£	£
2 cases Cape Glory Pears	25	50
Less 20% Trade Discount		10
		40

21.3 Example of a returns inwards day book

An example of a returns inwards day book showing the items posted to the sales ledger and the general ledger is shown below:

Returns Inwards Day Book

		Note No	Folio	(page 10)
2000				£
Sept 2	D Poole	9/37	SL 12	40
17	A Brewster	9/38	SL 58	120
19	C Vickers	9/39	SL 99	290
29	M Nelson	9/40	SL 112	160
Transferred to returns inwards account			GL 114	610

Sales Ledger

D Poole Account (page 12)

Dr				Cr
	2000			£
	Sept 8	Returns inwards	RI 10	40

A Brewster Account (page 58)

Dr				Cr
	2000			£
	Sept 17	Returns inwards	RI 10	120

Dr		C Vickers Account			(page 99) Cr
		2000			£
		Sept 19	Returns inwards	RI 10	290

Dr		M Nelson Account			(page 112) Cr
		2000			£
		Sept 29	Returns inwards	RI 10	160

General Ledger
Returns Inwards Account

Dr				(page 114) Cr
2000			£	
Sept 30	Returns for the month	RI 10	610	

Alternative names in use for the returns inwards day book are returns inwards journal or sales returns book.

21.4 Returns outwards and debit notes

If the supplier agrees, goods which have been bought previously by a customer may be returned. When this happens a **debit note** is sent by the customer to the supplier detailing the goods being returned and the reason for their return. Occasionally, the supplier may give the customer an allowance for goods previously sold, if for example the goods are faulty or damaged in some way. In these cases the customer will send the supplier a debit note. Exhibit 21.2 shows an example of a debit note.

21.5 Returns outwards day book

The debit notes are listed in a returns outwards day book. This is then used for posting the items, as follows:

1   **Purchases ledger.** Debit the amounts of debit notes, one by one, to the accounts of the suppliers in the purchases ledger.

2   **General ledger.** At the end of the period, the total of the returns outwards day book is posted to the credit of the returns outwards account.

Using 'IN' and 'OUT' the entries would be as follows: the goods returned by us to the supplier go 'IN' to the suppliers' accounts and come 'OUT' of the returns outwards account.

Exhibit 21.2

<table>
<tr><td colspan="4" align="center">**DEBIT NOTE**</td></tr>
<tr><td colspan="4" align="center">**R GRANT (CATERING SUPPLIES)**
HIGHER SIDE PRESTON PR1 2NL</td></tr>
<tr><td colspan="2"></td><td colspan="2">**Telephone:** (01703) 33122
Fax: (01703) 22331</td></tr>
<tr><td colspan="2">B Hamilton Food Supplies
20 Fourth Street
Kidderminster
KD2 4PP</td><td colspan="2">**Debit Note No**   9/34
Account No   H/3752
Date: 11 September 2000</td></tr>
<tr><td align="center">*Quantity*</td><td></td><td align="center">*Per unit*</td><td align="center">*Total*</td></tr>
<tr><td rowspan="2">4 cases Canadian Salmon
Less 25% Trade Discount

Returned damaged in transit</td><td></td><td align="center">£
60</td><td align="center">£
240
60
──
180
══</td></tr>
</table>

21.6 Example of a returns outwards day book

An example of a returns outwards day book, showing the items posted to the purchases ledger and the general ledger, is shown below.

Returns Outwards Day Book

2000			Note No	Folio	(page 7) £
Sept	11	B Hamilton	9/34	PL 29	180
	16	B Rose	9/35	PL 46	100
	28	C Blake	9/36	PL 55	30
	30	S Saunders	9/37	PL 87	360
Transferred to returns outwards account				GL 116	670

Purchases Ledger

B Hamilton Account   *(page 29)*

Dr					Cr
2000				£	
Sept	11	Returns outwards	RO 7	180	

B Rose Account   *(page 46)*

Dr					Cr
2000				£	
Sept	16	Returns outwards	RO 7	100	

			C Blake Account	(page 55)

Dr   Cr

| 2000 | | | £ | |
| Sept 28 | Returns outwards | RO 7 | 30 | |

S Saunders Account   *(page 87)*

Dr   Cr

| 2000 | | | £ | |
| Sept 30 | Returns outwards | RO 7 | 360 | |

General Ledger
Returns Outwards Account   *(page 116)*

Dr   Cr

| | | 2000 | | | £ |
| | | Sept 30 | Returns for the month | RO 7 | 670 |

Other names in use for the returns outwards day book are returns outwards journal or purchases returns book.

21.7 Double entry and returns

Exhibit 21.3 shows how double entry is made for both returns inwards and returns outwards.

Exhibit 21.3 Posting returns inwards and returns outwards

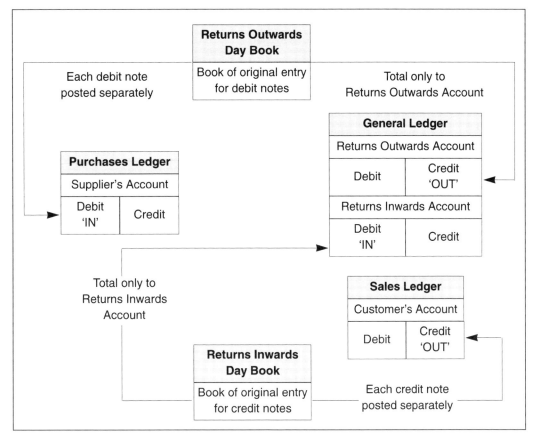

NEW TERM

Debit note A document sent by a business to a supplier giving details of a claim for an allowance in respect of damaged goods received or faulty goods, or where an overcharge has been made.

STUDENT ACTIVITIES

21.1 You are to enter up the purchases day book and the returns outwards day book from the following details, then to post the items to the relevant accounts in the purchases ledger and to show the transfers to the general ledger at the end of the month.

May 1 Credit purchase from H Lloyd £119
May 4 Credit purchases from the following: D Scott £98; A Simpson £114;
         A Williams £25; S Wood £56
May 7 Goods returned by us to the following: H Lloyd £16; D Scott £14
May 10 Credit purchase from A Simpson £59
May 18 Credit purchases from the following: M White £89; J Wong £67; H Miller £196;
         H Lewis £119
May 25 Goods returned by us to the following: J Wong £5; A Simpson £11
May 31 Credit purchases from: A Williams £56; C Cooper £98

21.2X Enter up the sales day book and the returns inwards day book from the following details. Then post to the customer's accounts and show the transfers to the general ledger.

June 1 Credit sales to: A Simes £188; P Tulloch £60; J Flynn £77; B Lopez £88
June 6 Credit sales to: M Howells £114; S Thompson £118; J Flynn £66
June 10 Goods returned to us by: A Simes £12; B Lopez £17
June 20 Credit sales to M Barrow £970
June 24 Goods returned to us by S Thompson £5
June 30 Credit sales to M Parkin £91

21.3 You are to enter the following items in the books, post to personal accounts, and show transfers to the general ledger:

July 1 Credit purchases from: K Hill £380; M Norman £500; N Senior £106
July 3 Credit sales to: E Rigby £510; E Phillips £246; F Thompson £356
July 5 Credit purchases from: R Morton £200; J Cook £180; D Edwards £410;
         C Davies £66
July 8 Credit sales to: A Green £307; H George £250; J Ferguson £185
July 12 Returns outwards to: M Norman £30; N Senior £16
July 14 Returns inwards from: E Phillips £18; F Thompson £22
July 20 Credit sales to: E Phillips £188; F Powell £310; E Lee £420
July 24 Credit purchases from: C Ferguson £550; K Ennevor £900
July 31 Returns inwards from E Phillips £27; E Rigby £30
July 31 Returns outwards to: J Cook £13; C Davies £11

21.4X Michael Newton runs a small printing business from rented premises in Newcastle. On 1 June 2002 his sales ledger contained the following debtors:

	£
T Cosgrove	416
C Moore	550
D Woolham	184

During the month of June 2002 the following transactions took place:

Sales invoices

June		Goods £
4	D Woolham	200
11	C Moore	312
23	T Cosgrove	178

Returns inward (credit notes)

June		Goods £
16	D Woolham	34
30	C Moore	143

Payments received by cheque

June		Cheque £	Discount allowed £
12	C Moore	536	14
28	D Woolham	179	5
30	T Cosgrove	402	14

Tasks

(a) Open ledger accounts for the debtors and enter the balances as at 1 June 2002.
(b) Draw up a sales day book and enter the invoices sent to the debtors during June 2002.
(c) Draw up a returns inwards day book and enter the returns for June 2002.
(d) Post the invoices and credit notes to the debtors' accounts in the sales ledger.
(e) Post the total sales to the sales account in the general ledger and the total returns to the returns inwards account in the general ledger.
(f) Finally, post the cash received and discounts allowed to the debtors' accounts and balance off at the end of June.

21.5 On 30 September 2000 the trial balance of Maurice Norman was as follows:

	Dr £	Cr £
Capital		9,151
A Birch	4,251	
H Jameson	1,260	
Cash at bank	7,200	
S Franklin		1,780
P Greenbank		670
E Oliver		1,110
	12,711	12,711

The following transactions, as shown in the books of original entry, took place during the month of October 2000.

Sales Day Book

Oct		£
9	A Birch	1,095
15	H Jameson	740
19	H Jameson	205

Purchases Day Book

Oct		£
8	E Oliver	348
12	S Franklin	206
23	E Oliver	1,050

Returns Outwards Day Book

Oct		£
19	S Franklin	80

Returns Inwards Day Book

Oct		£
24	H Jameson	140

Payments Made by Cheque

Oct	To	Discounts received £	Cheque value £
2	P Greenbank	67	603
18	S Franklin	120	1,080
29	E Oliver		1,110

Payments Received by Cheque

Oct	From	Discounts allowed £	Cheque value £
7	A Birch	151	4,100
23	H Jameson		900

You are required to:

(a) open the accounts in the appropriate ledgers for all the above items shown in the trial balance (including Bank) and enter the balances shown as at 30 September 2000;

(b) post the transactions indicated in the books of original entry direct to the appropriate ledger accounts, indicating the subdivisions of the ledger involved;

(c) balance the personal accounts and bank accounts as at the end of the month.

(RSA)

21.6 Framework Ltd is a small company which specialises in framing pictures, photographs, certificates, etc. At the beginning of the new financial year 1 January 2003 the following balances appeared in the ledgers:

Sales Ledger

	£
J Forbes (Fancy Gifts)	745 Dr
J Goodwin & Co	276 Dr
L & P Moss	390 Dr

Purchases Ledger

	£
M & P Fitzsimons	800 Cr
L Horne	450 Cr
M Ward & Sons	245 Cr

During January 2003 the following transactions took place:

Jan	Details
2	Purchased goods from L Horne £650
3	Purchased goods from M Ward & Sons £334
11	Sold goods to J Goodwin & Co £328
12	Received credit note from L Horne £42 in respect of goods returned as unsuitable
22	Purchased goods from M & P Fitzsimons £756
23	Sold goods to J Forbes (Fancy Gifts) £1,234
27	Sold goods to L & P Moss £2,500
28	Received credit note from M & P Fitzsimons £200

On 31 January the company received a cheque from J Forbes (Fancy Gifts) for £745 and a cheque for £200 on account from L & P Moss.

On the same date the company paid cheques to M & P Fitzsimons £500 on account and M Ward & Sons £245.

Tasks

(a) You are required to open personal accounts for the debtors and creditors and enter the outstanding balances at 1 January 2003.

(b) Post the above transactions to the accounts in the sales and purchases ledgers.

(c) Balance off the accounts at 31 January and bring the balances down.

Note: Day books and postings to the general ledger are not required.

22 Further considerations regarding sales and purchases

AIMS

- To be able to prepare statements of account.

- To understand how payment via credit cards is recorded in the books of account.

- To understand the procedures for carrying out internal checks within an organisation.

- To understand the term 'factoring'.

- To be able to authorise and code invoices for payment.

22.1 Statements of account

At the end of each month a **statement of account** is normally sent to each debtor showing the amount outstanding at the end of the month. This is really a copy of the debtor's account which appears in the supplier's books of account. The statement should show:

- the amount owing at start of month;

- the amount of each sales invoice sent to the debtor during the month;

- the amount of any credit notes sent to them during the month;

- all cash and cheques received from the debtor during the month;

- the amount due from them at the end of the month;

- the due date by which payment of the amount owing should be made.

The debtor will use the statement of account to check that their accounting records agree with the supplier's records. For example, if the supplier's records show an amount outstanding of £798, then, depending on items in transit between supplier and debtor, the account in the debtor's books should also show an amount owing to the creditor of £798. The statement also acts as a reminder to the debtor that they owe money to their supplier. Chapter 18, section 18.10, also discusses statements of account.

Exhibit 22.1 shows an example of a statement of account.

Exhibit 22.1

STATEMENT OF ACCOUNT

R GRANT (CATERING SUPPLIES)
HIGHER SIDE PRESTON PR1 2NL

Telephone: (01703) 33122
Fax: (01703) 22331

Accounts Department
D Poole
Deansgate Restaurant
45 Charles Street
Manchester M1 5ZN

Date: 30 September 2000

Date	Details	Debit	Credit	Balance
2000		£	£	£
Sept 1	Balance b/f			880
Sept 2	Invoice 30956	560		1,440
Sept 3	Returns 9/37		40	1,400
Sept 25	Bank		880	520
Sept 30	Balance owing c/f			520

All accounts due and payable within one month

22.2 Sales and purchases via credit cards

Various banks, building societies and other financial organisations issue credit cards to their customers. Examples are Visa, Access and American Express. The holder of the credit card purchases items or services without giving cash or cheques, but simply signs a special voucher used by the store or selling organisation. Later on, usually several weeks later, the credit card holder pays the organisation for which they hold the card, e.g. Visa, for all/or part of their previous month's outgoings.

The sellers of the goods or services then present the vouchers to the credit card company and the total of the vouchers, less commission, is paid to them by that credit card company.

In effect the sales are 'cash sales' for as far as the purchasers are concerned they have seen goods (or obtained services) and have received them, and in their eyes they have paid for them by using their credit card. Such sales are very rarely sales to anyone other than the general public, as compared with sales to professionals in a specific trade.

Once the customer has received the goods or services from the seller, they do not need to be entered in the sales ledger as a debtor. All the selling company is then interested in, from a recording point of view, is collecting the money from the credit card company.

The double entry needed is:

Sale of items via credit cards:	Dr: Credit card company
	Cr: Cash sales
Receipt of money from credit card company:	Dr: Bank
	Cr: Credit card company
Commission charged by credit card company:	Dr: Selling expenses
	Cr: Credit card company

Chapter 12, sections 12.10 and 12.11, gives a full description of credit cards.

22.3 Internal check

When sales invoices are being made out they should be scrutinised very carefully. A system is usually set up so that each stage of the preparation of the invoice is checked by someone other than the person whose job it is to send out the invoice. If this was not done then it would be possible for someone inside a firm to send out an invoice, as an instance, at a price less than the true price. Any difference could then be split between that person and someone outside the firm. If an invoice should have been sent to Ivor Twister & Co for £2,000, but the invoice clerk made it out deliberately for £200, then, if there was no cross-check, the difference of £1,800 could be split between the invoice clerk and Ivor Twister & Co.

Similarly outside firms could send invoices for goods which were never received by the firm. This might be in collaboration with an employee within the firm, but there are firms sending false invoices which rely on the firms receiving them being inefficient and paying for items never received. There have been firms sending invoices for such items as advertisements which have never been published. The cashier of the firm receiving the invoice, if the firm is an inefficient one, might possibly think that someone in the firm had authorised the advertisements and would pay the bill.

Besides these there are, of course, genuine errors, and these should also be detected. A system is, therefore, set up whereby the invoices have to be subject to scrutiny, at each stage, by someone other than the person who sends out the invoices or is responsible for paying them (refer to section 22.4).

Naturally in a small firm, simply because the office staff might be quite small, this cross-check may be in the hands of only one person other than the person who will pay it. A similar sort of check will be made in respect of sales invoices being sent out.

22.4 Authorisation and coding of invoices

Authorisation of purchase invoices

When purchase invoices are received from various suppliers of goods or services it is important to check the invoice for accuracy in the calculations and to ensure that the goods invoiced have been received and agree with the purchase order and specifications.

On receipt the purchase invoice should be numbered, recorded and stamped with an appropriate rubber stamp (*see* Exhibit 22.2), to enable the invoice to be checked and coded.

Exhibit 22.2

Invoice no	
Purchase order no	
Goods received	
Extensions	
Passed for payment	
Code	

Coding of invoices

After stamping, the invoice is sent to the department responsible for ordering the goods, the invoice is checked and if everything is satisfactory it is coded (*see* Exhibit 22.3), passed for payment by a department head and returned to the accounts department for entry into the books and payment.

Organisations using computer accounting systems need to give unique numbers to all their various accounts which the computer can easily recognise.

Exhibit 22.3

Purchases Ledger
    Suppliers are given account numbers, i.e.:

	Account number
Blackshaws	0207
Harvey Construction Ltd	0243
Morridge Products	0275
Travis and Humphreys	0284

Sales Ledger
    Customers' account numbers may be:

	Account number
Heath Manufacturing Ltd	1084
Office Supplies Ltd	1095
Seddon & Sons	1098
Yeoman's Supplies	1099

General Ledger
    Examples of account codes are as follows:

	Account number
Capital account	4003
Motor expenses account	4022
Printing and stationery account	4074
Sales account	4098

A register of code numbers allocated to specific accounts must be maintained and updated as necessary. This register may be a manual one or held on the computer system.

22.5 Factoring

One of the problems that many businesses face is the time taken by debtors to pay their accounts. Few businesses have so much cash available to them that they do not mind how long the debtor takes to pay. It is a fact that a lot of businesses which become bankrupt do so, not because the business is not making profits, but because the business has run out of cash funds. Once that happens, the confidence factor in business evaporates, and the business then finds that very few people will supply it with goods, and it also cannot pay its employees. Closure of the firm then happens fairly quickly in many cases.

In the case of debtors, the cash problem may be alleviated by using the services of a financial intermediary called a factor.

Factoring is a financial service designed to improve the cash flow of healthy, growing companies, enabling them to make better use of management time and the money tied up in trade credit to customers.

In essence, factors provide their clients with three closely integrated services covering sales accounting and collection, credit management which can include protection against bad debts, and the availability of finance against sales invoices.

NEW TERMS

Factoring A system used by a business to improve its cash flow. This involves 'selling' its debtors to a factoring company, which is then responsible for collecting debts as they become due and which keeps a percentage of the money collected, usually around 10 per cent.

Coding of invoices A process used, particularly in computerised accounting, to code the invoice to the supplier or purchaser, and also to the relevant account in the general ledger.

STUDENT ACTIVITIES

22.1 Study the statement shown in Exhibit 22.4.

Exhibit 22.4

		STATEMENT			
In account with		J Hunt			
		24 Coventry Road			
		Nuneaton C4			
Mr R J Cook					
14 Thorn Street					
Derby DE3					31 March
			£	£	£
February	1	Balance			130.42
"	6	Invoice 512	140.64		271.06
"	8	Cheque		127.16	
		Discount		3.26	140.64
"	12	Returns		16.30	124.34
"	26	Invoice 540	184.42		308.76
"	28	Undercharge	3.60		312.36

(a) Name the person who is supplying goods.

(b) Explain in simple terms the meaning of each item in the statement from February 1–26 and state the document used for the item on February 28 and the names of the sender and the receiver.

(c) Give the names of the debtor and the creditor and the amount owed on 28 February.

(RSA)

22.2 Why is it important to ensure that sales invoices are thoroughly checked before being sent out to the customer?

22.3 What is meant by the term 'factoring'?

22.4 You are employed as accounts clerk for Elder's Printing Co, 36 High Street, Shrewsbury SH4 8JK. One of your tasks is to prepare statements of account which are sent out to customers at the end of each month. Two of the customers' accounts are shown below:

Sales Ledger

Dr   *D Hammond Ltd Account*   Cr

2002			£	2002			£
Jan	1	Balance b/d	1,403	Jan	7	Bank	1,380
Jan	3	Sales	177	Jan	12	Credit note	23
Jan	10	Sales	527				
Jan	25	Sales	200				

Dr   *Alex Richards Ltd Account*   Cr

2002			£	2002			£
Jan	1	Balance b/d	346	Jan	7	Bank	292
Jan	7	Sales	27	Jan	7	Discount	8
Jan	9	Sales	521	Jan	12	Credit note	46
Jan	27	Sales	400				
Jan	31	Sales	53				

The addresses of the above customers are as follows:

D Hammond Ltd	Alex Richards Ltd
Bay House	Unit 12
Heath Road	Greenways Industrial Estate
Shrewsbury	Chester
SH7 3KL	CE21 9HU

Tasks:
(*a*) Balance each of the above accounts off and state the amount owing by each of the customers.
(*b*) Draft a statement of account to be sent to each customer.

22.5X On 1 May 2004 T Gray Ltd's purchases ledger showed a credit balance of £789 on S Brown's account. In S Brown's books his sales ledger showed T Gray Ltd as owing £789. The following transactions occurred during May:

May   11   T Gray Ltd paid a cheque for £777 in full settlement of the account, and this was received by S Brown on 13 May.

May   15   T Gray Ltd buys £480 goods on credit from S Brown, they are sent by Brown on that date and reach T Gray Ltd on 18 May.

May   22   Some of the goods just bought by T Gray Ltd are found to be faulty and are returned on this date, reaching Brown on 24 May. The allowance made by Brown is £24.

May   29   Goods to the value of £1,560 are sold by Brown on credit to T Gray Ltd, the goods being sent on this date and reaching T Gray Ltd on 2 June.

May   30   T Gray Ltd sends a cheque for £200 on account to Brown, but unfortunately sends it by second-class post. The cheque is received by Brown on 3 June.

May   31   A further £35 goods are returned to Brown by T Gray Ltd on this date, arriving at Brown's premises on 3 June.

All transactions are recorded at the time of receipt or despatch in each firm. You are required to:

(a) Write up the account of T Gray Ltd as it would appear in the books of S Brown for the month of May 2004. Balance off as at 31 May 2004.

(b) Write up the account of S Brown as it would appear in the books of T Gray Ltd for the month of May 2004. Balance off as at 31 May 2004.

(c) Draw up the statement that S Brown would send to T Gray Ltd at the end of the month.

(d) Reconcile the balances on the two accounts as at 31 May 2004.

23 Value added tax (sales tax)

AIMS

- To be able to enter value added tax (VAT) in the necessary books of account.

- To be able to distinguish between taxable businesses and other businesses where special regulations apply.

- To be able to prepare sales invoices including charges for VAT.

23.1 Introduction

This chapter looks at the accounting requirements when a tax is levied on sales by the government. The system in operation in the United Kingdom is called value added tax (VAT). Students studying in the UK will be examined on their knowledge and understanding of this system. For students studying in other countries it is important to be familiar with the appropriate sales tax in operation and also advisable to seek the advice of a teacher or lecturer.

Value added tax (VAT) is a tax on turnover, not on profits. It is described as an indirect tax, and ultimately the tax is paid by the final consumer of the goods or services. VAT is administered by HM Customs and Excise department of the government.

23.2 The scope of VAT

VAT is charged on the supply of most goods or services by a VAT registered business. A VAT registered business may be a sole proprietor, partnership or limited company.

Not all goods and services are subject to VAT. Some goods and services are **zero rated**. This means that VAT is charged at the rate of 0%. Examples of zero-rated supplies are:

- human and animal food

- water and sewerage charges

- books and periodicals

- clothing and footwear for young children.

Some goods and services are **exempt** from VAT. This means such supplies are outside the scope of VAT, and VAT cannot be charged. Examples of exempt supplies are:

- financial services
- postal services provided by the post office
- education.

It is very important to differentiate between zero-rated and exempt supplies, as we will see later.

23.3 The rate of VAT

The rate of VAT is decided by Parliament in the Finance Acts, passed each year after the budget(s). The rates at the publication of this book were:

All zero-rated goods and services	0%
Fuel and power for domestic or charity use only	5%
All other standard rated supplies	17.5%

The VAT charged *by* a business on its supplies (**outputs**), is called **output VAT**, and is payable by the business to the Customs and Excise.

The VAT charged *to* a business on its purchases and expenses (**inputs**), is called **input VAT**, and is reclaimable by the business from the Customs and Excise.

23.4 Example: how the VAT system works

A toymaker manufactures toys from scraps of material and sells them to a wholesaler for £200 plus VAT. The wholesaler sells these toys to a chain of retailers for £280 plus VAT, who in turn retail the toys in their shops for £400 plus VAT.

1   The toymaker accounts for VAT as follows:

	Net £	VAT @ 17.5% £
Sale of toys to wholesaler	200.00	35.00
Cost	–	–
VAT payable to Customs and Excise		35.00

2   The wholesaler accounts for VAT as follows:

	Net £	VAT @ 17.5% £
Sale of toys to retailer	280.00	49.00
Cost of toys	200.00	35.00
VAT payable to Customs and Excise		14.00

3   The retailer accounts for VAT as follows:

	Net £	VAT @ 17.5% £
Sale of toys to the public	400.00	70.00
Cost of toys	280.00	49.00
VAT payable to Customs and Excise		21.00

It will be seen that the total output VAT paid to Customs and Excise is £70.00, as charged by the retailer to its customers. The VAT, however, has been paid to the Customs and Excise at various stages in the distribution of the toys as follows:

	£
Toymaker has paid	35.00
Wholesaler has paid	14.00
Retailer has paid	21.00
	70.00

23.5 Zero-rated supplies

In section 23.2 the concept of zero-rated supplies was introduced. The important matter to note is that items are charged to VAT at 0 per cent which is a rate of VAT. In some European Union countries, supplies which are zero-rated in the UK, are charged to VAT at that country's VAT rate.

As the supplies are sold at a rate of VAT (even though it is 0 per cent), any input VAT incurred relating to the business can all be reclaimed.

Example 1

A book dealer sells £100,000 worth of books in a year, and during that year, purchases book shelving for £10,000 plus VAT.

The VAT reclaimable is therefore:

	Net	VAT @ 17.5%
	£	£
Sales	100,000	Nil
Purchases	10,000	1,750
VAT reclaimable		1,750

23.6 Exempt supplies

In section 23.2 the concept of exempt supplies was also introduced. There are two types of exempt supplies:

1   supplies of specifically exempted items, examples of which are stated in section 23.2;

2   all supplies of goods and services by non-VAT registered businesses, for example:

(a)   exempt businesses like bank and insurance companies;

(b)   businesses who do not need to register, as their turnover is below the VAT registration limit.

The important matter to note is that input VAT directly attributable to exempt supplies, or non-VAT registered businesses, cannot be reclaimed from the Customs and Excise.

Example 2

An insurance company sells £100,000 worth of insurance, and purchases furniture for its office for £10,000 plus VAT.

This business cannot reclaim the £1,750 input VAT on the furniture as it does not have any vatable supplies. The total amount paid for the furniture of £11,750 will be the cost to the business.

Note: Contrast this with the zero-rated supplier in Example 1 above who was able to reclaim £1,750.

23.7 Partly exempt traders

Some VAT registered traders will sell some goods which are exempt from VAT, and some which are either standard rated or zero-rated. These businesses may reclaim part of the input VAT paid by them, but not all of it. The rules are complicated, but in essence, the input VAT reclaimable will be proportionate to the standard and zero-rated percentage of the business's total turnover.

23.8 Firms which can recover VAT paid

Taxable firms

Value added tax and sales invoices

A taxable firm will have to add VAT to the value of the sales invoices. It must be pointed out that this is based on the amount of the invoice *after* any trade discount has been deducted. Exhibit 23.1 is an invoice drawn up from the following details:

On 2 March 2000, W Frank & Co, Hayburn Road, Stockport, sold the following goods to R Bainbridge Ltd, 267 Star Road, Colchester: Bainbridge's order no was A/4/559, for the following items:

> 220 Rolls T56 Black Tape at £6 per 10 rolls
> 600 Sheets R64 Polythene at £10 per 100 sheets
> 7000 Blank Perspex B49 Markers at £20 per 1000

All of these goods are subject to VAT at the rate of 17.5 per cent.

A trade discount of 25 per cent is given by Frank & Co. The sales invoice is numbered 8851.

Exhibit 23.1

W Frank & Co
Hayburn Road
Stockport SK2 5DB

To: R Bainbridge   INVOICE No 8851
        267 Star Road
        Colchester CO1 1BT
                                                        VAT Registration No: 469 2154 42
                                                        Date/tax point: 2 March 2000
                                                        Your order no: A/4/559
                                                        Account no: F/1896

	£
200 Rolls T56 Black Tape @ £6 per 10 rolls	120
600 Sheets R64 Polythene @ £10 per 100 sheets	60
7,000 Blank Perspex B49 Markers @ £20 per 1,000	140
	320
Less Trade Discount 25%	80
	240
Add VAT	42
	282

The sales day book will normally have an extra column for the VAT contents of the sales invoice (*see* Chapter 24). This is needed to make it easier to account for VAT. The entry of several sales invoices in the sales book and in the ledger accounts can now be examined.

W Frank & Co sold the following goods during the month of March 2000:

			Total of invoice, after trade discount deducted but before VAT added	VAT 17.5%
2000			£	£
March	2	R Bainbridge Ltd (*see* Exhibit 23.1)	240	42
March	10	S Lange & Son	200	35
March	17	K Bishop	160	28
March	31	R Andrews & Associates	80	14

Sales Day Book						Page 58
		Invoice No	Folio	Total	Net	VAT
2000				£	£	£
March 2 R Bainbridge Ltd		8851	SL 77	282	240	42
March 10 S Lange & Son		8852	SL 119	235	200	35
March 17 K Bishop		8853	SL 185	188	160	28
March 31 R Andrews & Associates		8854	SL 221	94	80	14
Transferred to General Ledger				799	680	119
					GL 76	GL 90

Now that the sales day book has been written up, the next task is to enter the amounts of the invoices in the individual customer's accounts in the sales ledger. These are simply charged with the full amounts of the invoices including VAT.

As an instance of this K Bishop will be shown as owing £188. When he pays his account he will pay £188. It will then be the responsibility of W Frank & Co to ensure that the figure of £28 VAT in respect of this item is included in the total cheque payable to the Customs and Excise.

Sales Ledger

R Bainbridge Ltd Account   Page 77

Dr						Cr
2000				£		
March	2	Sales	SB 58	282		

S Lange & Son Account   Page 119

Dr						Cr
2000				£		
March	10	Sales	SB 58	235		

K Bishop Account   Page 185

Dr						Cr
2000				£		
March	17	Sales	SB 58	188		

Dr   Cr

2000			£	
March 31	Sales	SB 58	94	

In total, therefore, the personal accounts have been debited with £799, this being the total of the amounts which the customers will have to pay. The actual sales of the firm are not £799, the amount which is actually sales is £680, the other £119 being simply the VAT that W Frank & Co are collecting on behalf of the government.

The double entry is made in the general ledger:

1   Credit the sales account with the sales content only, i.e. £680

2   Credit the value added tax account with the VAT content only, i.e. £119

These are shown as:

General Ledger

Sales Account   Page 76

Dr   Cr

	2000			£
	March 31	Credit sales		
		for the month	SB 58	680

Value Added Tax Account   Page 90

Dr   Cr

	2000			£
	March 31	Sales book:		
		VAT content	SB 58	119

Value added tax and purchases

In the case of a taxable firm, the firm will have to add VAT to its sales invoices, but it will **also** be able to get a refund of the VAT which it pays on its purchases.

Instead of paying VAT to the Customs and Excise and then claiming a refund of the VAT on purchases, the firm can set off the amount paid as VAT on purchases against the amount payable as VAT on sales. This means that only the difference has to be paid to the Customs and Excise. It is shown as:

£

1   Output VAT collected on sales invoices   xxx
2   *Less* Input VAT already paid on purchases   xxx
3   Net amount to be paid to the Customs and Excise   xxx

In certain fairly rare circumstances **1** may be less than **2**. If that was the case then it would be the Customs and Excise that would refund the difference **3** to the firm. Such a settlement between the firm and the Customs and Excise will take place at least every three months.

The recording of purchases in the purchases day book and purchases ledger follows a similar method to that of sales, but with the personal accounts being debited instead of credited. This can be seen in the records of purchases for the same firm whose sales have been dealt with, W Frank & Co. The firm made the following purchases for March 2000.

			Total invoice, after trade discount deducted but before VAT added	VAT 17.5%
2000			£	£
March	1	E Lyal Ltd (see Exhibit 23.2)	200	35
March	11	P Portsmouth & Co	280	49
March	24	J Davidson	40	7
March	29	B Cofie & Son Ltd	80	14

Before looking at the recording of these in the purchases records, compare the first entry for E Lyal Ltd with Exhibit 23.2 to ensure that the correct amounts have been shown.

Exhibit 23.2

E Lyal Ltd
College Avenue
St Albans
Hertfordshire ST2 4JA

INVOICE No K 453/A

Date/tax point: 1 March 2000
Your order No: BB/667
VAT Reg No: 236 4054 56

To: W Frank & Co   Terms: Strictly net 30 days
        Hayburn Road
        Stockport

	£
50 metres of BYC plastic 1 metre wide × £3.60 per metre	180
1,200 metal tags 500mm × 10p each	120
	300
Less Trade Discount 33 ⅓%	100
	200
Add VAT 17½%	35
	235

The purchases day book can now be entered up.

Purchases Day Book								*Page 38*
			Folio		Total		Net	VAT
2000					£		£	£
March	1	E Lyal Ltd	PL	15	235		200	35
March	11	P Portsmouth & Co	PL	70	329		280	49
March	24	J Davidson	PL	114	47		40	7
March	29	B Cofie & Son Ltd	PL	166	94		80	14
Transferred to General Ledger					705	GL 54	600	GL 90 105

These are entered in the purchases ledger. Once again there is no need for the VAT to be shown as separate amounts in the accounts of the suppliers.

Purchases Ledger

E Lyal Ltd Account   *Page 15*

Dr					Cr
	2000				£
	March	1	Purchases	PB 38	235

In the final accounts of W Frank & Co the following entries would be made:

Trading account for the month ended 31 March 2000:
    Debited with £600 as a transfer from the purchases account.
    Credited with £680 as a transfer from the sales account.

Balance sheet as at 31 March 2000:
    Balance of £14 (credit) on the VAT account would be shown as a current liability, as it represents the amount owing to the Customs and Excise for VAT.

Zero-rated firms

These firms:

1   do not have to add VAT on to their sales invoices, as their rate of VAT is zero or nil;

2   they can, however, reclaim from the Customs and Excise any VAT paid on goods or services bought.

Accordingly, because of **1** no VAT is entered in the sales day book. VAT on sales does not exist. Because of **2** the purchases day book and purchases ledger will appear exactly in the same manner as for taxable firms, as already shown in the case of W Frank & Co.

The VAT account will only have debits in it, being the VAT on purchases. Any balance on this account will be shown in the balance sheet as a debtor.

P Portsmouth & Co Account   *Page 70*

Dr					Cr
	2000				£
	March	11	Purchases	PB 38	329

J Davidson Account   *Page 114*

Dr					Cr
	2000				£
	March	24	Purchases	PB 38	47

B Cofie & Son Ltd   *Page 166*

Dr					Cr
	2000				£
	March	29	Purchases	PB 38	94

The personal accounts have been credited with a total of £705, this being the total of the amounts which W Frank & Co will have to pay to them.

The actual cost of purchases is not, however, £705. You can see that the correct amount is £600. The other £105 is the VAT which the various firms are collecting for the Customs and Excise. This amount is also the figure for VAT which is reclaimable from the Customs and Excise by W Frank & Co. The debit entry in the purchases account is, therefore, £600, as this is the actual cost of the goods to the firm. The other £105 is entered on the debit side of the VAT account.

Notice that there is already a credit of £119 in the VAT account in respect of the VAT added to sales.

General Ledger

Purchases Account   *Page 54*

Dr					Cr
2000		£			
March 31	Credit purchases for the month	600			

Value Added Tax Account   *Page 90*

Dr					Cr
2000		£	2000		£
March 31	Purchases day book: VAT content PB 38	105	March 31	Sales day book: VAT content SB 58	119
March 31	Balance c/d	14			
		119			119
			April 1	Balance b/d	14

23.9 VAT and cash discounts

Where a cash discount is offered for speedy payment, VAT is calculated on an amount represented by the value of the invoice less such a discount. Even if the cash discount is lost because of late payment, the VAT will not change.

Exhibit 23.3 shows an example of such a sales invoice, assuming a cash discount offered of 2.5 per cent.

Exhibit 23.3

ATC Ltd
18 High Street
London WC2E 9AN

INVOICE No ZT48910

VAT Reg No: 313 5924 71
Date/tax point: 11 May 2002
Your order no: TS/778

To: R Noble
        Belsize Road
        Edgeley
        Stockport

	£
500 paper dispensers @ £20 each	10,000
Less Trade Discount @ 20%	2,000
	8,000
Add VAT 17.5%	1,365 *
	9,365

Note: The VAT has been calculated on the net price £8,000 *less* cash discount 2.5 per cent,
   i.e. £8,000 (less 2.5% cash discount of £200)   = £7,800
   VAT at 17.5% on £7,800   = £1,365

23.10 Firms which cannot get refunds of VAT paid

As these firms do not add VAT on to the value of their sales invoices, there is obviously no entry for VAT in the sales day book or the sales ledger. They do not get a refund of VAT on purchases. This means that there will not be a VAT account. All that will happen is that VAT paid is included as part of the cost of the goods bought.

In the purchases day book, goods bought for £80 + VAT £14 will simply appear as purchases £94. The double entry will show a credit of £94 in the supplier's account.

Both the sales and purchases records will, therefore, not show anything separately for VAT. For comparison let us look at the accounting records of two firms for an item which costs £120 + VAT £21, the item being bought from D Oswald Ltd. The records for the month of May 2003 would appear as follows:

1   Firm which cannot recover VAT:

Purchases Day Book

			£
2003			
May	16	D Oswald Ltd	141

Purchases Ledger
D Oswald Ltd Account

Dr							Cr
				2003			£
				May	16	D Oswald Ltd	141

General Ledger
Purchases Account

Dr			£				£
2003				2003			
May	31	Credit purchases for the month	141	May	31	Transfer to trading account	141

Trading Account for the month ended 31 May 2003 (extract)

	£	
Purchases	141	

2   Firm which can recover VAT (e.g. zero-rated firm):

Purchases Day Book

			Net	VAT
			£	£
2003				
May	16	D Oswald Ltd	120	21

Purchases Ledger
D Oswald Ltd Account

Dr							Cr
				2003			£
				May	16	Purchases	141

General Ledger

Purchases Account

Dr					Cr
2003			£	2003	£
May	31	Credit purchases for the month	120	May 31 Transfer to trading account	120

Value Added Tax Account

Dr				Cr
2003			£	
May	31	Purchases book	21	

Trading Account for the month ended 31 May 2003 (extract)

	£	
Purchases	120	

Balance Sheet as at 31 May 2003 (extract)

	£	
Debtor	21	

23.11 VAT included in gross amount

Often only the gross amount of an item will be known, this figure being made up of the net amount plus VAT. To find the amount of VAT which has been added to the net amount, a formula capable of being used with any rate of VAT is:

$$\frac{\% \text{ rate of VAT}}{100 + \% \text{ rate of VAT}} \times \text{Gross amount} = \text{VAT in £}$$

Suppose that the gross amount of sales was £940 and the rate of VAT was 17.5 per cent. Find the amount of VAT and the net amount before VAT was added. Using the formula:

$$\frac{17.5}{100 + 17.5} \times £940 = \frac{17.5}{117.5} \times £940 = £140$$

Therefore, the net amount was £800, which with VAT £140 added becomes £940 gross.

23.12 VAT on items other than sales and purchases

VAT is not just paid on purchases. It is also payable on many items of expense and on the purchase of fixed assets.

Firms which **can** get refunds of VAT paid will not include VAT as part of the cost of the expense or fixed asset. Firms which **cannot** get refunds of VAT paid will include the VAT cost as part of the expense or fixed asset. For example, two firms buying similar items would treat the following items as shown:

	Firm which can reclaim VAT			Firm which cannot reclaim VAT	
Buys Machinery	Debit Machinery	£200		Debit Machinery	£235
£200 + VAT £35	Debit VAT Account	£35			
Buys Stationery	Debit Stationery	£160		Debit Stationery	£188
£160 + VAT £28	Debit VAT Account	£28			

23.13 VAT owing

VAT owing by or to the firm can be included with debtors or creditors, as the case may be. There is no need to show the amount(s) owing as separate items.

23.14 Relief from VAT on bad debts

It is possible to claim relief on any debt which is more than one year old and has been written off in the accounts. Should the debt later be paid, the VAT refunded will then have to be paid back to the Customs and Excise.

23.15 VAT Records

VAT records must be retained by the business for six years.

NEW TERMS

Exempted firms Firms which do not have to add VAT to the price of goods and services supplied by them and which cannot obtain a refund of VAT paid on goods and services purchased by them.

Inputs The value of goods and services purchased by a business.

Input tax The VAT charged to a business on its purchases and expenses (inputs).

Outputs The value of goods and services sold to a business.

Output tax The VAT charged *by* a business on its supplies (outputs).

Value added tax (VAT) A tax charged on the supply of most goods and services. The tax is borne by the final consumer of the goods or services, not by the business selling them to the consumer. VAT is administered by the Customs and Excise.

Zero-rated firms Firms which do not have to add VAT to goods and services supplied by them to others, and which receive a refund of VAT paid on goods and services purchased by them.

STUDENT ACTIVITIES

23.1 On 1 May 2001, D Wilson Ltd, 1 Hawk Green Road, Stockport, sold the following goods on credit to G Christie & Son, The Golf Shop, Hole-in-One Lane, Marple, Cheshire:

Order No A/496
3 sets of 'Boy Michael' golf clubs at £240 per set.
150 Watson golf balls at £8 per 10 balls.
4 Faldo golf bags at £30 per bag.
Trade discount is given at the rate of 33⅓%.
All goods are subject to VAT at 17.5%.

(a) Prepare the sales invoice to be sent to G Christie & Son. The invoice number will be 10586.
(b) Show the entries in the personal ledgers of D Wilson Ltd and G Christie & Son.

23.2 The following sales have been made by S Thompson Ltd during the month of June 2004. All the figures are shown net after deducting trade discount, but before adding VAT at the rate of 17.5%.

2004
August	1	to M Sinclair & Co	£160
August	8	to M Brown & Associates	£240
August	19	to A Axton Ltd	£80
August	31	to T Christie	£40

You are required to enter up the sales day book, sales ledger and general ledger in respect of the above items for the month.

23.3 The following sales and purchases were made by R Colman Ltd during the month of May 2002.

			Net	VAT added
2002			£	£
May	1	Sold goods on credit to B Davies & Co	160	28
May	4	Sold goods on credit to C Grant Ltd	200	35
May	10	Bought goods on credit from:		
		G Cooper & Son	400	70
		J Wayne Ltd	240	42
May	14	Bought goods on credit from B Lugosi	40	7
May	16	Sold goods on credit to C Grant Ltd	120	21
May	23	Bought goods on credit from S Hayward	40	7
May	31	Sold goods on credit to B Karloff	80	14

Enter up the sales and purchases day books, sales and purchases ledgers and the general ledger for the month of May 2002. Carry the balance down on the VAT account.

23.4X On 1 March 2003 C Black, Curzon Road, Manchester, sold the following goods on credit to J Booth, 89 Andrew Lane, Stockport. Order No 1697.

20,000 Coils Sealing Tape	@ £4.70 per 1,000 coils
40,000 Sheets Bank A5	@ £4.50 per 1,000 sheets
30,000 Sheets Bank A4	@ £4.20 per 1,000 sheets

All goods are subject to VAT at 17½%.

(a) Prepare the sales invoice to be sent to J Booth.
(b) Show the entries in the personal ledgers of J Booth and C Black.

23.5 C Emberson, a sole trader, buys and sells goods on credit. A bank account is kept through which all amounts received and paid are entered. On 30 November 2005 the following balances remain in the books:

	£	£
C Hills		154
L Lowe		275
K Harris	330	
Bank	740	
Capital		641
	1,070	1,070

You are required to:

(a) open appropriate ledger accounts for the above and enter the balances as at 1 December 2005;

(b) post the transactions indicated in the day books direct to the ledger and open any other accounts which may be required;

(c) balance the accounts where necessary and extract a trial balance on 31 December 2005.

Purchases Day Book

December		Net	VAT	Total
13	C Hills	80	14	94
20	C Hills	160	28	188
21	L Lowe	40	7	47
		280	49	329

Sales Day Book

December		Net	VAT	Total
11	K Harris	240	42	282
15	K Harris	80	14	94
		320	56	376

Payments received

December		£
16	K Harris	612

Payments made

December		£
8	C Hills	154
15	Printing	20

(RSA)

23.6X At 1 February 2004 K Murphy's debtors included D Hanson £103.30 and P Newbury £48.60. His creditors included E Goodman £178.20. The balance on Murphy's value added tax account was £237.14 credit. During February his credit transactions with those named above were as follows:

		Sales					Purchases	
Feb	4	P Newbury	£217.10		Feb	6	E Goodman	£83.00
Feb	20	D Hanson	£133.50					

All of these transactions were subject to value added tax at 17.5 per cent. In the bank account in Murphy's books were recorded the following:

		Debit					Credit	
Feb	8	P Newbury	£48.60		Feb	10	E Goodman	£178.20

You are required to write up in the books of Murphy the accounts of Hanson, Newbury and Goodman, and the VAT account, all for the month of February 2004.

(RSA)

23.7 The following is a summary of purchases and sales and the relevant figures for VAT for the three months ended 31 March 2005.

Purchases

		£	VAT £
2005	January	20,000	3,500
	February	21,000	3,675
	March	22,000	3,850

Sales	£	£
January	21,000	3,675
February	20,000	3,500
March	15,000	2,625

Required

(a) Write up and balance the VAT account for the three months to 31 March 2005.

(b) Explain briefly the significance of the balance and how it will be cleared.

(RSA)

23.8 Comart Supplies Ltd recently purchased from Ace Import Ltd 10 printers originally priced at £200 each. A 10 per cent trade discount was negotiated together with a 5 per cent cash discount if payment was made within 14 days. Calculate the following:

(a) the total of the trade discount;

(b) the total of the cash discount;

(c) the total of the VAT.

(AAT (part of Central Assessment))

23.9 A manufacturer sells a product to a wholesaler for £200 plus VAT of £35. The wholesaler sells the same product to a retailer for £280 plus VAT of £49. The retailer then sells the product to a customer for £320 plus VAT of £56. What is the amount of VAT collectable by the Customs and Excise?

(AAT (part of Central Assessment))

23.10 (a) Should the total of the VAT column in the petty cash book be debited or credited to the VAT account in the general ledger?

(b) For what period of time must VAT records be retained?

(c) MMS Textiles Ltd is a VAT registered firm. Should they charge VAT on good supplied to a customer who is not VAT registered?

(d) What bookkeeping entries would be necessary to record a cash refund of £94 (inclusive of VAT) to a customer?

(AAT (part of Central Assessment))

23.11X Bloomers Ltd purchases 40 glass crystal vases for £7.50 each plus VAT. The vases are then all sold to a hotel gift shop for £517 inclusive of VAT. How much is owed by Bloomers to the Customs and Excise in respect of the vases?

(AAT (part of Central Assessment))

24 Analytical sales and purchases day books and analytical cash books

AIMS

- To be able to enter invoices into analytical sales and purchases day books.

- To be able to post transactions from analytical sales and purchases day books to the personal accounts in the sales and purchases ledgers.

- To be able to post totals from the analytical day books to the general ledger.

- To be able to enter transactions into an analytical cash book and post the entries into the general ledger.

24.1 Introduction

In Chapters 19 and 20 the sales and purchases day books were shown using only one total column for the value of the goods sold or purchased. Sometimes goods are subject to VAT, as discussed in Chapter 23. Here you will have noticed that additional columns were used to take account of the VAT, as shown in the sales day book in Exhibit 23.1 and the purchases day book in Exhibit 23.2.

In addition to accounting for VAT many businesses find it useful to analyse their sales and purchases between different types of goods bought and sold or perhaps between different departments. For example, a coffee shop may sell refreshments and gifts and wish to ascertain the profit on the two different sales areas. In this example it would be advantageous to analyse both sales and purchases to reflect the goods/services bought or sold in each area. The purchases day book could be ruled as follows:

Purchases Day Book						
Date	Details	Folio	Total	Gifts	Food	VAT
			£	£	£	£

24.2 Entering sales invoices into a columnar sales day book

When a business requires additional information from its records then the books can easily be adapted to meet the particular needs.

Let us consider a retail computer shop which sells hardware and software to the public, local businesses and schools.

The proprietor, Mr Harlow, wishes to monitor the sales of each of these lines separately.

Exhibit 24.1 shows an example of Mr Harlow's **columnar sales day book**.

Exhibit 24.1

Sales Day Book						
Date	Details	Folio	Total	Software	Hardware	VAT
			£	£	£	£
April 1	Mount Hey School	SL 1	705		600	105
April 3	Ashby Marketing	SL 2	564	480		84
April 15	Davenport Manufacturing	SL 3	4,700		4,000	700
April 20	St James College	SL 4	23,500		20,000	3,500
			29,469	480	24,600	4,389
				GL 1	GL 2	GL 3

24.3 Posting credit sales

Each sale now has to be posted to the individual debtors' accounts in the sales ledger as follows:

1 The total of each sales invoice (i.e. the net price of the goods plus VAT) is posted to each individual debtor's account on the debit side, since the goods are going 'IN' to their account.

2 At the end of the period the sales day book is added up and the totals posted on the credit side, or 'OUT' side of the following accounts:

   - sales of software account

   - sales of hardware account

   - VAT account.

This is shown in Exhibit 24.2.

Exhibit 24.2 Posting credit sales

Sales Ledger
Mount Hey School Account

Dr				SL 1 Cr
April	1	Sales	£ 705	

Ashby Marketing Co Account

Dr				SL 2 Cr
April	3	Sales	£ 564	

Davenport Manufacturing Co Account

Dr				SL 3 Cr
April	15	Sales	£ 4,700	

St James College Account

Dr				SL 4 Cr
April	22	Sales	£ 23,500	

General Ledger
Sale of Software Account

Dr			GL 1 Cr
	April 30	Credit Sales for April	£ 480

Sale of Hardware Account

Dr			GL 2 Cr
	April 30	Credit Sales for April	£ 24,600

VAT Account

Dr			GL 3 Cr
	April 30	VAT on credit sales for April	£ 4,389

24.4 Entering purchases invoices into a columnar purchases day book

Another business might wish to monitor its purchases which may include the purchase of goods for resale and business expenses such as electricity, motor expenses, etc.

Exhibit 24.3 illustrates how a business would analyse its purchases invoices.

Exhibit 24.3

				Purchases Day Book			
Date	Details	Folio	Total	Goods	Motor Exp	Stationery	VAT
			£	£	£	£	£
Nov 1	Bould & Co	PL 1	4,230	3,600			630
Nov 10	Sigley's (Stat)	PL 2	47			40	7
Nov 17	T Adams Ltd	PL 3	940	800			140
Nov 30	Robinson's Garage	PL 4	188		160		28
			5,405	4,400	160	40	805
				GL 1	GL 2	GL 3	GL 4

24.5 Posting credit purchases

Each purchase now has to be posted to the individual creditors' accounts in the purchase ledger as follows:

1   The **total** of each purchase invoice (i.e. the net price of the goods plus VAT) is posted to each individual creditor's account on the **Credit** side, since the goods are coming 'OUT' of their accounts.

2   At the end of the period the purchases day book is added up and the totals posted on the **Debit** side, or 'IN' side of the following accounts:

- purchases account
- motor expenses account
- stationery account
- VAT account.

This is shown in Exhibit 24.4.

24.6 Analytical cash book

Many businesses use an analytical cash book in a similar way to the analytical petty cash book. This has several advantages.

One advantage is that it enables the business to have the use of a VAT (value added tax) column to record payments/receipt of VAT. At the end of the month the VAT columns are added up and the totals transferred to the VAT account in the general ledger. This VAT column is especially useful if the business buys and sells goods and/or services for immediate payment. The topic of value added tax was dealt with in Chapter 23.

Another advantage is that it allows for analysis of, say, sales or purchases. In the example below (Exhibit 24.5) Whiteheads Electrical Co sells television sets, radios and videos as well as washing machines, dryers, fridges, etc. To monitor the sales and profit margins of the various lines, the owner of Whiteheads uses four analysis columns.

Payments made from the cash book are analysed in a similar way.

Exhibit 24.4 Posting credit purchases/expenses

Purchases Ledger

Bould & Co Account

Dr			PL 1 Cr
			£
	Nov 1	Purchases	4,230

Sigley's Stationers Account

Dr			PL 2 Cr
			£
	Nov 10	Purchases	47

T Adams Ltd Account

Dr			PL 3 Cr
			£
	Nov 17	Purchases	940

Robinson's Garage Account

Dr			PL 4 Cr
			£
	Nov 30	Purchases	188

General Ledger

Purchases Account

Dr				GL 1 Cr
		£		
Nov 30	Credit purchases for November	4,400		

Motor Expenses Account

Dr				GL 2 Cr
		£		
Nov 30	Purchases day book	160		

Stationery Account

Dr				GL 3 Cr
		£		
Nov 30	Purchases day book	40		

VAT Account

Dr				GL 4 Cr
		£		
Nov 30	Purchases day book	805		

Exhibit 24.5 A worked example

Whiteheads Electrical Co is an independent electrical shop which sells television sets, radios, videos, etc., as well as selling washing machines, dryers and refrigerators. All the sales are cash sales. The company pays for all its purchases immediately and does not need to maintain sales and purchases ledgers. In order to monitor sales and profit margins, Mr Whitehead operates an analytical cash book, as follows:

Receipts:
These are divided into four accounts, namely:

- VAT Account
- Sales – Electrical Goods Account (televisions, radios and videos)
- Sales – White Goods Account (washing machines, dryers and refrigerators)
- Sundry Sales Account (small items, e.g. plugs, light bulbs, etc.).

Payments
The payments side of the cash book has headings as follows:

- VAT Account
- Purchases – Electrical Goods Account (as described above)
- Purchases – White Goods Account (as described above)
- Wages and Salaries Account
- General Overheads Account.

During October 2002 the following transactions took place:

2002
Oct 1 Balance of cash in hand £64.92
         Balance at bank £416.17
Oct 2 Bought radios from Shaws Ltd, £187.36 plus VAT of £32.78 paid by cheque
Oct 4 Sold goods as follows:
         – Washing machine £360.00 plus VAT of £63 to K Walters who paid by cheque
         – Video to S Worrall who paid by cheque £330.00 plus VAT of £57.75
         Both cheques were paid into the bank
         – Sundry cash sales, plugs, etc., £27.50 including VAT of £4.10
Oct 7 Paid electricity account £76.30 by cheque
         Paid wages £245. Drew cash from bank for this purpose
Oct 10 Sold goods as follows:

         Mrs J White – Colour TV   £550   (including VAT £81.92)
         Dr V Ford – Fridge   £180   (including VAT £26.81)
         Mr J Summers – Dryer   £225.50   (including VAT £33.59)

         Cheques were received in respect of the above and duly banked
Oct 12 Cash sales: radio, £80.00 (including VAT £11.91)
Oct 14 Purchased the following goods from Allan Ltd, and paid by cheque. This totalled £2,056.25.

         – Fridges   £   450.00 plus VAT
         – Televisions   £1,300.00 plus VAT

Oct 14 Paid wages £245.00. Drew cash from bank
Oct 18 Cash sale, one fridge £163.50 (including VAT)
Oct 20 Paid cash for petrol £20.00 (including VAT)
Oct 23 Paid wages £252.00. Drew cash from bank
Oct 24 Sold TV and video to J Pratt £964.67 (including VAT £143.67). He paid by cheque
Oct 26 Bought electrical clocks and radios from B Donald Ltd for £327.50 (including VAT). Paid by cheque
Oct 30 Sundry cash sales of small items paid direct into the bank £367.00 (including VAT)
Oct 31 Paid rent £200.00 in cash

Exhibit 24.5 *(continued)*

The entries in the cash book would be as follows:

Cash Book (debit side only) *CB1*

Date		Details	Folio	VAT	Sales Electrical Goods	Sales White Goods	Sundry Sales	Cash	Bank
2002				£	£	£	£	£	£
Oct	1	Balances b/d						64.92	416.17
Oct	4	K Walters		63.00		360.00			423.00
Oct	4	S Worrall		57.75	330.00				387.75
Oct	4	Cash Sales		4.10			23.40	27.50	
Oct	10	Mrs J White		81.92	468.08				550.00
Oct	10	Dr V Ford		26.81		153.19			180.00
Oct	10	J Summers		33.59		191.91			225.50
Oct	12	Cash sales		11.91	68.09			80.00	
Oct	18	Cash sales		24.35		139.15		163.50	
Oct	24	J Pratt		143.67	821.00				964.67
Oct	30	Cash sales		54.66			312.34		367.00
				501.76	1,687.17	844.25	335.74	335.92	3,514.09
Nov	1	Balances b/d						115.92	91.90
				GL 1	GL 2	GL 3	GL 4		

Cash Book (credit side only) *CB1*

Date		Details	Folio	VAT	Purchases Electrical Goods	Purchases White Goods	Wages and Salaries	General Overheads	Cash	Bank
2002				£	£	£	£	£	£	£
Oct	2	Shaws Ltd		32.78	187.36					220.14
Oct	7	Electricity						76.30		76.30
Oct	7	Wages					245.00			245.00
Oct	14	Allan Ltd		306.25	1,300.00	450.00				2,056.25
Oct	14	Wages					245.00			245.00
Oct	20	Petrol		2.98				17.02	20.00	
Oct	23	Wages					252.00			252.00
Oct	26	B Donald Ltd		48.78	278.72					327.50
Oct	31	Rent						200.00	200.00	
Oct	31	Balances c/d							115.92	91.90
				390.79	1,766.08	450.00	742.00	293.32	335.92	3,514.09
				GL 1	GL 5	GL 6	GL 7	GL 8		

24.7 Posting the cash book to the general ledger

At the end of the month the cash book is balanced off in the normal way as shown in Chapter 11, but in addition to balancing off, each analysis column is also totalled (*see* Exhibit 24.5). At the end of the month these totals are then posted to the general ledger as illustrated in Exhibit 24.6.

Exhibit 24.6 Posting from the Cash Book

General Ledger

VAT Account — GL 1

Dr						Cr
2002				2002		
Oct	31	Bank	390.79	Oct	31	Bank	501.76

Sales – Electrical Goods Account — GL 2

Dr						Cr
				2002		
				Oct	31	Bank	1,687.17

Sales – White Goods Account — GL 3

Dr						Cr
				2002		
				Oct	31	Bank	844.25

Sundry Sales Account — GL 4

Dr						Cr
				2002		
				Oct	31	Bank	335.74

Purchases – Electrical Goods Account — GL 5

Dr						Cr
2002						
Oct	31	Bank	1,766.08			

Purchases – White Goods Account — GL 6

Dr						Cr
Oct	31	Bank	450.00			

Wages and Salaries Account — GL 7

Dr						Cr
2002						
Oct	31	Bank	742.00			

General Overheads Account — GL 8

Dr						Cr
2002						
Oct	31	Bank	293.32			

24.8 Posting from the cash book when a sales ledger and a purchases ledger are maintained

Some businesses have separate sales and purchases ledgers whose accuracy is checked by the use of control accounts (to be discussed in Chapter 25). Analysis columns are used in the analytical cash book to record monies received from debtors or paid to creditors. The items are then posted to the respective personal accounts in the sales ledger or purchase ledger – *see* Exhibit 24.7.

Exhibit 24.7

Dr   *Extract from Cash Book*   Cr

Date	Details	Debtors	Other items	Cash	Bank	Date	Details	Creditors	Other items	Cash	Bank
2000						2000					
Jan 1	Balance b/d			200	1,763	Jan 10	H Clifton	67			67
Jan 8	T Smart	52			52	Jan 11	A Street	230			230
Jan 15	C Cox	85			85	Jan 13	Sundry		120	120	
Jan 22	Cash Sales		751	751		Jan 30	Wages		400	400	
Jan 30	J Lee	842			842	Jan 31	S Ford	125			125
						Jan 31	Balance c/d			431	2,320
		979	751	951	2,742			422	520	951	2,742
Feb 1	Balance b/d			431	2,320						

Posting from the cash book – debtors:

	Sales Ledger	SL 1
Dr	*T Smart Account*	Cr

2000				2000			
Jan	1	Balance b/d	52	Jan	8	Bank	52

		SL 2
Dr	*C Cox Account*	Cr

2000				2000			
Jan	1	Balance b/d	85	Jan	15	Bank	85

		SL 3
Dr	*J Lee Account*	Cr

2000				2000			
Jan	1	Balance b/d	842	Jan	30	Bank	842

(*continued*)

Exhibit 24.7 (*continued*)

Posting from the cash book – creditors:

Dr			**Purchase Ledger** *H Clifton Account*					*PL 1* *Cr*
2000				2000				
Jan	10	Bank	67	Jan	1	Balance b/d		67

Dr			*A Street Account*					*PL 2* *Cr*
2000				2000				
Jan	11	Bank	230	Jan	1	Balance b/d		230

Dr			*S Ford Account*					*PL 3* *Cr*
2000				2000				
Jan	31	Bank	125	Jan	1	Balance b/d		125

At the end of the month the columns are added up and the total amount of money received from the **debtors**, i.e. £979, is posted to the sales ledger control account and the total amount paid to **creditors**, i.e. £422, is posted to the purchase ledger control account. (This is dealt with more fully in the next chapter.) Other items included in Exhibit 24.7 are posted to the general ledger as described in Exhibit 24.6.

There is no set format for the number and names of the columns which may be used in an analytical cash book. It is up to the business to adapt the cash book to meet its own requirements.

NEW TERMS

Analytical cash book Book of original entry for cash and bank receipts and payments; also contains analysis columns to make postings to ledger accounts easier.

Analytical day books Book of original entry in which invoices are entered. The book has various analysis columns which are totalled at the end of the month and posted to the general ledger and control accounts.

STUDENT ACTIVITIES

24.1 The Curtain Design Company sells both ready-made and custom-made curtains to local hotels, nursing homes and the public.

It operates a columnar sales day book where it analyses the sales into sales of ready-made curtains and custom-made curtains.

The following invoices were sent during November 2002.

Date		Customer	Ready-made £	Custom-made £
Nov	1	Jarvis Arms Hotel		2,300
Nov	8	Springs Nursing Home	1,000	
Nov	15	J P Morten	220	
Nov	17	Queen's Hotel		1,500
Nov	30	W Blackshaw	90	

All goods are subject to VAT at 17.5 per cent.

You are required to:

(a) record the above transactions in a columnar sales day book;

(b) post the invoices to the personal accounts in the sales ledger;

(c) post the totals to the appropriate accounts in the general ledger.

24.2 The Hall Engineering Company manufactures small engineering components for the motor car industry. It operates a columnar purchases day book in which the purchases invoices are recorded.

During May 2000 the following invoices were received:

				£
May	1	Black's Engineering Co	Engineering goods	520
May	3	Ace Printing Co	Printing catalogues	145
May	24	Morgan's Garage	Petrol account	120
May	26	Martin's Foundry	Engineering parts	700
May	28	Office Supplies	Stationery	126
May	29	Black's Engineering Co	Engineering parts	220

All goods are subject to VAT at 17.5 per cent.

You are required to:

(a) Enter the purchases invoices in a columnar purchases day book using the following analysis columns:

- Engineering parts
- Printing and stationery
- Motor expenses
- VAT.

(b) Post the transactions to the personal accounts in the purchases ledger.

(c) Post the totals to the appropriate accounts in the general ledger.

24.3X Harkers Electrical Wholesalers Ltd, Brighton, employs you as accounts assistant responsible for the purchases ledger.

The following details relate to the purchases invoices and credit notes received for April. The company uses an analytical day book with the following column headings and references for spreadsheet purposes.

	Account reference
Total	E
Electrical goods	F
Motor expenses	G
Office expenses	H
Telephone	I
Sundries	J
VAT	K

Suppliers' account nos are as follows:

Supplier	Account no
British Telecom	007
Leigh Electrics	030
Office Cleaning Co	043
Peak Electrical Installations Ltd	051
PCD Electrical	060
Smith Stationers	079
Star Manufacturing Co	080
Thomas Motors	090

Purchases invoices and credit notes for April

Invoices

Our inv no	Date 2001	Supplier	Details
2306	April 6	Leigh Electrics	Electrical goods £723.52 including VAT £107.75
2307	April 8	PCD Electrical	Cable, etc. £299.13 plus VAT £52.35
2308	April 10	Star Manufacturing Co	Plugs, sockets, etc. £32.17 including VAT £4.79
2309	April 12	British Telecom	Telephone A/c £112.70 including VAT £16.78
2310	April 14	Peak Electrical Installations Ltd	Electrical goods £425.00 plus VAT @ 17½%
2311	April 16	Office Cleaning Co	Cleaning offices (as per contract) £105.00 plus VAT @ 17½%
2312	April 17	Leigh Electrics	Electrical goods £663.68 including VAT
2313	April 19	Thomas Motors	Petrol for March £84.10 including VAT £12.52
2314	April 21	Star Manufacturing Co	Cable, sockets, etc. £160.38 including VAT
2315	April 25	Thomas Motors	Repairs to Renault £131.93 plus VAT £23.09 MOT £24.00 (zero-rated)
2316	April 28	Smith Stationers	Office stationery £68.95 including VAT £10.27

Credit notes

| 27CN | April 16 | Leigh Electrics | Credit re: faulty goods £57.00 including VAT |
| 28CN | April 30 | Star Manufacturing Co | Credit re: overcharge £2.25 including VAT 34p |

Required

As accounts assistant, you are required to record the purchases invoices and credit notes, but these need to be done in a specific sequence.

(a) Using the headings shown in Exhibit 24.8, draw up an account postings schedule for both the invoices and credit notes, making sure that you check the VAT calculations given in the list of invoices and credit notes. The first item has been entered as an example.

Exhibit 24.8

ACCOUNTING POSTINGS – INVOICES   **Date** _APRIL 2001_

Date	Supplier	Supplier A/c No	A/c Ref	Total	Goods	VAT
2001 April 6	Leigh Electrics	030	F	723.52	615.77	107.75

ACCOUNTING POSTINGS – CREDIT NOTES   **Date**

Date	Supplier	Supplier A/c No	A/c Ref	Total	Goods	VAT

(b) Rule up a columnar purchases day book and returns outward day book and enter the purchases invoices and credit notes for April 2001. Ensure that all the totals and cross-totals agree.

(c) Post the invoices and credit notes to the suppliers' accounts in the purchases ledger.

(d) Post the totals to the respective accounts in the general ledger.

(NVQ Level 2)

24.4 The Peakdale Café and Craft Centre is situated in one of the Peak District's villages and has a reputation for providing good wholesome refreshments which are very popular with hikers and visitors. In addition to selling refreshments the centre also sells home-made ice cream, and local crafts such as pottery items, artists' pictures and ornaments.

To enable the proprietors to monitor sales of food and craft items they maintain an analytical cash book with columns as follows:

Debit side

Date	Details	Sale of food	Sale of crafts	Cash	Bank

Credit side

Date	Details	Purchase of food	Purchase of craft items	Other expenses	Cash	Bank

During July 2001 the following transactions took place:

2001

July	1	Balance of cash in hand £150.00
		Balance of cash in the bank £2,687.50
July	3	Paid sundry expenses in cash £67.90
July	5	Paid cash to Restaurant Supplies Co £56.23 for sundry items of table napkins etc.
July	6	Paid cheque £2,480.00 to Food Wholesalers Ltd for food supplies
July	7	Cash takings from the restaurant for the week £1,923.56
July	7	Paid £1,750 cash into the bank
July	8	Paid wages in cash £120
July	14	Sold paintings totalling £400 and banked the cheques immediately
July	15	Cash takings from the restaurant for the week £2,100.00
July	16	Banked cash £1,500
July	16	Paid wages in cash £150.00
July	19	Paid cheque to Ash (Butchers) & Co £360.00 for meat supplies
July	20	Paid cash for petrol £25.00
July	22	Sold sundry craft items £267.50, received cheques which were banked immediately
July	22	Cash takings from the restaurant for the week £2,356.00
July	23	Banked cash £2,000
July	24	Sold painting by cheque £378.00, the cheque was banked immediately
July	25	Purchased additional craft items and paintings and paid cheque to Artcraft Designs £3,100
July	27	Sold paintings and craft items and banked cheques immediately totalling £990
July	30	Paid salaries by cheque as follows: M Chapman £ 980.00
		S Kerr £1,550.00
July	30	Restaurant cash takings for the week £2,500
July	30	Banked cash £2,700.00

Task

Draw up an analytical cash book with columns as mentioned above and enter the transactions for July 2001; balance off at the end of the month and bring down the cash and bank balances as at 1 August 2001.

25 Control accounts

AIMS

- To be able to draw up sales ledger control account.

- To be able to draw up a purchase ledger control account.

- To know the source of information for control accounts.

- To understand the double-entry aspect of control accounts.

25.1 Need for control accounts

When all accounts are kept in one ledger a trial balance can be drawn up as a test of the arithmetical accuracy of the accounts though it must be remembered that certain errors are not revealed by such a trial balance. If the trial balance totals disagree for a small business the books can easily and quickly be checked to find the errors.

However, when the firm has grown and the accounting work has been so divided up that there are several or many ledgers, any errors could be very difficult to find. Every item in every ledger would have to be checked. What is required is a type of trial balance for each ledger, and this requirement is met by the **control account**. Thus it is only the ledgers whose control accounts do not balance that need detailed checking to find errors.

25.2 Principle of control accounts

The principle on which the control account is based is simple, and is as follows. If the opening balance of an account is known, together with information of the additions and deductions entered in the account, the closing balance can be calculated.

Applying this to a complete ledger, the total of opening balances together with the additions and deductions during the period should give the total of closing balances. This can be illustrated by reference to a sales ledger for entries for a month.

	£
Total of opening balances at 1 January 2001	3,000
Add Total of entries which have increased the balances	9,500
	12,500
Less Total of entries which have reduced the balances	8,000
Total of closing balances at 31 January 2001 should be	4,500

It must be emphasised that control accounts are **not** necessarily a part of the double-entry system (*see* section 25.7). They are merely arithmetical proofs performing the same function as a trial balance to a particular ledger.

25.3 Form of control accounts

Sales ledger control account

It is usual to find control accounts in the same form as any other account, with the totals of the debit entries in the ledger on the left-hand side and the totals of the various credit entries in the ledger on the right-hand side.

Exhibit 25.1 shows an example of a sales ledger control account for a sales ledger in which all the entries are arithmetically correct.

Exhibit 25.1

Sales ledger	£
Debit balances on 1 January 2001	1,894
Total credit sales for the month	10,290
Cheques received from customers in the month	7,284
Cash received from customers in the month	1,236
Returns inwards from customers during the month	296
Debit balances on 31 January 2001 as extracted from the sales ledger	3,368

Sales Ledger Control Account

Dr					Cr
2001			£	2001			£

2001			£	2001			£
Jan	1	Balances b/d	1,894	Jan	31	Bank	7,284
Jan	31	Sales	10,290			Cash	1,236
						Returns inwards	296
						Balances c/d	3,368
			12,184				12,184

We have proved the ledger to be arithmetically correct, because the totals of the control account equal each other. If the totals are not equal, then this proves there is an error somewhere.

Purchase ledger control account

Exhibit 25.2 shows an example where an error is found to exist in a purchases ledger. The ledger will have to be checked in detail, the error found and the control account then corrected.

Exhibit 25.2

Purchases ledger	£
Credit balances on 1 January 2001	3,890
Cheques paid to suppliers during the month	3,620
Returns outwards to suppliers in the month	95
Bought from suppliers in the month	4,936
Credit balances on 31 January as extracted from the purchases ledger	5,151

Purchases Ledger Control Account

Dr			£	Cr			£
2001				2001			
Jan	31	Bank	3,620	Jan	1	Balances b/d	3,890
Jan	31	Returns outwards	95	Jan	31	Purchases	4,936
Jan	31	Balances c/d	5,151				
			8,866*				8,826*

*There is a £40 error in the purchases ledger. We will have to check that ledger in detail to find the error.

25.4 Information for control accounts

The following tables show where information is obtained from to draw up control accounts.

Sales Ledger Control		Source
1	Opening debtors	List of debtors drawn up at end of previous period
2	Credit sales	Total from sales day book
3	Returns inwards	Total of returns inwards day book
4	Cheques received	Cash book: bank column on received side. List extracted
5	Cash received	Cash book: cash column on received side. List extracted
6	Closing debtors	List of debtors drawn up at end of the period

Purchases Ledger Control		Source
1	Opening creditors	List of creditors drawn up at end of previous period
2	Credit purchases	Total from purchases day book
3	Returns outwards	Total of returns outwards day book
4	Cheques paid	Cash book: bank column on payments side. List extracted
5	Cash paid	Cash book: cash column on payments side. List extracted
6	Closing creditors	List of creditors drawn up at end of the period

25.5 Other transfers

Transfers to bad debt accounts will have to be recorded in the sales ledger control account as they involve entries in the sales ledgers.

Similarly, a contra account whereby the same firm is both a supplier and a customer, and inter-indebtedness is set off, will also need entering in the control accounts. An example of this follows:

1　The firm has sold A Hughes £600 goods.

2　Hughes has supplied the firm with £880 goods.

3　The £600 owing by Hughes is set off against £880 owing to him.

4　This leaves £280 owing to Hughes.

Sales Ledger

Dr				A Hughes Account			Cr
			£				
Sales	**1**		600				

Purchases Ledger

Dr				A Hughes Account			Cr
							£
				Purchases	**2**		880

The set-off now takes place.

Sales Ledger

Dr				A Hughes Account			Cr
			£				£
Sales	**1**		600	Set-off: Purchases ledger	**3**		600

Purchases Ledger

Dr				A Hughes Account			Cr
			£				£
Set-off: Sales ledger	**3**		600	Purchases	**2**		880
Balance c/d	**4**		280				
			880				880
				Balance b/d	**4**		280

The transfer of the £600 will therefore appear on the credit side of the sales ledger control account and on the debit side of the purchases ledger control account.

25.6　**A more complicated example**

Exhibit 25.3 shows a worked example of a more complicated control account.

You will see that there are sometimes credit balances in the sales ledger as well as debit balances. Suppose, for instance, we sold £500 goods to W Young. He then paid in full for them, and then afterwards he returned £40 goods to us. This would leave a credit balance of £40 on the account, whereas usually the balances in the sales ledger are debit balances.

There may also be reason to write off a debt as bad where a business finds it impossible to collect the debt. If this happens the double entry would be as follows:

Debit　　Bad debts account
Credit　　Individual debtors' accounts

Ultimately, the bad debts account would be credited and the profit and loss account would be debited. If the business uses control accounts, then the Sales Ledger Control Account would also be credited as shown in Exhibit 25.3.

Exhibit 25.3

2001			£
Aug	1	Sales ledger – debit balances	3,816
Aug	1	Sales ledger – credit balances	22
Aug	31	Transactions for the month:	
		Cash received	104
		Cheques received	6,239
		Sales	7,090
		Bad debts written off	306
		Discounts allowed	298
		Returns inwards	664
		Cash refunded to a customer who had overpaid his account	37
		Dishonoured cheques	29
		Interest charged by us on overdue debt	50
		At the end of the month:	
		Sales ledger – debit balances	3,429
		Sales ledger – credit balances	40

Sales Ledger Control Account

Dr				£					Cr £
2001				£	2001				£
Aug	1	Balances b/d		3,816	Aug	1	Balances b/d		22
Aug	31	Sales		7,090	Aug	31	Cash		104
		Cash refunded		37			Bank		6,239
		Bank: dishonoured					Bad debts		306
		cheques		29			Discounts allowed		298
		Interest on debt		50			Returns inwards		664
		Balances c/d		40			Balances c/d		3,429
				11,062					11,062

25.7 Control accounts as part of double entry

A **sales ledger control account** shows, in total form, all the individual items debited and credited in the sales ledger for a particular period. A **purchases ledger control account** does exactly the same thing but for the purchases ledger. If both the control accounts and the ledgers contain exactly the same information, one by using totals and the other containing a large number of individual entries, then the question arises as to whether it is the ledgers that are part of the double entry or the control accounts.

One way of looking at this question is to say that the sales ledger and the purchases ledger are part of the double entry, while the control accounts are classed as 'memorandum accounts' and act as a form of trial balance checking on whether the ledgers 'balance' – *see* Exhibit 25.4.

Exhibit 25.4 Control account as a memorandum account

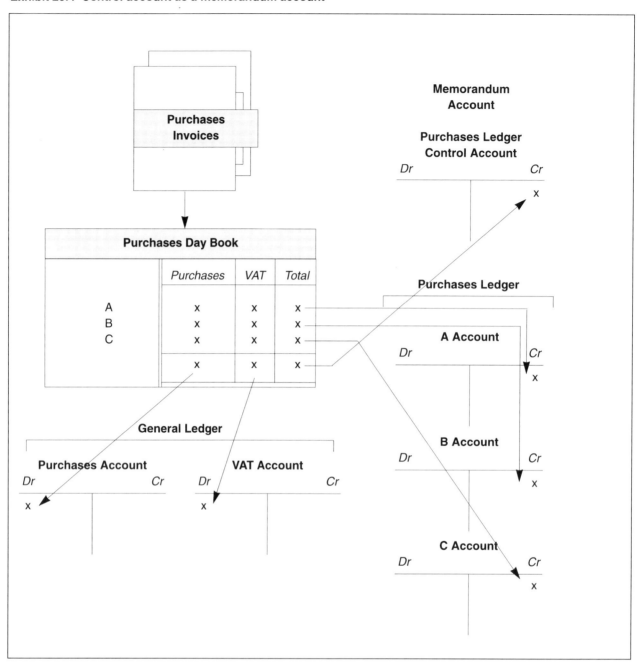

Another way of looking at it is to say that the sales and purchases ledger control accounts are part of the double entry, while the sales ledger and the purchases ledger contain memorandum accounts only – *see* Exhibit 25.5. Obviously there is a need for a sales ledger and purchases ledger otherwise the identity and amount owing in respect of each individual debtor and creditor would not be known.

Exhibit 25.5 Control account as part of a double-entry system

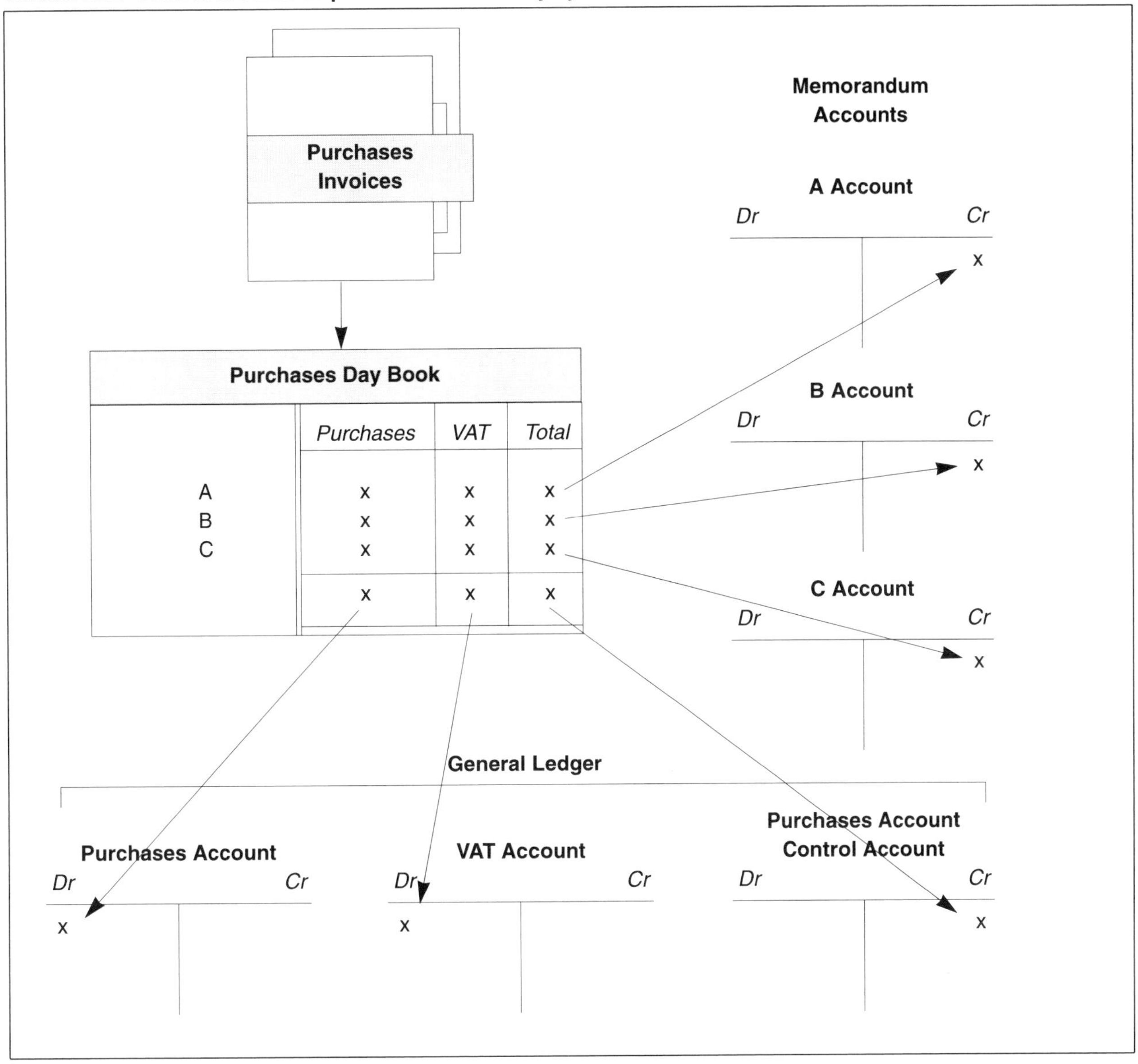

In Exhibit 25.5 the balance of outstanding debtors and creditors is taken from the control accounts and included in the trial balance at the end of the month or year end, as required. In this case the personal accounts of the debtors and creditors, i.e. A Account, B Account, C Account, etc., are not part of the double entry and are referred to as memorandum accounts. It is, however, important to balance the memorandum accounts periodically with the sales and purchases ledger control accounts so that errors can be located and corrected.

In larger organisations it would be normal to find that control accounts are an integral part of the double-entry system, the balances of the control accounts being taken for the purpose of extracting a trial balance. In this case the personal accounts are used as subsidiary records or memorandum accounts.

This view which the larger organisation takes is the one that is most favoured by the various examining bodies. In practical terms, as a student, it will be necessary to draw up both control accounts and the sales and purchases ledgers. The way in which control accounts are used within an organisation does have an effect on the way certain questions in an assessment should be answered. This will be considered further in section 27.9 of Chapter 27 and section 30.3 in Chapter 30.

Note: Many students become confused when making postings to control accounts and might find it useful to remember that when posting entries to control accounts the entry goes on the same side as it would in the personal account. Another useful hint can also be applied when entering 'contra' or 'set-off' items – here think of the contra or set-off as **cash** and enter the item where you would normally enter cash on the respective control account.

NEW TERMS

Control account An account which contains the total of the various individual personal account balances which are held in subsidiary ledgers such as the 'sales ledger' or 'purchases ledger'. By comparing the balance on the control account with the total outstanding balances in a subsidiary ledger the arithmetical accuracy can be checked. Errors can easily be located and rectified.

Memorandum accounts An account which is not part of the double-entry system. These may be the personal accounts of debtors or creditors where the control account is part of the double entry and the personal accounts are classified as 'memorandum accounts'. Alternatively, the sales and purchases ledgers may be part of the double entry and the control accounts classified as 'memorandum accounts'.

STUDENT ACTIVITIES

25.1 You are required to prepare a sales ledger control account from the following:

2001				£
May	1	Sales ledger balances		4,560
		Total of entries for May:		
		Sales day book		10,870
		Returns inwards day book		460
		Cheques and cash received from customers		9,615
		Discounts allowed		305
May	31	Sales ledger balances		5,050

25.2 You are to prepare a sales ledger control account from the following. Deduce the closing figure of sales ledger balances as at 31 March 2001.

2001				£
Mar	1	Sales ledger balances		6,708
		Totals for March:		
		Discounts allowed		300
		Cash and cheques received from debtors		8,970
		Sales day book		11,500
		Bad debts written off		115
		Returns inwards day book		210
Mar	31	Sales ledger balances		?

25.3X Draw up a purchases ledger control account from the following:

2001				£
June	1	Purchases ledger balances		3,890
		Totals for June:		
		Purchases day book		5,640
		Returns outwards day book		315
		Cash and cheques paid to creditors		5,230
		Discounts received		110
June	30	Purchases ledger balances		?

25.4X You are to prepare a purchases ledger control account from the following. As the final figure of purchases ledger balances at 30 November 2001 is missing, you will have to deduce that figure.

2001			£
Nov	1	Purchases ledger balances	7,560
		Totals for November:	
		Discounts received	240
		Returns outwards day book	355
		Cash and cheques paid to creditors	9,850
		Purchases day book	11,100
Nov	30	Purchases ledger balances	?

25.5 The following balances have been extracted from the books of R Stevenson at 31 December 2001:

1 January 2001	£
Sales ledger balances	6,840
Further balances:	
Sales	46,801
Discounts allowed	420
Bad debts written off	494
Receipts from customers	43,780
Returns inwards	296

Required

(a) Prepare the sales ledger control account for R Stevenson, showing clearly the balance carried forward at 31 December 2001.

(b) An explanation of the meaning and use of the final balance.

(RSA)

25.6 Ann Bannister has a small business which makes a wide range of designer sportswear. On 1 April 2001 her sales ledger contained the following debtors:

	£
Atlantis Sport	909.36
T L Maleta	495.68
Lenton Leisurewear	736.29
Sportime	574.73

During the month of April 2001 the following transactions took place:

Sales on credit

			Goods	VAT	Total
			£	£	£
April	2	Lenton Leisurewear	463.72	46.37	510.09
April	7	Atlantis Sport	782.34	78.23	860.57
April	19	Sportime	850.63	85.06	935.69

Returns inward

			Goods	VAT	Total
			£	£	£
April	10	Lenton Leisurewear	56.24	5.62	61.86
April	25	Sportime	70.64	7.06	77.70

Payments received by cheque

			Discount allowed	Cheque value
			£	£
April	15	Atlantis Sport	45.46	863.90
April	28	Sportime	28.74	545.99
April	30	Lenton Leisurewear	36.82	699.47

On 29 April notification was received that T L Maleta had been declared bankrupt and his account was written off as a bad debt.

You are required to:
(a) Open ledger accounts for all debtors and enter the balances as at 1 April 2001.
(b) Post the transactions which have taken place during the month of April 2001 to the appropriate ledger accounts and balance the accounts at the end of the month.
(c) Prepare a sales ledger control account for April 2001 and reconcile the balance with the total debtors balances in the sales ledger.

(RSA)

25.7 (a) List **three** reasons for maintaining a sales ledger (debtors) control account.
(b) Would the following errors cause a difference to occur between the balance on the purchases ledger control account and the total of the balances in the purchases ledger?
   (i) The purchases day book has been overcast by £50.
   (ii) A purchase for £65 has been debited to the supplier's account.
   (iii) A purchase invoice received from Tapes and Braids Ltd has been credited to the account of Tapes and Tassels Ltd

(AAT (part of Central Assessment))

25.8X (a) Would the following errors cause a difference between the balance of the sales ledger control account and the total of the balances in the sales ledger?
   (i) The sales returns day book has been undercast by £10.
   (ii) A credit note issued to Midgems Ltd for £32 has been credited to Middletons Ltd.
   (iii) One of the sales ledger accounts has been balanced off incorrectly.

(b) Briefly explain the purpose of control accounts.

(AAT (part of Central Assessment))

25.9 On 30 June the balances on Shaun Edwards' Purchase Ledger were as follows:

	£
K Skerrett	3,240 Cr
M Cassidy	3,160 Cr
N Cowie	64 Dr

During the month ended 31 July the following transactions took place:

	Credit purchases	Cash purchases	Purchase returns	Payments made on account	Discount received
	£	£	£	£	£
K Skerrett	16,302	2,000	–	17,088	100
M Cassidy	9,518	–	162	8,700	–
N Cowie	8,662	–	58	6,337	83

You are required to:
(a) Write up the purchases ledger accounts for the month ended 31 July.
(b) Prepare the purchases ledger control account for the month ended 31 July.
(c) Reconcile the control account balance with the ledger account balances.

(Pitman Qualifications)

25.10X On 1 December Lauren Hau's Purchase Ledger contained the following balances only:

	£
T Biswas	1,415 Cr
R Yapp	1,070 Cr
M Dibb	1,235 Cr

During December Lauren Hau made the following transactions:

	Credit purchases £	Purchases returns £	Payments made £	Discount received £
T Biswas	550	50	950	50
R Yapp	–	–	700	70
M Dibb	300	60	800	–

You are required to:

(a) Write up Lauren Hau's purchases ledger accounts for December.

(b) Prepare the purchases ledger control account for December.

(c) Reconcile the purchases ledger with the control account.

(Pitman Qualifications)

26 Reconciling ledger accounts

AIMS

- **To be able to reconcile a supplier's statement of account with the ledger account in the business's own books of account.**

- **To be able to produce an 'aged debtors analysis'.**

26.1 Statement of account

As already mentioned in Chapter 18, section 18.10, a statement of account is usually sent to each debtor at the end of each month stating the amount outstanding at the month end. The statement contains the following:

- the balance brought forward from the previous month;

- details of invoices issued during the month – representing the sales to the debtor for the month, these amounts are added to the opening balance;

- any amount paid, together with any cash discount allowed, is deducted from the balance outstanding;

- if a credit note has been issued this too is deducted from the balance outsanding;

- lastly, the final balance shown is a request for payment to be made against the statement;

- the terms and conditions of payment are usually printed at the foot of the statement.

An example of a statement of account was shown in Chapter 18, Exhibit 18.9, and a further example is shown below in Exhibit 26.1.

26.2 Reconciliation of ledger accounts with the supplier's statement of account

On receipt by a debtor of a statement of account from a supplier it is necessary to check or reconcile the statement balance with the business's own ledger accounts of the supplier's account.

Sometimes, because of the difference in timing, the balance on a supplier's statement on a certain date can differ from the balance on that supplier's account in the business's purchases ledger. This is similar to a bank statement whose balance may differ from that in the cash book and require the preparation of a 'bank reconciliation statement' to reconcile the two balances. If the balance on the statement of account does differ from the supplier's account in the purchase ledger then it will be necessary to check the statement against the ledger account and reconcile the difference by preparing a 'supplier's reconciliation statement'. This is illustrated below using the details provided in Exhibit 26.1.

Exhibit 26.1

Books of A Hall Ltd

Dr					2003				£

C Young Ltd Account — Cr

2003				£	2003				£
Jan	10	Bank		1,550	Jan	1	Balance b/d		1,550
Jan	29	Returns	**(1)**	116	Jan	6	Purchases		885
Jan	31	Balance c/d		1,679	Jan	18	Purchases		910
				3,345					3,345
					Feb	1	Balance b/d		1,679

C YOUNG LTD
Market Place, Leeds, LD23 7TR

Telephone: 01987 872490
Fax: 01987 872400

To: A Hall Ltd
Bridge End Industrial Estate
Hathersage Road
Leeds LD33 4TT

Account No: H93

Date 31 January 2003

				Debit £	Credit £	Balance £
2003						
Jan	1	Balance				1,550 Dr
Jan	4	Invoice No 3250		885		2,435 Dr
Jan	13	Payment received			1,550	885 Dr
Jan	18	Invoice No 3731		910		1,795 Dr
Jan	31	Invoice No 3894	**(2)**	425		2,220 Dr

TERMS NET MONTHLY

Comparing the account of A Hall Ltd in the purchases ledger with the supplier's statement, **two** differences can be seen.

1. A Hall Ltd returned goods totalling £116 to C Young Ltd on 29 January 2003, but they had not received them nor recorded them in their books by the end of January.

2. C Young Ltd sent goods to A Hall Ltd on 31 January, invoice no 3894, totalling £425. However, A Hall Ltd had not received the goods or the invoice and were therefore unable to enter the invoice in their books by the end of January.

A reconciliation statement can now be drawn up by A Hall Ltd, as on 31 January 2003.

Reconciliation of Supplier's Statement
C Young Ltd as on 31 January 2003

	£	£
Balance per our purchases ledger		1,679
Add Purchases not received by us **(1)**	425	
Returns not received by supplier **(2)**	116	541
Balance per supplier's statement		2,220

The **two** differences highlighted in the above example are differences due to timing and will be corrected within a few days when the documentation is received by the respective buyer and seller and entered in their books of account.

26.3 Other reasons for differences in balances

In addition to the two items mentioned above differences in balances may occur as a result of one of the following:

- **Payments in transit.** When a payment is made by a buyer, either by cheque or perhaps by BACS, it is usually entered in the buyer's cash book and purchases ledger immediately; however, it may be several days before the payment reaches the supplier. Therefore, if the supplier sends out a statement of account before receipt of the payment it will not have been entered in the supplier's books and will not appear on the statement.

- **Other errors.** Occasionally errors may be made when data is entered into either the supplier's or buyer's books of account; for example, a figure can easily be transposed. If the accounts are kept on a manual system then errors in calculating balances may occur. Statements of account may also be prepared manually and again errors in copying data from the ledger account may be made or perhaps in calculating the balance outstanding.

26.4 How often should supplier's statements be reconciled

As previously stated statements of account are usually sent out by suppliers on a monthly basis. It is, therefore, recommended that the statement be reconciled with the purchase ledger monthly. This enables the buyer to pay the supplier promptly and take advantage of any settlement discount. Errors can also be identified and brought to the attention of the creditor and the necessary amendments made.

26.5 Filing statements of account

It is usual to file statements of account alphabetically and retain them in case a query arises with the supplier. Occasionally statements of account are checked by the **external auditor** to ascertain the creditors' outstanding balances when preparing the business's annual accounts.

26.6 Aged debtors analysis

It is important for a business to know how much is owed to it by its debtors and the length of time that each debt has been outstanding. It is a well known fact that the longer a debt has been owing the more likely it is that it will become a bad debt. To help with credit control many businesses find it useful to draw up an **aged analysis of debtors** which shows the individual balances outstanding and how long the debt has been outstanding, i.e. up to one month, up to three months, from four to six months and so on. An example of an aged debtors schedule is shown in Exhibit 26.2.

Exhibit 26.2

Aged analysis of debtors as at 31 December 2001						
Account No	Name	Up to 1 month	From 4–6 months	From 7–12 months	Over 1 year	Total
		£	£	£	£	£
B73	K Bates & Co	345.00				345.00
D44	Derbyshire Plant Co			200.10		200.10
G32	Grants Ltd	1,543.00				1,543.00
J17	Johnsons & Co		79.50			79.50
P21	J K Perkins Ltd			678.00		678.00
R55	J G Roberts Ltd	17.44				17.44
		1,905.44	79.50	878.10		2,863.04

Many computer accounting packages have the facility to produce an 'aged analysis of debtors' which enables long outstanding debts to be identified and measures taken to collect the debt.

26.7 Aged creditors analysis

In the same way that debtors are analysed into the length of time the debt has been owing many businesses like to know how much they owe their creditors and how long the account has been outstanding. Again, a schedule called an 'aged creditors analysis' may be drawn up which shows each individual creditor's balance and the length of time the debt has been outstanding. Again this information can be obtained very easily if the company uses a computer accounting package.

NEW TERMS

Aged analysis of debtors or creditors A list of individual debtors' or creditors' outstanding balances, analysed into the length of time the debt has been outstanding from, say, less than one month, up to three months, from four to six months and so on.

Reconciling a supplier's statements Checking supplier's statements of account with a business's own ledger account for the individual creditor and preparing a 'reconciliation statement' to identify the differences.

STUDENT ACTIVITIES

26.1 Squires Sports is a small family business run by Mr G Squires and his son, Matthew. They sell a wide variety of goods ranging from the usual sports equipment for football, rugby, swimming, etc., and also provide uniforms for the local grammar schools and scout and guide movement.

On 31 January 2002 the business receives statements of account from two of its customers, Silver Sports Ltd and Zoom Sports Ltd. These are shown in Exhibits 26.3 and 26.4 together with each creditor's ledger account.

Exhibit 26.3

Creditors Ledger						
						A/c No S23
Dr			Silver Sports Ltd a/c			Cr
2002				2002		
Jan 3	Cheque	10.00		Jan 1	Balance b/f	10.00
21	Credit Note No 423	57.30		7	Purchases Inv No 1001	321.60
				13	Purchases Inv No 1290	470.90
				20	Purchases Inv No 1814	79.80

STATEMENT

SILVER SPORTS LTD
Mercury Industrial Estate
Birmingham

Tel: 0121 - 73209

VAT No: 228 139 484

Customer:
   Squires Sports
   Booth Avenue
   Birmingham

Date: 31st Jan 2002

DATE	DESCRIPTION		DR	CR	BALANCE
2001					
Dec 31	Balance				10.00
2002					
Jan 3	Cheque			10.00	–
7	Invoice No	1001	321.60		321.60
13		1290	470.90		792.50
20		1814	79.80		872.30
21	Credit Note	423		57.30	815.00
29	Invoice No	2137	142.57		957.57

AMOUNT DUE WITHIN 30 DAYS

Exhibit 26.4

Creditors Ledger

A/c No Z1

Dr				Zoom Sports Ltd a/c				Cr
2002				2002				
Jan	2	Cheque	330.50	Jan	1	Balance b/f		372.50
	7	Credit Note No 73	42.00		3	Purchases		12.30
						Inv No 323		
	12	Credit Note No 87	13.40		17	Purchases		
						Inv No 450		79.10
					24	Purchases		
						Inv No 501		62.70
						Inv No 502		111.30

STATEMENT OF ACCOUNT

ZOOM SPORTS LTD
Haydock Lane
Birmingham

Tel: 0121 - 763401
Fax:
VAT No: 616 517 242

Customer:
 Squires Sports
 Booth Avenue
 Birmingham

Date: 31st Jan 2002

DATE		DESCRIPTION		DR	CR	BALANCE
2002						
Jan	1	Balance				372.50
	3	Invoice No	323	12.30		384.80
	7	Credit Note No	73		42.00	342.80
	2	Bank			330.50	12.30
	17	Invoice No	450	79.10		91.40
	24		501	62.70		154.10
			502	111.30		265.40
	12	Credit Note No	87		13.40	252.00

AMOUNT DUE WITHIN 30 DAYS – TERMS NET

Required:

(a) Balance the ledger accounts of Silver Sports Ltd and Zoom Sports Ltd.
(b) Carry out a reconciliation of the ledger accounts with the creditors' statements.
(c) State the amount Squires Sports owes each of the creditors at 31 January 2002.

26.2X As accounts clerk for Perris Design Co one of your tasks is to reconcile the company's suppliers' statements of account with the purchases ledger accounts prior to payment.

Exhibits 26.5 and 26.6 show two statements of account which have just been received from two of the company's suppliers, Kirkhams Mfr Ltd and Elders Ltd. Your task is to reconcile the statements with the ledger accounts shown in Exhibit 26.7 and state the amount outstanding at the end of the month.

Exhibit 26.5

<table>
<tr><td colspan="5" align="center">STATEMENT OF ACCOUNT</td></tr>
<tr><td colspan="3">KIRKHAMS MFR LTD
Riverside Works, Romford</td><td>Tel:
Date:</td><td>01708 649685
31 July 2001</td></tr>
<tr><td colspan="3">Customer:
   Perris Design Co
   Deansgate
   Ipswich</td><td colspan="2">Account No PX/32971</td></tr>
<tr><td>Date</td><td>Description/reference</td><td>Debit
£ p</td><td>Credit
£ p</td><td>Balance
£ p</td></tr>
<tr><td>2001</td><td>Balance   b/f</td><td></td><td></td><td>1,829.00</td></tr>
<tr><td>15.07</td><td>Invoice No 49606</td><td>531.75</td><td></td><td></td></tr>
<tr><td>13.07</td><td>Invoice No 822663</td><td>54.62</td><td></td><td></td></tr>
<tr><td>21.07</td><td>Invoice No 84133</td><td>459.23</td><td></td><td></td></tr>
<tr><td>24.07</td><td>Invoice No 82624</td><td>68.42</td><td></td><td>2,943.02</td></tr>
<tr><td>30.07</td><td>Cash</td><td></td><td>1,432.30</td><td>1,510.72</td></tr>
<tr><td colspan="2">AMOUNT NOW DUE</td><td colspan="3">NB: Our Invoice No 821503 for £396.70 is overdue</td></tr>
<tr><td colspan="5" align="center">Interest will be charged on overdue accounts</td></tr>
</table>

Exhibit 26.6

STATEMENT OF ACCOUNT

ELDERS LTD
The Green, Brentwood, Essex

Tel: 01277 371832
Date: 31 July 2001

Customer:
  Perris Design Co
  Deansgate
  Ipswich

Account No   47310

Date	Description/reference		Debit £ p	Credit £ p	Balance £ p
2001					
30 June	Balance	b/f			252.41
2 July	002361 Inv		84.96		
9 July	003123 Inv		42.50		379.87
16 July	Cash			252.41	127.46
23 July	003972 Inv		696.32		823.78
30 July	003989 Inv		121.50		945.28

AMOUNT NOW DUE

Interest will be charged on overdue accounts

Exhibit 26.7

Purchases Ledger

Dr   Elders Ltd a/c   Cr

2001				2001			
Jul	10	Bank	252.41	Jul	1	Balance b/d	252.41
	27	Returns	63.50		2	Purchases	84.96
	31	Balance c/d	760.28		9	Purchases	42.50
					23	Purchases	696.32
			1,076.19				1,076.19
				Aug	1	Balance b/d	760.28

Dr   Kirkhams Mfr Ltd a/c   Cr

2001				2001			
Jul	30	Bank	1,432.30	Jul	1	Balance b/d	1,829.00
	30	Purchases Returns	54.62		15	Purchases	531.75
	31	Balance c/d	1,387.68		13	Purchases	54.62
					21	Purchases	459.23
			2,874.60				2,874.60
				Aug	1	Balance b/d	1,387.68

26.3 Excel Products are one of your suppliers. Their account in your ledger is as follows:

2001			£	2001			£
Oct	14	Purchases returns	95	Oct	1	Balance b/d	1,350
	29	Bank	1,330		6	Purchases	1,850
	29	Discount	20		20	Purchases	1,050
	30	Purchases returns	75				
	31	Balance c/d	2,730				
			4,250				4,250
				Nov	1	Balance b/d	2,730

On 2 November the following statement of account is received from Excel Products:

			Debit £	Credit £	Balance £
2001					
Oct	1	Balance			2,775
	3	Bank		1,400	1,375
	3	Discount		25	1,350
	6	Sales	1,850		3,200
	14	Returns inwards		95	3,105
	20	Sales	1,050		4,155
	28	Sales	1,550		5,705

You are required to:

(a) Prepare a reconciliation statement, starting with the balance in your books of **£2,730**, to explain the difference between the balance in your ledger and the closing balance on the statement of account.

(b) Briefly explain why a supplier may disallow a cash discount.

(RSA)

26.4X M Marchand is one of your suppliers. His account in your books is set out below:

M Marchand Account

2001			£	2001			£
May	6	Bank	6,780	May	1	Balance	6,800
		Discount	20		13	Purchases	1,350
	12	Purchase returns	150		18	Purchases	1,120
	23	Bank	1,325				
		Discount	25				
		Balance	970				
			9,270				9,270
				June	1	Balance	970

During the first week of June the following statement of account is received from M Marchand:

			Dr £	Cr £	Balance £
2001					
May	1	Balance			6,800
	9	Bank		6,780	20
	9	Sales	1,350		1,370
	14	Returns inward		150	1,220
	17	Sales	1,120		2,340
	30	Sales	1,470		3,810

You are required to:

(a) Prepare a reconciliation statement, **starting with the balance in your books of £970,** to explain the difference between the balance in your books and the closing balance of the statement of account.

(b) Give **two** reasons why a supplier may disallow any cash discount.

26.5 On 30 April 2001, James Hamilton Ltd receives a statement of account from one of its suppliers, Ward & Worrell Ltd. The statement showed the amount owing to be quite different from the credit balance on Ward & Worrell Ltd's account in James Hamilton's ledger.

Assuming no errors have been made, give and explain **three** possible reasons for the difference.

26.6 You have just been appointed credit controller for Apex Marketing Consultants. Recently the company has been experiencing difficulty obtaining payment from its debtors. Your job is to review the situation and make recommendations to the company secretary.

Task 1

The company's accountant issues you with the attached list of outstanding debtors. Your first task is to prepare an 'aged debtors analysis' using the following categories:

- Up to 1 month
- Up to 3 months
- From 4–6 months
- From 7–12 months
- Over 1 year.

You may wish to prepare this information using a spreadsheet.

APEX MARKETING CONSULTANTS
Debtors Outstanding as at 31 January 2003

Account No	Customer's name	Amount £	Date
B12	G Black & Co Ltd	162.00	Jan 2003
G37	O Gregson	748.18	Nov 2002
S23	J Samuels & Son	78.50	Jan 2002
R12	Redfern Marketing Services	2,345.00	Sep 2002
H52	Haslin, Saint & Partners	750.00	Oct 2002
M63	McDonald Consultants	4,756.00	Jan 2003
N27	Nice One Fashions	1,450.00	Dec 2002
A32	Ashlea Services	355.00	Nov 2002
P17	Platt Jones & Co	1,763.50	Sep 2002
G65	Grand Mfr Co	300.00	May 2002
B29	Bowdler Harris	621.00	June 2002
G51	Gold Signs Co	521.00	Nov 2002
J32	Jones, Jepson & Ford	230.00	Dec 2002
T7	Triton & Son Ltd	262.00	Feb 2002
P21	PCD Dynamics	1,700.00	Oct 2002

Task 2

(a) On completion of the 'aged debtors analysis' you are asked to make recommendations to the company secretary in the form of a memo.

(b) Draft a suitable letter to customers who fall in the category 'from 1 to 3 months'.

27 The journal

AIMS

- To be able to identify the journal as a book of original entry.
- To be able to use the journal for entering a range of different transactions.
- To be able to post items from the journal to the ledgers.
- To consider examination questions based on control accounts and the journal.

27.1 Main books of original entry

It has already been shown in earlier chapters that most transactions are entered in one of the following books of original entry:

- cash book;
- sales day book;
- purchases day book;
- returns inwards day book;
- returns outwards day book.

These books have grouped together similar things, e.g. all credit sales in the sales day book. To trace any of them would be relatively easy, since it is known exactly which book would contain the item.

27.2 The journal: the other book of original entry

The other items which do not pass through the above books are much less common, and sometimes much more complicated. It would be easy for a bookkeeper to forget the details of these transactions or perhaps the bookkeeper may leave the company making it impossible at a later date to understand such bookkeeping entries.

It is, therefore, important to record such transactions in a form of diary prior to entries being made in the double-entry accounts. The book used to record these transactions is called the **journal** and contains the following details for each transaction:

- the date;
- the name of the account(s) to be debited and the amount(s);

- the name of the account(s) to be credited and the amount(s);

- a description and explanation of the transaction (this is called a '**narrative**');

- a reference number for the source of the documents giving proof of the transaction.

The use of the journal makes errors or fraud by bookkeepers more difficult. It also reduces the risk of entering the item once only instead of having the complete double entry. Despite these advantages there are many firms which do not use the journal.

27.3 Typical uses of the journal

Some of the main uses of the journal are listed below. It must not be thought that this list is a fully detailed one.

1 The purchase and sale of fixed assets on credit.

2 The correction of errors.

3 Writing off bad debts.

4 Opening entries – the entries needed to open a new set of books.

5 Other items.

The layout of the journal can be shown:

The Journal

Date	Folio	Dr	Cr
The name of the account to be debited. The name of the account to be credited. The narrative.			

It can be seen that on the first line the name of the account to be **debited** is entered while the second line gives the account to be **credited**. The name of the account to be **credited** is indented slightly and **not** shown directly under the name of the account to be debited as this makes it easier to distinguish between the debit and credit items.

It should be remembered that the journal is not a double-entry account; it is a form of diary, and entering an item in the journal is not the same as recording an item in an account. Once the journal entry has been made then the entry into the double-entry accounts can be made. Examples of the uses of the journal are now given.

27.4 Purchase and sale on credit of fixed assets

1 A machine is bought on credit from Toolmakers for £550 on 1 July 2003:

	Folio	Dr	Cr
2003		£	£
July 1 Machinery		550	
Toolmakers			550
Purchase of milling machine on credit, Capital			
Purchases invoice no 7/159			

2 Sale of a motor vehicle for £300 on credit to K Lamb on 2 July 2003:

	Folio	Dr	Cr
2003		£	£
July 2 K Lamb		300	
Motor vehicles disposal			300
Sales of motor vehicles per Capital			
Sales invoice no 7/43			

27.5 Correction of errors

Correction of errors not affecting trial balance agreement

It is inevitable that errors will occur when data are entered into the books of account. One of the main uses of the journal is to record such errors and show the corrective entry necessary to amend the double-entry accounts.

One of the ways in which errors are identified is through the trial balance. In Chapter 8 a trial balance was drawn up from a list of balances in the books of account at the end of an accounting period. Each side of the trial balance was then added up and, provided no error had occurred, the two sides should equal each other, i.e.

> **Total debit balances = Total credit balances**

While both sides of the trial balance may agree, complete accuracy cannot be guaranteed. Certain errors can still be made which do not affect the balancing of a trial balance, i.e. the trial balance would still appear to balance even though certain errors may have occurred.

Examples of the different types of errors under this category are as follows:

- errors of commission
- errors of principle
- errors of original entry
- errors of omission
- compensating errors
- complete reversal of entries.

Each one of the above errors will now be discussed and the corrected entries shown.

Errors of commission

An error of commission arises when the correct amounts are entered, but in the wrong person's account.

Example

D Long paid us by cheque £50 on 18 May 2001. It is correctly entered in the cash book, but it is entered by mistake in the account for D Lee.

This means that there had been both a debit of £50 and a credit of £50. It has appeared in the personal account as:

D Lee Account

Dr					Cr
			2001		£
			May	18 Cash	50

The error was found on 31 May 2001. This will now have to be corrected and needs two entries:

1　A debit of £50 in the account of D Lee to cancel out the error on the credit side in that account.

2　A credit of £50 in the account of D Long. This is where it should have been entered.

The accounts will now appear:

D Lee Account

Dr					Cr
2001			£	2001	£
May	31 D Long:				
	Error corrected (**1**)	50	May	18 Cash	50

D Long Account

Dr			£	2001		£
2001				May	31 Cash entered in error	
May	1 Balance b/d	50			in D Lee's account (**2**)	50

The journal

The ways by which errors have been corrected should all be entered in the journal. The correction has already been shown above in double entry. The journal entry will be:

The Journal

2001		Folio	Dr	Cr
			£	£
May 31	D Lee		50	
	D Long			50
	Cash received … entered in wrong			
	personal account, now corrected.			

Errors of principle

This is where a transaction is entered in the wrong class of account.

For instance, the purchase of a fixed asset should be debited to a fixed asset account. If in error it is debited to an expense account, then it has been entered in the wrong class of account.

Example

The purchase of a motor lorry £5,500 by cheque on 14 May 2001 has been debited in error to a motor expenses account. In the cash book it is shown correctly. This means that there has been both a debit of £5,500 and a credit of £5,500.

It will have appeared in the expense account as:

Motor Expenses Account

Dr				Cr
2001		£		
May 14	Bank	5,500		

The error is found on 31 May 2001. We will now correct it. Two entries are needed:

1 A debit in the motor lorry account of £5,500 to put it where it should have been entered.

2 A credit of £5,500 in the motor expenses account to **cancel** the error. The accounts will now appear as:

Motor Expenses Account

Dr						Cr
2001		£	2001			£
May 14	Bank	5,500	May 31	Motor lorry error corrected	(2)	5,500

Motor Lorry Account

Dr				Cr
2001			£	
May 31	Bank: entered originally in Motor expenses	(1)	5,500	

The journal

The journal entries to correct the error will be shown as:

The Journal

		Folio	Dr	Cr
2001			£	£
May 31	Motor lorry		5,500	
	Motor expenses			5,500
	Correction of error whereby purchase of motor lorry was debited to motor expenses account.			

Errors of original entry

This occurs when an incorrect figure is posted to the correct sides of the correct accounts.

Example

If sales of £150 to T Higgins on 13 May 2001 had been entered as both a debit and a credit of £130, the accounts would appear:

T Higgins Account

Dr				Cr
2001		£		
May 13	Sales	130		

Sales Account

Dr					Cr
		2001			£
		May 31	Sales journal (part of total)		130

The error is found on 31 May 2001. The entries to correct it are now shown:

T Higgins Account

Dr				Cr
2001			£	
May	13	Sales	130	
May	31	Sales: error	20	

Sales Account

Dr				Cr
	2001			£
	May	31	Sales journal	130
	May	31	T Higgins:	
			error corrected	20

The journal

To correct the error the journal entries will be:

The Journal

		Folio	Dr	Cr
2001			£	£
May 31	T Higgins		20	
	Sales account			20
	Correction of error. Sales of £150			
	had been incorrectly entered as £130.			

Errors of omission

This type of error occurs when the bookkeeper 'omits' to record a transaction.

Example

If we purchased goods from T Hope for £250 but did not enter it in the accounts there would be nil debits and nil credits. We find the error on 31 May 2001. The entries to record it will be:

Purchases Account

Dr				Cr
2001			£	
May	13	T Hope:		
		error corrected	250	

T Hope Account

Dr				Cr
	2001			£
	May	31	Purchases:	
			error corrected	250

The journal

The journal entries to correct the error will be:

The Journal

		Folio	Dr	Cr
2001			£	£
May 31	Purchases		250	
	T Hope			250
	Correction of error. Purchases omitted from books.			

Compensating errors

These are where errors cancel each other out. They are known as compensating errors.

Example

Let us take a case where the sales day book is added up to be £100 too much. In the same period the purchases day book is also added up to be £100 too much.

If these were the only errors in our books the trial balance totals would equal each other. Both totals would be wrong – they would both be £100 too much, but they would be equal totals.

If in fact the **incorrect** totals had purchases £7,900 and sales £9,900, the accounts would have appeared as:

Purchases Account

Dr				Cr
2001			£	
May	13	Purchases	7,900	

Sales Account

Dr					Cr
			2001		£
			May	31 Sales	9,900

When corrected, the accounts will appear as:

Purchases Account

Dr						Cr
2001			£	2001		£
May	13	Purchases	7,900	May 31	The Journal:	
					error corrected	100

Sales Account

Dr						Cr
2001			£	2001		£
May	31	The Journal:		May 31	Sales	9,900
		error corrected	100			

The journal

Journal entries to correct these two errors will be:

The Journal

		Folio	Dr	Cr
2001			£	£
May 31	Sales account		100	
	Purchases account			100
	Correction of compensating errors. Totals of both purchases and sales day books incorrectly added up £100 too much.			

Complete reversal of entries

This is where the correct amounts are entered in the correct accounts, but each item is shown on the wrong side of each account. There has therefore been both a debit and a credit.

Example

For instance, we pay a cheque for £200 on 28 May 2001 to D Charles. We enter it as follows in accounts with the letter (A):

Cash Book (A)

Dr		Cash £	Bank £			Cash £	Bank £	Cr
2001								
May 28	D Charles		200					

D Charles (A)

Dr				Cr
		2001		£
		May	28 Bank	200

This is incorrect. It should have been debit D Charles £200, credit Bank £200. Both items have been entered in the correct accounts, but each is on the wrong side of its account.

The way to correct this is more difficult to understand than with other errors. Let us look at how the items would have appeared if we had done it correctly in the first place. We will show the letter (B) after the account names:

Cash Book (B)

Dr		Cash £	Bank £			Cash £	Bank £	Cr
				2001				
				May	28 D Charles		200	

D Charles (B)

Dr		£		Cr
2001				
May	28 Bank	200		

We have found the error on 31 May 2001. By using double entry we have to make the amounts shown to cancel the error by twice the amount of the error. This is because:

1 First we have to cancel the error. This would mean entering these amounts:

   Dr D Charles   £200
   Cr Bank   £200

2 The we have to enter up the transaction:

   Dr D Charles   £200
   Cr Bank   £200

Altogether then, the entries to correct the error are twice the amounts first entered.

When corrected the accounts appear as follows, marked (C):

Cash Book (C)

Dr			*Cash* £	*Bank* £				*Cash* £	*Bank* £ Cr
2001					2001				
May	8	D Charles		200	May	31	D Charles: error corrected		400

D Charles (C)

Dr			£				Cr £
2001				2001			
May	28	Bank: error corrected	400	May	28	Bank	200

You can see that accounts (C) give the same final answer as accounts (B):

				£	£
(B)	*Dr*	Dr Charles		200	
	Cr	Bank			200
(C)	*Dr*	D Charles (£400 – £200)		200	
	Cr	Bank (£400 – £200)			200

The journal

Journal entries would be shown as follows:

The Journal

			Folio	*Dr*	*Cr*
2001				£	£
May 31	D Charles			400	
	Bank				400
	Payment of £200 on 28 May 2001 to D Charles incorrectly credited to his account, and debited to bank. Error now corrected.				

Correction of errors affecting trial balance agreement

In the previous section errors which did not affect the balancing of the trial balance were discussed. However, there are many errors which occur that do affect the balancing of the trial balance, for example:

- incorrect additions in any account;

- making an entry on only one side of the accounts, e.g. a debit but no credit; a credit and no debit;

- entering a different amount on the debit side from the amount on the credit side.

Suspense account

If a trial balance does not balance it is important that errors are located and corrected as soon as possible. When they cannot be found, then the trial balance totals should be made to agree with each other by inserting the amount of the difference between the two sides in a **suspense account**. This occurs in Exhibit 27.1 where there is a difference of £40.

Exhibit 27.1

<table>
<tr><td colspan="3">Trial Balance as on 31 December 2001</td></tr>
<tr><td></td><td>Dr</td><td>Cr</td></tr>
<tr><td></td><td>£</td><td>£</td></tr>
<tr><td>Totals after all the accounts have been listed</td><td>100,000</td><td>99,960</td></tr>
<tr><td>Suspense account</td><td></td><td>40</td></tr>
<tr><td></td><td>100,000</td><td>100,000</td></tr>
</table>

To make the two totals the same, a figure of £40 for the suspense account has been shown on the credit side. A suspense account is opened and the £40 difference is also shown there on the credit side.

Suspense Account

Dr			*Cr*
	2001		£
	Dec 31	Difference per trial balance	40

Suspense account and the balance sheet

If the errors are not found before the final accounts are prepared, the suspense account balance will be included in the balance sheet. Where the balance is a credit balance, it should be included under current liabilities on the balance sheet. When the balance is a debit balance it should be shown under current assets on the balance sheet.

Correction of errors

When the errors are found they must be corrected, using double entry. Each correction must also have an entry in the journal describing it.

One error only

We will look at two examples:

Example 1

Assume that the error of £40 shown in Exhibit 27.1 is found in the following year on 31 March 2002, the error being the sales account which was undercast by £40. The action taken to correct this is:

Debit suspense account to close it: £40.
Credit sales account to show item where it should have been: £40.

The accounts and journal entry now appear as in Exhibit 27.2.

Exhibit 27.2

	Suspense Account		
Dr			*Cr*

2002		£	2001				£
			Dec	31	Difference per		
Mar	31	Sales	40			trial balance	40

	Sales Account		
Dr			*Cr*

		2002			£
		Mar	31	Suspense	40

The Journal

			Folio	Dr	Cr
2002				£	£
Mar	31	Suspense		40	
		Sales			40
		Correction of undercasting of sales by £40			
		in last year's accounts.			

Example 2

The trial balance on 31 December 2001 had a difference of £168. It was a shortage on the debit side.

A suspense account is opened and the difference of £168 is entered on the debit side.

On 31 May 2002 the error was found. We had made a payment of £168 to K Leek to close his account. It was correctly entered in the cash book, but it was not entered in K Leek's account.

To correct the error, the account of K Leek is debited with £168, as it should have been in 2001 and the suspense account is credited with £168 so that the account can be closed.

The accounts and journal entry now appear as in Exhibit 27.3.

Exhibit 27.3

	K Leek Account		
Dr			*Cr*

2002			£	2002			£
May	31	Bank	168	Jan	1	Balance b/d	168

	Suspense Account		
Dr			*Cr*

2002			£	2002			£
May	31	Difference per		May	31	K Leek	168
		trial balance	168				

The Journal

			Folio	Dr	Cr
2002				£	£
May	31	K Leek		168	
		Suspense			168
		Correction of non-entry of payment last			
		year in K Leek's account.			

More than one error

We can now look at Exhibit 27.4 where the suspense account difference was caused by more than one error.

Exhibit 27.4

The trial balance at 31 December 2001 showed a difference of £77, being a shortage on the debit side. A suspense account is opened, and the difference of £77 is entered on the debit side of the account.

On 28 February 2002 all the errors from the previous year were found.

1   A cheque of £150 paid to L Kent had been correctly entered in the cash book but had not been entered in Kent's account.
2   The purchases account had been undercast by £20.
3   A cheque of £93 received from K Sand had been correctly entered in the cash book but had not been entered in Sand's account.

These three errors resulted in a net error of £77, shown by a debit of £77 on the debit side of the suspense account.

These are corrected by:

● making correcting entries in the accounts for (**1**), (**2**) and (**3**);
● recording the double entry for these items in the suspense account.

L Kent Account

Dr		£		Cr
2002				
Feb 28	Suspense (**1**)	150		

Purchases Account

Dr		£		Cr
2002				
Feb 28	Suspense (**2**)	20		

K Sand Account

Dr				£	Cr
		2002			
		Feb 28	Suspense (**3**)	93	

Suspense Account

Dr		£			Cr £
2002			2002		
Jan 1	Balance b/d	77	Feb 28	L Kent (**1**)	150
Feb 28	K Sand (**3**)	93	Feb 28	Purchases (**2**)	20
		170			170

The Journal

			Folio	Dr £	Cr £
2002					
Feb 28	L Kent			150	
	Suspense				150
	Cheque paid omitted from Kent's account				
Feb 28	Purchases			20	
	Suspense				20
	Undercasting of purchases by £20 in last year's accounts				
Feb 28	Suspense			93	
	K Sand				93
	Cheque received omitted from Sand's account				

Only those errors which make the trial balance totals different from each other have to be corrected via the suspense account.

27.6 Bad debts

A debt of £78 owed to the business from H Mander is written off as a bad debt on 31 August 2003:

The Journal

		Folio	Dr	Cr
2003			£	£
Aug 31	Bad debts		78	
	H Mander			78
	Debt written off as bad. See letter in file 7/8906			

27.7 Opening entries

J Brew, after being in business for some years without keeping proper records, now decides to keep a double-entry set of books. On 1 July 2003 he establishes that his assets and liabilities are as follows:

Assets: Motor van £840, Fixtures £700, Stock £390,
Debtors – B Young £95, D Blake £45,
Bank £80, Cash £20.

Liabilities: Creditors – M Quinn £129, C Walters £41.

The assets therefore total £840 + £700 + £390 + £95 + £45 + £80 + £20 = £2,170 and the liabilities total £129 + £41 = £170. The capital consists of: Assets – Liabilities = £2,170 – £170 = £2,000.

To write up the books of account on 1 July 2003 the following actions are carried out:

1 Open asset accounts, one for each asset. Each opening asset is shown as a debit balance.

2 Open liability accounts, one for each liability. Each opening liability is shown as a credit balance.

3 Open an account for the capital. Show it as a credit balance.

The journal is used to record these transactions and the reason. Exhibit 27.5 shows:

● the journal;

● the opening entries in the double-entry accounts.

Exhibit 27.5

		The Journal	Folio	Dr	Page 5 Cr
2003				£	£
July 1	Motor van		GL 1	840	
	Fixtures		GL 2	700	
	Stock		GL 3	390	
	Debtors – B Young		SL 1	95	
	D Blake		SL 2	45	
	Bank		CB 1	80	
	Cash		CB 1	20	
	Creditors – M Quinn		PL 1		129
	C Walters		PL 2		41
	Capital		GL 4		2,000
	Assets and liabilities at the date entered to open the books			2,170	2,170

Exhibit 27.5 *(continued)*

General Ledger
Motor Van Account

Dr   Page 1
                                                                          Cr

2003				£	
July	1	Balance	J 5	840	

Fixtures Account

Dr   Page 2
                                                                          Cr

2003				£	
July	1	Balance	J 5	700	

Stock Account

Dr   Page 3
                                                                          Cr

2003				£	
July	1	Balance	J 5	390	

Capital Account

Dr   Page 4
                                                                          Cr

					2003				£
					July	1	Balance	J 5	2,000

Sales Ledger
B Young Account

Dr   Page 1
                                                                          Cr

2003				£	
July	1	Balance	J 5	95	

D Blake

Dr   Page 2
                                                                          Cr

2003				£	
July	1	Balance	J 5	45	

Purchases Ledger
M Quinn Account

Dr   Page 1
                                                                          Cr

					2003				£
					July	1	Balance	J 5	129

C Walters Account

Dr   Page 2
                                                                          Cr

					2003				£
					July	1	Balance	J 5	41

Cash Book

Page 1

Dr   Cash   Bank   Cr

2003				£	£	
July	1	Balances	J 5	20	80	

27.8 Other items

These can be of many kinds and it is impossible to write out a complete list. Several examples are now shown:

1. K Young, a debtor, owed £2,000 on 1 July 2003. He was unable to pay his account in cash, but offers a motor car in full settlement of the debt. The offer is accepted on 5 July 2003.

   The personal account is, therefore, not now owed and needs crediting. On the other hand the firm now has an extra asset, a motor car, therefore the motor car account needs to be debited.

The Journal

	Folio	Dr	Cr
2003		£	£
July 5 Motor car		2,000	
K Young			2,000
Accepted motor car in full settlement of debt			
per letter dated 5/7/2003			

2. T Jones is a creditor. On 10 July 2003 his business is taken over by A Lee to whom the debt now is to be paid.

   Here one creditor is being exchanged for another. The action needed is to cancel the amount owing to T Jones by debiting his account, and to show it owing to Lee by opening an account for Lee and crediting it.

The Journal

	Folio	Dr	Cr
2003		£	£
July 10 T Jones		150	
A Lee			150
Transfer of indebtedness as per letter			
ref G/1335			

3. We had previously bought an office typewriter for £310. It is faulty. On 12 July 2003 we return it to the supplier, RS Ltd. An allowance of £310 is agreed, so that we will not have to pay for it.

The Journal

	Folio	Dr	Cr
2003		£	£
July 12 RS Ltd		310	
Office machinery			310
Faulty typewriter returned to supplier			
Full allowance given. See letter 10/7/2003			

27.9 Examinations and control account questions

In Chapter 25 on control accounts, section 25.7, the question as to whether control accounts formed part of the double entry was discussed. To recap:

- If the sales ledger and purchases ledger are part of the double entry then the control accounts are classed as 'memorandum accounts'.

- If the sales ledger control account and purchases ledger control account are maintained in the general ledger then they are part of the double-entry system and the sales ledger accounts and purchases ledger accounts are classed as 'memorandum accounts'.

As already stated in Chapter 25, the view of most large organisations and indeed the one most favoured by the various examining bodies is the latter, i.e. that the control accounts should be maintained in the general ledger and are, therefore, part of the double-entry system.

It is important for students to be aware of this when answering examination questions since the answer required can differ depending upon whether the control accounts are part of the double-entry system or not. Consider the example outlined in Exhibit 27.6.

Exhibit 27.6

> Wesley Davies & Co receive a cheque for £525 from one of their debtors, Clive Johnson Ltd. They bank the cheque on 4 April 2001. However, on 15 April 2001 the company is advised that the cheque has been dishonoured. Show the journal entries necessary to record the dishonoured cheque.

If Wesley Davies & Co maintain sales and purchases ledgers which are part of the double-entry system, then the control accounts will be classed as memorandum accounts and the answer would be as follows:

The Journal

	Folio	Dr	Cr
2001			
April 15 Clive Johnson Ltd		525	
Cash Book			525
Cheques received from Clive Johnson Ltd dishonoured by the bank.			

Sales Ledger

Dr			Clive Johnson Ltd Account			Cr
2001				2001		
April	1	Balance b/d	525	April	1 Bank	525
April	15	Bank dishonoured cheque	525			

Dr		Cash Book		Cr
		2001		
		April	15 Clive Johnson Ltd	
			dishonoured cheque	525

If, however, Wesley Davies & Co. maintain the sales and purchases ledger control accounts in the general ledger and they are part of the double-entry system, with the sales and purchases ledger accounts being memorandum accounts, then the answer to the question would be as follows:

The Journal

	Folio	Dr	Cr
2001			
April 15 Sales ledger control A/c		525	
Cash book			525
Cheque received from Clive Johnson Ltd			
dishonoured by the bank.			

General Ledger

Dr   *Sales Ledger Control Account*   *Cr*

2001		
April 15 Bank – dishonoured cheque		
Clive Johnson Ltd	525	

Dr   **Cash Book**   *Cr*

	2001	
	April 15 Dishonoured cheque	
	Clive Johnson Ltd	525

The student will notice that if the control accounts **are part of the double-entry system** then any entry affecting an individual debtor or creditor account is posted direct to the control account for the purpose of answering examination questions. If, however, the control accounts are **not part of the double-entry system** but are classed as memorandum accounts then any entry necessary would be made to the individual debtor or creditor account.

It is very important that students familiarise themselves with this topic, and when answering questions on control accounts in an examination ensure they read the question carefully to ascertain whether the control accounts are part of the double entry or not, as this will affect the answer.

27.10 Casting

Students will notice the use of the expression **to cast**, which means to add up. Overcasting means incorrectly adding up a column of figures to give an answer which is **greater** than it should be. Undercasting means incorrectly adding up a column of figures to give an answer which is **less** than it should be.

NEW TERMS

Casting Adding up figures.

Suspense account Account showing balance equal to difference in trial balance.

STUDENT ACTIVITIES

27.1   You are to show the journal entries necessary to record the following items:

2001

(a) May 1   Bought a motor vehicle on credit from Kingston Garage for £6,790

(b) May 3   A debt of £34 owing from H Newman was written off as a bad debt

(c) May 8   Office furniture bought by us for £490 was returned to the supplier, Unique Offices, as it was unsuitable. Full allowance will be given to us

(d) May 12   We are owed £150 by W Charles. He is declared bankrupt and we receive £39 in full settlement of the debt

(e) May 14   We take £45 goods out of the business stock without paying for them

(f) May 28   Some time ago we paid an insurance bill thinking that it was all in respect of the business. We now discover that £76 of the amount paid was in fact insurance of our private house

(g) May 29   Bought machinery £980 on credit from Systems Accelerated

27.2X   Show the journal entries for April 2001 necessary to record the following items:

April 1   Bought fixtures on credit from J Harper £1,809

April 4   We take £500 goods out of the business stock without paying for them

April 9   £28 worth of the goods taken by us on 4 April are not returned back into stock by us. We do not take any money for the return of the goods

April 12   K Lamb owes us £500. He is unable to pay his debt. We agree to take some office equipment from him at the value and so cancel the debt

April 18   Some of the fixtures bought from J Harper, £65 worth, are found to be unsuitable and are returned to him for full allowance

April 24   A debt owing to us by J Brown of £68 is written off as a bad debt

April 30   Office equipment bought on credit from Super Offices for £2,190

27.3   On 1 May 2001 the financial position of Carol Green was as follows:

	£
Freehold premises	45,000
Fixtures and fittings	12,500
Motor vehicles	9,500
Bank overdraft	2,800
Cash in hand	650
Stock in hand	1,320
F Hardy (a trade debtor)	160
A Darby (a trade creditor)	270

Required

(a) Make a journal entry for the above showing clearly the capital of Carol Green on 1 May 2001.

(b) On examination of her books on 1 May 2001 Sue Baker discovered the following adjustments were necessary:

(i) When Parker, a debtor for £350, paid his account he was allowed discount of 2 per cent for prompt payment. The actual amount of cash received has been entered in Parker's account and in the cash book, no entry having been made for the discount allowed.

(ii) The purchase of a motor van for £4,500 had not been entered in the books. The van was purchased from Supervans Ltd paying a deposit of 25 per cent, the balance being due in six months' time.

(iii) I M Broke, a debtor for £250, has been declared bankrupt. On 1 May 2001 a payment of 20p in the pound was received with notification that it will be the only payment. The remaining balance on the account is therefore to be written off as a bad debt.

Make journal entries giving effect to all of the above transactions including the payment received from Broke and the writing off of the bad debt.

(c) Show I M Broke's account and the bad debts account in the ledger.

Note: Narratives must be given with all journal entries.

(RSA)

27.4 Write the journal entries needed to effect the following:

(a) 1 July   Interest at 6 per cent per annum charged to the account of James Crawford whose debit balance was due to be paid by the previous 31 March when he owed us £120.

(b) 30 Aug   Purchased on credit from 'Mechweights' a new weighing machine worth £1,500, less (i) 10 per cent trade discount, and (ii) less a second-hand weighing machine from us worth £400, in part exchange.

(c) 10 Sept   A dividend of £0.35p in the £ received from the bankrupt estate of Thomas Watson whose debt of £150 had previously been written off as irrecoverable. The amount received had been entered in the cash book and posted to Thomas Watson's old account in the ledger, which had been reopened for the purpose.

(d) 31 Dec   The proprietor of the business, A Walker, had taken stock from the shop for his own use to the value of £39.50.

(Pitman Qualifications)

27.5 You are to open the books of K Mullings, a trader, via the journal to record the assets and liabilities, and are then to record the daily transactions for the month of May. A trial balance is to be extracted as on 31 May 2002.

2002

May   1   *Assets* – Premises £2,000; Motor van £450; Fixtures £600; Stock £1,289.
Debtors – N Hardy £40; M Nelson £180. Cash at bank £1,254;
Cash in hand £45
Liabilities – Creditors: B Blake £60; V Reagan £200.

May   1   Paid rent by cheque £15

May   2   Goods bought on credit from B Blake £20; C Harris £56; H Gordon £38;
N Lee £69

May   3   Goods sold on credit to: K O'Connor £56; M Benjamin £78; L Staines £98;
N Duffy £48; B Green £118; M Nelson £40

May   4   Paid for motor expenses in cash £13

May   7   Cash drawings by proprietor £20

May   9   Goods sold on credit to: M Benjamin £22; L Pearson £67

May 11   Goods returned to Mullings by: K O'Connor £16; L Staines £18

May 14   Bought another motor van on credit from Better Motors Ltd £300

May 16   The following paid Mullings their accounts by cheque less 5 per cent cash discount: N Hardy; M Nelson; K O'Connor; L Staines

May 19   Goods returned by Mullings to N Lee £9

May 22   Goods bought on credit from: J Johnson £89; T Best £72

May 24   The following accounts were settled by Mullings by cheque less 5 per cent cash discount: B Blake; V Reagan; N Lee

May 27   Salaries paid by cheque £56

May 30   Paid rates by cheque £66

May 31   Paid Better Motors Ltd a cheque for £300

27.6 Show the journal entries necessary to correct the following errors:

(a) A sale of goods £678 to J Harkness had been entered in J Harker's account.

(b) The purchase of a machine on credit from L Pearson for £4,390 had been completely omitted from our books.

(c) The purchase of a motor van £3,800 had been entered in error in the motor expenses account.

(d) A sale of £221 to E Fletcher had been entered in the books, both debit and credit, as £212.

(e) Commission received £257 had been entered in error in the sales account.

27.7X Show the journal entries needed to correct the following errors:

(a) Purchases £699 on credit from K Webb had been entered in H Weld's account.

(b) A cheque of £189 paid for advertisements had been entered in the cash column of the cash book instead of in the bank column.

(c) Sale of goods £443 on credit to B Maxim had been entered in error in B Gunn's account.

(d) Purchase of goods on credit from K Innes £89 entered in two places in error as £99.

(e) Cash paid to H Mersey £89 entered on the debit side of the cash book and the credit side of H Mersey's account.

27.8X J Jones extracted the following trial balance from his books on 31 January 2003:

	£	£
Capital		7,450
Drawings	3,000	
Stock 1 February 2002	2,500	
Trade debtors	2,950	
Trade creditors		2,684
Shop fittings	1,530	
Purchases	5,140	
Sales		7,460
General expenses	860	
Discount received		40
Cash at bank	1,660	
Returns outwards		40
	17,640	17,674

The following errors and omissions were subsequently discovered:

(a) A purchase of shop fittings £320 had been debited to purchases account.

(b) A sales invoice of £150 entered in the sales day book had not been posted to the customer's personal account.

(c) A credit note for £30 issued by J Jones to a customer had been completely omitted from the books.

(d) A credit balance of £16 in the purchases ledger had been omitted from the trial balance.

(e) The sales day book was undercast by £100 in December 2002.

Draw up a corrected trial balance. Show all workings.

(RSA)

27.9X For question 27.8X show the journal entries necessary to correct the errors.

Other
considerations and
supporting topics

28 Payroll procedures

- **To understand the functions of the payroll.**

- **To be able to calculate employees' pay using various methods.**

- **To be able to distinguish between statutory deductions and voluntary deductions.**

- **To be able to understand the basic outline of PAYE income tax and national insurance contributions (NIC).**

- **To be able to calculate the net pay of an employee given details of their gross pay and PAYE income tax and other deductions and be able to complete a wages book and cash analysis.**

28.1 Introduction

To enable the payment of **wages** and **salaries** to be carried out efficiently and accurately, all organisations, whether large or small, need to keep records of their **employees**. The need for this is essential not only for recording the payment of wages and income tax etc. but also for recording basic personal details. Such personal records are usually kept in the personnel department of an organisation.

28.2 Functions of the payroll

The payroll is a list of employees that specifies the wage or salary that each employee receives.

The procedures and calculations that are necessary to produce this list need to be fully understood and applied to ensure that all employees are paid promptly and correctly.

The responsibility for producing the payroll will depend on the size of the organisation. A large organisation will probably have a wages department, whereas a small one will rely on a wages clerk. Irrespective of who carries out the function they must ensure that the payments are:

1 **Accurate**
   - Correct basic payment for work done.
   - Additional entitlements such as **bonus**, overtime, expenses, etc.
   - Deduction of taxes, national insurance contributions due to the government.

- Deduction of contributions to pension and medical schemes.
- Wage cost information for the **employer**.

2 **Regular and on time**
   - Enables the employees to meet their own financial commitments and plan their future expenditure.
   - Late or irregular payment would harm the morale of the employees and cause them to doubt the financial stability of the organisation.

3 **Confidential**
   - Staff involved in preparing the payroll must not divulge any of its contents except to authorised people, i.e. company executives, the Inland Revenue.
   - Staff must only discuss with an employee that employee's wage/salary details.

4 **Secure**
   - The handling of cash and cheques must be done in a secure environment to prevent loss, theft or loss of confidentiality.
   - Checks must be built into the procedures to guard against the possibility of fraud by wages staff.
   - The distribution of wages must be organised so that each employee receives their own wage.
   - All employee records must be kept securely. If a manual system is used it should be held in a locked cabinet with access limited to staff from the personnel/wages department. If a computerised system is used, a password should be given to authorised personnel only so that the information may be accessed only by them.

28.3 Payments to employees

Payments to employees may be made by wage or salary. Wages are usually paid weekly, in cash, often to manual workers. Salaries are paid monthly by cheque, credit transfer (i.e. paid direct into the employee's bank account) or direct into a building society account.

Pay may also be referred to as remuneration, which simply means to reward or pay for work carried out. This term 'remuneration' is often attached to pay given to the directors of a company where their pay is recorded in the accounts as directors' remuneration.

28.4 Gross pay and net pay

All employees are subject to income tax (PAYE: Pay As You Earn) and national insurance contributions (NIC). These and other deductions have to be made by the employer from the gross pay so it is important to distinguish between the gross pay and net pay.

- Gross pay is the amount of wage or salary due to the employee before deductions are made.

- Net pay is the amount of wage or salary received by the employee after all deductions have been made. Many employees talk about 'take-home pay'; this is in fact the net pay.

28.5 Methods of calculating pay

The methods of calculating pay vary between employers and also the employees within an organisation. The main methods are as follows.

Fixed amount salary or wage

These are an agreed annual or weekly wage.

Example

For an annual salary of £11,604 the monthly salary would be:

$$\frac{£11,604}{12} = £967 \text{ per month}$$

whereas a weekly wage would be a set figure, e.g. £200 per week.

Time rates

Here a fixed basic rate per hour is paid multiplied by the number of hours worked.

Example A

A bricklayer receives £5.20 per hour: if he works for 40 hours during a particular week his gross pay =

40 hours × £5.20 = £208 per week

If additional hours are worked it is usual to pay the workers overtime; this payment is normally at a higher rate. Extra hours worked during the week are often paid at 'time and a half' and 'double time' is frequently paid for weekend work.

Example B

Richard Kerr worked the following hours during the week ended 31 March 2002:

	Hours
Monday	9
Tuesday	8
Wednesday	8.5
Thursday	10
Friday	8
Saturday	4

His basic rate of pay is £4.60 per hour and he works a standard week of 40 hours (i.e. 8 hours a day). Overtime is paid at time and a half during the week and double time on Saturday and Sunday.

Richard Kerr's **gross wage** for the week ending 31 March 2002 is calculated as follows:

		£
Basic pay 40 hours at £4.60	=	184.00
Overtime:		
Week 3.5 hours at (4.60 × 1.5) = £6.90 per hour	=	24.15
Saturday 4 hours at (£4.60 × 2) = £9.20 per hour	=	36.80
Gross wage	=	£244.95

Basic rate plus bonus

Many organisations offer bonus payments as an incentive to workers to reach and exceed set targets. Sometimes the bonus is referred to as a 'productivity bonus' and can be either a set sum of money or a percentage of the basic wage.

Example

Electronic Supreme Ltd manufacture television sets for both the home and overseas markets. They pay their workers a basic wage of £168 per week plus a productivity bonus of £20 per worker if 1,500 televisions are produced in the factory per week; this increases to £30 per week if production exceeds 2,000 televisions.

During the first week of November the company produces 1,600 televisions, therefore the workers will receive:

	£
Basic wage	168.00
Bonus	20.00
	£188.00

Piece rate

Here payment is based on the number of units produced or operations completed. The employee is paid only for work completed although most employers agree a minimum wage regardless of work completed. **Piece rate** payment is an incentive to encourage workers to work faster although it is important to ensure that quality does not suffer as a result of faster production.

Example

Lowe Production Co manufacture parts for the motor car industry. They pay their workers piecework rates as follows:

    Part PCD 27   = £2.10 per unit
    Part JB 103   = £7.45 per unit

They also have a minimum wage agreement of £175.00 per week.

During the first week of January one of the workers, Jack Murphy, produced 60 Part PCD 27s and 12 Part JB 103s.

His wage for the week would be:

		£
60 × £2.10	=	126.00
12 × £7.45	=	89.40
		£215.40

Another worker, Thomas Hobson, produced 50 Part PCD 27s and 8 Part JB 103s; his wage would be:

		£
50 × £2.10	=	105.00
8 × £7.45	=	59.60
		£164.60

but because there is a minimum wage agreement Thomas Hobson would receive £175.00.

Commission

Commission is a percentage based on the amount of sales made by an employee. Commission may be paid in addition to a basic salary or instead of a salary.

Example

Carol Chapman and Dianne Dawson work for a computer software company. Their salaries were £12,000 and £10,800 a year respectively, plus commission of 1 per cent of total sales made each month.

During July, Carol's sales totalled £30,000 and Dianne's £17,000. Their July salaries would be as follows:

Carol	$\dfrac{£12,000}{12}$	=	£1,000 per month
	Plus 1% of £30,000	=	300
	Salary	=	£1,300
Dianne	$\dfrac{£10,800}{12}$	=	£900
	Plus 1% of £17,000	=	170
	Salary	=	£1,070

28.6 Clock cards

Some organisations require their workers to 'clock in and out' of work to enable accurate payment to be made in respect of time spent at work.

On arrival at work each employee removes their personal **clock card** from a rack and slots it into a time recorder clock which records the time of arrival. The same procedure is carried out on leaving work.

At the end of the week the card is passed to the wages department to enable them to calculate the actual hours worked by each employee.

A clock card prior to handing to the wages department is shown in Exhibit 28.1. The card, after completion by the wages department, is given in Exhibit 28.2, showing the hours worked and calculation of gross pay.

Exhibit 28.1 A clock card prior to handing to wages department

CLOCK CARD

Name: _B. Sullivan_   No: _98_

Week ending: _11 April_   _2003_

Day	In	Out	In	Out	Total hours
Mon	8.00	12.01	1.00	5.03	
Tue	8.10	12.00	1.00	5.00	
Wed	8.01	12.02	12.57	5.01	
Thu	8.03	12.00	12.59	5.30	
Fri	8.00	12.01	1.01	4.00	
Sat	7.30	12.00			
Total					

Ordinary time

Overtime

Bonus

Gross pay

Exhibit 28.2 A clock card after completion by wages department

CLOCK CARD

Name: _B. Sullivan_   No: _98_

Week ending: _11 April_   _2003_

Day	In	Out	In	Out	Total hours
Mon	8.00	12.01	1.00	5.03	_8_
Tue	8.10	12.00	1.00	5.00	_7 3/4_
Wed	8.01	12.02	12.57	5.01	_8_
Thu	8.03	12.00	12.59	5.30	_8 1/2_
Fri	8.00	12.01	1.01	4.00	_7_
Sat	7.30	12.00			_4 1/2_
Total					_43 3/4_

Ordinary time	_39 hrs x £3.60_	_140.40_
Overtime	_1/2 hr x £5.00 plus 4 1/4 hrs x £7.20_	_33.10_
Bonus		
	Gross pay	_£173.50_

Note: Any employee clocking in more than five minutes late has pay calculated from the next quarter hour

28.7 Time sheets

Time sheets are usually used by employees who work away from the main business premises. For example, in a decorating company the workers will be employed at various locations according to the requirements of the individual jobs. Exhibits 28.3 and 28.4) show time sheets completed by an employee called Gary Lester. You will notice that Gary is required to complete details of work carried out, the hours worked on the job, together with the time spent on travelling to the job.

At the end of the week the time sheet will be checked by the supervisor or foreman before being passed to the wages department for completion.

Time sheets can also be used by workers based at the main office but involved in work for various clients or customers. A typical example here would be a firm of solicitors or accountants who carry out specific duties for clients and need to record the time spent on each particular job to enable correct costings to be carried out prior to invoicing the client.

Exhibit 28.3 Time sheet completed by employee

<table>
<tr><th colspan="5" style="text-align:center">TIME SHEET</th></tr>
<tr><td colspan="2">Name: Gary Lester</td><td colspan="3">Week ending: 20 March 2003</td></tr>
<tr><th>Day</th><th>Job description</th><th>Hours worked</th><th>Travel time</th><th>Total</th></tr>
<tr><td>**Mon**</td><td>Decorating Casino</td><td>8</td><td>$^1/_2$</td><td></td></tr>
<tr><td>**Tue**</td><td>"</td><td>8$^1/_2$</td><td>$^1/_2$</td><td></td></tr>
<tr><td>**Wed**</td><td>"</td><td>8</td><td>$^1/_2$</td><td></td></tr>
<tr><td>**Thu**</td><td>External work at Stanton offices</td><td>9</td><td>1</td><td></td></tr>
<tr><td>**Fri**</td><td>"</td><td>8$^1/_2$</td><td>1</td><td></td></tr>
<tr><td>**Sat**</td><td>Decorating office – Black's Estate Agents</td><td>6</td><td>1</td><td></td></tr>
<tr><td>**Sun**</td><td>"</td><td>4</td><td>1</td><td></td></tr>
<tr><td colspan="2" style="text-align:right">**Totals**</td><td></td><td></td><td></td></tr>
<tr><td colspan="2">**Basic** _____ hrs × _____</td><td colspan="3">**Total**</td></tr>
<tr><td colspan="2">**O/T** – **Week:** _____ hrs × _____</td><td colspan="3"></td></tr>
<tr><td colspan="2"> – **Weekend:** _____ hrs × _____</td><td colspan="3"></td></tr>
<tr><td colspan="2">**Travel:** _____ hrs × _____</td><td colspan="3"></td></tr>
<tr><td colspan="2">**Foreman:** _____</td><td colspan="3">**Gross pay**</td></tr>
</table>

One of the main advantages of using this method of recording time spent on each job is that employees are more conscious of their time and deploy time more effectively. Also clients are charged fairly according to the time spent on a particular job. However, one of the disadvantages is that clients could be overcharged if an employee records their time inaccurately or charges time to a particular client's job when that time was spent in other areas of work or inactivity.

Many organisations also require payroll information and data to be fed into the costing system to enable management information to be available for budgeting, costing and profitability analysis.

Exhibit 28.4 Time sheet showing calculations of hours worked and gross pay

TIME SHEET

Name: _Gary Lester_   Week ending: _20 March 2003_

Day	Job description	Hours worked	Travel time	Total
Mon	_Decorating Casino_	8	$^1/_2$	$8^1/_2$
Tue	"	$8^1/_2$	$^1/_2$	9
Wed	"	8	$^1/_2$	$8^1/_2$
Thu	_External work at Stanton offices_	9	1	10
Fri	"	$8^1/_2$	1	$9^1/_2$
Sat	_Decorating office – Black's Estate Agents_	6	1	7
Sun	"	4	1	5
	Totals	52	$5^1/_2$	$57^1/_2$

Basic	40	hrs ×	£5.20	**Total**	208.00
O/T – Week:	2	hrs ×	£7.80		15.60
– Weekend:	10	hrs ×	£10.40		104.00
Travel:	$5^1/_2$	hrs ×	£4.00		22.00
Foreman: _R. Derbyshire_				**Gross pay**	349.60

28.8 Computer cards

Many organisations are adapting **computerised card** systems whereby employees carry computer cards which they insert into a computerised time clock on arrival and departure. In the same way as clock cards the computerised card automatically records their hours of work.

This method of recording hours worked is often used by employers using a **flexitime system** (*see* section 28.9).

28.9 Flexitime system

Flexitime is a system permitting flexibility of working hours at the beginning or end of the day provided an agreed period of time, called the core time, is spent at work.

Staff are usually free to choose their starting and finishing times but must work the normal number of hours per week. However, it is possible to carry forward time worked in excess of the normal time, or owed, to another period and then take time off in lieu, although the time allowed to be carried forward is usually limited, say only one day per fortnight.

Flexitime is widely used in many large organisations and local authorities while not so popular in smaller private companies.

28.10 Deductions from pay

There are two types of deductions which are made from wages and salaries:

1   **statutory**

2   **voluntary**

Statutory deductions

Deductions which an employer has to make by law (statute) from their employees' gross pay are:

- income tax
- national insurance contributions.

Income tax

In the United Kingdom the wages and salaries of all employees are liable to **income tax** deductions. This does not mean, however, that everyone will pay income tax; it depends upon the amount of earnings and the **tax allowances** that can be offset against that **income**. If income tax is found to be payable then the employer will deduct the tax from the employee's wage or salary. This is then paid to the Inland Revenue, the government department responsible for collection of income tax.

National insurance contributions (NIC)

National insurance contributions (NIC) are also deducted by the employer from the employee in a similar way to income tax deductions but the employer also has to contribute a certain amount of money, again depending upon the amount of gross pay.

All contributions are again sent to the Inland Revenue, which collects them on behalf of the government Department of Social Security.

Voluntary deductions

As the name suggests these are deductions made from pay at the employee's request. They include payments to:

- occupational **pension funds** or **superannuation schemes**
- charitable organisations

- savings schemes
- trade unions and/or social clubs.

28.11 Income tax (PAYE)

Introduction

PAYE is the system used in the United Kingdom for the calculation and collection of income tax and Class 1 national insurance contributions (NIC) from employees' gross wages. As previously mentioned, the income tax and NIC collected are then paid to the Inland Revenue by the employer.

The PAYE system simply means that workers pay tax as they earn their wages or salaries. In other words they pay income tax weekly, if paid weekly wages, and monthly if salaried. This avoids a large tax bill at the end of each year, which is what some self-employed people are faced with.

Note: PAYE applies to all employees of a business including directors, both full-time and part-time staff, casuals and pensioners who are being paid superannuation/pension from an approved company scheme.

Tax year

The income tax year runs from 6 April of one year to the 5 April of the following year. The tax year for 2000/01 is as follows:

6 April 2000 to 5 April 2001

and for 2001/02:

6 April 2001 to 5 April 2002

For PAYE purposes each tax year is divided into either weeks (for weekly paid staff) or months for salaried staff.

Pay/income (for PAYE purposes)

It is important to be aware of what counts as pay for PAYE tax purposes.

Examples of such pay include:

- salaries, wages, fees, overtime, bonuses, commission
- cash payments such as Christmas gifts
- payment in respect of absence from work
- statutory sick pay
- statutory maternity pay
- holiday pay
- lump sum payments (i.e. when an employee leaves)
- tips paid in addition to normal pay.

Tax allowances

All of the above items under the heading 'pay' constitute income which is subject to income tax. However, each individual is given a personal allowance. This is a tax-free allowance (i.e. an amount of money that a person can earn without paying tax). This amount is deducted from the income to arrive at the **taxable income**. The personal allowance is known as a tax allowance and is announced each year by the Chancellor of the Exchequer in the Budget. The Chancellor also announces the rates of income tax each year. These allowances and **rates of tax** can change each year according to the Budget.

In addition to the personal allowance individuals may be entitled to other allowances such as relief on mortgage interest, maintenance payments, etc. People may also claim for professional expenses incurred in employment such as fees paid to a professional body like the Chartered Institute of Management Accountants. Allowance may also be given for expenditure on specialist equipment and working clothes such as safety shoes, overalls, etc. It is the employee's responsibility to ensure that he or she receives the right amount of allowances.

Rates of tax

When the tax allowance is deducted from the total income the difference is the taxable income; this is the amount of income which is subject to income tax. As already mentioned above, the Chancellor of the Exchequer also announces any changes in the rates of tax in his annual budget.

For the income tax year 1998/99 the rates of tax and bands of taxable income are as follows:

Lower rate at	20%	£0–£4,300
Basic rate at	23%	on the next £22,800
Higher rate at	40%	on income over £27,100

Calculation of income tax by the PAYE system

We will now look at the income tax payable in the following examples:

1   Matthew Roberts earns £3,000 a year as a part-time gardener. His personal allowance is £4,195 for the year; therefore, no tax will be payable as his personal allowance exceeds his income.

2   Adrian Duffy earns £12,400 a year as a joiner; his personal relief totals £5120. This means Adrian can earn £5,120 tax free. Therefore, Adrian's taxable pay will be as follows:

	£
Gross pay	12,400
Less Tax allowance	5,120
Taxable pay	7,280

We can now see that the amount of pay Adrian has to pay tax on is £7,280; if we were to deduct the tax under the PAYE system, Adrian would pay an amount of tax each week as he earns his wages. To enable us to calculate the amount of tax payable we would use the various tax tables, code numbers and the income tax form P11: Deductions Working Sheet.

For the time being we will calculate the total amount of income tax Adrian has to pay for the year as follows:

Tax due =	£
Income tax at 20% on £4,300	860.00
Basic rate at 23% on £2,980	685.40
Tax payable	1,545.40

3   Let us consider another example by looking at the case of Alice McGuire who, as director of a marketing company, earns considerably more than either of the two previous examples. Her salary amounts to £34,000 a year and she has allowances of £5,165; the tax payable for the year is as follows:

	£
Gross pay	34,000
Less Tax allowance	5,165
Taxable pay	28,835

Tax due =	£
Income tax at 20% on £4,300	860.00
Basic rate at 23% on £22,800	5,244.00
Higher rate at 40% on £1,735	694.00
Tax due	6,798.00

Now we have calculated the amount of income tax due for the above employees let us assume that national insurance contributions are 5 per cent of gross pay. In addition we will assume that two of the employees, Adrian Duffy and Alice McGuire, also contribute 10 per cent of their gross salary to the company pension scheme.

The **net wage/salary** each employee would receive is calculated as follows:

1   **Matthew Roberts**

	£	£
Gross wage		3,000
Less Income tax	Nil	
Less NIC	Nil	
Less Pension fund	Nil	Nil
Net wage for the year		3,000

Note: As Matthew earns less than the amount on which NIC is payable, he is not liable for NIC.

2   **Adrian Duffy**

	£	£
Gross wage/salary		12,400.00
Less Income tax	1,545.40	
Less NIC	620.00	
Less Pension fund	1,240.00	3,405.40
Net wage/salary for the year		8,994.60

3   **Alice McGuire**

	£	£
Gross wage/salary		34,000
Less Income tax	6,798	
Less NIC	1,700	
Less Pension fund	3,400	11,898
Net wage/salary for the year		22,102

Tax code numbers

To enable employers to calculate the correct amount of taxable income and tax payable by their employees they need to know each individual employee's tax allowance. This allowance is communicated to both the employee and employer by the Inland Revenue using Income Tax Form P6 in the form of a tax code.

The tax code will incorporate all the reliefs to which the employee is entitled, i.e. personal allowance, married couples allowance, plus relief for mortgage interest, etc. The way the tax codes are arrived at is very simple to understand:

- The total of all the allowances is added up, i.e. £4,195, then the last digit is removed, so £4,195 becomes 419.

- The number will also be followed by a letter. The most common letter used is *L* (for Lower) where an individual is entitled to the basic personal allowance. *H* (for Higher) is used for a person entitled to both the personal and married couples allowance.

- So the **tax code number** of 419 becomes *419L*, indicating that it is a single person's allowance.

There are other tax code numbers but at this stage of your studies it is not necessary to consider these.

Tax Tables

Tax Tables are issued by the Inland Revenue to enable organisations to operate the PAYE system as easily and smoothly as possible, always ensuring that the correct amount of tax is deducted from or refunded to employees.

The tables help employers to work out how much to deduct from, or refund to, each of their employees every time they are paid. Tax Tables are used in conjunction with the employee's tax code (*see* previous section).

A set of Tax Tables consists of:

- **Table A** – called Pay Adjustment Tables;
- **Tables LR and B to D** – called Taxable Pay Tables.

28.12 Worked example

The following example shows the preparation of a wages book, cash analysis and finally the cheque for withdrawing the money from the bank.

Example

Spencers (Exhibition Suppliers) Co of Nottingham is a small company specialising in the supply of exhibition display units and materials to industrial and commercial organisations. They employ a small workforce of four people, details of which are as follows:

Employee's name	Gross weekly wage	Income tax due	NIC employee	NIC employer
Julie L Gibbons	£185.00	£25.17	£13.91	£12.98
David R Hall	£265.00	£40.17	£21.91	£27.08
Andrew M Turner	£250.00	£35.92	£20.41	£25.55
Amanda Whitehouse	£220.00	£33.42	£17.41	£22.49

Each of the above employees also contributes £1.00 per week each to the company's social club.

The completed wages book for Spencers (Exhibition Suppliers) Co is shown in Exhibit 28.5.

Exhibit 28.5 Completed wages book for Spencers (Exhibition Suppliers) Co

WAGES BOOK

Week ending: _6 April 2002_

Number	Name	Earnings				Deductions				Net pay	Employer's NI contri-butions
		Basic	Over-time	Bonus	Total gross pay	PAYE (income tax)	National insur-ance	Other deduc-tions	Total deduc-tions		
		£	£	£	£	£	£	£	£	£	£
	J L Gibbons	185.00			185.00	25.17	13.91	1.00	40.08	144.92	12.98
	D R Hall	265.00			265.00	40.17	21.91	1.00	63.08	201.92	27.08
	A M Turner	250.00			250.00	35.92	20.41	1.00	57.33	192.67	25.55
	A Whitehouse	220.00			220.00	33.42	17.41	1.00	51.83	168.17	22.49
	Totals	920.00			920.00	134.68	73.64	4.00	212.32	707.68	88.10

The wages clerk would then prepare a cash analysis to ensure that the notes and coins obtained from the bank will enable the wage packets to be filled with correct amount of money.

Note: The company pays the first £100 in £20 notes and any amount thereafter in £10 and £5 notes or £1 coins as appropriate.

To carry out the calculation it is necessary to make a list of the note and coin values across the top and list the employees down the side. After working out what is needed for each single employee the quantities required for all the employees is added up; this is shown in Exhibit 28.6.

Exhibit 28.6 Completed cash analysis for Spencers (Exhibition Suppliers) Co

CASH ANALYSIS

Week ending: *6 April 2002*

Name	£20	£10	£5	£1	50p	20p	10p	5p	2p	1p	Amount £ p
J L Gibbons	5	4		4	1	2			1		144.92
D R Hall	5	10		1	1	2			1		201.92
A M Turner	5	9		2	1		1	1	1		192.67
A Whitehouse	5	6	1	3			1	1	1		168.17
Number of notes and coins required	20	29	1	10	3	4	2	2	4		
Totals cross-check	400	290	5	10	1.50	0.80p	0.20p	0.10p	0.8p		707.68

Now we need to check that we have carried out the cash analysis correctly by adding up the notes and coins required as follows:

Notes and coins required

				£
20	×	£20	=	400.00
29	×	£10	=	290.00
1	×	£5	=	5.00
10	×	£1	=	10.00
3	×	50p	=	1.50
4	×	20p	=	0.80
2	×	10p	=	0.20
2	×	5p	=	0.10
4	×	2p	=	0.08
				707.68

The total of the cash analysis agrees with the net pay figure as shown in the wages book (Exhibit 28.5) so we can assume that the analysis has been carried out correctly.

Finally, a cheque is made out to enable the cash to be withdrawn from the bank (*see* Exhibit 28.7).

Exhibit 28.7 Completed cheque for payment of the wages

NEW TERMS

Bonus An additional amount paid to an employee if a set target is achieved.

Clock card Card issued to employees to enable them to 'clock in and out' of work. The card is then used to calculate the employees' wages according to the number of hours spent at work.

Commission A percentage, based on the amount of sales made by an employee, which may be paid in addition to a basic salary or instead of a salary.

Computer card Card used by staff to record the time spent on the business premises by inserting the card into a computerised time clock on arrival and departure.

Flexitime system System of permitting flexibility of working hours at the beginning and end of the day provided an agreed 'core time' is spent on the premises.

Employee A person who is hired to work for an organisation in return for payment.

Employer A person or organisation that employs workers and pays them wages or salaries in return for services rendered.

Gross pay This is the amount of wages or salary before deductions are made.

Income Pay which is subject to income tax.

Income tax (PAYE) System used in the UK for the calculation and collection of income tax and Class 1 national insurance contributions (NIC) from payments made to employees.

Net pay This is the amount of wages or salary after deductions are made (the net wage is often referred to as 'take home pay').

Pension fund/superannuation scheme Schemes set up by employers to provide their employees with a pension.

Personnel department An organisation's department that deals with interviewing and appointing staff together with the keeping of accurate employee records.

Piece rate Pay based on the number of units produced or operations completed.

Rates of tax The rates of income tax which are levied by the government through the Inland Revenue.

Salary Fixed payment, usually paid monthly, to an employee for professional or office work.

Statutory deductions Deductions which an employer has to make by law (statute) from their workers' gross pay.

Tax allowance An allowance of tax-free income to which an individual is entitled. Also known as the personal allowance.

Tax code numbers A PAYE code number issued by the Inland Revenue which reflects the tax allowances to which the employee is entitled.

Taxable income The difference between income and the tax allowance is known as taxable income. This amount is subject to income tax and is known as the taxable income.

Time rate A fixed basic rate per hour is paid multiplied by the number of hours worked.

Time sheet Form used by employees, who often work away from the main business premises, to record the time spent on various jobs and the overall weekly attendance.

Voluntary deductions Deductions made from pay at the employee's request.

Wage Payment made to a worker in return for services rendered, usually paid weekly.

STUDENT ACTIVITIES

28.1 Kevin Chandler is employed by a firm of joiners and is paid at the rate of £7.50 per hour. During the week to 18 May 2001 he worked a basic week of 40 hours. The income tax due on his wages was £55, he is also liable to pay national insurance contributions of 6 per cent of his gross wage. Calculate Kevin's net wages.

28.2 Michael Ford works as an electrician and is paid a basic rate of £7.20 per hour for a 40-hour week; overtime is paid at a rate of 1½ times the basic pay. During the week ending 28 April 2001 Michael worked 50 hours. He pays national insurance at 6 per cent of his gross pay, pension contributions at 8 per cent of the basic pay and income tax at 23 per cent on all earnings after deducting £80 tax-free pay. Michael also pays £2 per week for his union subscriptions.

You are required to:
(a) Calculate Michael Ford's gross pay.
(b) Calculate each of the deductions.
(c) Show the amount Michael Ford will take home.

28.3 You are employed in the wages department of Adelwood Builders. The basic working week is 38 hours. Overtime is paid at time and a quarter for the first six hours; any further hours are paid at time and a half.

During the week ended 7 June 2001, David Rogers worked 46 hours. His basic rate is £6.80 per hour. National insurance is calculated at 9 per cent of gross pay and the weekly contribution to the pension fund is based on 5 per cent of the basic pay. Income tax is £70.45. David makes a weekly contribution of £1.50 to the Building Workers' Union.

The company's national insurance contribution to be paid on behalf of David Rogers is £17.50.

You are required to:
Complete the pay slip given in Exhibit 28.8.

(RSA)

Exhibit 28.8

Week ending

Name	Hours	Rate	Gross pay	Deductions				Total deductions	Net	Employer's national insurance contribution
				Income tax	National insurance	Pension	Others			

Exhibit 28.9

Clock No   Week No   Week ending

Name	Numbers produced	Rate	Gross pay	Deductions				Total deductions	Net pay	Employer's national insurance contribution
				Tax	National insurance	Pensions	Others			

28.4 A local business employs assembly line workers who are paid piece rates of £8 for every 50 items produced.

During week 29, ending 25 October 2001, J Sanders, whose clock number is 42, assembled 2,200 items.

Deductions from pay are to be calculated as follows:

- Company pension scheme £21.12.
- National insurance 8½ per cent of gross pay.
- PAYE 25 per cent of all earnings over £164.
- Trade union dues £3.50.

The company's national insurance contribution to be paid on behalf of J Sanders is £18.50.

You are required to:
Complete the pay slip given in Exhibit 28.9.

(RSA)

28.5 Howarth's Office Equipment Ltd employs four members of staff who each work for the company on a part-time basis. During the week ended 30 June 2002 each employee earned the following net pay:

Net wages payable for the week ended 30 June 2002

	£
W Y Chung	124.97
A Patel	154.47
L Hinds	134.37
S Jones	138.67
B Hart	124.72
	677.20

Using the following columns £20, £10, £5, £1, 50p, 20p, 10p, 5p, 2p, 1p you are requested to draw up and complete a cash analysis form and calculate the number and denominations of notes and coins required to pay the above employees. Ensure that each employee has at least one £10 note in their wage packet.

28.6X D Burton manages a small firm employing six staff. The net wages for the week ending 5 July 2001 is shown below:

Net wages for the week ending 5 July 2001

	£
D Ball	93.86
P Crofts	154.16
J Henshaw	158.26
H Stevens	151.01
K Webster	181.66
D Martin	132.56
	871.51

You are required to:
(a) Rule up and complete a note and coin analysis in table form using columns as follows:
£20, £10, £5, £1, 50p, 20p, 10p, 5p, 2p and 1p.
(b) Reconcile the value of the total notes and coins with the total wages.

28.7 Clifton Garden Services employ Gary Holland and Neil Simpson to lay grass turves on new housing estates. Each employee is paid £10 for every 100 turves laid and if any week a worker lays more than 2,000 turves he receives a bonus of 50 per cent for laying the extra turves, in addition to the normal rate for all turves laid.

In the week ended 29 May 2002 Gary Holland laid 2,200 turves and Neil Simpson 2,600 turves. Each employee has to pay national insurance contributions of 6 per cent of gross wage plus income tax at 23 per cent on all earnings after deducting £75 tax-free pay. Both Gary and Neil contribute £2 per week to the company's social club.

Calculate the net wages each employee will receive for the week ended 29 May 2002.

28.8X Calculate the gross wages for each of the following employees using the following information:

Normal working week is 40 hours.

Overtime is paid as follows:

Weekdays	Time and a quarter
Saturdays	Time and a half
Sundays	Double time

Employee	Hours worked			
	Normal	Weekday	Sat	Sun
R Giles	40	4	4	–
R Paskes	40	6	–	4
I Hargreaves	40	–	–	4
S Worrall	40	3	4	4

The basic rate of pay is £4.28 per hour

28.9 R & R Production Co manufactures exhaust clips for the motor car industry. They pay their workers £3.75 per hour – plus a weekly bonus of £2.50 for every 500 clips produced. You are required to calculate the gross wages for the week ending 30 November for the following workers:

Employee	Hours worked	Clips produced
S Crawley	40	5,000
D Brookes	44	8,000
J Burns	40	7,000
V Newman	42	4,000

28.10 Calculate the gross pay which each of the following workers would receive from the details below:

The pay rate is: £5.20 per hour plus incentive bonus scheme of 75 pence for each unit of output.

Employee	Hours worked	Output
A Taylor	35	30
S McKenzie	42	40
R Brindley	40	36
W Baseley	44	36
W Warburton	45	52

28.11X Mortons Garages Ltd, who sell new and used cars, pay their sales representatives an annual salary of £12,300 plus commission of 1 per cent of sales.

You are required to calculate the gross wages of the area representatives for August 2002.

Area	Representative	Sales for month
		£
North West	M D Ross	50,000
Midlands	J T Cross	45,000
South East	P Kent	80,000
Wales	B Knott	40,000
Scotland	H McDonald	60,000

29 Communicating for accounting

AIMS

- **To understand the importance of effective communication.**

- **To understand the process of communication.**

- **To appreciate the various means used in communication and when to use them.**

- **To be able to draft memoranda (memos), notes and letters.**

29.1 Introduction

Proper communication by a business, both internally and externally, is vital for its continuing success. Essentially business communication means transmitting information that is:

- accurate;

- of the correct content;

- to the required timescale;

- concise;

- easily understood;

- courteous.

If the six aspects above are not complied with then problems will arise.

The person receiving the information may want clarification which can lead to delays and could cause loss of goodwill. This could occur if a customer received a number of incorrect invoices in a month and had to query each one. This could lead to doubts as to the competence generally of the supplier. It could also lead to the supplier receiving payments later than expected with the possibility of cash flow problems.

An organisation receives information as well as sending it and expects what it receives to meet the six aspects stated above. It will then be able to respond effectively and promptly.

29.2 The process of communication

The process of communication follows an accepted sequence of activities but people are not normally conscious of these in their daily work. However, understanding the principles involved in communication can help in preparing information for transmission.

Exhibit 29.1 One-way communication

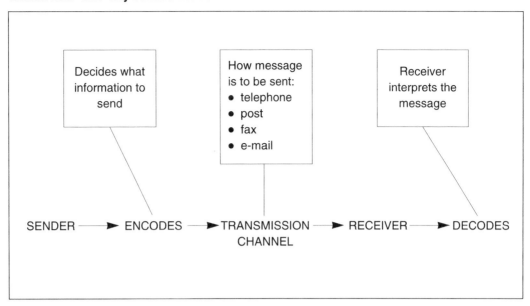

Exhibit 29.1 shows one-way communication but the sender does not know if the message has been received or if it has been understood. Only when the receiver responds will the sender know that the message has been successfully received.

Some organisations, following the receipt of a communication, may send an acknowledgement which lets the sender know that their message is being dealt with and usually indicates when the response might be given. This shows good practice by the organisation since the response is informative, immediate, courteous and leads to goodwill between the organisation and the sender.

The basic decision is how to communicate – should it be oral or written? The relative advantages of these are:

Written	**Oral**
Can be planned	Personal
Accurate	Can be two-way
Allows time for a response	Fast
Provides a record	Simple
Effective for complex information	Flexible

The demands of a business mean that a more formal approach to communication is needed than would be used in a social context.

There will also be a difference in internal communication in organisations which can be less formal than that used when dealing with external organisations. However, the size of an organisation will have an influence on internal communication – a large concern will usually have well-established procedures whereas a small one will leave the format of communication to individuals.

29.3 Internal communication

There will be a great deal of oral communication during the working day – face-to-face discussion, internal telephone calls and possibly external telephone calls where the organisation has many branches.

These will cover many situations and topics but will normally involve colleagues and be highly interactive relative to the work of the particular department. This form of communication is likely to be fairly informal but on occasions it will be necessary to make notes to record facts, instructions, etc., since it is unlikely that these can be memorised.

More formal internal communication will involve notes, memoranda (memos) and electronic mail (e-mail).

Notes

Notes are used to convey a message in an abbreviated form and tend to fall into two categories.

A very informal note will usually involve close colleagues, an example of which is shown in Exhibit 29.2.

Exhibit 29.2

> 2.30 p.m. 27.3.00
>
> Alan
>
>   Joan called from Sales, please ring.
>
>   Sue

The note is adequate for the purpose. It is brief but contains all the essential information. The time of the message is clearly stated and Sue knows that her colleague, Alan, has regular contact with Joan in Sales. The time taken to write the message is probably about 30 seconds which is time effective.

A more formal note will be necessary to convey a message with more important information. This might take the form shown in Exhibit 29.3.

Exhibit 29.3

> 9.30 a.m. 16.5.01
>
> Gary
>
>   Mr Wright, Dellaware Ltd, called about discount on Invoice 88140, thought it should be 20% not 15%. Please call 01998 641262 today or after 1 p.m. tomorrow.
>
>   Sue

Again, all necessary information has been conveyed. Mr Wright obviously expects a response by the following afternoon and the writer has given sufficient facts to allow Gary to check the invoice before calling him. However, the note is obviously intended for a close colleague due to the use of first names only.

All written communication must show the date that the message was initiated and the time if the writer considers this appropriate. It is surprising how many people omit this essential information. Without the date the receiver will have no idea how long the message has existed.

Memoranda (Memos)

These are normally considered vital to maintain proper communication in larger organisations A memo is a formal communication document and is used to pass information, i.e. one-way communication, or require a response, i.e. two-way communication.

The standard of English used in memos must be high but abbreviations can be used. These may be generally accepted abbreviations or they might be peculiar to a particular organisation.

Memos are normally kept short to convey only essential information. They may be handwritten, but are more usually typed and the sender keeps a copy.

A typical layout of a memo is shown in Exhibit 29.4.

Exhibit 29.4 Layout of a memo

MEMO	
To:	Date:
From:	
Subject:	

The person sending the memo may add their initials, full name or leave it unsigned depending on the practice in a particular organisation.

The memos in Exhibits 29.5 and 29.6 show how different information might be conveyed.

Exhibit 29.5 Memo conveying a single item of information

MEMO		
To:	All accounting staff	**Date:** 3.2.02
From:	M Johnson, Accounts Manager	
Subject:	Financial Audit	

The annual financial audit will start on 6 March 2002 and the auditors expect to be on the premises for seven days.

I will arrange a meeting during week commencing 15 February to ensure staff are aware of the requirements of the audit.

All members of the accounting staff will be required to attend.

M Johnson

Exhibit 29.6 Memo providing information and also asking for a response

<table>
<tr><td colspan="3" align="center">MEMO</td></tr>
<tr><td>To:</td><td>D Wood, Accounts Manager</td><td>Date: 6.4.02</td></tr>
<tr><td>From:</td><td colspan="2">S Ahktar, Budgetary Control Manager</td></tr>
<tr><td>Subject:</td><td colspan="2">Budget – Revenue expenses</td></tr>
</table>

The actual revenue expenses for the first three months of the year have exceeded the budget by 11 per cent. I am concerned about the effect on cash flow of this over-spend and would like to arrange a meeting soon to discuss the situation.

I suggest Friday, 8 April for this meeting at 9.30 a.m. in Committee Room 3.

Would you please let me know if this is convenient to you.

SA

It is important to remember that memos should be issued sparingly since they are time-consuming to prepare and they usually demand action from the recipient. Do not over-burden staff with an excess of memos otherwise their normal working routine will be disrupted.

Electronic mail (e-mail)

Many organisations now have sophisticated computer systems with staff able to communicate using e-mail. This is a fast interactive system for conveying information. It can be used internally in one building, for communication with departments remote from the building, for example the company's shops, or for communication with suppliers and customers.

E-mail uses a computer linked to a telephone line to communicate with other computers in almost any part of the world. The sender can type in a message or scan a document which can then be sent to the receiver's computer at any time. This is ideal for communicating with organisations in different time zones such as Australia and America.

The receiver's machine can store the message ready to be retrieved and, if required, a hard copy can be obtained via a printer. The receiver can reply to the on-screen message straight away or can amend or edit a document for return to the sender.

Both the fax (*see* section 29.4 below) and e-mail systems make economic use of the telephone network since neither need to locate an individual to convey messages.

E-mail is a fast-expanding system with many organisations and individuals having the necessary equipment even though it is much more expensive than a fax machine.

29.4 External communication

The usual documents used in day-to-day accounting communication were discussed in Chapter 18 on documents used in buying and selling (*see* pp. 173–89).

External communication will be by telephone, fax, e-mail and letter. Here we intend to deal with the more formal means – fax and letter – since these provide a record for the sender and receiver. E-mail has already been discussed – *see* section 29.3 above.

Fax (facsimile)

This form of communication consists of two machines which resemble small photocopiers linked by a telephone line. The sender places a document into the fax machine which scans it and turns it into a series of electronic impulses which are fed via the telephone line to the receiver's machine. This converts the impulses back into images to reproduce a facsimile of the original. The machines are relatively inexpensive, about £250, but the drawback is that the receiver's machine must be free to accept the sender's message.

An example of a typical fax is given in Exhibit 29.7 which shows a pre-printed form on which a message can be written or typed. The message should be as concise as possible so as to keep the time of transmission short thus keeping the cost to a minimum.

Exhibit 29.7 A typical fax

FAX	**DEAN END GARAGE**
DATE: 29 Oct 2000	**BELPER, DERBYSHIRE**
FROM: Paul Collins	**FAX NO 01954 767667**
TO: MEREGATE SUPPLIES LEEDS L34 7BJ	

FAX NO   01

ATTENTION OF: Jane Barlow

Re: Your Invoice No 107994 for £1,671.28

Your quotation of 23.9.2000 gave a total of £1,611.28. I consider an error of £60 has been made and a credit note is requested.

Please check and advise.

Paul Collins

Letters

Letters are extensively used in the business environment even though technology has had a great influence on communication over the last 20 years or so. Business letters usually have a letterhead printed on them giving all the details of the sender, such as name, address, telephone and fax numbers. They must convey information as quickly and efficiently as possible and a number of conventions have evolved which ensures this is done. A conventional business letter is shown in Exhibit 29.8.

Exhibit 29.8 Business letter

GLEESON PAINTS

**DEAN CROSS ROAD
DERBY DE14 9HQ**

Our ref: A/7452

Your ref: GP 4451

Tel: 01576 872001

Fax: 01576 877230

Ms G Bond
Adam Chemicals Ltd
Willow Road
Birmingham
B12 6ST

3 March 2001

Dear Ms Bond

Our O/No G 69121

We have experienced an increase in demand for our gloss paints and want to amend our order quantity for: White Spirit, Type AC 24, from 750 litres per month to 1,400 litres per month. This increase to take effect from 1 May 2001.

Please confirm that you are able to supply the increased amount. We propose to issue an amendment to the above order following your agreement that you can meet our request.

Yours sincerely

David Barlow

David Barlow, Purchasing Manager

How a letter is started will decide how it is to be closed:

- Letters beginning 'Dear Sir', 'Dear Madam' or 'Dear Sir or Madam' should end 'Yours faithfully'.

- Letters beginning 'Dear Mr/Mrs/Miss/Ms Ward' should end 'Yours sincerely'.

All letters should be signed by the sender and since many signatures cannot be read it has become normal practice to type the person's name below the signature followed by the position of the writer in the organisation.

 NEW TERMS

E-mail Electronic mail transmitted via the telephone network using computers.

Fax (facsimile) Communication using photocopier-like machines which are linked via telephone lines.

Memorandum Formal written internal communication used by organisations.

STUDENT ACTIVITIES

29.1 You work in the Accounts Dept of King Office Supplies and you have just taken a telephone call on behalf of your boss Jean Todd, sales accounts manager, from Derek Amos, one of the company's sales representatives. Jean is presently at a meeting with the directors.

Derek has just visited a very good customer, Sphere Products, and spoken to the buyer, Mr Stott, who complained about two incorrect invoices that had been received in the last few days. The invoices are 40169 and 40183.

Derek wants the complaint conveyed to Jean Todd urgently and for her to contact Mr Stott to explain the reason for the errors and to correct them.

(a) Decide on a suitable format for conveying the information to Jean Todd and draft this in your own name.

(b) What other action might you decide to take to assist Jean Todd in dealing with the complaint?

29.2 You work as an accounts assistant at Popular Plastics Ltd, Trent Road, Derby DE14 7MN. Your duties include the preparation of invoices, credit notes and statements of account. While preparing the statements of account for May 2001 you notice that Sentinel Signs Ltd, 142 King Street, Chester CH3 4PQ still owe £58. On investigation you find that it refers to Invoice no PP 4611 dating back to 7 February 2001.

Draft a letter to the company requesting payment of the overdue invoice.

29.3 As accounts clerk at Johnson Products Co, Park Industrial Estate, Knutsford, you find that the month end is particularly busy with suppliers requiring payments by the seventh day of the following month.

Check the calculations on the three invoices shown in Exhibit 29.9 and if any errors are found draft an appropriate letter to the supplier concerned.

Exhibit 29.9

SEDDON & SONS (Painters & Decorators) Northern Road, Middlewich	79
	23 June 2001

		£
To Decorating office and reception area including supply of materials		
	As per quotation	525.00
	VAT	91.87
		616.87

CITY SERVICES & SUPPLIES Invoice No 01782 Harwood Industrial Estate, Stockport Date: 17th June 2001 VAT 740 9452 20	
	Amount
7 – ½" SWITCH BOARD @ £49.00 each	343.00
3 – K71 ANGLE STRUTS @ £23.50 each	70.50
	413.50
VAT	27.36
	440.86

	Invoice No B39766
HEATH MFR CO LTD Knutsford Road, Macclesfield	Date 16th June 2001
To supplying Parts to your Drawing No ZS 37/5441	357.70
VAT	60.20
£	417.90
VAT 863 2730 33	

29.4X The financial controller, Don O'Connor, has received the letter shown in Exhibit 29.10 from a customer.

Exhibit 29.10

BD STEEL SERVICES LIMITED

Unit 27 Carlton Industrial Estate, Walsall,
West Midlands, WS7 2DZ
Telephone: 01563 938014
Fax: 01563 785013

Centro Steelstock Limited
18 Walsall Trading Estate
Walsall
West Midlands
WS8 9CF

For the attention of the Financial Controller

28 November 2001

Dear Sirs

It was with some concern that we received your statement of account this morning and noted that we will be unable to take any more goods on credit until a payment has been made as we are in excess of our credit limit.

The growth of our company over the last three years has been reflected in the amount of orders placed with you for steel. However, during this time our credit limit has remained the same and is now inadequate. Will you please arrange to increase our credit limit to £20,000 to allow our two companies to continue our good trading relationship.

Yours faithfully

B Daniels
Director

Registered in England number 4587978
Directors: B Daniels   G Chance   Company Secretary: C Laing

Don has investigated the account of B D Steel Services Limited and is satisfied that they have maintained their account in a satisfactory manner. Draft a letter, ready for Don's signature, confirming that B D Steel Services Limited's credit limit will be raised to £20,000 as requested, and thanking them for their valued custom.

Write a memo on behalf of Don O'Connor to the credit controller, Jan Pearce, briefly explaining the content of the letter from B D Steel Services Limited and the decision to increase their credit limit to £20,000. Ask Jan Pearce to ensure this increase is made with immediate effect.

(AAT (part of Central Assessment))

Practice assessments and multiple-choice questions

30 Practice assessments – cash and credit transactions

30.1 Introduction

This chapter contains two practice assessments which are typical of the AAT Foundation Level Assessment in Cash and Credit Transactions. Each assessment consists of three parts:

Section 1   Processing Exercise
Section 2   20 Short Answer Tasks
Section 3   Communicating Accounting Information

and the whole assessment should be completed in three hours.

30.2 Practice assessments

- **Practice assessment 1 – Summit Glazing Ltd**
  Section 1 (amended) has been reproduced by kind permission of the AAT while Sections 2 and 3 have been devised to represent a typical AAT format.

- **Practice assessment 2 – Medic Supplies Ltd**
  In this case, the whole assessment has been devised by the authors which should be very similar to those set by the AAT.

The purpose of the AAT central assessment is to test the knowledge and understanding which underpin the competences required by the Accounting Standards. Since the central assessment aims to cover the broader aspects of each unit students must be able to apply their knowledge and understanding to a variety of situations. Students must attain a high degree of accuracy and presentation and demonstrate competence with a high level of correct responses.

Students will notice that the practice assessment papers contain much larger figures than in the rest of the textbook. The purpose of this is to provide the student with plenty of practice prior to undertaking the central assessment rather than coming across larger figures for the first time in a live assessment.

30.3 Control accounts

Chapter 25 presented a full discussion of the treatment of control accounts within the double-entry system, while in Chapter 27, section 27.9, the topic was also covered in relation to answering assessment tasks. For the purpose of answering central assessment tasks the debtors control account and the creditors control account are maintained in the general ledger and are, therefore, part of the double-entry system. The individual personal accounts of the debtors and creditors are maintained in the debtors ledger and creditors ledger respectively and are classed as memorandum accounts only. This procedure is that favoured by many organisations and is more consistent with computerised methods of accounting.

30.4 Day books

The processing question which forms Section 1 of the central assessment paper, contains data which is in summary form. In many organisations the sales day books, purchases day books and returns day books are kept in analysed form, i.e. the sales day book may be divided into sales areas such as Scotland, England and Wales. The object of this section of the assessment is to test the student's understanding of the interrelationships within a basic double-entry system rather than repeat a more detailed and larger exercise which should have been covered within simulations or provided as work-based evidence.

30.5 Preparing for external assessment

In reaching this stage, students will have spent a considerable amount of time in mastering the art of double entry, dealing with cash and credit transactions, and learning new terms and theories. To benefit from all the hard work students need to decide upon a particular strategy in preparing to take a central assessment or a multiple-choice examination. The following tips should help in the preparation.

1   Know the subject and all the topics within it thoroughly.

2   Allow sufficient time for revision. Make a timetable which ensures the subject is covered but also provides for relaxation.

3   Make your own revision notes since these are most likely to be remembered and will aid your knowledge and understanding.

4   To develop competence, practise as many relevant questions as possible.

5   Check your understanding and competence by trying a practice paper of the type of final assessment you will be undertaking.

6   Study in a comfortable place but ensure that you are aware of your own concentration span. A short break or a different activity can help within a fairly long study period.

7   Make sure you have everything needed for the assessment. This can include assessment entry document, calculator, rule, pen and pencil.

The approach to actually taking a central assessment or multiple-choice examination will vary slightly. The technique for tackling multiple-choice examinations is dealt with in Chapter 31.

30.6 AAT Central Assessments

These were discussed at the beginning of the book in Chapter 1 but there are further points to be considered.

- **Section 1 – Processing Exercise**
  A very important aspect of this section is the application of double-entry principles and the way in which data reaches its correct destination within the ledgers. Competence in posting transactions is essential in being able to complete this section.

  It is suggested that in a central assessment this section be completed **after** tackling the short questions.

- **Section 2 – Short Answer Tasks**
  As already mentioned this section of the paper is best attempted **first**. Such is the broad nature of this section that tackling this section first means that the questions might help refresh the student's memory and instil confidence.

  Where a guide is given within the paper as to how long to spend on this section, say 60 minutes, divide the number of questions, say 20, into 60 minutes. This indicates that three minutes be spent on each question which should not be exceeded initially. Some questions are likely to be answered fairly quickly which can leave time to return to the more difficult questions. Make sure that all questions are attempted – even a guess could produce the right answer.

- **Section 3 – Communicating Accounting Information**
  This section requires the student to communicate accounting information in a formal way, usually by memoranda and letters. Chapter 29 covered all the aspects of business communication and provided the student with examples of the various forms of communication and the opportunity for developing competence by undertaking the student activities.

  It is important for the student not to neglect this important area since competence in all areas must be achieved in order to gain the qualification.

Practice assessment 1 – Summit Glazing Ltd

The time allowed for this practice assessment is 3 hours.

The assessment is in three sections:

Section 1 – Processing Exercise

Section 2 – 20 Short Answer Tasks

Section 3 – Communicating Accounting Information

Introduction

The tasks and questions are based on the transactions of Summit Glazing Ltd. The company provides a glazing service to commercial and domestic customers. It also constructs conservatories and installs replacement windows which are bought in from specialist manufacturers.

The Managing Director is Chris Cooper and Mary Owen is the Accountant/Company Secretary. You are employed as an Accounting Technician to assist Mary Owen.

Data

The following transactions all occurred on 1 December 2001 and have yet to be entered into the ledger system. VAT has been calculated at the rate of 17.5 per cent.

Sales invoices issued

	Total	VAT	Net
	£	£	£
G C J Builders Ltd	8,460	1,260	7,200
Acorn Housing Association	6,063	903	5,160
Cordington PLC	2,021	301	1,720
James Building Services	799	119	680
	17,343	2,583	14,760

Purchases invoices received

	Total	VAT	Net
	£	£	£
Georgian Conservatories	705	105	600
Diamond Glass Ltd	2,115	315	1,800
Russell Timber Supplies	423	63	360
Elite Windows	1,269	189	1,080
	4,512	672	3,840

Credit note received

	Total	VAT	Net
	£	£	£
Diamond Glass Ltd	47	7	40

Cheques received

	£	
Acorn Housing Association	6,200	
For cash sales	329	(Including £49 VAT)

Cheques issued

	£	
Georgian Conservatories	27,195	(Full settlement of an invoice for £27,750)
Elite Windows	13,995	

Journal entry

	Debit £	Credit £
Motor expenses	340	
Motor vehicles		340

Correction of error: Cost of repairs on delivery van debited in error to the motor vehicle account.

Account balances

The following balances are available to you at the start of the day on 1 December 2001.

	£
Purchases	897,953
Sales	1,138,325
Purchases returns	4,280
Bank (debit balance)	22,723
Petty cash	150
Bank charges	1,417
VAT (credit balance)	8,136
Discounts allowed	6,340
Discounts received	2,892
Sales ledger control (debtors)	85,995
Purchases ledger control (creditors)	78,237
Wages	282,500
Rent & rates	16,225
Electricity	4,106
Telephone	1,852
Motor expenses	6,857
Insurance	5,935
Sundry expenses	2,734
Motor vehicles	56,900
Machinery & equipment	15,120
Stocks	37,063
Capital	212,000

Section 1 Processing exercise

Task 1.1   Draw up the following accounts and enter in the opening balances:

- Sales ledger control account
- Purchases ledger control account
- Purchases
- Sales
- VAT
- Purchases returns
- Discounts received

- Motor vehicles
- Motor expenses

Task 1.2 Using the data already shown enter all the transactions into the accounts given in Task 1.1.

Task 1.3 Balance all the accounts in which you have made entries.

Note: You are not required to update any accounts other than those shown in Task 1.1.

Task 1.4 Show how the memorandum accounts would appear in the sales ledger and purchases ledger in respect of:

- Acorn Housing Association: Debit balance brought down to 1 December 2001 £6,200.

- Georgian Conservatories: Credit balance brought down to 1 December 2001 £48,920.

Balance down the accounts to the following day.

Task 1.5 Taking into account the transactions on 1 December, draw up a list of balances as it would appear at the close of business on 1 December 2001. Remember to take into account the balances shown in the list of opening balances which have not already been used in this processing exercise.

Note: If the list of balances totals do not agree, do not waste time looking for the errors but instead carry on with the rest of the simulation. When you have completed the remainder of the simulation then you can use any spare time to correct the trial balance.

Section 2 Short answer tasks

Answer all of the following questions

1 List three checks that should be made when accepting a credit card from a customer in payment for goods.

2 Summit Glazing has had some heavyweight shelving installed by Speedy Fixtures Ltd. There is a serious fault in the shelving. A fitter from Speedy Fixtures Ltd inspects it and says it is the fault of the manufacturer, and that Summit Glazing should contact the manufacturer to obtain satisfaction.

  (a) Was the fitter legally correct in telling them to contact the manufacturer?

  (b) Briefly explain the reason for your answer.

3 Give one reason only for maintaining a purchases ledger (creditors) control account.

4 Summit Glazing has recently bought five special steel drills. Would the purchase be regarded as revenue expenditure if:

  (a) The steel drills are to be kept in stock for sale to customers. Answer Yes or No.

  (b) The steel drills are to be used only by Summit Glazing. Answer Yes or No.

5 Would the following errors cause a difference to occur between the total of the balances in the sales ledger and the balance of the debtors' control account? Answer Yes or No.

(a) An invoice for £77 has been incorrectly added up as £277 and shown as such in the sales day book.

(b) A cheque for £186 has been entered in the wrong debtor's account.

(c) A debit balance on an account has been brought down as a credit balance.

(d) A cash discount, which should have been £15 was incorrectly calculated as £18.

6 State two advantages of using a computerised accounting system.

7 A cheque requisition form is used to request payment from a debtor by cheque. True or False?

8 Summit Glazing has bought five tonnes of steel bolts at £400 a tonne. A trade discount of 30 per cent was agreed as well as a 2.5 per cent cash discount if paid within seven days. Calculate the following figures:

(a) The total of the VAT.

(b) The total of the cash discount.

(c) The total of the trade discount.

(d) The total to be paid if payment is made after 14 days.

9 Classify the following ledger accounts according to whether they represent: Asset/Liability/Revenue/Expense.

(a) Rent

(b) Petty cash float

(c) Loan from V Flynn

(d) Discounts received

(e) Bank overdraft

10 A credit balance on a personal account normally denotes a liability. In view of this, explain briefly why, when the company has funds in the bank, it should receive a statement showing a credit balance.

11 Should the total of the VAT column in a returns inwards day book be debited or credited to the VAT account in the general ledger?

12 Which accounts are contained in the sales ledger?

13 Which of the following would not be entered in the sales ledger?

(a) Discounts received

(b) Payments for accounts outstanding more than one year

(c) Delivery notes

(d) Dishonoured cheques

14 Summit Glazing Ltd wants to pay for its business rates bill by ten instalments each year. The amount of rates varies each year. Which method of payment would be the most appropriate?

(a) Standing order

(b) Credit transfer

(c) Telegraphic transfers

(d) Direct debit

15 Give TWO examples of the use of the journal as a book of original entry.

16 Summit Glazing Ltd operate a petty cash imprest system. The float at the start of the period was £150. During the period the following payments were made:

	£
Stationery	8.96
Food for guard dog	7.22
Cleaning materials	18.47
Travelling expenses	29.36
Sundries	18.11

At the end of the period it was decided to reduce the float to £125. What amount of money will be required at the end of the period to reimburse the petty cashier?

17 When cheques are received from debtors it is important that certain measures are taken by the business to ensure that monies received are properly handled. Briefly describe three measures that the business should adopt.

18 Summit Glazing Ltd are planning to buy a new machine. Would the following items be classified as capital or revenue expenditure?

(a) Purchase price of the machine

(b) Cost of insurance against injury to machine operator

(c) Cost of extra attachment to the machine

(d) Carriage inwards on machinery bought

19 The only people who can get cash discounts are those who pay immediately by cash. True or False?

20 Complete the following sentences by inserting the name of the document to be used.

(a) Summit Glazing Ltd send out a .... to accompany the goods being delivered.

(b) Each month Summit Glazing sends out a ....to each of its customers showing the transactions between them and showing the amount, if any, owed by the customers.

(c) When petty cash is paid to any of Summit Glazing Ltd's staff they must complete a ....

Section 3 Communicating accounting information

Suggested time allocation: 45 minutes

Answer BOTH TASKS

Task 3.1 On 20 December 2001, Elite Windows delivered a consignment of double-glazed windows Model L400 to Summit Glazing Ltd against order no 6918. Their invoice no 232/12 was received by Summit Glazing on 21 December for a total of £3,243. This was calculated as follows:

	£
20 – Double Glazed Windows Model L400 at £138 each	2,760
VAT @ 17.5 %	483
	3,243

On 22 December 2001 you receive a copy of the goods received note from the Goods Inwards Dept which shows that an actual quantity of 18 windows was delivered.

Draft an appropriate letter to Elite Windows, Bolton Road, Bury BY10 6JJ, advising them of the discrepancy in the amount of windows received and ask for a credit note for the correct amount.

Task 3.2 You have been asked by Mary Owen to check the aged debtors list for accounts which have now been unpaid for more than six months. On checking you find that only one account over six months old exists, that of Abbott Building Co for £157.00. She asks you to investigate this account and propose a course of action.

You telephone the company but the line is dead. Your subsequent letter is returned with 'gone away' written on the envelope. You ask your sales representative to visit the company and she reports that the premises are now occupied by a garage repair business. The owner of the business told her that the owner of Abbott Building Co was rumoured to have gone abroad.

Draft a memorandum to Mary Owen with your findings and recommendations.

Practice assessment 2 Medic Supplies Ltd

The time allowed for this practice assessment is 3 hours.

The assessment is in three sections:

Section 1:   Processing exercise

Section 2:   20 short answer tasks

Section 3:   Communicating accounting information

Introduction

The tasks and questions are based on the transactions of Medic Supplies Ltd. The company is a wholesale chemist supplying goods entirely to retail chemists. It is located in London in the UK.

The Managing Director is Jane Mayall and Mark Hanson is the Accountant. You are employed as an Accounting Technician to assist Mark Hanson.

Data

The following transactions all occurred on 1 May 2002 and have yet to be entered in the ledger systems. VAT is at the rate of 17.5 per cent.

Sales invoices issued

	Total £	VAT £	Net £
Wilson & Co	2,115	315	1,800
Healthcheck Ltd	7,614	1,134	6,480
Kildare Ltd	4,418	658	3,760
Other customers	16,309	2,429	13,880
	30,456	4,536	25,920

Purchases invoices received (all goods for resale)

	Total £	VAT £	Net £
United Powders	4,465	665	3,800
Megax Ltd	2,491	371	2,120
Opex Ltd	9,729	1,449	8,280
Other suppliers	6,533	973	5,560
	23,218	3,458	19,760

Credit note issued

	Total £	VAT £	Net £
Kildare Ltd	282	42	240

Credit note received

	Total £	VAT £	Net £
United Powders	846	126	720

Cheques issued

	£	
Opex Ltd	4,178	(In full settlement of an invoice for £4,285)
Sundry expenses	235	(Including VAT £35)

Cheques received

	£	
Wilson & Co	11,079	(In full settlement of an invoice for £11,221)
Kildare Ltd	3,795	
Cash sales	1,598	(Including VAT £238)

Account balances

The following balances are available to you at the start of the day on 1 May 2002:

	£
Suppliers:	
Opex Ltd	4,285
Megax Ltd	1,650
United Powders	5,811
Other suppliers	255,057
Customers:	
Wilson & Co	22,490
Kildare Ltd	5,066
Healthcheck Ltd	13,875
Other customers	519,374
Other accounts:	
Purchases	1,346,217
Sales	1,895,105
Purchases returns	8,212
Sales returns	11,370
Bank (credit balance)	2,173
Discounts received	20,890
Discounts allowed	24,666
Creditors control account	266,803
Debtors control account	560,805
VAT (credit balance)	59,230
Sundry expenses	1,585
Various other credit balances – total	747,587
Various other debit balances – total	1,055,357

Section 1   Processing exercise

Complete ALL the following tasks: suggested time allocation 60 minutes

Task 1.1   Draw up the following accounts and enter in the opening balances:

- Bank (cash book)
- Debtors control account
- Creditors control account
- Sales
- Purchases
- VAT

- Sundry expenses
- Discounts received
- Discounts allowed
- Opex Ltd
- Kildare Ltd

Task 1.2   Using the data already shown, enter all relevant transactions in the accounts shown in Task 1.

The cash book should be divided into two sections, one to record receipts and the other to record payments.

Analysis columns in the cash book received and cash book payments should show as follows:

	Received		*Payments*
1	Discounts	1	Discounts
2	Total received	2	Total paid
3	VAT	3	VAT
4	Debtors	4	Creditors
5	Other	5	Other

Task 1.3   Total the various columns of the cash book and clearly show the closing bank balance.

Task 1.4   Transfer any relevant sums from the cash book into the other accounts shown in Task 1.1.

Task 1.5   Balance off all the remaining accounts in which you have made entries.

Note: You are **not** required to update any accounts other than those shown in Task 1.

Section 2   Short answer tasks

Using, where appropriate, the information given in Section 1, answer the following. Suggested time allocation: 75 minutes

ANSWER ALL THE QUESTIONS

1   If a cheque received from a customer was later dishonoured, would it then show as a debit or a credit on the bank statement of Medic Supplies Ltd?

2   In a sale of goods a contract must contain three basic elements. What are they?

3   Which of the following would not be recorded in the accounts?

   (a)   A promise to a supplier to order more goods in future

   (b)   Payment by postal order

   (c)   Cash donation to a local charity

   (d)   Payment to member of Parliament for advice

4   Medic Supplies Ltd has recently bought six electronic tablet counting machines, retail price being £500 each. A 20 per cent trade discount has been obtained, together with a 2.5 per cent discount if paid within seven days. VAT is at the rate of 17.5 per cent.

Calculate the following:

(a) The amount of trade discount.

(b) The total of the cash discount.

(c) How much would have to be paid if Medic Supplies Ltd paid for them two months later.

(d) The amount of VAT included in the total price.

5 Medic Supplies Ltd is going to retain three of the machines mentioned in question 4 above for its own use while the remaining two machines will be sold to customers. Explain how the purchase of these machines will be treated in the accounts.

6 State whether the following errors would cause a difference to occur between the balance of the sales control account and the total of the balances in the sales ledger.

		Answer
(a)	An invoice has been omitted from the sales day book.	Yes/No
(b)	A debtor's account has been incorrectly balanced off.	Yes/No
(c)	A bad debt has not yet been written off.	Yes/No

7 Medic Supplies Ltd paid out two cheques which meant that the bank account was overdrawn but was within the limit agreed by the bank. When presented the two cheques were dishonoured by the bank. The suppliers, to whom the cheques had been sent, have refused to supply any more goods in future. What could Medic Supplies Ltd do now to remedy the situation?

8 Why do Medic Supplies Ltd have a purchases ledger?

9 Cash discounts are not allowed if the rate of trade discount is 50 per cent or more. True/False.

10 When using a computer to process accounting data there are two main systems which can be adopted.

(a) The system where documents or transactions for a period are grouped and processed together is known as .... processing.

(b) The system where documents or transactions are input as they occur is known as .... processing.

11 What bookkeeping entries are necessary to record a cash refund of £188 (inclusive of VAT) to a cash sales customer who has returned the goods.

12 Would the following errors cause a difference to occur between the balance of the creditors control account and the total balance in the purchases ledger? Answer Yes or No.

(a) A creditor's account has been balanced off incorrectly.

(b) An invoice for £37 has been entered into the purchases day book as £39.

(c) An invoice has, in error, been omitted from the purchases day book.

13 A page in the purchases ledger has been partially destroyed. One item in the account has been torn away. What was it, and how much was the amount involved? The items shown are:

Returns outwards £404; Discounts received £48; Cheques paid £2,195;

Cash paid £96; Balance carried forward £1,944; Purchases £2,368.

14 Medic Supplies Ltd buys medical supplies from and sell supplies to Kildare Ltd. The two companies have agreed to set off a debt owing to Kildare Ltd against the balance which Kildare Ltd owes to Medic Supplies Ltd.

What entries would be required in the *general ledger* of Kildare Ltd to record this set-off?

15 Which of the following cannot be called 'purchases' by Medic Supplies Ltd?

(a) Buying pill boxes in which pills are to be sold.

(b) Buying a closed-circuit television system to help defend premises from possible criminal activities.

(c) Buying chemicals for cleaning tablet counting machinery after being used.

(d) Labels to put on bottles of tablets being sold.

16 Medic Supplies Ltd received a cheque from a credit customer which they banked. Unfortunately the cheque was out of date and was subsequently returned by the bank. What journal entries are necessary to record the returned cheque?

17 Which of the following are incorrect?

(a) Capital will always exceed liabilities.

(b) Assets can be greater than the capital.

(c) Fixed assets less liabilities equals capital.

(d) Profits increase capital; losses increase liabilities.

18 Give two reasons why a business should avoid settling its debts by sending cash through the post.

19 Sophie Ross checks her bank statement and realises that she has only £96 left in her account with bills to pay totalling £175. Her salary is due in two weeks' time and she does not anticipate similar problems again in the near future. Explain which bank service would seem the most appropriate to meet her needs at this present time.

20 Complete the following sentences:

(a) An .... is sent by Medic Supplies Ltd with the goods to the buyer of medical supplies to advise them how much is owed for the goods supplied.

(b) A .... is packed with goods so that the buyer can check that all items listed have been received.

(c) Medic Supplies Ltd sends a .... with a payment to a supplier to indicate which invoices are being paid.

(d) Medic Supplies Ltd sends out a .... to a credit customer to correct an overcharge of an invoice.

Section 3 Communicating accounting information

Suggested time allocation: 45 minutes

Answer BOTH TASKS

Task 3.1   One of your tasks as Accounting Technician is to maintain the company's petty cash imprest system which currently has a float of £100. You have to go into hospital for a few days and will probably be absent from work for two to three weeks. Mark Hanson asks you to write out a set of instructions in note form on the operation of the petty cash imprest system as Carol Dodd, Jane

Mayall's secretary, will be taking over in your absence. Ensure the instructions are clear, concise and easy to follow.

Task 3.2 Another of your tasks is to prepare the bank reconciliation statement at the end of each month. In preparing the statement as at 30 April 2002 you notice a standing order payment of £65.00 to Ace Insurance which is not a regular payment and you are not aware of any instruction which authorises this payment. Draft a letter to the company's bank, Oak Bank Ltd, 3 Market Square, Marple, Cheshire SK6 9MP pointing out that this appears to be an error on their part and asking for the amount of £65.00 to be credited to the company's account.

Medic Supplies Ltd is situated at Holdsworth Business Park, Heaton Way, Stockport, Cheshire SK6 7KL and their account number with Oak Bank Ltd is 01798321.

31 Multiple-choice questions

In recent times more and more examination boards have begun to use multiple-choice questions in examinations. Multiple-choice questions certainly give an examiner the opportunity to cover large parts of the syllabus briefly but in detail. Students who omit to study areas of the syllabus will be caught out by an examiner's use of multiple-choice questions. No longer will it be possible to say that it is highly probable a certain topic will not be tested – the examiner can easily cover it with a multiple-choice question.

Each multiple-choice question has a 'stem' – this is a part which poses the problem – a 'key' which is the one correct answer, and a number of 'distractors', i.e. incorrect answers. The key plus the distractors are known as the 'options'.

If a candidate fails to answer a particular question then they will not gain any marks. Where a candidate is not certain about the answer then they should guess at the answer. Often when a candidate has a good feeling for the subject then their answer will be the correct one.

The paper in Transaction Accounting for the ACCA Accounting Technician examination consists entirely of multiple-choice questions. It is a two-hour examination and can contain between 40 and 60 questions. The number of questions depends on the examiner's view of the time needed for the particular questions used in that paper.

In this book two specimen papers have been set which should be very similar to the ACCC Accounting Technician paper. Each paper consists of 50 questions. Paper 1 has the answers given on pp. 418–20 while Paper 2 can be used by teachers or lecturers to assess each student's ability and identify their revision needs prior to sitting the examination.

All readers of this book should attempt these papers since they will give a quick insight into their individual strengths and weaknesses in preparation for sitting a particular examination.

Note:
The following examination-type papers are fully the work of the authors of this book. They each represent the type and amount of work expected from a student in a two-hour examination.

Test paper 1

1   On 1 May 2002 Lucas Ltd owed £7,585 to its creditors as shown in the purchases ledger. During May, Lucas made cash purchases of £656 and also bought goods on credit for £16,940. At 31 May creditors were owed £9,171. How much was paid to suppliers during May 2002?

(A) £15,354   (B) £16,940   (C) £24,525   (D) £16,010

2   Of the following, which are correct?

		Account debited	Account credited
(i)	Goods sold on credit to R Hart	R Hart	Sales
(ii)	P Jones returns goods to us	P Jones	Returns inwards
(iii)	Goods bought for cash	Purchases	Cash
(iv)	We returned goods to C Smith	Returns Outwards	C Smith

(A) (i) and (iv) only   (B) (i) only   (C) (i) and (iii) only   (D) (iii) only

3   Which of the following cannot be called 'sales'?

(A) Goods sold for cash.
(B) Sale of an item previously included in purchases.
(C) Sale of computer when a new one is bought.
(D) Goods sold on credit.

4   Eight items retailing at £200 each plus VAT of 17.5 per cent are sold to traders with a trade discount of 25 per cent. A cash discount of 5 per cent is also given for prompt payment. How much will be received if all pay promptly?

(A) £940.50   (B) £1,339.50   (C) £1,057.50   (D) £1,459.50

5   Carmen thought that she had a £395 positive balance in her bank account. Her bank statement shows a different figure. Taking into account the following items calculate her bank statement's balance.

(i)   Carmen thought she had banked a £50 cheque but later she finds it is still in her purse.
(ii)   The bank had deducted £28 for bank charges but Carmen was not aware of this.
(iii) She did not take into account a standing order paid by herself of £55.
(iv) A cheque paid to her mother for £240 has not yet been banked.

(A) £502   (B) £288   (C) £602   (D) £612

6   Which of the following best describes a trial balance?

(A) Shows all the entries in the books.
(B) A special account for a special purpose.
(C) It is a list of balances in the books.
(D) Where the financial position of a business is shown.

7   Camden Ltd owe Rahman & Co for some goods. Camden Ltd are paying promptly and will get a cash discount. What is the correct double entry for this in the books of Camden Ltd?

(A) Debit Rahman & Co; Credit Bank; Credit Discount allowed.
(B) Debit Discount allowed; Credit Bank; Credit Rahman & Co.
(C) Debit Rahman & Co; Credit Bank; Debit Discount received.
(D) Debit Rahman & Co; Credit Bank; Credit Discount received.

8   In the sale of goods a contract must have various basic elements. Which of these is correct?

   (A) Agreement, intention, consideration.
   (B) Adequate consideration, offer and acceptance, case law.
   (C) Offer and acceptance, agreement, consideration.
   (D) Statute law, consideration, definite offer.

9   A stopped cheque is one which:

   (A) The bank refuses to pay because of lack of funds.
   (B) The bank returns because it has not been signed.
   (C) The drawer has requested that the bank should not pay it.
   (D) The drawee has negotiated it to someone without a bank account.

10 A credit balance of £100 on the cash columns of a cash book shows that:

   (A) There was £100 cash in hand.
   (B) Cash has been overspent by £100.
   (C) Capital will be increased by £100.
   (D) An error has been made in the books.

11 Given the following what is the amount of creditors?

   Fixtures £450; Capital £15,700; Bank overdraft £675; Cash balance £97;
   Buildings £10,000; Debtors ledger – Debit balances £3,175; Credit balances £66;
   Stock £5,170; Creditors?

   (A) £2,683   (B) £2,451   (C) £3,801   (D) £4,216

12 Emily is preparing her first set of accounts. She is not certain which assets are current assets. Of the following, which should she classify as current assets?

   (i)   Loan from mother
   (ii)   Fixtures
   (iii) Cash in hand
   (iv)   Bank overdraft

   (A) (i), (iii) and (iv)   (B) (i) and (iii)   (C) (iii) only   (D) (iii) and (iv)

13 What are recorded in nominal accounts?

   (A) Expenses, income and capital.
   (B) Expenses only.
   (C) All transactions concerning debtors.
   (D) Fixed assets.

14 A cheque payment by us of £185 to P Ahmed has been debited in our cash book (bank columns) and credited to P Ahmed. What correcting entries, if any, are needed?

   (A) None.
   (B) Debit P Ahmed £185; Credit Bank £185.
   (C) Credit Bank £185.
   (D) Debit P Ahmed £370; Credit Bank £370.

15 A new business started on 1 May. During the first month £4,800 goods (retail price) were bought at trade discount 20 per cent. Of these 75 per cent are sold at full retail price. Returns inwards (at retail price) amounted to £120. What is the cost price of stock the business should have on 31 May?

   (A) £960   (B) £864   (C) £990   (D) £1,056

16 Jack owns three taxis. He wants to know which of the following would be capital expenditure.

    (i)   Purchase of an additional second-hand taxi.
    (ii)   Payment of public taxi licences.
    (iii) Installing extra equipment for transporting people in wheelchairs.
    (iv) Replacement of engine and gear-box.

    (A) *(i)* and *(iv)* (B) *(i)* and *(iii)* (C) *(iii)* and *(iv)* (D) *(ii)* and *(iii)*

17 Which of the following should be entered in the journal?

    (i)   Sale of goods at discounted prices.
    (ii)   Cash purchase of motor van.
    (iii) Sale of unwanted office machinery.
    (iv) Fixtures bought on credit.

    (A) *(i)*, *(iii)* and *(iv)* (B) All of them (C) *(ii)*, *(iii)* and *(iv)* (D) *(iii)* and *(iv)*

18 The total of the purchases day book is entered on:

    (A)   The credit side of the purchase account in the general ledger.
    (B)   The debit side of the purchases day book.
    (C)   The credit side of the trial balance.
    (D)   The debit side of the purchases account in the general ledger.

19 A customer J Green is unable to pay his account. We agree to accept a computer from him in full settlement of the debt. The double entry needed is:

    (A)   Debit Office equipment; Credit J Green.
    (B)   Debit Bad debts recovered; Credit J Green.
    (C)   Debit J Green; Credit Office equipment.
    (D)   Enter it in the journal.

20 Which is the best definition of fixed assets?

    (A)   Are bought to be used in the business.
    (B)   Are expensive items bought for the business.
    (C)   Are of long life and are not bought specifically for resale.
    (D)   Are items which will not wear out quickly.

21 To make sure that your money will be safe if cheques sent by you are lost in the post, you should:

    (A)   Not use the postal service in future.
    (B)   Always pay by cash.
    (C)   Always take the money in person.
    (D)   Cross your cheques 'Account Payee Only, Not Negotiable'.

22 A contra item is where

    (A)   Cash is banked before it has been paid out.
    (B)   Where double entry is completed within the cash book.
    (C)   Where the proprietor has repaid his capital in cash.
    (D)   Where sales have been paid by cash.

23 Abdul's cash book shows a bank overdraft of £1,123. He has just received his bank statement and finds that there are unpresented cheques of £422, banking not yet recorded on the bank statement of £77, bank charges not yet recorded by him of £26 and a standing order not shown in his cash book of £110. What is the overdraft balance on his bank statement?

(A) £1,332 (B) £694 (C) £1,552 (D) £914

24 Lee & Co wants to buy goods from Chan Ltd. Which of the following would probably be the flow of documents to complete the purchase?

(A) Purchase order, delivery note, goods received note, invoice, cheque requisition.
(B) Purchase order, goods received note, invoice, delivery note, cheque requisition.
(C) Purchase order, invoice, delivery note, goods received note, cheque requisition.
(D) Delivery note, goods received note, invoice, cheque requisition.

25 Noble Ltd both sells goods to and buys goods from Scorer & Co. On 1 January Noble Ltd owed Scorer & Co £249 for purchases and Scorer & Co owed Noble Ltd £872 for goods received.

During January Noble Ltd buys further goods totalling £717 from Scorer & Co but also returns goods £65. Scorer & Co buys £421 goods from Noble Ltd.

Accounts are kept separately in sales and purchases ledgers. A cheque for £300 was paid to Noble Ltd and £600 was set off the balances in each ledger.

What was the balance at 31 January in Scorer & Co's account in the purchase ledger?

(A) Credit balance £393
(B) Debit balance £393
(C) Credit balance £301
(D) Debit balance £301

26 Which of the following are correct?

		Account debited	Accounted credited
(i)	Standing order paid to R Bain Ltd	Bank	R Bain Ltd
(ii)	Received refund of insurance by cheque	Insurance	Bank
(iii)	Repairs to car roof paid by cash	Motor vehicles	Cash
(iv)	Part of bank charges refunded	Bank	Bank charges

(A) *(i)* and *(iv)* (B) *(ii)* only (C) *(iii)* and *(iv)* (D) *(iv)* only

27 You post a letter to Brady on 1 June accepting his offer to sell you some goods. The letter was delivered to the wrong address by the post office on 3 June. When the letter is delivered to Brady on 5 June the postal authorities ask him for 50p as the letter had not been stamped correctly. What is the legal date of acceptance?

(A) 5 June
(B) 3 June
(C) 1 June
(D) There was no legal acceptance.

28 The total of the returns outwards day book is transferred to:

(A) The debit side of the returns outwards account in the nominal ledger.
(B) The credit side of the returns outwards account in the general ledger.
(C) The debit side of the returns outwards account in the general ledger.
(D) The credit side of the returns outwards account in the sales ledger.

29 The petty cash float on 1 May was £250. During May a total of £229 petty cash was spent, less a refund of overpaid travel expenses £17. On 1 June the float is to be increased to £325. How much should be paid to achieve this using the imprest system?

(A) £304 (B) £113 (C) £287 (D) £75

30 What figure should be shown as 'purchases' given the following facts:
6 items are bought for £300 each, less 35 per cent trade discount. Cash discount of 5 per cent is given if payment is made promptly. VAT is charged at 17.5 per cent.

(A) £1,111.50 (B) £1,306.01 (C) £1,364.51 (D) £1,170

31 Which of the following should not be found in the credit balances shown on the trial balance?

(i)   Returns inwards
(ii) Discounts allowed
(iii) Trade discount received
(iv) Bank overdraft

(A) *(i)* and *(ii)* (B) *(i)* and *(iii)* (C) *(i)*, *(ii)* and *(iv)* (D) *(i)*, *(ii)* and *(iii)*

32 Which of the following statements is incorrect?

(A) Liabilities + Assets   =   Capital
(B) Liabilities + Capital =   Assets
(C) Assets – Capital   =   Liabilities
(D) Assets – Liabilities   =   Capital

33 By how much would the trial balance totals disagree if the following errors had been made?

(i)   Sales overcast by £289.
(ii) Bank overdraft £200 shown as debit balance.
(iii) Motor expenses £68 debited in error to motor vehicles account.
(iv) Rent undercast by £85.

(A) £404 (B) £204 (C) £604 (D) £94

34 A bank draft is most likely to be used for payment:

(A) When speed of payment is needed.
(B) When it is feared that the debtor may become bankrupt.
(C) When the drawer does not have a bank account.
(D) When certainty of the draft not being dishonoured is required.

35 What errors are shown in the following debtors control account?

Dr			Debtors Control Account		Cr
Balance b/f	*(i)*	10,258	Balance b/f	*(ii)*	222
Discount allowed	*(iii)*	305	Bank	*(iv)*	12,236
Bad debts	*(v)*	116	Cash	*(vi)*	198
Sales	*(vii)*	21,967	VAT on Sales	*(viii)*	3,844
			Balance c/d	*(ix)*	19,148

(A) *(ii)*, *(iii)* and *(v)*   (B) *(ii)*, *(v)* and *(viii)*
(C) *(iii)*, *(v)* and *(viii)*   (D) *(iii)* and *(v)*

36 Which of the following are incorrect?

	Accounts	To record	Entry in the account
(i)	Liabilities	a decrease	Debit
		an increase	Credit
(ii)	Revenue	an increase	Debit
		a decrease	Credit
(iii)	Assets	a decrease	Credit
		an increase	Debit
(iv)	Expenses	an increase	Credit
		a decrease	Debit
(v)	Capital	a decrease	Credit
		an increase	Debit

(A) (ii) and (iv)   (B) (iii), (iv) and (v)

(C) (ii), (iv) and (v)   (D) (i), (iii) and (iv)

37 What is the closing balance on Peter's account? Credit balance brought forward £1,237; Sales to him £15,870; Cheques received from him £12,050; Discounts allowed £149; Returns by him £249; Discounts withdrawn (part of £149) £16; Cash received from him £114; Allowance given to him for 'best customer award' £200.

(A) £1,887 debit balance

(B) £2,287 credit balance

(C) £4,461 debit balance

(D) £1,396 debit balance

38 What document should be filled in when a payment has to be made without supporting evidence for it?

(A) A bank draft.

(B) A cheque marked 'Invoice not received'.

(C) A bank giro credit slip.

(D) A cheque requisition form.

39 For what uses may a columnar sales day book be useful?

(i) To find total of VAT included in sales.

(ii) To analyse sales between geographical areas.

(iii) To calculate cash discounts allowed to customers.

(iv) To analyse sales between different departments.

(A) (i), (ii) and (iii)   (B) (ii) and (iv)

(C) (i), (ii) and (iv)   (D) (i), (iii) and (iv)

40 In the books of Marks, a customer, our account on 31 March shows a credit balance of £795. Taking into account the following, what would be the balance on Marks' account in our books on that date?

(i) £44 goods returned by him but not received by us.

(ii) Cheque £498 sent by him but not received by us.

(iii) Goods £217 sent by us but not received by him.

(A) £1,120   (B) £1,554   (C) £558   (D) £1,032

41 Which of these would not be entered in the sales ledger?

   (i)   Pro-forma invoice.
   (ii)   A customer's dishonour of a cheque.
   (iii)   Cash refund to a customer who had overpaid his account.
   (iv)   Trade discount.

   (A) *(iv)* only   (B) *(i)* and *(iii)*   (C) *(ii)* and *(iv)*   (D) *(i)* and *(iv)*

42 Which of the following are not effective security procedures?

   (i)   Cash should be banked as soon as possible.
   (ii)   Cash should be counted by a responsible person who works on the cash register.
   (iii)   A key must be inserted into the cash register before it will operate. Keys are
         held by authorised personnel.
   (iv)   Cash reconciliations should not involve anyone who works on the cash register.

   (A) *(ii)* only   (B) *(iv)* only   (C) *(ii)* and *(iv)*   (D) *(i)* and *(ii)*

43 When may cheque payments for expenses be entered in the petty cash book?

   (i)   When the amount involved is small.
   (ii)   When only the petty cashier is on duty.
   (iii)   Never.
   (iv)   When the item is not deductible for tax purposes.

   (A) *(iii)* and *(iv)*   (B) *(ii)* only   (C) *(iii)* only   (D) *(i)*

44 We have sold goods to a credit customer, 20 items at £30 each less 30 per cent trade
   discount. All goods are subject to 17.5 per cent VAT. The customer now returns three
   items to us. How much should be credited to the customer for the returns?

   (A)   £90.00
   (B)   £51.98
   (C)   £74.02
   (D)   £63.00

45 Damage to an account page in the sales ledger has rendered one item completely
   unreadable. The items that can be read are: Balance b/f £1,866; Sales £2,177, Returns
   inwards £209; Discounts allowed £77; Balance c/f £1,007. What must be the missing
   item?

   (A)   Cash £2,904
   (B)   Cash £2,750
   (C)   Bad debts £2,750
   (D)   The journal £2,750

46 Binders Ltd ages its debtors in the debtors' ledger into four categories:

Under 1 month; 1 month to 2 months; 2 months to 3 months; Over 3 months.
Cash paid and credit notes sent are matched against invoices. From the two accounts shown below what is the correct classification of amounts owing as at 31 December 2002?

Dr				Boris Ltd			Cr
2002				2002			
Oct	4	Sales	307.85	Nov	18	Cash	141.29
Oct	18	Sales	141.29	Nov	21	Returns	88.41
Nov	16	Sales	88.41				
Nov	28	Sales	247.33				
Dec	14	Sales	111.22				

Dr				Ivan & Co			Cr
2002				2002			
Sept	18	Sales	104.00	Nov	5	Cash	210.50
Sept	25	Sales	210.50	Nov	29	Cash	142.50
Oct	28	Sales	160.00	Dec	29	Returns	58.00
Nov	28	Sales	142.50				
Dec	22	Sales	58.00				
Dec	31	Sales	58.00				

	Under 1 month	1 month to 2 months	2 months to 3 months	Over 3 months
	£	£	£	£
(A)	227.22	247.33	467.85	160.00
(B)	169.22	389.83	301.29	56.00
(C)	111.22	247.33	160.00	104.00
(D)	169.22	247.33	467.85	104.00

47 Joe is paid £6 an hour for a 35-hour week. Any time over that is paid at 1.5 times normal rate. He is also entitled to a bonus of £27 per week if he exceeds a production limit. During week 5 he works 42 hours and exceeds the production limit. His income tax amounted to 20 per cent of all earnings above £100 a week and he pays national insurance of £12 a week. What was his take-home pay for week 5?

(A) £300 (B) £248 (C) £273 (D) £260

48 When a cheque is paid in respect of an outstanding invoice, what should be sent with the cheque?

(A) An invoice.   (B)   The advice note.
(C) A remittance advice. (D)   Banker's code number.

49 The individual items in a columnar sales day book are posted to:
(A) Debit of the debtor's account in the debtor's ledger.
(B) Credit of the debtor's account in the debtor's ledger.
(C) Debit of the sales control account in the general ledger.
(D) Debit of the sales account in the nominal ledger.

50 The following is essential for credit notes sent to debtors.
(A) They must be printed in red ink.
(B) They must be sent only after a debit note has been received from the debtor.
(C) They will be invalid after six months.
(D) A copy must be kept by the sender.

Test paper 2

1 Which of the following are incorrect?

		Account debited	Account credited
(i)	Refund of part of insurance premium by cash	Cash	Insurance
(ii)	Cheque cashed for petty cash purposes	Bank	Petty cash
(iii)	Building new car park, paid by cheque	Motor expenses	Bank
(iv)	Sale of old fixtures for cash	Cash	Fixtures

(A) *(ii)*, *(iii)* and *(iv)*
(B) *(iii)* and *(iv)*
(C) *(ii)* and *(iii)*
(D) *(ii)* and *(iv)*

2 What errors are shown in the following creditors control account?

Dr			Creditors Control Account			Cr
Balances b/f	*(i)*	307	Balances b/f	*(ii)*	18,526
Trade discounts	*(iii)*	1,311	Discounts received	*(iv)*	236
Bank	*(v)*	16,170	Purchases	*(vi)*	19,990
Balances c/d	*(vii)*	22,220	Bad debts	*(viii)*	58
			Balances c/d	*(ix)*	417

(A) *(iii)* and *(viii)* (B) *(iii)*, *(iv)* and *(viii)*
(C) *(ii)*, *(iii)* and *(vii)* (D) *(i)*, *(iv)* and *(viii)*

3 Which of these would not be entered in the purchases ledger?

(i) Advice notes.
(ii) Discounts received.
(iii) Small accounts settled by petty cash.
(iv) Payments on accounts outstanding more than one year.

(A) *(iii)* only (B) *(iii)* and *(iv)* (C) *(i)* and *(iii)* (D) *(i)* only

4 Howells Ltd owe Beet & Co for goods bought a few days ago. Howells Ltd are paying the invoice early by cheque and are getting a cash discount. What is the correct double entry in Howells Ltd's books?

(A) Debit Beet & Co; Credit Bank; Credit Discount received.
(B) Debit Bank; Debit Discount allowed; Credit Beet & Co.
(C) Debit Beet & Co; Credit Bank; Credit Discount allowed.
(D) Debit Howells Ltd; Credit Bank; Credit Discount received.

5 Andrew's cash book shows that he has £1,595 in his bank account on 31 December. His bank statement, received the same day, shows otherwise. In fact there were two unpresented cheques £177 and £205. Not yet entered in the cash book were the following items: a standing order for £2,075, bank charges £115 and bank interest received £12. What balance was shown on his bank statement?

(A) £201 cash at bank (B) £87 overdraft
(C) £3,390 overdraft (D) £201 overdraft

6 Donald owns a small retail food store. He wants to know which of the following are fixed assets, and you are to advise him.

(i)   Scales and weighing equipment.
(ii) Debtors.
(iii) Motor van.
(iv) Stock of food stuffs.

(A) *(i)*, *(ii)* and *(iii)*   (B) *(iii)* only   (C) *(i)* and *(iii)*   (D) *(i)* and *(ii)*

7 What would be the totals on a trial balance given the following balances: Loan from uncle £2,000; Stock £3,955; Bank overdraft £368; Debtors £3,092; Fixtures £5,500; Petty cash balance £121; Creditors £2,766; Motor vehicles £3,900; Capital?

(A) £11,494 (B) £14,628 (C) £16,568 (D) £16,996

8 You see something on a shelf in a supermarket at a ridiculously low price. The store assistant refuses to sell it to you. Can you force the supermarket to let you buy it at that price? Which of the following is correct?

(A) No, because you should have known that could not be the correct price.
(B) Yes, because the Sale of Goods Act says so.
(C) Yes, because otherwise prices would be meaningless.
(D) No, because there is no contract.

9 The following are some of the details of an account for December. Debit balance 31 December £1,654; Sales £2,389; Discounts allowed £114; Cash received £207; Cheques received £2,222. What was the opening balance on 1 December?

(A) £1,856 (B) £1,808 (C) £1,654 (D) £1,605

10 Joshua sold Simpson goods £3,200 less trade discount of 25 per cent. Terms were 5 per cent cash discount seven days. VAT was at 17.5 per cent. The goods were paid for after 14 days. One-third of the goods were then returned by Simpson. What would be the total of the credit note sent to Simpson?

(A) £800 (B) £933 (C) £893 (D) Another figure

11 When Howard is paying Susan by bank giro credit, which of the following must be shown on the bank giro form?

(i)   Title of Susan's account.
(ii) Name of Howard's bank.
(iii) Name of Susan's bank.
(iv) Code number of Susan's account.

(A) All of them   (B) *(i)*, *(iii)* and *(iv)*
(C) *(i)*, *(ii)* and *(iii)*   (D) *(iii)* and *(iv)*

12 If the payer completes and signs a mandate form instructing the payee's bank to take funds from the payer's bank account, then this is known as:

(A) A standing order
(B) A bank giro credit.
(C) A direct debit.
(D) The BACS system.

13 If Scott lent his friend Clarke £5,000 in cash, then the entries in Clarke's books would be:

    (A) Debit Cash; Credit Creditors.
    (B) Debit Loan from Scott; Credit Cash.
    (C) Debit Capital; Credit Loan from Scott.
    (D) Debit Cash; Credit Loan from Scott.

14 Markham has an overdraft of £7,200 at the start of May. The following four transactions take place during May. Markham allows his customers 14 days to pay their invoices, and if they do so they are allowed 5 per cent cash discount.

    May 4   Goods sold to Hoe for £12,000 on credit. Hoe pays within the time limit.
    May 8   Markham buys goods on credit from Skermer for £1,400.
    May 12   Markham sells goods worth £4,400 to King who pays by cheque after two days, Markham allowing him a 10 per cent trade discount.
    May 26   Jones, who is closing down his business, settles his account by giving Markham a cheque for £295 plus a typewriter valued at £180.

What is the balance of Markham's account at the bank on 31 May?

    (A) £8,635 cash at bank
    (B) £8,455 overdraft
    (C) £8,257 cash at bank
    (D) £7,055 cash at bank

15 Moore Ltd keeps a bank cash book plus a petty cash book. Only cheques are banked. Oakley, a customer, pays Moore Ltd the balance on his account of £11 in cash. What double-entry records should be made?

    (A) Debit Petty cash; Credit Oakley.
    (B) Debit Cash sales; Credit Oakley.
    (C) No Debit needed; Credit Oakley.
    (D) Debit Oakley, Credit Petty cash.

16 Which of the following do not affect trial balance agreement?

    (i)   Purchases of £210 from P Cook entered in C Cook's account.
    (ii)   Sales £890 to J Lowe entered in both accounts as £809.
    (iii) Cheque payment to R Noble of £155 entered only in cash book.
    (iv) Motor vehicle purchased £5,000 entered in motor expenses account.

    (A) *(i)* and *(ii)*   (B) *(ii)* only (C) *(ii)* and *(iv)* (D) *(i), (ii)* and *(iv)*

17 Which of the following transactions might explain the existence of a credit balance on an individual debtor's account?

    (A) By mistake the bookkeeper posted a total from the returns inwards day book twice to the debtors control account.
    (B) The debtor settled his account in full and later on returned goods which were faulty and received a credit note.
    (C) The debtor paid £500 on account leaving a balance outstanding of £45.
    (D) The bookkeeper posted a bad debt written off to the debit of the debtors control account in error.

18 Given that capital is £4,800, stock equals 20 per cent of capital, debtors are twice the value of stock, current assets total £3,020 and liabilities equal 50 per cent of current assets, what must be the value of fixed assets?

    (A) £6,310 (B) £3,290 (C) £1,510 (D) £3,020

19 In the books of Lee, a supplier, our account shows a debit balance of £2,190. Taking into account the following, what would be the balance on Lee's account in our books at that date?

(i)   Cheque £950 sent by us but not received by him.
(ii)   Goods £377 sent by him but not received by us.
(iii) Returns from us of £55 not received by him.

(A) £808 debit balance   (B) £1,672 credit balance
(C) £808 credit balance   (D) £2,708 credit balance

20 Which of the following columns should not be found in a columnar sales day book?

(i)   Folio column
(ii)   Trade discount column
(iii) VAT column
(iv)   Sales returns column

(A) *(i)* and *(iii)*   (B) *(ii)*, *(iii)* and *(iv)*   (C) *(ii)* and *(iv)*   (D) *(i)*, *(ii)* and *(iv)*

21 Which of the following are incorrect?

	Accounts	To record	Entry in the account
(i)	Revenue	a decrease	Debit
		an increase	Credit
(ii)	Liabilities	an increase	Debit
		a decrease	Credit
(iii)	Capital	an increase	Credit
		a decrease	Debit
(iv)	Expenses	a decrease	Debit
		an increase	Credit
(v)	Assets	an increase	Debit
		a decrease	Credit

(A) *(ii)* and *(iv)*   (B) *(i)* and *(iii)*   (C) *(i)* and *(iv)*   (D) *(ii)*, *(iii)* and *(iv)*

22 Gordon's bank statement on 31 March shows that he has a credit balance of £1,724. He finds that there are the following differences between his bank statement and his cash book.

(i)   Cheques not yet presented by Gordon's suppliers £910.
(ii)   Bankings not shown on bank statement £2,620.
(iii) Direct debit not shown in cash book £188.
(iv)   Bank interest received not shown in cash book £77.

What was the balance in his cash book on 31 March?

(A) £3,545 credit balance   (B) £97 debit balance
(C) £97 credit balance   (D) £3,545 debit balance

23 Given a VAT rate of 17.5 per cent, an item sold on credit to Gray without an offer of cash discount but showing VAT of £63 would result in the following entry in Gray's account in the sales ledger:

(A) Debit   £360   (B) Debit   £423
(C) Debit   £297   (D) Credit   £389

24 Which of the following can be called 'purchases'?

(i) Buying goods to sell for cash.
(ii) Buying fixtures for display of goods.
(iii) Buying goods for resale overseas.
(iv) Buying back goods previously sold, to resell in the future.

(A) *(i), (iii)* and *(iv)*   (B) *(i), (ii)* and *(iii)*   (C) All of them   (D) *(i)* and *(iii)*

25 Draw up a debtors control account from the following information for the month of May: Debtors at 1 May £1,680; Sales were four times as much as opening debtors; Discounts allowed equalled 2.5 per cent of accounts paid; Bad debts equalled 1 per cent of sales plus opening debtors; Debtors at 31 May amounted to £2,316. How much was received from customers by cash and cheques?

(A) Cannot be calculated   (B) £6,000
(C) £5,850   (D) £5,934

26 Which is the best definition of 'real accounts'.

(A) The accounts which show the real value of a business.
(B) Account kept secret by the proprietors.
(C) Accounts in which errors or items of fraud have been corrected.
(D) Accounts for property of all kinds.

27 The petty cash balance at 1 June was £79, and the float was restored to £300 on that day. During June items paid were: Stationery £44; Travel expenses £115; Sundries £45; J Clayton a creditor £38. It was decided to reduce the float to £260. How much did the petty cashier then receive on 30 June using imprest system methods?

(A) £202   (B) £260   (C) £221   (D) £220

28 The termination of an offer occurs when:

(i) A reasonable period of time has taken place.
(ii) When the goods are sold to somebody else.
(iii) When a counter-offer is made by the prospective purchaser.
(iv) The person selling goods posts a letter saying that the offer has been withdrawn.

(A) *(i)* and *(ii)*   (B) *(ii)* only   (C) *(i)* and *(iii)*   (D) *(i), (iii)* and *(iv)*

29 Bagshaws Ltd sends out a document to a credit customer on a monthly basis summarising the transactions that have taken place during the month and showing the amount owed by the customer. What is the name of the document?

(A) Remittance advice   (B) Quotation
(C) Statement of account   (D) Invoice

30 The closing balances in a sales ledger:

(A) Are always debit balances.
(B) Are always credit balances.
(C) Can be both debit and credit balances.
(D) Must be shown on the creditors control account.

31 Which of the following obligations must a bank give to its customer?

   (i)   To provide a statement of the account showing the transactions which have occurred.
   (ii) To provide confirmation of the balance on the account when requested by the customer.
   (iii) To give a copy of the bank's balance sheet to the customer to illustrate its liquidity.
   (iv) To use a professional level of care and skill.

   (A) All of them (B) *(i)*, *(ii)* and *(iv)*   (C) *(i)* and *(ii)*   (D) *(i)*, *(iii)* and *(iv)*

32 Smith both sells goods to and buys goods from Kelly. Smith keeps accounts for Kelly in both sales and purchases ledgers. For May you are given the following information: Opening balances – Debit £115; Credit £970; Sales £2,980; Purchases £790; Returns outwards £165; Returns inwards £95; a set-off between the accounts of £1,000 is agreed. What are the closing balances in each of Smith's ledgers?

   (A) Sales ledger, debit £3,000   : Purchases ledger, credit £1,595.
   (B) Purchases ledger, debit £595   : Sales ledger, debit £2,095.
   (C) Purchases ledger, credit £595   : Sales ledger, debit £2,115.
   (D) Sales ledger, debit £2,000   : Purchases ledger, credit £595.

33 A customer who does not have an account with us wishes to pay by cheque, supported by a bank guarantee card with a limit of £100. The sale price of the item is £150. Which of the following is permissible?

   (i)   Pay cheque for £150.
   (ii) Pay one cheque of £100 and another for £50.
   (iii) Pay cheque of £75 and cash of £75.
   (iv) Pay cheque of £100 today and another of £50 tomorrow, collecting the goods tomorrow.

   (A) *(ii)*, *(iii)* and *(iv)*   (B) *(i)* *(iii)* and *(iv)*   (C) *(iii)* only   (D) *(ii)* and *(iii)*

34 Bray, one of our employees, is paid £8 an hour for a 35-hour week. Overtime is at time-and-a-quarter. He also gets a bonus of £2 per item produced for production over 500 units per week. He pays income tax at 25 per cent on all pay over £110 per week, and national insurance at 5 per cent of gross pay. In week 5 he worked 43 hours and produced 530 items. What was his net pay for the week?

   (A) £321.50 (B) £420.00 (C) £342.50 (D) £399.00

35 Gregg Ltd have a customer Barnes & Co who owe them £860. They agree to accept a cheque from Barnes & Co for 60 per cent of the money owing and transfer the remaining debt to Stevens Ltd. What journal entries are needed?

   (A) Debit Barnes & Co £860; Credit Stevens Ltd £344; Credit Bank £516.
   (B) Debit Bad debts £344; Debit Bank £516; Credit Barnes & Co £860.
   (C) Debit Bank £516; Debit Stevens Ltd £344; Credit Barnes & Co £860.
   (D) Debit Bank £516; Debit Stevens Ltd £344; Credit Purchases control £860.

36 A credit balance on an account in a sales ledger can mean that:

   (i)   The account was overpaid.
   (ii) A bad debt has been written off.
   (iii) An expensive item of goods had been returned to us.
   (iv) The debtor has become bankrupt.

   (A) *(i)* only (B) *(i)* and *(iii)* (C) *(iii)* and *(iv)* (D) *(i)* and *(iv)*

37 Which of the following are correct?

		Account debited	Account credited
(i)	Sale of fixture for cash	Cash	Fixtures
(ii)	Bank charges paid	Bank	Cash
(iii)	Refund of rates by cheque	Rates	Bank
(iv)	Goods returned by L Lee Ltd	Returns inwards	L Lee Ltd

(A) *(i)* and *(iv)* (B) *(i), (ii)* and *(iv)* (C) *(iv)* only (D) *(i), (ii)* and *(iii)*

38 In our books George, a customer, is shown as owing us £590. He had, however, sent a cheque to us of £310 and returned goods of £70 and £45, none of which has yet been received by us. What is the balance of our account in George's books?

(A) £165 debit (B) £395 credit (C) £165 credit (D) £395 debit

39 A remittance advice is always sent by us:

(A) When a creditor settles his account.

(B) When a standing order is cancelled.

(C) When the items needs to be entered in the journal.

(D) When a cheque is paid in respect of an outstanding invoice.

40 Complete the following: A stale cheque

(A) Must be banked immediately.

(B) Must be returned to the drawee.

(C) Should be replaced by a postdated cheque.

(D) Must be returned to the drawer.

41 Which of the following statements are correct?

(i) Assets – Capital = Liabilities

(ii) Liabilities + Capital = Assets

(iii) Liabilities + Assets = Capital

(iv) Capital + Liabilities = Assets

(A) *(i), (ii)* and *(iv)* (B) *(i)* and *(ii)* (C) All of them (D) *(i), (ii)* and *(iii)*

42 Malcolm makes the following expenditure on his lorry. How much of it is capital expenditure?

(i) Repairs to bodywork £4,500 of which £300 is for an additional safety alarm system.

(ii) Motor insurance £790.

(iii) Fix a towing bar £190 to enable the lorry to tow a trailer.

(iv) Replacement engine £1,400.

(A) £300 (B) £190 (C) £490 (D) £4,990

43 What will be the totals of the following trial balance after is has been corrected?

	Dr £	Cr £
Capital		18,936
Cash	146	
Bank overdraft	1,279	
Stock	3,690	
Debtors		6,873
Creditors	3,594	
Fixtures	6,000	
Motor vehicles	9,100	
Loan from uncle	2,000	
	25,809	25,809

(A) £27,115 both sides.
(B) £26,930 debits, £28,190 credits.
(C) £27,115 debits, £25,809 credits.
(D) £25,809 both sides.

44 When may a purchase of goods be included in a sales account?

(i) When the goods have been bought in error.
(ii) When an error has been made in the purchases journal.
(iii) When the items are capital instead of revenue expenditure.
(iv) Never.

(A) (i) and (ii)   (B) (ii) only   (C) (iii) only   (D) (iv) only

45 A business which started with £10,000 capital has now gone bankrupt and £15,000 more is owed than there are assets available to pay creditors. By how much will the balance sheet totals disagree?

(A) £15,000   (B) Nothing   (C) £5,000   (D) £25,000

46 A business's bank overdraft on 1 May was £3,690. During May it receives payment of cheques from debtors who owed £21,380, and who were allowed discounts of £616; cash sales amounted to £1,790 of which all but £119 was banked; a cheque of £500 was cashed to pay wages; creditors totalling £13,200 were paid and we were allowed 2.5 per cent discount; expenses £795 were paid by cheque. What was the balance at the bank on 31 May?

(A) £4,375 overdraft   (B) £5,375
(C) £4,575   (D) Another figure

47 Roger has owed us £3,600 for a long time. He agrees to a charge for interest on the debt at 5 per cent per annum. Assuming all months to be taken as the same length, what entry should we make for one month in respect of the interest?

(A) Debit Interest received £180; Credit Roger £180.
(B) Debit Roger £180; Credit Interest received £180.
(C) Credit Interest received £15; Debit Roger £15.
(D) Debit Bad debts £15; Credit Roger £15.

48 A new machine is bought for £5,600. During the first year of ownership the following expenditure occurs: repair broken shaft £205; fix new attachment £370; electricity used £497; wages of machine operator £3,920; instal new safety rails £217; costs of legal action when operator is injured £250. After the above what would be the balance on the machinery account?

(A) £6,187 (B) £5,970 (C) £5,817 (D) £6,437

49 What ledger entries would need to be made by the business to record cash taken by the proprietor for his personal use?

(A) Debit Bank; Credit Drawings.
(B) Debit Cash; Credit Capital.
(C) Debit Drawings; Credit Capital.
(D) Debit Drawings; Credit Cash.

50 Which one of the following transactions should be treated as capital expenditure in the accounts of a computer sales company?

(A) Purchase of ten new computers for stock.
(B) Installation of new security system for the building.
(C) Decoration of the accounts office.
(D) Drawings by the company director to buy a new colour television.

Answers to student activities, assessments and multiple-choice tests

Note: £ signs have not been used in the majority of answers in order to save space

Chapter 3

3.1 *(a)* 25,750 *(b)* 72,820 *(c)* 34,980 *(d)* 48,600 *(e)* 12,500 *(f)* 30,620

3.3 *(a)* Asset *(b)* Liability *(c)* Asset *(d)* Asset *(e)* Liabilities *(f)* Asset

3.5 Wrong: Assets: Loan from C Smith; Creditors; Liabilities: Stock of goods; Debtors.

3.7 Assets: Motor 2,000; Premises 5,000; Stock 1,000; Bank 700; Cash 100 = total 8,800. Liabilities: Loan from Bevan 3,000; Creditors 400 = Total 3,400. Capital 8,800 − 3,400 = 5,400.

3.9 Horizontal presentation:

T Lymer
Balance Sheet as at 31 December 2000

Assets		Capital & Liabilities	
Office furniture	8,640	Capital	34,823
Delivery van	12,000	Creditors	12,651
Stock	4,220		
Debtors	10,892		
Cash at bank	11,722		
	47,474		47,474

Vertical presentation:

Balance Sheet of T Lymer as at 31 December 2000

			Net book value
Fixed assets	£	£	£
Office furniture			8,640
Delivery van			12,000
			20,640
Current assets			
Stock	4,220		
Debtors	10,892		
Cash at bank	11,722	26,834	
Less Current liabilities			
Creditors	12,651	12,651	
Net current assets			14,183
			£34,823
Financed by			
Capital			34,823
			£34,823

3.11

	Assets	Liabilities	Capital
(a)	– Cash	– Creditors	
(b)	– Bank		
	+ Fixtures		
(c)	+ Stock	+ Creditors	
(d)	+ Cash		+ Capital
(e)	+ Cash	+ Loan from J Walker	
(f)	+ Bank		
	– Debtors		
(g)	– Stock	– Creditors	
(h)	+ Premises		
	– Bank		

3.13 Horizontal presentation:

C Sangster

Balance Sheet as at 7 May 2001

Assets		Capital & Liabilities	
Fixtures	4,500	Capital	18,900
Motor vehicle	4,200	Loan from	
Stock	5,720	T Sharples	2,000
Debtors	3,000	Creditors	2,370
Bank	5,450		
Cash	400		
	23,270		23,270

Vertical presentation:

C Sangster

Balance Sheet as at 7 May 2001

			Net book value £
Fixed assets			
Fixtures			4,500
Motor vehicle			4,200
			8,700
Current assets			
Stock	5,720		
Debtors	3,000		
Bank	5,450		
Cash	400	14,570	
Less Current liabilities			
Creditors	2,370	2,370	
Net current assets			12,200
			20,900
Less Long-term liability			
Loan from T Sharples			2,000
			£18,900
Financed by			
Capital			£18,900

Chapter 4

4.1

	Debited	Credited			Debited	Credited
(a)	Motor van	Cash	(b)		Office machinery	J Grant & Son
(c)	Cash	Capital	(d)		Bank	J Beach
(e)	A Barrett	Cash				

4.2

	Debited	Credited		Debited	Credited
(a)	Machinery	A Jackson & Son	(b)	A Jackson & Son	Machinery
(c)	Cash	J Brown	(d)	Bank	J Smith (Loan)
(e)	Cash	Office machinery			

4.5

Cash

(1) Capital	1,000	(14) Office mach	60
		(31) Speed & Sons	698

Motor Lorry

(3) Speed & Sons	698		

Capital

		(1) Cash	1,000

Speed & Sons

(31) Cash	698	(3) M Lorry	698

Office Machinery

(14) Cash	60		

4.6

Bank

(1) Capital	2,500	(2) Office furn	150
		(5) Motor van	600
		(15) Planers Ltd	750
		(31) Machinery	280

Capital

		(1) Bank	2,500

Office Furniture

(2) Bank	150	(8) J Walker & Sons	60

Machinery

(3) Planers Ltd	750		
(31) Bank	280		

Cash

(23) J Walker	60		

Planers Ltd

(15) Bank	750	(3) Machinery	750

Motor Van

(5) Bank	600		

J Walker & Sons

(8) Office F	60	(23) Cash	60

4.8

Bank

(1) Capital	5,000	(2) Motor van	1,200
(25) Cash	800	(12) Cash	100
		(19) Super Motors	800
		(30) Office fixtures	300

Office Fixtures

(5) Young Ltd	400		
(15) Cash	60		
(30) Bank	300		

Capital

		(1) Bank	5,000

Cash

(12) Bank	100	(15) Office fixtures	60
(21) Loan: Jarvis	1,000	(25) Bank	800

Motor Van

(2) Bank	1,200		
(8) Super Motors	800		

Young Ltd

		(5) Office fixtures	400

Super Motors

(19) Bank	800	(8) Motor van	800

Loan from Jarvis

		(21) Cash	1,000

Chapter 5

5.1   *(a)*   Dr Purchases, Cr Cash   *(b)*   Dr Purchases, Cr E Flynn

      (c)   Dr C Grant, Cr Sales   *(d)*   Dr Cash, Cr Motor Van

      (e)   Dr Cash, Cr Sales

5.3

	Debited	Credited		Debited	Credited
(a)	Purchases	J Reid	*(b)*	B Perkins	Sales
(c)	Motor vans	H Thomas	*(d)*	Bank	Sales
(e)	Cash	Sales	*(f)*	H Hardy	Returns outwards
(g)	Cash	Machinery	*(h)*	Returns inwards	J Nelson
(i)	Purchases	D Simpson	*(j)*	H Forbes	Returns outwards

5.5

Cash

(1) Capital	500	(3) Purchases	85
(10) Sales	42	(25) E Morgan	88
(31) A Knight	55		

Purchases

(3) Cash	85		
(7) E Morgan	116		
(18) A Moses	98		

Sales

		(10) Cash	42
		(24) A Knight	55

Returns Outwards

		(14) E Morgan	28
		(21) A Moses	19

A Knight

(24) Sales	55	(31) Cash	55

E Morgan

(14) Returns outwards	28	(7) Purchases	116
(25) Cash	88		

A Moses

(21) Returns outwards	19	(18) Purchases	98

Capital

		(1) Cash	500

5.6

Cash

(1) Capital	1,000	(2) Bank	900
(19) Sales	28	(7) Purchases	55

Purchases

(4) S Holmes	78		
(7) Cash	55		

Returns Outwards

		(12) S Holmes	18

S Holmes

(12) Returns	18	(4) Purchases	78
(29) Bank	60		

D Moore

(10) Sales	98		

Bank

(2) Cash	900	(5) Motor van	500
(24) D Watson (Loan)	100	(29) S Holmes	60
		(31) Kingston Equipment	150

Sales

		(10) D Moore	98
		(19) Cash	28

Fixtures

(22) Kingston Equipment	150		

Motor Van

(5) Bank	500		

D Watson (Loan)

		(24) Bank	100

Kingston Equipment

(31) Bank	150	(22) Fixtures	150

Capital

		(1) Cash	1,000

6.7

Cash

(1) Capital	1,500	(3) Rent	28
(11) Sales	49	(4) Bank	1,000
		(20) B repairs	18
		(28) Purchases	125
		(30) Motor exps	15

Bank

(4) Cash	1,000	(7) Stationery	15
		(27) A Hanson	279
		(29) Motor Van	395

Purchases

(2) A Hanson	296		
(28) Cash	125		

Sales

		(5) E Linton	54
		(11) Cash	49
		(17) S Morgan	29

Stationery

(7) Bank	15		

Returns Outwards

		(14) A Hanson	17

Fixtures

(31) A Webster	120		

Capital

		(1) Cash	1,500

Rent

(3) Cash	28		

Building Repairs

(20) Cash	18		

Motor Expenses

(30) Cash	15		

Motor Van

(29) Bank	395		

A Hanson

(14) Returns out	17	(2) Purchases	296
(27) Bank	279		

E Linton

(5) Sales	54	(22) Returns in	14

S Morgan

(17) Sales	29		

Returns Inwards

(22) E Linton	14		

A Webster

		(31) Fixtures	120

Chapter 7

7.1

H Harvey

(1) Sales	690	(10) Returns	40
(4) Sales	66	(24) Cash	300
		(31) Balance c/d	416
	756		756
(1) Balance b/d	416		

L Masters

(4) Sales	418	(31) Balance c/d	621
(31) Sales	203		
	621		621
(1) Balance b/d	621		

N Morgan

(1) Sales	153	(18) Bank	153

J Lindo

(1) Sales	420	(10) Returns	20
		(20) Bank	400
	420		420

7.2

J Young

(10) Returns	55	(1)	Purchases	458
(28) Cash	250	(15)	Purchases	80
(30) Balance c/d	233			
	538			538
		(1)	Balance b/d	233

L Williams

(30) Returns	17	(1)	Purchases	120
(30) Balance c/d	180	(3)	Purchases	77
	197			197
		(1)	Balance b/d	180

G Norman

(10) Returns	22	(1)	Purchases	708
(30) Balance c/d	686			
	708			708
		(1)	Balance b/d	686

T Harris

(19) Bank	880	(3)	Purchases	880

7.3

H Harvey

2001			Dr	Cr	Balance
May	1	Sales	690		690 Dr
May	4	Sales	66		756 Dr
May	10	Returns		40	716 Dr
May	24	Cash		300	416 Dr

N Morgan

2001			Dr	Cr	Balance
May	1	Sales	153		153 Dr
May	18	Bank		153	0

J Lindo

2001			Dr	Cr	Balance
May	1	Sales	420		420 Dr
May	10	Returns		20	400 Dr
May	20	Bank		400	0

L Masters

2001			Dr	Cr	Balance
May	4	Sales	418		418 Dr
May	31	Sales	203		621 Dr

7.5

D Williams

(1) Sales	458	(24)	Bank	300
		(28)	Cash	100
		(30)	Balance c/d	58
	458			458
(1) Balance b/d	58			

A White

(20) Bank	77	(2)	Purchases	77

J Moore

(1) Sales	235	(12)	Returns	26
(8) Sales	444	(20)	Balance c/d	653
	679			679
(1) Balance b/d	653			

H Samuels

(17) Returns	24	(2)	Purchases	231
(30) Balance c/d	219	(10)	Purchases	12
	243			243
		(1)	Balance c/d	219

G Grant

(1) Sales	98	(12)	Returns	9
		(30)	Balance c/d	89
	98			98
(1) Balance b/d	89			

P Owen

		(2)	Purchases	65

O Oliver

(17) Returns	12	(10)	Purchases	222
(26) Cash	210			
	222			222

F Franklin

(8) Sales	249	(30)	Bank	249

Chapter 8

8.1

Cash

(1)	Capital	250	(6)	Rent	12
			(15)	Carriage	23
			(31)	Balance c/d	215
		<u>250</u>			<u>250</u>

Bank

(9)	C Bailey	43	(12)	K Gibson	25
(10)	H Spencer	150	(12)	D Ellis	54
			(31)	Rent	18
			(31)	Balance c/d	96
		<u>193</u>			<u>193</u>

Capital

			(1)	Cash	250

Rent

(6)	Cash	12
(31)	Bank	18

Carriage

(15)	Cash	23

D Ellis

(12)	Bank	54	(2)	Purchases	54

C Mendez

(2)	Purchases	87
(18)	Purchases	43

K Gibson

(12)	Bank	25	(2)	Purchases	25

D Booth

(2)	Purchases	76
(18)	Purchases	110

L Lowe

(2)	Purchases	64

C Bailey

(4)	Sales	43	(9)	Bank	43

B Hughes

(4)	Sales	62
(21)	Sales	67

H Spencer

(4)	Sales	176	(10)	Bank	150

Purchases

(2)	D Ellis	54
(2)	C Mendez	87
(2)	K Gibson	25
(2)	D Booth	76
(2)	L Lowe	64
(18)	C Mendez	43
(18)	D Booth	110

Sales

(4)	C Bailey	43
(4)	B Hughes	62
(4)	H Spencer	176
(21)	B Hughes	67

Trial Balance as at 31 May 2002

	Dr	Cr
Cash	215	
Bank	96	
Capital		250
Rent	30	
Carriage	23	
C Mendez		130
D Booth		186
L Lowe		64
B Hughes	129	
H Spencer	26	
Purchases	459	
Sales		348
	<u>978</u>	<u>978</u>

8.2

Bank

(1)	Capital	800	(17)	M Hyatt	84
(24)	J Carlton	95	(21)	Betta Ltd	50
			(31)	Motor Van	400
			(31)	Balance c/d	361
		895			895

Cash

(5)	Sales	87	(6)	Wages	14
(30)	J King		(9)	Purchases	46
	(Loan)	60	(12)	Wages	14
			(31)	Balance c/d	73
		147			147

Capital

		(1) Bank	800

Motor Van

(31) Bank	400	

Wages

(6) Cash	14	
(12) Cash	14	

Shop Fixtures

(15) Betta Ltd	50	

J King (Loan)

	(30) Cash	60

H Elliott

(7) Sales	35	

L Lane

(7) Sales	42	
(13) Sales	32	

J Carlton

(7)	Sales	72	(24) Bank	95
(13)	Sales	23		

K Henriques

(27)	Returns	24	(2) Purchases	76

M Hyatt

(17)	Bank	84	(2) Purchases	27
			(10) Purchases	57

T Braham

(18)	Returns	20	(2) Purchases	56
			(10) Purchases	98

Betta Ltd

(21)	Bank	50	(15) S Fixtures	50

Sales

	(5)	Cash	87
	(7)	H Elliott	35
	(7)	L Lane	42
	(7)	J Carlton	72
	(13)	L Lane	32
	(13)	J Carlton	23

Purchases

(2)	K Henriques	76
(2)	M Hyatt	27
(2)	T Braham	56
(9)	Cash	46
(10)	M Hyatt	57
(10)	T Braham	98

Returns Outwards

	(18) T Braham	20
	(27) K Henriques	24

Trial Balance as on 31 March 2003

	Dr	Cr
Bank	361	
Cash	73	
Capital		800
Motor van	400	
Wages	28	
Shop fixtures	50	
J King (Loan)		60
H Elliott	35	
L Lindo	74	
K Henriques		52
T Braham		134
Sales		291
Purchases	360	
Returns outwards		44
	1,381	1,381

8.3

Bank

(1) Capital	600	(5) Motor van	256
(25) P Potter	43	(7) Motor exps	12
		(12) N Moss	62
		(21) O Hughes	46
		Balance	267
	643		643

Cash

(1) Capital	50	(4) Purchases	23
(23) H Henry	66	(15) Motor exps	5
(26) Sales	34	(20) Drawings	10
		(27) Drawings	24
		(29) Postages	4
		Balance	84
	150		150

Capital

		(1) Bank	600
		(25) Cash	50

Drawings

(20) Cash	10		
(27) Cash	24		

Sales

		(3) H Henry	66
		(3) N Neita	25
		(3) P Potter	43
		(9) B Barnes	24
		(9) K Lyn	26
		(9) M Moore	65
		(26) Cash	34
		(30) N Neita	43
		(30) M Edgar	67
		(30) K Lyn	45

Purchases

(2) C Jones	500		
(4) Cash	23		
(11) C Jones	240		
(11) N Moss	62		
(11) O Hughes	46		

Returns Inwards

(19) N Neita	11		

Returns Outwards

		(13) C Jones	25
		(28) C Jones	42

Motor Van

(5) Bank	256		

Motor Expenses

(7) Bank	12		
(15) Cash	5		

Postages

(29) Cash	4		

H Henry

(3) Sales	66	(23) Cash	66

N Neita

(3) Sales	25	(19) Returns in	11
(30) Sales	43		

P Potter

(3) Sales	43	(25) Bank	43

B Barnes

(9) Sales	24		

K Lyn

(9) Sales	26		
(30) Sales	45		

M Moore

(9) Sales	65		

M Edgar

(9) Sales	67		

C Jones

(13) Returns	25	(2) Purchases	500
(28) Returns	42	(11) Purchases	240

N Moss

(21) Bank	62	(11) Purchases	62

O Hughes

(21) Bank	46	(11) Purchases	46

Trial Balance 30 June 2005

Bank	267	
Cash	84	
Capital		650
Drawings	34	
Sales		438
Purchases	871	
Returns inwards	11	
Returns outwards		67
Motor van	256	
Motor expenses	17	
Postages	4	
N Neita	57	
B Barnes	24	
K Lyn	71	
M Moore	65	
M Edgar	67	
C Jones		673
	1,828	1,828

8.7   **Trial Balance of P Brown as at 31 May 2003**

| | Dr | Cr |
	£	£
Capital		20,000
Drawings	7,000	
General expenses	500	
Sales		38,500
Purchases	29,000	
Debtors	6,800	
Creditors		9,000
Bank	15,100	
Cash	200	
Plant and equipment	5,000	
Heating and lighting	1,500	
Rent	2,400	
	67,500	67,500

8.8   **Trial Balance of S Higton as at 30 June 2004**

| | Dr | Cr |
	£	£
Capital		23,820
Sales		119,439
Stationery	1,200	
General expenses	2,745	
Motor expenses	4,476	
Cash at bank	1,950	
Wages and salaries	9,492	
Rent and rates	10,500	
Office equipment	6,000	
Purchases	89,421	
Heating and lighting	2,208	
Debtors	10,353	
Drawings	4,200	
Creditors		10,230
Motor vehicle	7,500	
Insurance	3,444	
	153,489	153,489

8.9   **Trial Balance of Ms Anita Hall as at 31 December 2003**

| | Dr | Cr |
	£	£
Plant and machinery	21,450	
Motor vehicles	26,000	
Premises	80,000	
Wages	42,840	
Purchases	119,856	
Sales		185,944
Telephone, printing and stationery	3,600	
Creditors		27,200
Debtors	30,440	
Cash at bank	624	
Capital		131,250
Drawings	10,680	
General expenses	3,584	
Lighting and heating	2,960	
Motor expenses	2,360	
	344,394	344,394

Chapter 10

10.1 Difference – *see* section 10.2. A deposit account would be the best for regular savings.

10.4 *See* Exhibit A1.

Exhibit A1

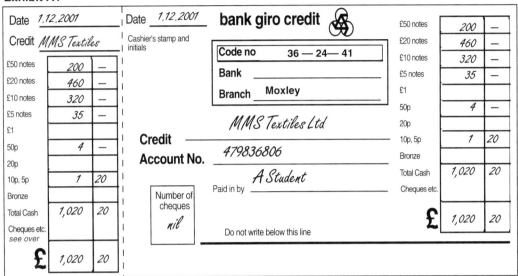

10.5 *See* section 10.7.

10.7 *See* section 10.10.

Chapter 11

11.1

Cash Book

Dr			Cash	Bank				Cash	Bank	Cr
(1)	Capital		100		(2)	Rent		10		
(3)	F Lake (Loan)			500	(4)	B McKenzie			65	
(5)	Sales		98		(9)	B Burton		22		
(7)	N Miller			62	(16)	Bank C		50		
(11)	Sales			53	(19)	F Lake (Loan)			100	
(15)	G Moores		65		(26)	Motor expenses			12	
(16)	Cash C			50	(30)	Cash C			100	
(22)	Sales			66	(31)	Wages		97		
(30)	Bank C		100		(31)	Balances c/d		184	454	
			363	731				363	731	

11.2

Cash Book

Dr   Cr

			Cash	Bank				Cash	Bank
(1)	Balances b/d		56	2,356	(2)	Rates			156
(5)	Sales		74		(3)	Postages		5	
(7)	Cash	C		60	(7)	Bank	C	60	
(12)	J Moores		50	100	(8)	T Lee			75
(20)	P Jones			79	(10)	C Brooks		2	
(22)	Bank	C	200		(17)	Drawings		20	
(31)	Sales			105	(22)	Cash	C		200
					(24)	Motor van		195	
					(28)	Rent			40
					(31)	Balance c/d		98	2,229
			380	2,700				380	2,700

11.5

Cash Book

Dr   Cr

		Disct	Cash	Bank			Disct	Cash	Bank
(1)	Capital			6,000	(1)	Fixtures			950
(3)	Sales		407		(2)	Purchases			1,240
(5)	N Morgan	10		210	(4)	Rent		200	
(9)	S Cooper	20		380	(7)	S Thompson			
(14)	L Curtis			115		& Co	4		76
(20)	P Exeter	2		78	(12)	Rates			410
(31)	Sales			88	(16)	M Monroe	6	114	
					(31)	Balance c/d		93	4,195
		32	407	6,871			10	407	6,871

In general ledger:
Debit discounts allowed 32: Credit discounts received 10.

11.6

Cash Book

Dr   Cr

		Disct	Cash	Bank			Disct	Cash	Bank
(1)	Balance b/d		230	4,756	(4)	Rent			120
(2)	R Burton	7		133	(8)	N Black	9		351
(2)	E Taylor	11		209	(8)	P Towers	12		468
(2)	R Harris	15		285	(8)	C Rowse	20		780
(6)	J Cotton: loan			1,000	(10)	Motor expenses		44	
(12)	H Hankins	3		74	(15)	Wages		160	
(18)	C Winston	13		247	(21)	Cash			350
(18)	R Wilson				(24)	Drawings		120	
	& Son	17		323	(25)	T Briers	7	133	
(18)	H Winter	23		437	(29)	Fixtures			650
(21)	Bank		350		(31)	Balances c/d		123	4,833
(31)	Commission			88					
		89	580	7,552			48	580	7,552

Discounts Received

	(31) Total for month	48

Discounts Allowed

(31) Total for month	89	

Chapter 12

12.1 *See* section 12.2.

12.2 *(a)* The purpose of issuing a receipt for payment received is twofold. First, it is proof that the person paying the money has actually paid it. Without it, if payment was made by cash the payer would have no evidence that payment had been made. Second, if receipts are given and copies are automatically produced, then it can help protect the firm receiving the money from fraud committed by its own employees. Otherwise they could steal the money received, especially cash if there was no record that the cash had been received.

(b) First, it acts as proof that they have actually paid the money involved. This could protect them against a claim by the store that they had stolen goods and not paid for them. Second, it acts as proof of purchase if the goods have to be returned if they are faulty or not suitable for the purpose or some such similar reason – some large stores will let customers return goods for any reason whatsoever, provided they have proof of original purchase and the goods are returned within a 'reasonable time'.

(c) Not normally – at least in the United Kingdom. Here returned cheques are treated as proof of payment.

12.4 *(a)* *See* section 12.9, parts **1** to **7**.

(b) Customer no. 1, Trasler: not acceptable – the date on the cheque is later than the expiry date on the guarantee card.

Customer No. 2, Blackshaw: payment accepted.

12.6 Possible measures include (depending on circumstances):

(a) Arrange with bank so as to be able to lodge the takings on a daily basis in the bank's night safe.

(b) Whether taking them home or to the bank, take different routes (if possible) and be accompanied by someone else (if possible).

(c) If kept at the café ensure that they are kept in a secure safe, preferably one whose location is disguised not to look like a safe. Ensure that it cannot easily be picked up and transported elsewhere.

(d) If kept at home, same precautions as *(c)*.

(e) Install burglar alarms at café/home.

(f) Ensure that property has locks that cannot easily be opened; similarly with windows and any other means of access.

(g) Install security lights which come on when someone approaches the premises.

Will obviously depend on amounts of takings involved, and also costs of preventative measures.

Chapter 13

13.1 *(a)* *See* section 13.2.

(b) *(i)* Check details against purchases order.

(ii) Check against delivery note and ensure that goods received are of correct quantity and quality, and that breakages etc. have been taken into account. Warehouse staff to have initialled for each of these things.

(iii) Check prices against any quotation and purchases order. Additions and calculations to be checked.

(iv) Ensure that any cash discounts available are taken.

(v) Ensure that payment is made on time, but not earlier than it need be.

(vi) Check that VAT has been correctly charged (if any) and that VAT no of supplier is stated on the invoice.

(vii) Check that our company's name and address is correctly stated.

13.2 (a) *See* section 13.4.

(b) *See* section 13.6.

13.3 Cheques before being signed by Miss Howson and the company secretary are shown in Exhibit A2.

Exhibit A2

Exhibit A2 (*continued*)

13.4 *See* Exhibit A3.

13.5 Any four from:

- cheques – *see* section 10.3;
- bank giro credits – *see* section 10.6;
- BACS – *see* section 10.7;
- direct debits – *see* section 10.8;
- standing orders – *see* section 10.8;
- petty cash;
- bank drafts – *see* section 13.7;
- telegraphic transfers – *see* section 13.7.

13.6 *See* section 13.8.

13.7 Cheque ready for signature is shown in Exhibit A4.

Exhibit A3

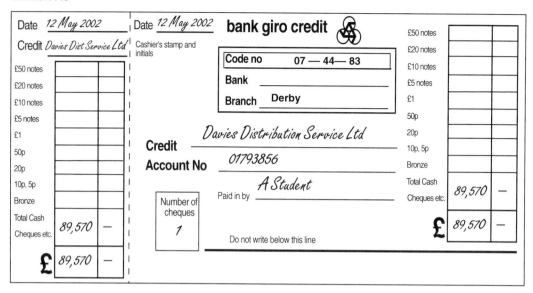

Exhibit A4

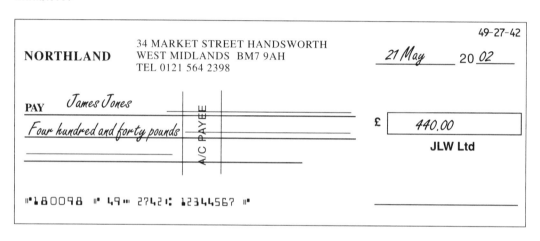

Chapter 14

14.1

Bank Reconciliation as on 31 December 2005

Cash at bank as per cash book		678
Add Unpresented cheques	256	
Credit transfers	56	312
		990
Less Bank lodgements		115
Cash at bank as per bank statement		875

14.5

Cash Book

Dr   Cr

Dec	31	Balance b/d	2,200	Dec	31	Standing order	40
Dec	31	Credit transfer	175	Dec	31	Bank charges	40
						Balance c/d	2,295
			2,375				2,375
Jan	1	Balance b/d	2,295				

Mitchell: Bank Reconciliation as at 31 December

	£
Balance per bank statement	2,245
Less Unpresented cheques	250
	1,995
Add Deposit	300
Balance per cash book	2,295

14.6 *(a) (i)*

Cash Book (Bank Column Only)

Dr   Cr

Date 2003	Details	Folio	Bank	Date 2003	Details	Folio	Bank
July 31	Balance	b/d	1,069.68	July 7	D/D United Insurance		35.00
25	Wheeldons		217.00	9	S/O Uttoxeter CC		76.00
				18	Bank Charges		24.40
				31	Balance	c/d	1,151.28
			1,286.68				1,286.68
Aug 1	Balance	b/d	1,151.28				

(ii)   *Bank Reconciliation Statement as at 31 July 2003*

		£
Balance per bank statement		3,225.63
Add Cash not credited		34.10
		3,259.73
Less Unpresented cheques		
00236	54.00	
00241	450.25	
00242	125.00	
00244	1,427.30	
00245	51.90	2,108.45
Balance per cash book		1,151.28

(b) Standing orders are payments made by the bank on the customer's behalf by deducting a regular amount of money from the customer's account to pay for such things as a mortgage payment, insurance premium, etc. The customer requests the bank to make the payment on a regular, often monthly, basis until such time as he or she wishes to cancel the order.

Direct debits are also used to enable regular payments to be made by the bank on the customer's behalf. These, however, differ slightly from standing orders in that authority is given to the person/firm receiving the money to make the request for payment to the bank from the payer's account. Often the payment will vary from one payment to another, whereas standing orders remain fixed until altered at the customer's request.

(c) As you are an employee of the firm it is not your duty to divulge confidential information about the business's financial stability to anyone, be they employees or outside personnel. Therefore, to protect both yourself and the firm you should refuse this request.

14.9 Any three from:

- unpresented cheques;
- bankings not yet credited on bank statement;
- bank charges not yet entered in cash book;
- BACS and giro credits paid into the bank by customers, not yet entered in cash book;
- standing orders not entered in cash book;
- direct debits not entered in cash book;
- errors.

14.10 Debit.

Chapter 15

15.1

Petty Cash Book

Receipts			Total	Cleaning	Motor Expenses	Postages	Stationery	Travelling
300	(1)							
	(2)	Postages	18			18		
	(3)	Travelling	12					12
	(4)	Cleaning	15	15				
	(7)	Petrol	22		22			
	(8)	Travelling	25					25
	(9)	Stationery	17				17	
	(11)	Cleaning	18	18				
	(14)	Postages	5			5		
	(15)	Travelling	8					8
	(18)	Stationery	9				9	
	(18)	Cleaning	23	23				
	(20)	Postages	13			13		
	(24)	Motor service	43		43			
	(26)	Petrol	18		18			
	(27)	Cleaning	21	21				
	(29)	Postages	5			5		
	(30)	Petrol	14		14			
			286	77	97	41	26	45
	(31)	Balance c/d	14					
300			300					
14	(1)	Balance b/d						
286	(1)	Bank						

15.3 *(a)*

Petty Cash Book

Receipts	Date		Details	Voucher No	Total payment	Travel-ling	Post-age	Station-ery	Office expenses	VAT	Ledger postings
£	2004				£	£	£	£	£	£	£
120.00	Mar	1	Cash								
		2	Postage stamps	1	6.50		6.50				
		3	Rail fare	2	23.00	23.00					
		7	Parcel	3	4.00		4.00				
		9	Window cleaning	4	8.00				8.00		
		12	Envelopes	5	3.10			2.64		.46	
		14	Office tea, etc	6	6.40				6.40		
		16	Petrol	7	10.00	8.51				1.49	
		19	Disks – computer	8	13.00				11.06	1.94	
		20	Dusters and polish	9	1.73				1.47	.26	
		23	Postage stamps	10	2.40		2.40				
		27	Ledger a/c J Cheetham	11	7.30						7.30
		31	Magazine	12	6.40				6.40		
91.83	Mar	31	Cash	CB 1		31.51	12.90	2.64	33.33	4.15	7.30
		31	Balance	c/d	28.17						
120.00					120.00						
28.17	Apr	1	Balance	b/d		GL 1	GL 2	GL 3	GL 4	GL 5	
91.83	"	1	Cash	CB 1							

(b)

General Ledger

Dr		Travelling Expenses Account				GL 1		Cr
Date	Details		Fol	£	Date	Details	Fol	£
2004								
Mar 31	Petty cash		PCB 1	31.51				

Dr		Postages Account				GL 2		Cr
Date	Details		Fol	£	Date	Details	Fol	£
2004								
Mar 31	Petty cash		PCB 1	12.90				

Dr		Stationery Account				GL 3		Cr
Date	Details		Fol	£	Date	Details	Fol	£
2004								
Mar 31	Petty cash		PCB 1	2.64				

Dr		Office Expenses Account				GL 4		Cr
Date	Details		Fol	£	Date	Details	Fol	£
2004								
Mar 31	Petty cash		PCB 1	33.33				

Dr		VAT Account				GL 5		Cr
Date	Details		Fol	£	Date	Details	Fol	£
2004								
Mar 31	Petty cash		PCB 1	4.15				

Dr		Cash Book (Bank Column Only)				CB 1		Cr
Date	Details		Fol	£	Date	Details	Fol	£
					2004			
					Mar 31	Petty cash	PCB 1	91.83

Purchase Ledger

Dr		J Cheetham Account						Cr
Date	Details		Fol	£	Date	Details	Fol	£
2004					2004			
Mar 31	Petty cash		PCB 1	7.30	Feb 1	Purchases	PDB 1	7.30

(c)

MEMORANDUM

To	Ms S Dickinson	**Ref**	
From	Student's Name	**Date**	31 March 2004
Subject	Petty Cash Imprest System		

Advantages of Imprest System

1   *Control*: The petty cash can be checked easily at any time because cash in hand plus vouchers paid out for the period should always equal the amount of the 'float'.
2   *Responsibility*: It is an ideal opportunity to appoint junior staff and give them some responsibility and test their honesty.
3   It relieves the accountant of dealing with numerous small cash payments and reduces the posting to the general ledger.

15.5

Petty Cash Book   PCB 1

Receipts	Date	Details	Voucher No	Total Payment	Workshop Materials	Station-ery	Postages	Travel	Sundries	VAT
£				£	£	£	£	£	£	£
9.25	1 June	Balance b/d								
140.75	1 June	Cash								
150.00	1 June	Stationery	21	18.30		15.57				2.73
	3 June	Sundry Expenses	22	6.27					6.27	
	4 June	Stationery	23	16.70		14.21				2.49
	8 June	Postages	24	2.40			2.40			
	11 June	Travelling Exp	25	4.35				4.35		
	12 June	Purchase of Materials	26	42.65	36.30					6.35
	20 June	Cleaning Windows	27	12.50					12.50	
	16 June	Stationery	28	2.20		1.87				0.33
	21 June	Light Bulbs	29	2.47					2.10	0.37
	23 June	Parcel Post	30	3.52			3.52			
	27 June	First Aid	31	4.20					3.57	0.63
	30 June	Travelling Expenses	32	29.50				29.50		
				145.06	36.30	31.65	5.92	33.85	24.44	12.90
	30 June	Balance	c/d	4.94						
150.00				150.00						
4.94	1 July	Balance	b/d							
145.06	1 July	Cash								

Chapter 16

16.1   Case law refers to decisions based on previous law cases brought before the courts. Statute law is based entirely on the law shown in Acts of Parliament.

16.2   Briefly: agreement, intention and consideration.

16.3   No, he cannot be sued. The offer must be clear, must be complete and must be final. In this case his offer was conditional and was not made final.

16.5   Elgin was informed of the true nature of the slabs. As the 'defect' of the goods was notified to Elgin then he has no legal rights and cannot insist on either a return of his money or the replacement marble slabs.

16.7   The conditions were that an acceptance had to be made by **fax**. This was not done, and though it was not due to your fault, the fact remains that you did not use fax for the acceptance and therefore Jenkins is entitled to ignore it. You have no legal rights to enforce the contract.

16.9 No. There has been no offer and acceptance. You originally made an offer, but this was not accepted. You then made a counter-offer and this was also not accepted. Without an offer and an acceptance there is no contract and you cannot force him to sell the item to you.

16.11 You are entitled to full damages. The garage did not exercise the due 'care and skill' which should be expected of them. One would not expect a motorist to check his rear wheels when collecting a repaired car from a garage.

Chapter 17

17.1 Capital: *(a) (c) (d) (f) (j) (l)*.
Revenue: *(b) (e) (g) (h) (i) (k)*.

17.3 Capital: *(a) (b) (e)*.
Explanation – *see* text.

17.4 Capital: £4,500 of *(a)*; £1,000 of *(b)*; £2,300 of *(c)*; £100 of *(e)*; £4,000 of *(f)*.
Revenue: £13,500 of *(a)*; £3,000 of *(b)*; £200 of *(c)*; £1,400 of *(d)*; £700 of *(e)*.

17.8 *(a)*   Capital. *(b)* Revenue.

17.9 *(a)*   Capital. *(b)* Capital. *(c)* Revenue.

17.10 *(a)*   Total expenses would be too high and the net profit would be reduced.
      (b)   The value of the assets in the balance sheet would be too low.

17.11 *(a)*   Capital. *(b)* Capital. *(c)* Revenue.

Chapter 18

18.1 Quotation for Halshaw Printing Co:

	£
2 × Super Zoom Photocopier Z-90 @ £600 each	1,200.00
Less 20% Trade discount	240.00
	960.00

18.2 *See* Exhibit A5.

18.5 *(a)*   Remittance Advice – *see* section 18.11.

      (b)   Goods received note (GRN) – *see* section 18.12.

      (c)   Credit note – *see* section 18.9.

18.7 *(a)*   Advice note.

      (b)   Delivery note/despatch note/packing note.

      (c)   Invoice.

Exhibit A5

ROBERTS SUPPLIERS CO Liverpool Road Liverpool			Invoice No S.9270	
Telephone: 0151 307128 Fax: 0151 307824 VAT Reg No 224 36658			Date/Tax point 7 October 2002	
Customer: Burgess & Son 27 Frith Street Birkenhead B21 3RZ			Your Order No 1079	

Product code	Description	Quantity	Unit price £ p	Total amount £ p
LM 713	Easi-ride mower complete with collection boxes	2	1,527.30	3,054.60
Comments:			**Net Total**	3,054.60
			Total	3,054.60

Registered office **Park Avenue, Liverpool**	Registered No: **263120**

ROBERTS SUPPLIERS CO Liverpool Road Liverpool			Invoice No S.9271	
Telephone: 0151 307128 Fax 0151 307824 VAT Reg No. 224 36658			Date/Tax point 7 October 2002	
Customer: Rudkins Superstores Market Place Runcorn			Your Order No KT 27	

Product code	Description	Quantity	Unit price £ p	Total amount £ p
	Garden forks Wheelbarrows 24″ Quickmow machines (electric) with cable	6 10 2	22.30 67.95 324.00	133.80 679.50 648.00
Comments:			**Net Total**	1,461.30
			Total	1,461.30

Registered office **Park Avenue, Liverpool**	Registered No: **263120**

Chapter 19

19.1

	Sales Day Book	
(1)	J Gordon	187
(3)	G Abrahams	166
(6)	V White	12
(10)	J Gordon	55
(17)	F Williams	289
(19)	U Richards	66
(27)	V Wood	28
(31)	L Simes	78
		881

Sales Ledger

J Gordon

(1) Sales	187	
(10) Sales	55	

G Abrahams

(3) Sales	166	

V White

(6) Sales	12	

F Williams

(17) Sales	289	

U Richards

(19) Sales	66	

V Wood

(27) Sales	28	

L Simes

(31) Sales	78	

General Ledger

Sales Account

		(31) Total for month	881

19.3 Workings of invoices:

(1)	F Gray	3 rolls white tape × 10 =	30		
		5 sheets blue cotton × 6 =	30		
		1 dress length × 20 =	20	80	
		Less trade discount 25%		20	60
(4)	A Gray	6 rolls white tape × 10 =	60		
		30 metres green baize × 4 =	120	180	
		Less trade discount × 33⅓%		60	120
(8)	E Hines	1 dress length black silk × 20 =			20
(20)	M Allen	10 rolls white tape × 10 =	100		
		6 sheets blue cotton × 6 =	36		
		3 dress lengths black silk × 20 =	60		
		11 metres green baize × 4 =	44	240	
		Less trade discount × 25%		60	180
(31)	B Cooper	12 rolls white tape × 10 =	120		
		14 sheets blue cotton × 6 =	84		
		9 metres green baize × 4 =	36	240	
		Less trade discount 33⅓%		80	160

19.3 (*cont*)

<table>
<tr><td colspan="2">Sales Day Book</td><td></td></tr>
<tr><td>(1)</td><td>F Gray</td><td>60</td></tr>
<tr><td>(4)</td><td>A Gray</td><td>120</td></tr>
<tr><td>(8)</td><td>E Hines</td><td>20</td></tr>
<tr><td>(20)</td><td>M Allen</td><td>180</td></tr>
<tr><td>(31)</td><td>B Cooper</td><td>160</td></tr>
<tr><td></td><td></td><td>540</td></tr>
</table>

Sales Ledger

F Gray

(1)	Sales	60	

A Gray

(4)	Sales	120	

E Hines

(8)	Sales	20	

M Allen

(20)	Sales	180	

B Cooper

(31)	Sales	160	

General Ledger

Sales Account

		(31) Total for month	540

19.4 Morton's Garage:

(*a*)   *Sales Day Book*

2003		Invoice No	£
2 Jan	D Woolham & Co	37542	230
6 Jan	C Crawford	37543	345
7 Jan	S Brocklehurst	37544	1,980
9 Jan	L Price & Partners	37545	523
13 Jan	D Woolham & Co	37546	56
18 Jan	L Price & Partners	37547	200
21 Jan	C Crawford	37548	340
24 Jan	C Crawford	37549	45
29 Jan	S Brocklehurst	37550	845
31 Jan	L Price & Partners	37551	721
			5,285

(*b*) & (*c*)   **Sales Ledger**

C Crawford Account

(1)	Balance b/d	1,078	(31)	Bank	1,078
(6)	Sales	345	(31)	Balance c/d	730
(21)	Sales	340			
(24)	Sales	45			
		1,808			1,808
(1)	Balance b/d	730			

L Price & Partners Account

(1)	Balance b/d	321	(31)	Bank	321
(9)	Sales	523	(31)	Balance c/d	1,444
(18)	Sales	200			
(31)	Sales	721			
		1,765			1,765
(1)	Balance b/d	1,444			

S Brocklehurst Account

(1)	Balance b/d	563	(31)	Balance c/d	3,388
(7)	Sales	1,980			
(29)	Sales	845			
		3,388			3,388
(1)	Balance b/d	3,388			

D Woolham & Co Account

(1)	Balance b/d	146	(31)	Bank	146
(2)	Sales	230	(31)	Balance c/d	286
(13)	Sales	56			
		432			432
(1)	Balance b/d	286			

General Ledger

Sales Account

	(31) Total sales for the month	5,285

Chapter 20

20.1 Workings of purchases invoices

(1)	K King	4 radios × 30 =	120		
		3 music centres × 160 =	480	600	
		Less Trade discount 25%		150	450
(3)	A Bell	2 washing machines × 200 =	400		
		5 vacuum cleaners × 60 =	300		
		2 dish dryers × 150 =	300	1,000	
		Less Trade discount 20%		200	800
(15)	J Kelly	1 music centre × 300 =	300		
		2 washing machines × 250 =	500	800	
		Less trade discount 25%		200	600
(20)	B Powell	6 radios × 70 =		420	
		Less Trade discount 33⅓%		140	280
(30)	B Lewis	4 dish dryers × 200 =		800	
		Less Trade discount 20%		160	640

Purchases Day Book

(1) K King	450
(3) A Bell	800
(15) J Kelly	600
(20) B Powell	280
(30) B Lewis	640
	2,770

Purchases Ledger

K King

	(1) Purchases 450

A Bell

	(3) Purchases 800

J Kelly

	(15) Purchases 600

B Powell

	(20) Purchases 280

B Lewis

	(30) Purchases 640

General Ledger

Purchases Account

(31) Total for month	2,770	

20.3

Purchases Day Book		
(1)	Smith Stores	90
(23)	C Kelly	105
(31)	J Hamilton	180
		375

Sales Day Book		
(8)	A Grantley	72
(15)	A Henry	240
(24)	D Sangster	81
		393

Purchases Ledger

Smith Stores

	(1) Purchases	90

C Kelly

	(23) Purchases	105

J Hamilton

	(31) Purchases	180

Sales Ledger

A Grantley

(8) Sales	72

A Henry

(15) Sales	240

D Sangster

(24) Sales	81

General Ledger

Sales Account

	(31) Total for month	393

Purchases Account

(31) Total for month	375

20.4 *(a)*

	Product A		Product B	
Manufacturers' recommended retail price		1,500		4,000
Less Trade discount	(20%)	300	(25%)	1,000
Price paid per product		1,200		3,000

(b) Profit per product (equals trade discount when sold at MRRP)

Product A	Product B
300	1,000

(c)

$$\frac{300}{1,200} \times \frac{100}{1} = 25\% \qquad \frac{1,000}{3,000} \times \frac{100}{1} = 33\tfrac{1}{3}\%$$

20.6 *(a)*

Purchases Day Book

Date	Details	Folio	Invoice	Total
2004				
Nov 1	Bould & Co	PL1	SR2103	104.26
Nov 3	Hambleton's	PL2	SR2104	140.57
Nov 7	Farm Supplies Co	PL3	SR2105	448.12
Nov 10	Worthington's Ltd	PL4	SR2106	169.91
Nov 12	Sigley Bros	PL5	SR2107	47.00
Nov 15	Hambleton's	PL2	SR2108	259.09
Nov 20	Harlows Mfr	PL6	SR2109	84.96
Nov 20	Bould & Co	PL1	SR2110	29.14
Nov 25	Clark & Robinson	PL7	SR2111	61.63
Nov 30	T Adam Ltd	PL8	SR2112	233.83
				1,578.51

(b)

Purchases Ledger

Bould & Co Account

Nov 30	Balance c/d	133.40	Nov 1	Purchases	SR2103	104.26
			Nov 20	Purchases	SR2110	29.14
		133.40				133.40
			Dec 1	Balance		133.40

Hambleton's Account

Nov 30	Balance c/d	399.66	Nov 3	Purchases	SR2104	140.57
			Nov 15	Purchases	SR2108	259.09
		399.66				399.66
			Dec 1	Balance	b/d	399.66

Farm Supplies Co Account

	Nov 7	Purchases	SR2105	448.12

Worthington's Ltd Account

	Nov 10	Purchases	SR2106	169.91

Sigley Bros Account

	Nov 12	Purchases	SR2107	47.00

Harlows Mfr Account

	Nov 20	Purchases	SR2109	84.96

Clark & Robinson Account

	Nov 25	Purchases	SR2111	61.63

T Adam Ltd Account

	Nov 30	Purchases	SR2112	233.83

(c)

General Ledger

Purchases Account

Nov 30	Total Purchases for November	PDB1	1,578.51

Chapter 21

21.1

<table>
<tr><td colspan="2" align="center">Purchases Day Book</td></tr>
<tr><td>(1) H Lloyd</td><td align="right">119</td></tr>
<tr><td>(4) D Scott</td><td align="right">98</td></tr>
<tr><td>(4) A Simpson</td><td align="right">114</td></tr>
<tr><td>(4) A Williams</td><td align="right">25</td></tr>
<tr><td>(4) S Wood</td><td align="right">56</td></tr>
<tr><td>(10) A Simpson</td><td align="right">59</td></tr>
<tr><td>(18) M White</td><td align="right">89</td></tr>
<tr><td>(18) J Wong</td><td align="right">67</td></tr>
<tr><td>(18) H Miller</td><td align="right">196</td></tr>
<tr><td>(18) H Lewis</td><td align="right">119</td></tr>
<tr><td>(31) A Williams</td><td align="right">56</td></tr>
<tr><td>(31) C Cooper</td><td align="right">98</td></tr>
<tr><td></td><td align="right">1,096</td></tr>
</table>

Returns Outwards Day Book

(7) H Lloyd	16
(7) D Scott	14
(25) J Wong	5
(25) A Simpson	11
	46

General Ledger
Purchases Account

(31) Total for month 1,096		

Returns Outwards Account

	(31) Total for month 46

Purchases Ledger
H Lloyd

(7) Returns	16	(1) Purchases	119

D Scott

(7) Returns	14	(4) Purchases	98

A Simpson

(25) Returns	11	(4) Purchases	114
		(10) Purchases	59

A Williams

		(4) Purchases	25
		(31) Purchases	56

S Wood

		(4) Purchases	56

M White

		(18) Purchases	89

J Wong

(25) Returns	5	(18) Purchases	67

H Miller

		(18) Purchases	196

H Lewis

		(18) Purchases	119

C Cooper

		(31) Purchases	98

21.3

Sales Day Book

(3)	E Rigby	510
(3)	E Phillips	246
(3)	F Thompson	356
(8)	A Green	307
(8)	H George	250
(8)	J Ferguson	185
(20)	E Phillips	188
(20)	F Powell	310
(20)	E Lee	420
		2,772

Returns Inwards Day Book

(14)	E Phillips	18
(14)	F Thompson	22
(31)	E Phillips	27
(31)	E Rigby	30
		97

Purchases Day Book

(1)	K Hill	380
(1)	M Norman	500
(1)	N Senior	106
(5)	R Morton	200
(5)	J Cook	180
(5)	D Edwards	410
(5)	C Davies	66
(24)	C Ferguson	550
(24)	K Ennevor	900
		3,292

Returns Outwards Day Book

(12)	M Norman	30
(12)	N Senior	16
(31)	J Cook	13
(31)	C Davies	11
		70

Sales Ledger

E Rigby

(3)	Sales	510	(31)	Returns in	30

E Phillips

(3)	Sales	246	(14)	Returns in	18
(20)	Sales	188	(31)	Returns in	27

F Thompson

(3)	Sales	356	(14)	Returns in	22

A Green

(8)	Sales	307

H George

(8)	Sales	250

J Ferguson

(8)	Sales	185

F Powell

(20)	Sales	310

E Lee

(20)	Sales	420

Purchases Ledger

K Hill

			(1)	Purchases	380

M Norman

(13)	Returns out	30	(1)	Purchases	500

N Senior

(12)	Returns out	16	(1)	Purchases	106

R Morton

			(5)	Purchases	200

J Cook

(31)	Returns out	13	(5)	Purchases	180

D Edwards

			(5)	Purchases	410

C Davies

(31)	Returns out	11	(5)	Purchases	66

C Ferguson

			(24)	Purchases	550

K Ennevor

			(24)	Purchases	900

General Ledger

Sales

	(31) Sales book	2,772

Returns Inwards

(31) Returns in book	97	

Purchases

(31) Purchases book	3,292	

Returns Outwards

	(31) Returns out book	70

21.5

Sales Ledger

A Birch

(1)	Balance b/d	4,251	(7)	Bank		4,100
(9)	Sales	1,095	(7)	Discount		151
			(31)	Balance		
				c/d		1,095
		5,346				5,346

H Jameson

(1)	Balance b/d	1,260	(23)	Bank	900
(15)	Sales	740	(24)	Returns	140
(19)	Sales	205	(31)	Balance	
				c/d	1,165
		2,205			2,205

General Ledger

Capital

			(1)	Balance	
				b/d	9,151

Sales

			(31)	Sales	
				book	2,040

Purchases

(31)	Purchases		
	book	1,604	

Returns Inwards

(31)	Returns in		
	book	140	

Returns Outwards

			(31)	Returns	
				out book	80

Discounts Allowed

(31)	Cash		
	book	151	

Discounts Received

			(31)	Cash	
				book	187

Purchases Ledger

S Franklin

(18)	Bank	1,080	(1)	Balance	
				b/d	1,780
(18)	Discount	120	(12)	Purchases	206
(19)	Returns	80			
(31)	Balance c/d	706			
		1,986			1,986

P Greenbank

(2)	Bank	603	(1)	Balance	
(2)	Discount	67		b/d	670
		670			670

E Oliver

(29)	Bank	1,110	(1)	Balance	
(31)	Balance c/d	1,398		b/d	1,110
			(8)	Purchases	348
			(23)	Purchases	1,050
		2,508			2,508

Cash Book

		Disct	Bank			Disct	Bank
(1)	Balance b/d		7,200	(2)	P Greenbank	67	603
(7)	A Birch	151	4,100	(18)	S Franklin	120	1,080
(23)	H Jameson		900	(29)	E Oliver		1,110
				(31)	Balance c/d		9,407
		151	12,200			187	12,200

21.6 Framework Ltd:

Sales Ledger
J Forbes (Fancy Gifts) Account

(1)	Balance b/d	745	(31)	Bank	745
(23)	Sales	1,234	(31)	Balance c/d	1,234
		1,979			1,979
(1)	Balance b/d	1,234			

Goodwin & Co Account

(1)	Balance b/d	276	(31)	Balance c/d	604
(11)	Sales	328			
		604			604
(1)	Balance b/d	604			

L & P Moss Account

(1)	Balance b/d	390	(31)	Bank	200
(27)	Sales	2,500	(31)	Balance c/d	2,690
		2,890			2,890
(1)	Balance b/d	2,690			

Purchases Ledger
M & P Fitzsimmons Account

(28)	Returns Outward	200	(1)	Balance b/d	800
(31)	Bank	500	(22)	Purchases	756
(31)	Balance c/d	856			
		1,556			1,556
			(1)	Balance b/d	856

L Horne Account

(12)	Returns outwards	42	(1)	Balance b/d	450
(31)	Balance c/d	1,058	(2)	Purchases	650
		1,100			1,100
			(1)	Balance b/d	1,058

M Ward & Sons Account

(31)	Bank	245	(1)	Balance b/d	245
(31)	Balance c/d	334	(31)	Purchases	334
		579			579
			(1)	Balance b/d	334

Chapter 22

22.1 *(a)* J Hunt

(b) Feb 1 Amount owing brought forward from previous month.
Feb 6 Goods bought from Hunt on this date.
Feb 8 Cook paid Hunt a cheque for £127.16. Hunt allowed Cook to deduct this discount from payment because payment was made in good time.
Feb 12 Cook returns goods to Hunt.
Feb 26 Goods brought from Hunt on this date.
Feb 28 Cook was charged extra amount by Hunt because of an undercharge on a past invoice.
Sender: Hunt; Receiver: Cook. An invoice.

(c) Debtor is R J Cook.
Creditor is J Hunt.
Amount owed at 28 February is £312.36.

22.2 *See* section 22.3

22.3 *See* section 22.5

22.4 *(a)* Balances outstanding: D Hammond Ltd's Account £904 Dr
Alex Richards Ltd's Account £1,001 Dr

(b)

Statement of Account
Elder's Printing Co, 36 High Street
Shrewsbury SH4 8JK

D Hammond Ltd
Bay House, Heath Road
Shrewsbury SH7 3KL   31 January 2002

Date		Details	Debit	Credit	Balance
2002			£	£	£
Jan	1	Balance			1,403
Jan	3	Invoice	177		1,580
Jan	4	Bank		1,380	200
Jan	10	Invoice	527		727
Jan	12	Credit note		23	704
Jan	25	Invoice	200		904

Statement of Account
Elder's Printing Co, 36 High Street
Shrewsbury SH4 8JK

Alex Richards Ltd
Unit 12, Greenways Industrial Estate
Chester CE21 9HU   31 Janaury 2002

Date		Details	Debit	Credit	Balance
2002			£	£	£
Jan	1	Balance			346
Jan	7	Invoice	27		373
Jan	7	Bank		292	81
Jan	7	Discount		8	73
Jan	9	Invoice	521		594
Jan	12	Credit note		46	548
Jan	27	Invoice	400		948
Jan	31	Invoice	53		1,001

Chapter 23

23.1 *(a)*   Style of invoice will vary.
      Calculations:

3 sets of Boy Michael Golf Clubs × £240	720
150 Watson golf balls at £8 per 10 balls	120
4 Faldo golf bags at £30	120
	960
Less Trade discount 33⅓%	320
	640
Add VAT 17½%	112
	752

(b)

D Wilson Ltd Ledger

G Christie & Sons

Dr			Cr
2001		£	
May 1 Sales		752	

G Christie & Son Ledger

D Wilson Ltd

Dr		Cr	
	2001		£
	May 1 Purchases		752

23.2

Sales Book

2004			Net	VAT
Aug	1	M Sinclair & Co	160	28
Aug	8	M Brown & Associates	240	42
Aug	19	A Axton Ltd	80	14
Aug	31	T Christie	40	7
			520	91

Sales Ledger

M Sinclair & Co

(1)	Sales	188	

M Brown & Associates

(8)	Sales	282	

A Axton Ltd

(19)	Sales	94	

T Christie

(31)	Sales	47	

General Ledger

Sales

		(31) Credit sales for the month	520

Value Added Tax

		(31) Sales book: VAT content	91

23.3

Sales Day Book

		Net	VAT
(1)	B Davies & Co	160	28
(4)	C Grant Ltd	200	35
(16)	C Grant Ltd	120	21
(31)	B Karloff	80	14
		560	98

Purchases Day Book

		Net	VAT
(10)	G Cooper & Son	400	70
(10)	J Wayne Ltd	240	42
(14)	B Lugosi	40	7
(23)	S Hayward	40	7
		720	126

Sales Ledger
B Davies & Co

| (1) | Sales | 188 | | |

C Grant Ltd

| (4) | Sales | 235 | | |
| (16) | Sales | 141 | | |

B Karloff

| (31) | Sales | 94 | | |

Purchases Ledger
G Cooper & Son

| | | | (10) | Purchases | 470 |

J Wayne Ltd

| | | | (10) | Purchases | 282 |

B Lugosi

| | | | (14) | Purchases | 47 |

S Hayward

| | | | (23) | Purchases | 47 |

General Ledger
Sales

| | | | (31) | Credit sales for month | 560 |

Purchases

| (31) | Credit purchases for month | 720 | | | |

Value Added Tax

(31)	VAT content in purchases book	126	(31)	VAT content in sales book	98
			(31)	Balance c/d	28
		126			126

23.5

C Hills

(8) Bank	154	(1) Balance b/d	154
(31) Balance c/d	282	(13) Purchases	94
		(20) Purchases	188
	436		436
		(1) Balance b/d	282

L Lowe

(31) Balance c/d	322	(1) Balance b/d	275
		(21) Purchases	47
	322		322
		(1) Balance b/d	322

K Harris

(1) Balance b/d	330	(16) Bank	612
(11) Sales	282	(31) Balance c/d	94
(15) Sales	94		
	706		706
(1) Balance b/d	94		

Printing

(15) Bank	20	

Value Added Tax

(31) Purchases Book	49	(31) Sales Book	56
(31) Balance c/d	7		
	56		56
		(1) Balance b/d	7

Bank

(1) Balance b/d	740	(8) C Hills	154
(16) K Harris	612	(15) Printing	20
		(31) Balance c/d	1,178
	1,352		1,352
(1) Balance b/d	1,178		

Capital

	(1) Balance b/d	641

Purchases

(31) Day book	280	

Sales

	(31) Day Book	320

Trial Balance as at 31.12.2005

	Dr	Cr
C Hills		282
L Lowe		322
K Harris	94	
Printing	20	
Value Added Tax		7
Bank	1,178	
Capital		641
Purchases	280	
Sales		320
	1,572	1,572

23.7 *(a)* **VAT Account**

2005				2005			
Jan	31	Tax on inputs	3,500	Jan	31	Tax on outputs	3,675
Jan	31	Balance c/d	175				
			3,675				3,675
Feb	28	Tax on inputs	3,675	Feb	1	Balance b/d	175
				Feb	28	Tax on outputs	3,500
			3,675				3,675
Mar	31	Tax on inputs	3,850	Mar	31	Tax on outputs	2,625
				Mar	31	Balance c/d	1,225
			3,850				3,850
Apr	1	Balance b/d	1,225				

(b) The balance of £1,225 on 31 March 2005 is the amount owing by Customs & Excise (VAT) to the firm. This will be cleared by Customs & Excise sending a remittance for £1,225.

23.8 *(a)* Trade discount £200

(b) Cash discount £90

(c) VAT £299.25

23.9 VAT payable to Customs & Excise:

Manufacturer	35
Wholesaler (49 – 35)	14
Retailer (56 – 49)	7
	56

23.10 *(a)* Debited
(b) Six years
(c) Yes
(d) Debit – Sales returns/Returns inwards 80
Debit – VAT 14
Credit – Bank/cash 94

Chapter 24

24.1 *(a)*

Curtain Design Company

Sales Day Book

Date	Details	Folio	Total	Ready-made	Custom-made	VAT
2002			£	£	£	£
Nov 1	Jarvis Arms Hotel	SL 1	2,702.50		2,300.00	402.50
8	Springs Nursing Home	SL 2	1,175.00	1,000.00		175.00
15	J P Morten	SL 3	258.50	220.00		38.50
17	Queen's Hotel	SL 4	1,762.50		1,500.00	262.50
30	W Blackshaw	SL 5	105.75	90.00		15.75
			6,004.25	1,310.00	3,800.00	894.25
				GL1	GL2	GL3

(b)

Sales Ledger

Jarvis Arms Hotel Account SL 1

Dr   Cr

Nov 1 Sales   2,702.50

Spring's Nursing Home Account SL 2

Dr   Cr

Nov 8 Sales   1,175.00

J P Morten Account SL 3

Dr   Cr

Nov 15 Sales   258.50

Queen's Hotel Account SL 4

Dr   Cr

Nov 17 Sales   1,762.50

W Blackshaw Account SL 5

Dr   Cr

Nov 30 Sales   105.75

(c)
General Ledger

Sales – Ready-Made Account   GL 1
Dr   Cr

	Nov 30 Day book 1,310.00

Sales – Custom-Made Account   GL 2
Dr   Cr

	Nov 30 Day book 3,800.00

Value Added Tax Account   GL 3
Dr   Cr

	Nov 30 VAT on sales 894.25

24.2 (a)
Hall Engineering Co
Purchases Day Book

Date		Details	Folio	Total	Engin-eering parts	Printing and stationery	Motor expenses	VAT
2002				£	£	£	£	£
May	1	Black's Engineering Co	PL1	611.00	520.00			91.00
May	3	Ace Printing Co	PL2	170.37		145.00		25.37
May	24	Morgan's Garage	PL3	141.00			120.00	21.00
May	26	Martin's Foundry	PL4	822.50	700.00			122.50
May	28	Office Supplies	PL5	148.05		126.00		22.05
May	29	Black's Engineering Co	PL1	258.50	220.00			38.50
				2,151.42	1,440.00	271.00	120.00	320.42
					GL1	GL2	GL3	GL4

(b)
Purchases Ledger

Blacks Engineering Account   PL 1
Dr   Cr

	May 1 Purchases 611.00
	May 29 Purchases 258.50

Ace Printing Co Account   PL 2
Dr   Cr

	May 3 Purchases 170.37

Morgan's Garage Account   PL 3
Dr   Cr

	May 24 Purchases 141.00

Martin's Foundry Account   PL 4
Dr   Cr

	May 26 Purchases 822.50

Office Supplies Account   PL 5
Dr   Cr

	May 28 Purchases 148.05

(c)

General Ledger

Purchases – Engineering Parts Account   GL 1

Dr   Cr

May	31	Day book	1,440.00	

Printing and Stationery Account   GL 2

Dr   Cr

May	31	Day book	271.00	

Motor Expenses Account   GL 3

Dr   Cr

May	31	Day book	120.00	

VAT Account   GL 4

Dr   Cr

May	31	VAT on purchases	320.42	

24.4 Peakdale Cafe and Craft Centre:

Cash Book (Debit Side)

Date		Details		Food Sales	Craft Sales	Cash	Bank
2001							
July	1	Balance b/d				150.00	2,687.50
July	7	Takings		1,923.56		1,923.56	
July	7	Cash	C				1,750.00
July	14	Sale of paintings			400.00		400.00
July	15	Takings		2,100.00		2,100.00	
July	16	Cash	C				1,500.00
July	22	Sale of crafts			267.50		267.50
July	22	Takings		2,356.00		2,356.00	
July	23	Cash	C				2,000.00
July	24	Sale of painting			378.00		378.00
July	27	Sale of painting etc.			990.00		990.00
July	30	Takings		2,500.00		2,500.00	
July	30	Cash	C				2,700.00
				8,879.56	2,035.50	9,029.56	12,673.00
Aug	1	Balance b/d				660.43	4,203.00

Cash Book (Credit Side)

Date		Details		Food Purchases	Craft Item Purchases	Other Expenses	Cash	Bank
2001								
July	3	Sundry expenses				67.90	67.90	
July	5	Restaurant suppliers				56.23	56.23	
July	6	Food wholesalers		2,480.00				2,480.00
July	7	Bank	C				1,750.00	
July	8	Wages				120.00	120.00	
July	16	Bank	C				1,500.00	
July	16	Wages				150.00	150.00	
July	19	Ash & Co		360.00				360.00
July	20	Petrol				25.00	25.00	
July	23	Bank	C				2,000.00	
July	25	Artcraft			3,100.00			3,100.00
July	30	Salaries:						
		M Chapman				980.00		980.00
		S Kerr				1,550.00		1,550.00
July	30	Bank	C				2,700.00	
July	31	Balance	c/d				660.43	4,203.00
				2,840.00	3,100.00	2,949.13	9,029.56	12,673.00

Chapter 25

25.1

Sales Ledger Control Account

Dr   Cr

(1)	Balance b/f	4,560	(31)	Returns inwards	460
(31)	Sales journal	10,870	(31)	Cheques and cash	9,615
			(31)	Discount allowed	305
			(31)	Balances c/d	5,050
		15.430			15,430

25.2

Sales Ledger Control Account

Dr   Cr

(1)	Balances b/f	6,708	(31)	Discounts	300
(31)	Sales journal	11,500	(31)	Cash and cheques	8,970
			(31)	Bad debts	115
			(31)	Returns inwards	210
			(31)	Balances c/d	8,613
		18,208			18,208

25.5 (a)

Sales Ledger Control Account

Dr   Cr

(1)	Balances b/f	6,840	(31)	Discounts	420
(31)	Sales	46,801	(31)	Bad debts	494
			(31)	Receipts	43,780
			(31)	Returns in	296
			(31)	Balances c/f	8,651
		53,641			53,641

(b)   *See* text

25.6

Sales Ledger

Atlantis Sport Ltd Account

Dr   Cr

Apr	1	Balance b/d	909.36	Apr	15	Bank	863.90
Apr	7	Sales	860.57	Apr	15	Discount	45.46
				Apr	30	Balance c/d	860.57
			1,769.93				1,769.93

Dr   *T L Maleta Account*   Cr

Apr	1	Balance b/d	495.68	Apr	29	Bad debts	495.68

Dr   *Lenton Leisurewear Account*   Cr

Apr	1	Balance b/d	736.29	Apr	10	Returns	61.86
Apr	2	Sales	510.09	Apr	30	Bank	699.47
				Apr	30	Discount	36.82
				Apr	30	Balance c/d	448.23
			1,246.38				1,246.38

Dr   *Sportime Account*   Cr

Apr	1	Balance b/d	574.73	Apr	25	Returns	77.70
Apr	19	Sales	935.69	Apr	28	Bank	545.99
				Apr	28	Discount	28.74
				Apr	30	Balance c/d	857.99
			1,510.42				1,510.42

Dr		Sales Ledger Control Account				Cr
Apr	1	Balance b/d	2,716.06	Apr 30	Returns Book	139.56
Apr	30	Sales Day Book	2,306.35	Apr 30	Bank	2,109.36
				Apr 30	Discounts	111.02
				Apr 30	Bad debts	495.68
				Apr 30	Balance c/d	2,166.79
			5,022.41			5,022.41

Debtors outstanding as at 30 April 2002

Atlantis Sports Ltd	860.57
Lenton Leisurewear Ltd	448.23
Sportime	857.99
	2,166.79

25.7 (a) (i) A sales ledger control account enables the total of debtors outstanding to be obtained quickly when required for trial balance purposes.

(ii) They assist in the location of errors.

(iii) They enable checks to be made on the accuracy of entries made in the personal accounts in the sales ledger.

(b) (i) Yes

(ii) Yes (the account should have been credited)

(iii) No

25.9

Purchases Ledger

Dr		K Sherrett Account				Cr
July 31	Bank	17,088	July	1	Balance b/d	3,240
July 31	Discount	100	July	31	Purchases	16,302
July 31	Balance c/d	2,354				
		19,542				19,542

Dr		M Cassidy Account				Cr
July 31	Returns	162	July	1	Balance b/d	3,160
July 31	Bank	8,700	July	31	Purchases	9,518
July 31	Balance b/d	3,816				
		12,678				12,678

Dr		N Cowie Account				Cr
July	1	Balance b/d	64	July 31	Purchases	8,662
July	31	Returns	58			
July	31	Bank	6,337			
July	31	Discount	83			
July	31	Balance b/d	2,120			
			8,662			8,662

Dr		Purchase Ledger Control Account				Cr
July	1	Balance b/d	64	July	1	Balance b/d	6,400
July	31	Returns	220	July	31	Purchases	34,482
July	31	Bank	32,125			
July	31	Discounts	183			
July	31	Balance c/d	8,290			
			40,882			40,882

List of outstanding creditors as at 31 July

K Sherrett	2,354
M Cassidy	3,816
N Cowie	2,120
	8,290

Chapter 26

26.1 (a)

Creditors Ledger

Dr   *Silver Sports Mfrs Ltd Account*   Cr

2002				2002			
Jan	3	Cheque	10.00	Jan	1	Balance b/f	10.00
Jan	21	Credit note: No 423	57.30	Jan	7	Purchases: Inv No 1001	321.60
Jan	31	Balance c/d	815.00	Jan	13	Purchases: Inv No 1290	470.90
				Jan	20	Purchases: Inv No 1814	79.80
			882.30				882.30
				Feb	1	Balance b/d	815.00

Dr   *Zoom Sports Ltd Account*   Cr

2002				2002			
Jan	2	Cheque	330.50	Jan	1	Balance b/f	372.50
Jan	7	Credit note: No 73	42.00	Jan	3	Purchases: Inv No 323	12.30
Jan	12	Credit note: No 87	13.40	Jan	17	Purchases: Inv No 450	79.10
Jan	31	Balance c/d	252.00	Jan	24	Purchases: Inv No 501	62.70
						Inv No 502	111.30
			637.90				637.90
				Feb	1	Balance b/d	252.00

(b)   *Reconciliation of Creditors Accounts*

     (i)   *Silver Sports Mfrs Ltd as at 31 January*

Balance per our purchases ledger	815.00
Add Purchases not received by us	142.57
Balance as per supplier's statement	957.57

     (ii)   *Zoom Sports Ltd as at 31 January*

Balance per our purchases ledger	252.00
Same as supplier's statement	

(c)   *Outstanding creditors as at 31 January 2002*

Silver Sports Ltd	815
Zoom Sports Ltd	252

26.3 (a)

Balance as per ledger account		2,730
Add Invoice not yet received		1,550
Amount outstanding		4,280
Balance as per Excel Products Statement		5,705
Less Payment not yet entered	1,330	
Less Discount not yet entered	20	1,350
		4,355
Less Returns not yet entered		75
Amount outstanding		4,280

(b)   Cash discount may be disallowed by a supplier if the payment is received later than the agreed/stated credit period which is usually 30 days.

26.5 *(a)* An invoice may have been sent by the supplier and not yet received by James Hamilton Ltd.

(b) James Hamilton may have sent a payment to the supplier, Ward & Worrell Ltd, but it had not been received by them at the time the statement of account was prepared.

(c) James Hamilton Ltd may have returned goods to the supplier and they had not yet issued a credit note.

(d) The supplier may have disallowed a cash discount.

(e) An error may have been made in calculating the balance outstanding.

26.6 Task 1

Debtors Aged Analysis as at 31 January 2003

Account no	Name	Up to 1 month	Up to 3 months	From 4–6 months	From 7–12 months	Over 1 year	Total
B12	G Black & Co Ltd	162.00					162.00
G37	O Greyson		748.18				748.18
S23	J Samuels & Son					78.50	78.50
R12	Redfern Marketing Ser			2,345.00			2,345.00
H52	Haslim, Sant & Partners			750.00			750.00
M63	McDonald Consultants	4,756.00					4,756.00
N27	Nice One Fashions		1,450.00				1,450.00
A32	Ashlea Services		355.00				355.00
P17	Platt, Jones & Co			1,763.50			1,763.50
G65	Grand Mfr Co				300.00		300.00
B29	Bowdler Harris & Partners				621.00		621.00
G51	Gold Signs Co		521.00				521.00
J32	Jones, Jepson & Ford		230.00				230.00
T7	Triton & Son Ltd				262.00		262.00
P21	PCD Dynamics			1,700.00			1,700.00
		4,918.00	3,304.18	6,558.50	1,183.00	78.50	16,042.18

Task 2

(a)

MEMORANDUM

To: Company Secretary   *Date:* January 2003

From:

Re: Aged Debtors

An analysis of outstanding debtors has been carried out (*see* detailed list attached) showing a total of £16,042.18 owing.

Of this £78.50 has been outstanding for over one year. I recommend this item be written off as a bad debt.

The amounts outstanding from 7–12 months should be dealt with via our solicitors.

Items outstanding totalling £6,558.50 fall in the category 4–6 months. It is suggested that personal contact be made with these clients initially to encourage payment or discover the reason for non-payment. Failing this the matter will have to be referred to our solicitors. The same procedure could be applied for the category of items outstanding up to 3 months.

Items just falling due should be sent on a statement of account.

(b)   Draft letter – re: outstanding items:

Apex Marketing Consultants

Dear Sirs

We enclose a statement of account showing a total of _____ outstanding, some items now being three months overdue.

Your attention is drawn to our terms of trading, net payment within 30 days of invoice. We would appreciate receipt of your cheque in full settlement by return, otherwise we will have no option but reluctantly to place this matter in the hands of our solicitors.

Yours faithfully

Apex Marketing Consultants

Chapter 27

27.1	(a)		Motor vehicles	Dr	6,790	:	Kingston Garage	Cr	6,790
	(b)		Bad debts	Dr	34	:	H Newman	Cr	34
	(c)		Unique Offices	Dr	490	:	Office furniture	Cr	490
	(d)	(i)	Bank	Dr	39	:	W Charles	Cr	39
		(ii)	Bad debts	Dr	111	:	W Charles	Cr	111
	(e)		Drawings	Dr	45	:	Purchases	Cr	45
	(f)		Drawings	Dr	76	:	Insurance	Cr	76
	(g)		Machinery	Dr	980	:	Systems accelerated	Cr	980

27.3   (a)   *The Journal (dates omitted)*

	Dr	Cr
Freehold premises	45,000	
Fixtures and fittings	12,500	
Motor vehicles	9,500	
Bank (overdraft)		2,800
Cash	650	
Stock	1,320	
F Hardy	160	
A Derby		270
Capital		66,060
	69,130	69,130

(b)	Discounts Allowed	7	
	Parker		7
	Being discount allowed to Parker		
	Motor van	4,500	
	Supervans Ltd		4,500
	Being purchase of van		
	Supervans Ltd	1,125	
	Bank		1,125
	Being payment of deposit on van		
	Bank	50	
	I M Broke		50
	Being final payment by Broke		
	Bad debts	200	
	I M Broke		200
	Being bad debt written off		

(c)

Bad Debts Account

Dr			Cr
I M Broke	200		

I M Broke Account

Dr				Cr
Balance b/d	250	Bank	50
		Bad debts	200
	250		250

27.4

The Journal (narratives omitted)

			Dr	Cr
(a)	Jul 1	James Crawford	1.80	
		Interest receivable (6% × 120 × ½₂)		1.80
(b)	Aug 30	Weighing machines	1,350.00	
		Mechweights		1,350.00
		Mechweights	400.00	
		Weighing machines		400.00
(c)	Sept 10	Bank	52.50	
		Bad debt recovered		52.50
(d)	Dec 31	Drawings	39.50	
		Purchases		39.50

27.5

The Journal

		Dr	Cr
(1)	Premises	2,000	
	Motor van	450	
	Fixtures	600	
	Stock	1,289	
	Debtors: N Hardy	40	
	M Nelson	180	
	Bank	1,254	
	Cash	45	
	Creditors: B Blake		60
	V Reagan		200
	Capital		5,598
		5,858	5,858
(14)	Motor van	300	
	Better Motors		300

Returns Inwards Day Book

(11)	K O'Connor		16
(11)	L Staines		18
			34

Returns Outwards Day Book

(19)	N Lee		9

Purchases Day Book

(2)	B Blake	20
(2)	C Harris	56
(2)	H Gordon	38
(2)	N Lee	69
(22)	J Johnson	89
(22)	T Best	72
		344

Sales Day Book

(3)	K O'Connor	56
(3)	M Benjamin	78
(3)	L Staines	98
(3)	N Duffy	48
(3)	B Green	118
(3)	M Nelson	40
(9)	M Benjamin	22
(9)	L Pearson	67
		527

Cash Book

Dr		Disct	Cash	Bank			Disct	Cash	Bank	Cr
(1)	Balances		45	1,254	(1)	Rent			15	
(16)	N Hardy	2		38	(4)	Motor expenses		13		
(16)	M Nelson	11		209	(7)	Drawings		20		
(16)	K O'Connor	2		38	(24)	B Blake	4		76	
(16)	L Staines	4		76	(24)	V Reagan	10		190	
					(24)	N Lee	3		57	
					(27)	Salaries			56	
					(30)	Rates			66	
					(31)	Better Motors			300	
					(31)	Balance c/d		12	855	
		19	45	1,615			17	45	1,615	

B Blake Account

Dr					Cr
(24)	Bank	76	(1)	Balance	60
(24)	Discount	4	(2)	Purchases	20
		80			80

V Reagan Account

Dr					Cr
(24)	Bank and Disct	200	(1)	Balance b/d	200

C Harris Account

Dr				Cr
			(2) Purchases	56

H Gordon Account

Dr				Cr
			(2) Purchases	38

N Lee Account

Dr					Cr
(19)	Returns	9	(2)	Purchases	69
(24)	Bank and disct	60			
		69			69

M Benjamin Account

Dr					Cr
(3)	Sales	78			
(9)	Sales	22			

L Staines Account

Dr					Cr
(3)	Sales	98	(11)	Returns	18
			(16)	Bank & disct	80
		98			98

N Duffy Account

Dr				Cr
(3)	Sales	48		

B Green Account

Dr				Cr
(3)	Sales	118		

L Pearson Account

Dr				Cr
(9)	Sales	67		

Better Motors Account

Dr					Cr
(31)	Bank	300	(14)	Motor van	300

J Johnson Account

Dr				Cr
		(22)	Purchases	89

T Best Account

Dr				Cr
		(22)	Purchases	72

N Hardy Account

Dr					Cr
(1)	Balance	40	(16)	Bank & disct	40

M Nelson Account

Dr					Cr
(1)	Balance	180	(16)	Bank & disct	220
(3)	Sales	40			
		220			220

K O'Connor Account

Dr					Cr
(3)	Sales	56	(11)	Returns	16
			(16)	Bank & disct	40
		56			56

General Ledger

Capital Account

Dr						Cr
			(1)	Balance		5,598

Rent Account

Dr					Cr
(1)	Bank	15			

Motor Expenses Account

Dr					Cr
(4)	Cash	13			

Drawings Account

Dr					Cr
(7)	Cash	20			

Salaries Account

Dr					Cr
(27)	Bank	56			

Rates Account

Dr					Cr
(30)	Bank	66			

Sales Account

Dr					Cr
			(31)	Total for month	527

Purchases Account

Dr					Cr
(31)	Total for month	344			

Returns Inwards Account

Dr					Cr
(31)	Total for month	34			

Returns Outwards Account

Dr					Cr
			(31)	Total for month	9

Premises Account

Dr					Cr
(1)	Balance	2,000			

Motor Vans Account

Dr					Cr
(1)	Balance	450			
(14)	Better Motors	300			

Fixtures Account

Dr					Cr
(1)	Balance	600			

Stock Account

Dr				Cr
(1)	Balance	1,289		

Discounts Allowed Account

Dr				Cr
(31)	Total for month	19		

Discounts Received Account

Dr				Cr
			(31) Total for month	17

Trial Balance as at 31 May 2002

C Harris		56
H Gordon		38
J Johnson		89
T Best		72
M Benjamin	100	
N Duffy	48	
B Green	118	
L Pearson	67	
Capital		5,598
Rent	15	
Motor expenses	13	
Drawings	20	
Salaries	56	
Rates	66	
Sales		527
Purchases	344	
Returns inwards	34	
Returns outwards		9
Premises	2,000	
Motor vans	750	
Fixtures	600	
Stock	1,289	
Discounts allowed	19	
Discounts received		17
Bank	855	
Cash	12	
	6,406	6,406

27.6 To economise on space, all narratives for journal entries are omitted.

(a)	J Harkness	Dr	678	:	J Harker	Cr	678
(b)	Machinery	Dr	4,390	:	L Pearson	Cr	4,390
(c)	Motor van	Dr	3,800	:	Motor expenses	Cr	3,800
(d)	E Fletcher	Dr	9	:	Sales	Cr	9
(e)	Sales	Dr	257	:	Commissions received	Cr	257

Chapter 28

28.1 Kevin Chandler:

40 hrs at £7.50		300.00
Less deduction		
Income tax	55.00	
NIC (6% of 300.00)	18.00	73.00
Net pay		227.00

28.2 *(a)* Michael Ford:

	40 hrs at £7.20	288.00
	10 hrs × 1.5 = 15 hrs at £7.20	108.00
	Gross pay	396.00

(b) *Less deduction*

Income tax 23% (396–80)	72.68	
NIC (6% of 396)	23.76	
Pension (8% of 288)	23.04	
Union subscription	2.00	121.48
(c) *Net pay*		274.52

28.3 David Rogers:

Basic 38 hrs at £6.80	258.40
Overtime 6 hrs at 1.25 = 7.5 hrs at £6.80	51.00
Overtime 2 hrs at 1.50 = 3 hrs at £6.80	20.20
	329.80

Gross pay
Less deductions

Income tax	70.45	
NIC (9% of 329.80)	29.68	
Pension (5% of £258.40)	12.92	
Union subscriptions	1.50	114.55
Net pay		215.25

28.4 J Sanders – Clock No 42:

2,200 items at £8 per 50		352.00
Less deductions		
Income tax 25% (352–164)	47.00	
NIC (8.5% of 352)	29.92	
Pension	21.12	
Trade union subscriptions	3.50	101.54
Net pay		250.46

28.5 *Howarth's Office Equipment Ltd: see* Exhibit A6 for cash analysis.

Exhibit A6

CASH ANALYSIS											
Week ending: 30 June 2002											
Name	£20	£10	£5	£1	50p	20p	10p	5p	2p	1p	**Amount** £ p
W Y Chung	5	2		4	1	2		1	1		124.97
A Patel	7	1		4		2		1	1		154.47
L Hinds	6	1		4		1	1	1	1		134.37
S Jones	6	1	1	3	1		1	1	1		138.67
B Hart	5	2		4	1	1			1		124.72
Number of notes and coins required	29	7	1	19	3	6	2	4	5		
Total Cross-check	580	70	5	19	1.50	1.20	20p	20p	10p		677.20

28.5 *(cont)*   *Notes and coins required:*

29 × £20	=	580.00
7 × £10	=	70.00
1 × £5	=	5.00
19 × £1	=	19.00
3 × 50p	=	1.50
6 × 20p	=	1.20
2 × 10p	=	0.20
4 × 5p	=	0.20
5 × 2p	=	0.10
		677.20

28.7   Gary Holland:

2,000 turves laid at £10 per 100		200.00
200 turves laid at £15 per 100		30.00
Gross pay		230.00
Less deductions		
Income tax 23% (230–75)	35.65	
NIC (6% of 230)	13.80	
Social club	2.00	51.45
Net pay		178.55

Neil Simpson:

2,000 turves laid at £10 per 100		200.00
600 turves laid at £15 per 100		90.00
Gross pay		290.00
Less deductions		
Income tax 23% (290–75)	49.45	
NIC (6% of 290)	17.40	
Social club	2.00	68.85
Net pay		221.15

28.9

R&R Production Co

Employee	Basic pay		Bonus	Total
S Crawley	(40 hrs × £3.75) =	150.00	25.00	175.00
D Brookes	(44 hrs × £3.75) =	165.00	40.00	205.00
J Burns	(40 hrs × £3.75) =	150.00	35.00	185.00
V Newman	(42 hrs × £3.75) =	157.50	20.00	177.50
		£622.50	£120.00	£742.50

28.10

Employee			Gross pay
A Taylor	35 hrs × £5.20 =	182.00	
	30 hrs × £0.75 =	22.50	204.50
S McKenzie	42 hrs × £5.20 =	218.40	
	40 hrs × £0.75 =	30.00	248.40
R Brindley	40 hrs × £5.20 =	208.00	
	36 hrs × £0.75 =	27.00	235.00
W Baseley	44 hrs × £5.20 =	228.80	
	36 hrs × £0.75 =	27.00	255.80
W Warburton	45 hrs × £5.20 =	234.00	
	52 hrs × £0.75 =	39.00	273.00
			£1,216.70

Chapter 29

29.1   (a)   A memorandum would probably be too formal and a brief note should suffice. A suitable format might be as follows:

> Jean   *Time*   *Date*
>
> Derek Amos telephoned re: Sphere Products. Their Mr Stott has complained about two incorrect invoices, Nos 40169 and 40183. Derek asks that these are checked and Mr Stott contacted as quickly as possible.
>
>   *Your name*

(b)   Since Jean Todd is in a meeting with the directors it would be very helpful to her if you checked the two invoices to find out what was wrong and report what action needed to be taken.

29.2   The letter should be structured in a formal manner as suggested in the chapter.

> Dear Sirs
>
> We enclose a statement of account showing an outstanding total of £58 in respect of invoice no PP 4611 dated 7 February 2001.
>
> This amount is now considerably overdue and we would ask for immediate payment.
>
> Yours faithfully

29.3   *Seddon & Sons*:

On checking your invoice no 79, dated 23 June 2001, we note that VAT of £91.87 has been charged but no VAT registration number is shown on the invoice.

Would you please confirm that you are VAT registered and let us have your VAT number.

City Services & Supplies:

We note that an error has been made in the VAT calculation on your invoice no. 01782.

VAT at 17.5% on £413.50 = £72.36 not £27.36 as shown on the invoice. Would you please forward an amended invoice.

Heath Mfr Co Ltd:

On checking your invoice no B39766 we note that the VAT amount of £60.20 should, in fact, be £62.59. This will increase the invoice total to £420.29. Would you please forward an amended invoice.

Chapter 30

Practice assessment 1: Summit Glazing Ltd

Section 1 Processing exercise

Tasks 1.1, 1.2 and 1.3

General Ledger

Sales Ledger Control Account

Dr							Cr
2001				2001			
Dec	1	Balance b/d	85,995	Dec	1	Bank	6,200
	1	Sales (net)	14,760		1	Balance c/d	97,138
	1	VAT on sales	2,583				
			103,338				103,338
	2	Balance b/d	97,138				

Purchases Ledger Control Account

Dr						Cr
2001				2001		
Dec	1	Purchases returns (net)	40	Dec 1	Balance b/d	78,237
	1	VAT on returns	7	1	Purchases (net)	3,840
	1	Bank	41,190	1	VAT on purchases	672
	1	Discounts received	555			
	1	Balance c/d	40,957			
			82,749			82,749
				Dec 2	Balance b/d	40,957

Sales Account

Dr						Cr
2001				2001		
Dec	1	Balance c/d	1,153,365	Dec 1	Balance b/d	1,138,325
				1	Sales control	14,760
				1	Cash book	280
			1,153,365			1,153,365
				2	Balance b/d	1,153,365

Purchases Account

Dr						Cr
2001				2001		
Dec	1	Balances b/d	897,953	Dec 1	Balance c/d	901,793
	1	Purchases control	3,840			
			901,793			901,793
	2	Balance b/d	901,793			

Value Added Tax Account

Dr						Cr
2001				2001		
Dec	1	Purchases control	672	Dec 1	Balance b/d	8,136
		Balances c/d	10,103	1	Sales control	2,583
				1	Sales control (Returns)	7
				1	Bank: cash sales	49
			10,775			10,775
				Dec 2	Balance b/d	10,103

Purchases Returns Account

Dr						Cr
2001				2001		
Dec	1	Balance c/d	4,320	Dec 1	Balance b/d	4,280
				1	Purchases control	40
			4,320			4,320
				Dec 2	Balance b/d	4,320

Discounts Received Account

Dr						Cr
2001				2001		
Dec	1	Balance c/d	3,447	Dec 1	Balance b/d	2,892
				1	Sales control	555
			3,447			3,447
				Dec 2	Balance b/d	3,447

Motor Vehicles Account

Dr								Cr
2001				2001				
Dec	1	Balance b/d	56,900	Dec	1	Motor expenses	340	
					1	Balance c/d	56,560	
			56,900				56,900	
	2	Balance b/d	56,560					

Motor Expenses Account

Dr							Cr
2001				2001			
Dec	1	Balance b/d	6,857	Dec	1	Balance c/d	7,197
	1	Motor vehicles	340				
			7,197				7,197
	1	Balance b/d	7,197				

Task 1.4

Sales Ledger

Acorn Housing Association Account

Dr							Cr
2001				2001			
Dec	1	Balance b/d	6,200	Dec	1	Bank	6,200
	1	Sales	6,063		1	Balance c/d	6,063
			12,263				12,263
	2	Balance b/d	6,063				

Purchases Ledger

Georgian Conservatories Account

Dr							Cr
2001				2001			
Dec	1	Bank	27,195	Dec	1	Balance b/d	48,920
	1	Discount received	555		1	Purchases	705
	1	Balance c/d	21,875				
			49,625				49,625
					2	Balance b/d	21,875

Task 1.5

List of updated balances:

	Debit balances	Credit balances
Purchases	901,793	
Sales		1,153,365
Purchases returns		4,320
Bank (*see* workings below)*		11,938
Bank charges	1,417	
Petty cash	150	
VAT		10,103
Discounts allowed	6,340	
Discounts received		3,447
Sales ledger control (debtors)	97,138	
Purchases ledger controls (creditors		40,957
Wages	282,500	
Rent & rates	16,225	
Electricity	4,106	
Telephone	1,852	
Motor expenses	7,197	
Insurance	5,935	
Sundry expenses	2,734	
Motor vehicles	56,560	
Machinery & equipment	15,120	
Stocks	37,063	
Capital		212,000
Totals	1,436,130	1,436,130

*Workings:

Bank:	Dr			Cr
Balance b/d	22,723	Georgian		27,195
Cash sales	329	Elite		13,995
Acorn	6,200			
Balance c/d	11,938			
	41,190			41,190

Section 2 Answers to Short Answer Tasks

1   Any three from:
   (a)   Ensuring signatures on credit and on voucher correspond.
   (b)   Check that signature panel on card has not been tampered with.
   (c)   See that card being used within valid dates.
   (d)   Ensure that card does not exceed credit limits.
   (e)   Check against list of stolen/lost cards.

2   (a)   No
   (b)   Contract is between Summit Glazing and Speedy Fixtures Ltd, not with manufacturer. Legal rights are, therefore, against Speedy Fixtures.

3   Any from:
   (a)   Check on balances on creditors' ledger equalling balance of control account.
   (b)   Quick method for ascertaining total of creditors' balances.
   (c)   Makes fraud more difficult.

4   (a) Yes   (b) No

5   (a) No   (b) No   (c) Yes   (d) No

6   Any two from:
    (a)   Speed of processing.
    (b)   Versatility (can be used for various purposes).
    (c)   Accuracy.
    (d)   Storage – lot of information kept in a small space.

7   False

8   (a)   Based on price after trade and cash discounts. Is therefore $5 \times £400 = £2,000$ – trade discount $£600 = £1,400$ – cash discount $£35 = £1,365 \times 17.5\%$ VAT $= £238.87$.
    (b)   £35   (c) £600   (d) £1,400 + VAT £238.87 = £1,638.87

9   (a) Expense.   (b) Asset.   (c) Liability.   (d) Revenue.   (e) Liability.

10 The funds held are owed by the bank to the company. From the bank's point of view they are, therefore, a liability.

11 Debited.

12 Memorandum accounts for our credit customers.

13 (a)   (c)

14 (d)

15 Any two of the following:
    (a)   To record the purchase of fixed assets on credit.
    (b)   To correct errors.
    (c)   To record opening entries in a new set of books.
    (d)   To record transfers between accounts.
    (e)   To write off bad debts.

16 £150 – total payments £82.12 = £67.88. Payment to be received of £57.12 to bring float to £125.

17 Measures to ensure monies received are properly handled – any three from:
    (a)   Drawn as payable to the business.
    (b)   Check the amount is correct, both in words and figures.
    (c)   Ensure the cheque is not stale or postdated.
    (d)   Ensure the cheque is properly signed.

18 (a) Capital.   (b) Revenue.   (c) Capital.   (d) Capital.

19 False

20 (a) Delivery note.   (b) Statement.   (c) Petty cash voucher.

Section 3 Answers to Communicating Accounting Information

Task 3.1

The letter should be structured in a formal manner as suggested in Chapter 29.

Dear Sirs

We are in receipt of your invoice no 232/12, dated 21 December 2001, totalling £3,243. However, we notice that you have invoiced us for 20 – Double Glazed Windows Model L 400 at £138 each, plus VAT, when, in fact our Goods Inwards Department has advised that only 18 were received.

Could you please send us a credit note to correct the discrepancy.

Yours faithfully

Task 3.2

Memorandum

To: Mary Owen   **Date:** Current date

From: .... Accounts Clerk

Re: Abbott Building Co, outstanding balance £157.00

I have tried to contact this company by telephone and by letter but have had no success. I also asked our sales representative to visit the company and she has reported that there is no sign of the company.

The premises are, in fact, now occupied by a garage repair business whose owner told her that the owner of Abbott Building Co was rumoured to have gone abroad. Having regard to the small amount outstanding I consider that we should not incur any further expense in investigating the matter and should write off the debt.

Note: The answers to Practice assessment 2 are given in the *Lecturer's Guide*.

Chapter 31

Workings will not be shown on your answer paper. They are shown here for your guidance only.

Answers to Multiple-choice questions: Test Paper 1

1

Purchases Ledger Control Account

Dr				Cr
Cash paid (difference)	15,354	Balances b/f		7,585
Balances c/d	9,171	Purchases		16,940
	24,525			24,525

Cash paid to credit customers 15,354 + cash purchases 656 = total 16,010.
Answer therefore (D).

2   (C)

3   (C)

4   1,600 – trade discount 400 = 1,200 – cash discount 60 = 1,140 + VAT 199.50 = 1,339.50.
Answer therefore (B).

5   395 + 240 – 50 – 28 – 55 = 502. Answer therefore (A).

6   (C)

7   (D)

8   (A)

9   (C)

10   (D)

11   Assets = 450 + 97 + 10,000 + 3,175 + 5,170 = 18,892.
Capital and Liabilities = 15,700 + 675 + 66 = 16,441. Difference 2,451 is, therefore, creditors.
Answer (B).

12   (C)

13   (A)

14   (D)

15 Cost of purchases 4,800 – (20%) 960 = 3,840. Not sold 3,840 × 25% = 960 + returns at cost (120 – 24) 96 = 1,056.
Answer is (D)

16 (B)

17 (C)

18 (D)

19 (A)

20 (C)

21 (D)

22 (B)

23 Overdraft = 1,123 + 77 + 26 + 110 – 422 = 914.
Answer (D).

24 (A)

25 Answer is (C).

Scorer (Sales Ledger) Account

Dr			Cr
Balance b/f	872	Set-off	600
Sales	421	Bank	300

Scorer (Purchases Ledger) Account

Dr			Cr
Returns	65	Balance b/f	249
Set-off	600	Purchases	717
Balance c/d	301		
	966		966

26 (D)

27 (A): When actually received by Brady. Posting date could only be used if letter had correct stamps on it.

28 (B)

29 (C)

30 (D)

31 (D)

32 (A)

33 (B)

34 (D)

35 (C)

36 (C)

37 (A)

38 (D)

39 (C)

40 (B)

41 (D)

42 (A)

43 (C)

44 (C)

45 (B)

46 (D)

47 Basic 210 + overtime 63 + bonus 27 = 300 less income tax 40 – national insurance 12 = 248. Answer (B).

48 (C)

49 (A)

50 (D)

Note: The answers to Test paper 2 are given in the *Lecturer's Guide*.

Appendix: Useful names and addresses

The Association of Accounting Technicians (AAT)
154 Clerkenwell Road
London EC1R 5AD
Tel: 0171 837 8600
Fax: 0171 837 6970
Email: aatuk@dial.pipex.com
Web site: www.aat.co.uk

The Association of Chartered Certified Accountants (ACCA)
29 Lincoln's Inn Fields
London WC2A 3EE
Tel: 0171 396 5891
Fax: 0171 396 5880
Email: training@acca.co.uk
Web site: www.acca.co.uk

Association of Taxation Technicians
12 Upper Belgrave Street
London SW1X 8BB
Tel: 0171 235 2544
Fax: 0171 235 2562

The Chartered Institute of Management Accounts (CIMA)
63 Portland Place
London W1N 4AB
Tel: 0171 637 2311

The Chartered Institute of Public Finance and Accountancy (CIPFA)
3 Robert Street
London WC2N 6BH
Tel: 0171 543 5600
Fax: 0171 543 5700
Email: marketing@cipfa.org
Web site: www.cipfa.org.uk

Edexcel Foundation
BTEC
Stewart House
32 Russell Square
London WC1B 5DW
Tel: 0171 393 4444

The Institute of Chartered Accountants in England and Wales (ICAEW)
Chartered Accountant's Hall
PO Box 433 Moorgate Place
London
EC2P 2BJ
Tel: 0171 920 8100

Institute of Chartered Accountants in Ireland
11 Donegall Square South
Belfast BT1 5JE
Tel: 01232 321600

The Institute of Chartered Accountants in Scotland
27 Queen Street
Edinburgh
EH2 1LA
Tel: 0131 225 5673
Fax: 0131 247 4872

Pitman Qualifications
1 Giltspur Street
London EC1A 9DD
Tel: 0171 294 2471
Fax: 0171 294 2403

London Chamber of Commerce & Industry Examination Board (LCCI)
6 Graphite Street
London SE11 5EE
Tel: 0171 793 3850
Fax: 0171 582 1806

Royal Society of Arts (RSA)
Westwood Way
Coventry
CV4 8HS
Tel: 01203 470033
Fax: 01203 468080

Accounting standards

The accounting standards have been devised by the Lead Body for Accounting (LBA) and the following have been reproduced with the permission of the LBA:

Qualification Structure for NVQ Level 2
Unit 1: Recording and accounting for cash transactions
Unit 2: Recording and accounting for credit transactions.

The qualification structure at Level 2 consists of the following:

Unit Number	Unit Title
1	Recording and accounting for cash transactions
2	Recording and accounting for credit transactions
3	Recording payroll transactions
20	Data processing
24	Communicating for accounting
25	Create and maintain effective working relationships
26	Store, retrieve and supply information
27	Contribute to the effectiveness of the workflow.

As stated in the preface, the book deals comprehensively with recording and accounting for cash and credit transactions, Units 1 and 2. The requirements of the two units have been produced after a thorough analysis by the LBA of the accounting activity at this first level. The requirements of each unit are based on three fundamental aspects: Competence, Knowledge and Understanding, and these are fully stated in each particular unit.

To gain a qualification for each unit the student's work must be assessed and approved by an awarding body such as the AAT, Edexcel, RSA, etc. who have been approved by the LBA to make such awards. Candidates normally gain qualifications through a training provider such as a further education college or through their workplace if a trained assessor and verifier are available. Employers will be able to guide their employees as to the most appropriate method to follow.

UNIT 1: RECORDING AND ACCOUNTING FOR CASH TRANSACTIONS

UNIT COMMENTARY

What is this unit about?

This unit is concerned with receiving and making payments, keeping records of the transactions, checking transactions against the relevant documentation and preparing bank reconciliation statements. The candidate is required to perform in accordance with the organisation's policies, regulations, procedures and timescales at all times, and to obtain authorisation for any payments or claims.

Elements contained within this unit are:

ELEMENT 1.1 RECORD AND BANK MONIES RECEIVED
ELEMENT 1.2 MAKE AND RECORD PAYMENTS
ELEMENT 1.3 MAINTAIN PETTY CASH RECORDS
ELEMENT 1.4 ACCOUNT FOR CASH AND BANK TRANSACTIONS

Element 1.1 Record and bank monies received

Performance Criteria

(i)   Monies are banked in accordance with organisation's policies, regulations, procedures and timescales
(ii)   Incoming monies are checked against relevant supporting documentation
(iii)   Cash is correctly counted and correct change given where applicable
(iv)   Monies received are correctly and legibly recorded
(v)   Written receipts are correctly issued where required
(vi)   Totals and balances are correctly calculated
(vii)   Paying-in documents are correctly prepared and reconciled to relevant records
(viii) Documentation is correctly filed
(ix)   Cash handling, security and confidentiality procedures are followed
(x)   Discrepancies, unusual features or queries are identified and either resolved or referred to the appropriate person

Range Statement

1   **Monies received**: cash; cheques; inter-bank transfers; payable orders; credit card transactions; but not foreign currency

2   **The primary recording of monies received**: remittance lists; cash books; cash registers; other methods with a similar purpose

3   **Discrepancies, unusual features or queries**: wrongly completed cheques; out-of-date validation cards; credit limits exceeded; disagreement with supporting documentation

Knowledge and Understanding

The Business Environment:
- Types of business transactions and documents involved
- General principles of VAT
- Trade discounts and cash
- Legal aspects of cheques including crossings and endorsements
- Legal relationship of banker and customer
- General bank services and operation of clearing bank system
- Characteristics of forms of payment (as in Range Statement)
- Function and form of banking documentation

Accounting Techniques:
- Calculation facility, including use of equipment provided
- Methods of posting from primary records to ledger accounts
- Methods of coding data
- Operation of manual and computerised accounting systems

- Methods of handling and storing money, security
- Functioning of cash register equipment
- Credit card procedures

Accounting Principles and Theory:
- Functions of a ledger account system
- Main types of ledger account
- Interrelationship of accounts – double-entry system
- Nature and function of primary records
- Distinction between capital and revenue (in general terms)
- Principles of internal check

The Organisation:
- Background understanding that the accounting systems of an organisation are affected by its organisational structure, its administrative systems and procedures and the nature of its business transactions

Evidence Requirements

- Competence must be demonstrated consistently, over a period of time with evidence of performance being provided of monies being recorded and banked

Sources of Evidence

These are examples of sources of evidence, but candidates and assessors may be able to identify other, appropriate sources.

- **Observed performance**, e.g.
  - Incoming monies being checked against relevant supporting documentation
  - Counting cash and giving change
  - Recording monies received
  - Issuing receipts
  - Calculating totals and balances
  - Preparing paying-in documents
  - Filing documentation

- **Work produced by candidate**, e.g.
  - Written receipts
  - Calculations of totals and balances
  - Paying-in documents
  - Remittance lists
  - Cash books
  - Cash registers

- **Authenticated testimonies from relevant witnesses**

- **Personal accounts of competence**, e.g.
  - Report of performance

- **Other sources of evidence to prove competence or knowledge and understanding where it is not apparent from performance**, e.g.
  - Reports
  - Performance in simulation
  - Responses to verbal questioning

Element 1.2 Make and record payments

Performance Criteria

(i)   Payments are made and recorded in accordance with the organisation's policies, regulations, procedures and timescales
(ii)   Payments are properly authorised
(iii)   Cheques are prepared correctly and are signed by designated person(s) prior to despatch

(iv) Standing orders and other inter-bank transfers are correctly documented
(v) Remittance advices are correctly prepared and despatched with payments
(vi) Totals and balances are correctly calculated and checked against documentation
(vii) Available cash discounts are identified and deducted
(viii) Documentation is correctly filed
(ix) Safety and security procedures for the handling of cash and cheques are followed
(x) Discrepancies, unusual features or queries are identified and either resolved or referred to the appropriate person

Range Statement

1 **Payments**: cash; cheque; inter-bank transfers; payable orders; but not foreign currency

2 **The documentation against which payments are made**: suppliers' statements or invoices; authorised internal payment requests or claims

3 **Discrepances, unusual features or queries**: unauthorised claims; statements not reconciling with invoices and credit notes; calculation errors

Knowledge and Understanding

The Business Environment:
- Types of business transactions and documents involved
- General principles of VAT
- Trade discounts and cash
- Legal aspects of cheques including crossings and endorsements
- Legal relationship of banker and customer
- General bank services and operation of clearing bank system
- Characteristics of forms of payment (as in Range Statement)
- Function and form of banking documentation
- Evidence of payment

Accounting techniques:
- Calculation facility, including use of equipment provided
- Methods of posting from primary records to ledger accounts
- Methods of coding data
- Operation of manual and computerised accounting systems
- Methods of handling and storing money, security

Accounting Principles and Theory:
- Functions of a ledger account system
- Main types of ledger account
- Interrelationship of accounts – double-entry system
- Nature and function of primary records
- Distinction between capital and revenue (in general terms)
- Principles of internal check

The Organisation:
- Background understanding that the accounting systems of an organisation are affected by its organisational structure, its administrative systems and procedures and the nature of its business transactions

Evidence Requirements

- Competence must be demonstrated consistently, over a period of time with evidence of performance being provided of payments being made and recorded

Sources of Evidence

These are examples of sources of evidence, but candidates and assessors may be able to identify other, appropriate sources.

- **Observed performance**, e.g.
  - payments being made and recorded

- Preparing cheques
- Documenting standing orders and other inter-bank transfers
- Preparing and despatching remittance advices
- Calculating totals and balances
- Filing documentation

- **Work produced by candidate**, e.g.
  - Records of payments
  - Cheques signed by the designated person(s)
  - Calculations of totals and balances
  - Remittance advices
  - Cash book

- **Authenticated testimonies from relevant witnesses**

- **Personal accounts of competence**, e.g.
  - Report of performance

- **Other sources of evidence to prove competence or knowledge and understanding where it is not apparent from performance**, e.g.
  - Reports
  - Performance in simulation
  - Responses to verbal questioning

Element 1.3 Maintain petty cash records

Performance Criteria

(i)   Transactions are accurately recorded and analysed to the correct expenditure heads
(ii)   Cash withdrawals from the main cash account are accurately recorded
(iii)   Claims are properly authorised, are within prescribed limits and are supported by adequate evidence
(iv)   Totals and balances are correctly calculated
(v)   The balance of cash in hand is reconciled with the petty cash records at appropriate intervals
(vi)   Documentation is correctly filed
(vii)   Analysed totals of petty cash expenditure are transferred to the correct ledger accounts
(viii) Cash handling, security and confidentiality procedures are followed
(ix)   Any discrepancies, unusual features or queries are identified and either resolved or referred to the appropriate person

Range Statement

1   **The handling of petty cash transactions and records using an imprest system**

2   **Analysis**: items of petty cash expenditure appropriate to the organisation, including VAT charges

3   **Discrepancies, unusual features or queries**: claims for payment not properly authorised; insufficient supporting evidence; claims exceeding prescribed limit; uncertainty in coding

Knowledge and Understanding

The Business Environment:
- Types of business transactions and documents involved
- General principles of VAT
- Trade discounts and cash
- Legal aspects of cheques including crossings and endorsements
- Legal relationship of banker and customer
- General bank services and operation of clearing bank system
- Documentation for petty cash transactions
- The need for authorisation procedures and expenditure limits

Accounting Techniques:
- Calculation facility, including use of equipment provided
- Methods of posting from primary records to ledger accounts

- Methods of coding data
- Operation of manual and computerised accounting systems
- Imprest method and control features
- Methods of handling and storing money, security
- Credit card procedures

Accounting Principles and Theory:
- Functions of a ledger account system
- Main types of ledger account
- Interrelationship of accounts – double-entry system
- Nature and function of primary records
- Distinction between capital and revenue (in general terms)
- Principles of internal check
- Relationship of petty cash records to the main cash book and ledger system

The Organisation:
- Background understanding that the accounting systems of an organisation are affected by its organisational structure, its administrative systems and procedures and the nature of its business transactions

Evidence Requirements

- Competence must be demonstrated consistently, over a period of time with evidence of performance being provided of petty cash records being maintained

Sources of Evidence

These are examples of sources of evidence, but candidates and assessors may be able to identify other, appropriate sources.

- **Observed performance**, e.g.
  - Recording and analysing transactions
  - Recording cash withdrawals from the main cash account
  - Calculating totals and balances
  - Balancing cash in hand with petty cash records
  - Filing documentation
  - Transferring analysed totals of petty cash expenditure to ledger accounts

- **Work produced by candidate**, e.g.
  - Records and analysis of transactions
  - Records of cash withdrawals
  - Authorisation for claims
  - Petty cash records
  - Ledger accounts

- **Authenticated testimonies from relevant witnesses**

- **Personal accounts of competence**, e.g.
  - Report of performance

- **Other sources of evidence to prove competence or knowledge and understanding where it is not apparent from performance,** e.g.
  - Reports
  - Performance in simulation
  - Responses to verbal questioning

Element 1.4 Account for cash and bank transactions

Performance Criteria

(i)   Entries in the cash book are accurately transferred to correct ledger accounts

(ii)   Bank reconciliation statements are accurately prepared and are presented within specified timescales

(iii) Recorded transactions are supported by properly authorised primary documentation

(iv) Details for the relevant primary documentation are recorded in the cash book and analysed accurately

(v) Totals and balances are correctly calculated

(vi) Security and confidentiality procedures are followed

(vii) The organisation's policies, regulations, procedures and timescales are observed

(viii) Any discrepancies, unusual features or queries are identified and either resolved or referred to the appropriate person

Range Statement

1 **Cash book analysis of**: cash and bank entries; cash discounts; VAT; debtors and creditors total account entries

2 **Primary documentation**: cheque counterfoils; paying-in slips remittance lists; credit transfer and standing order schedules

3 **Transfers to ledger accounts**: individual receipts and payments; total for control accounts

4 **Discrepancies, unusual features or queries**: differences arising from preparation of bank reconciliations; uncertainty in coding

Knowledge and Understanding

The Business Environment:
- Types of business transactions and documents involved
- General principles of VAT
- Trade discounts and cash
- Legal aspects of cheques including crossings and endorsements
- Legal relationship of banker and customer
- General bank services and operation of clearing bank system
- Function and form of banking documentation

Accounting Techniques:
- Calculation facility, including use of equipment provided
- Methods of posting from primary records to ledger accounts
- Methods of coding data
- Operation of manual and computerised accounting systems
- Preparation of bank reconciliation statements

Accounting Principles and Theory:
- Functions of a ledger account system
- Main types of ledger account
- Interrelationship of accounts – double-entry system
- Nature and function of primary records
- Distinction between capital and revenue (in general terms)
- Principles of internal check
- Function of the cash book and its relationship to ledger accounts

The Organisation:
- Background understanding that the accounting systems of an organisation are affected by its organisational structure, its administrative systems and procedures and the nature of its business transactions

Evidence Requirements

- Competence must be demonstrated consistently, over a period of time with evidence of performance being provided of cash and bank transactions being accounted for

Sources of Evidence

These are examples of sources of evidence, but candidates and assessors may be able to identify other, appropriate sources.

- **Observed performance**, e.g.
  - Transferring entries in the cash book to ledger accounts
  - Preparing and presenting bank reconciliation statements
  - Recording and analysing details for the primary documentation
  - Calculating totals and balances

- **Work produced by candidate**, e.g.
  - Cash book
  - Ledger account
  - Bank reconciliation statement
  - Authorised primary documentation
  - Calculations of totals and balances

- **Authenticated testimonies from relevant witnesses**

- **Personal accounts of competence**, e.g.
  - Report of performance

- **Other sources of evidence to prove competence or knowledge and understanding where it is not apparent from performance**, e.g.
  - Reports
  - Performance in simulation
  - Responses to verbal questioning

UNIT 2: RECORDING AND ACCOUNTING FOR CREDIT TRANSACTIONS

UNIT COMMENTARY

What is this unit about?

This unit is concerned with processing documents relating to, and accounting for, goods and services supplied and received on credit. It involves the candidate coding and checking the calculations on invoices and credit notes, entering them as primary records, transferring entries on primary records to ledger accounts and reconciling the control account in the general ledger with the balances in the sales and purchases ledgers. The candidate is required to obtain authorisation for invoices and credit notes despatched to customers and adjustments involving debtors' and creditors' accounts. The candidate is responsible for filing documentation and is required to handle communications with creditors and debtors regarding accounts.

Elements contained within this unit are:

ELEMENT 2.1 PROCESS DOCUMENTS RELATING TO GOODS AND SERVICES SUPPLIED ON CREDIT
ELEMENT 2.2 PROCESS DOCUMENTS RELATING TO GOODS AND SERVICES RECEIVED ON CREDIT
ELEMENT 2.3 ACCOUNT FOR GOODS AND SERVICES SUPPLIED ON CREDIT
ELEMENT 2.4 ACCOUNT FOR GOODS AND SERVICES RECEIVED ON CREDIT

Element 2.1 Process documents relating to goods and services supplied on credit

Performance Criteria

(i)   Invoices and credit notes are correctly authorised and coded, and despatched to customers
(ii)   The calculations on invoices and credit notes, including discounts and VAT, are correct
(iii)   Invoices and credit notes are correctly entered as primary accounting records in a form acceptable to the organisation
(iv)   The analysis and totalling of the primary record is completed accurately
(v)   Documentation is correctly filed
(vi)   The organisation's procedures and timescales are observed
(vii)   Discrepancies, unusual features or queries are identified and either resolved or referred to the appropriate person

Range Statement

1   Goods and services supplied on credit other than those supplied under leasing and hire purchase contracts; returns

2   **Primary records**: analysed sales and returns day books; any other listing which serves the same purpose

3   **Calculations to be checked**: pricing; price extensions; discounts; VAT calculations

4   **Discrepancies, unusual features or queries**: incorrect calculations; VAT charges or discounts; incorrect coding

Knowledge and Understanding

The Business Environment:
- Trade discounts and cash discounts
- Types of business transactions and documents involved
- Basic law of contract
- General principles of VAT

Accounting Techniques:
- Calculation facility, including use of equipment provided
- Methods of posting from primary records to ledger accounts
- Methods of coding data
- Operation of manual and computerised accounting systems

Accounting Principles and Theory:
- Functions of a ledger account system and main types of account
- Interrelationship of accounts – double-entry principles
- Function of primary records
- Distinction between capital and revenue expenditure (in general terms)
- Internal check, control and security principles

The Organisation:
- Background understanding that the accounting systems of an organisation are affected by its organisational structure, its administrative systems and procedures and the nature of its business transactions

Evidence Requirements

- Competence must be demonstrated consistently, over a period of time with evidence of performance being provided of documents relating to goods and services supplied on credit being processed

Sources of Evidence

These are examples of sources of evidence, but candidates and assessors may be able to identify other, appropriate sources.

- **Observed performance**, e.g.
  - Coding and despatching invoices and credit notes
  - Analysing and totalling the primary record
  - Filing documentation

- **Work produced by candidate**, e.g.
  - Coded invoices and credit notes
  - Authorisation for invoices and credit notes
  - Calculations on invoices and credit notes
  - Primary accounting record
  - Analysed sales and returns day book

- **Authenticated testimonies from relevant witnesses**

- **Personal accounts of competence**, e.g.
  - Report of performance

- **Other sources of evidence to prove competence or knowledge and understanding where it is not apparent from performance**, e.g.
  - Reports
  - Performance in simulation
  - Responses to verbal questioning

Element 2.2 Process documents relating to goods and services received on credit

Performance Criteria

(i)   Suppliers' invoices and credit notes are correctly checked against ordering documentation and evidence that goods/services have been received
(ii) Suppliers' invoices and credit notes are correctly coded
(iii) Calculations on suppliers' invoices and credit notes are correct
(iv) Documents are correctly entered as primary accounting records in a form acceptable to the organisation
(v)   Documents are correctly filed
(vi) The organisation's procedures and timescales are observed
(vii) Discrepancies, unusual features or queries are identified and either resolved or referred to the appropriate person

Range Statement

1 Goods and services received on credit other than those supplied under leasing and hire purchase contracts; returns

2 **Primary records**: analysed sales and returns day books; any other listing which serves the same purpose

3 **Documentation against which invoices and credit notes are checked**: copy purchase orders or returns notes; delivery notes or goods received notes; other documents which serve similar purposes

4 **The calculations to be checked**: pricing; price extensions; discounts; VAT calculations

5 **Discrepancies, unusual features or queries**: incorrect calculations; non-delivery of goods charged; duplicated invoices; incorrect VAT charges or discounts

Knowledge and Understanding

The Business Environment:
- Trade discounts and cash discounts
- Types of business transactions and documents involved
- Basic law of contract
- General principles of VAT

Accounting Techniques:
- Calculation facility, including use of equipment provided
- Methods of posting from primary records to ledger accounts
- Methods of coding data
- Operation of manual and computerised accounting systems

Accounting Principles and Theory:
- Functions of a ledger account system and main types of account
- Interrelationship of accounts – double-entry principles
- Function of primary records
- Distinction between capital and revenue expenditure (in general terms)
- Internal check, control and security principles

The Organisation:
- Background understanding that the accounting systems of an organisation are affected by its organisational structure, its administrative systems and procedures and the nature of its business transactions

Evidence Requirements

- Competence must be demonstrated consistently, over a period of time with evidence of performance being provided of documents relating to goods and services received on credit being processed

Sources of Evidence

These are examples of sources of evidence, but candidates and assessors may be able to identify other, appropriate sources.

- **Observed performance**, e.g.
  - Checking suppliers' invoices and credit notes against ordering documentation and evidence that goods/services have been received
  - Coding suppliers' invoices and credit notes
  - Checking calculations on suppliers' invoices·and credit notes
  - Entering documents as primary accounting records
  - Filing documentation

- **Work produced by candidate**, e.g.
  - Coded suppliers' invoices and credit notes
  - Calculations on suppliers' invoices and credit notes
  - Primary accounting record
  - Analysed sales and returns day book

- **Authenticated testimonies from relevant witnesses**

- **Personal accounts of competence**, e.g.
  – Report of performance

- **Other sources of evidence to prove competence or knowledge and understanding where it is not apparent from performance**, e.g.
  – Reports
  – Performance in simulation
  – Responses to verbal questioning

Element 2.3 Account for goods and services supplied on credit

Performance Criteria

(i)   Entries in the primary records are correctly transferred to the correct ledger accounts
(ii)   Adjustments involving debtors' accounts are properly authorised and documented, and are correctly transferred to the correct ledger accounts
(iii)   The control account in the general ledger is reconciled with the total of balances in the sales (debtors ledger)
(iv)   Where required, statements of account are sent to debtors promptly
(v)   The organisation's procedures and timescales are observed
(vi)   Discrepancies, unusual features or queries are identified and either resolved or referred to the appropriate person
(vii)   Communications with debtors regarding accounts are handled promptly, courteously and effectively

Range Statement

1   **Primary records**: analysed sales and returns day books; other listings which serve the same purpose

2   **Adjustments**: to correct errors within the accounting system; to write off bad debts

3   **Discrepancies, unusual features or queries**: arising from reconciliation of the control account; from the age analysis; from preparation of statements

Knowledge and Understanding

The Business Environment:
- Trade discounts and cash discounts
- Types of business transactions and documents involved
- Basic law of contract
- General principles of VAT

Accounting Techniques:
- Calculation facility, including use of equipment provided
- Methods of posting from primary records to ledger accounts
- Methods of coding data
- Operation of manual and computerised accounting systems
- Procedures for writing off bad debts
- Function and form of age analysis reports
- Use of transfer journal

Accounting Principles and Theory:
- Functions of a ledger account system and main types of account
- Interrelationship of accounts – double-entry principles
- Function of primary records
- Distinction between capital and revenue expenditure (in general terms)
- Internal check, control and security principles

The Organisation:
- Background understanding that the accounting systems of an organisation are affected by its organisational structure, its administrative systems and procedures and the nature of its business transactions

Evidence Requirements

- Competence must be demonstrated consistently, over a period of time with evidence of performance being provided of goods and services supplied on credit being accounted for

Sources of Evidence

These are examples of sources of evidence, but candidates and assessors may be able to identify other, appropriate sources.

- **Observed performance**, e.g.
  - Transferring entries in the primary records to the ledger account
  - Transferring adjustments involving debtors' accounts to the ledger account
  - Reconciling the control account in the general ledger with the total of balances in the sales (debtors) ledger
  - Sending statements of accounts to debtors
  - Communicating with debtors

- **Work produced by candidate**, e.g.
  - Analysed sales and returns day book
  - Primary record
  - Ledger account
  - Authorisation for adjustments involving debtors' accounts
  - Statements of account
  - Written communication with debtors

- **Authenticated testimonies from relevant witnesses**

- **Personal accounts of competence**, e.g.
  - Report of performance

- **Other sources of evidence to prove competence or knowledge and understanding where it is not apparent from performance**, e.g.
  - Reports
  - Performance in simulation
  - Responses to verbal questioning

Element 2.4 Account for goods and services received on credit

Performance Criteria

(i)   Entries in the primary records are correctly transferred to the correct ledger accounts
(ii)   Adjustments involving creditors' accounts are properly authorised and documented, and are correctly transferred to the correct ledger accounts
(iii)   The control account in the general ledger is reconciled with the total of balances in the purchases (creditors) ledger
(iv)   The organisation's procedures and timescales are observed
(v)   Discrepancies, unusual features or queries are identified and either resolved or referred to the appropriate person
(vi)   Communications with creditors regarding accounts are handled promptly, courteously and effectively

Range Statement

1   **The primary records**: analysed purchase and return day books; other listing which serves the same purpose

2   **Adjustments**: those to correct errors within the accounting system

3   **Discrepancies, unusual features or queries**: arising from reconciliation of the control account; from the age analysis; from the receipt of statements

Knowledge and Understanding

The Business Environment:
- Trade discounts and cash discounts

- Types of business transactions and documents involved
- Basic law of contract
- General principles of VAT

Accounting Techniques:
- Calculation facility, including use of equipment provided
- Methods of posting from primary records to ledger accounts
- Methods of coding data
- Operation of manual and computerised accounting systems
- Use of transfer journal

Accounting Principles and Theory:
- Functions of a ledger account system and main types of account
- Interrelationship of accounts – double-entry principles
- Function of primary records
- Distinction between capital and revenue expenditure (in general terms)
- Internal check, control and security principles

The Organisation:
- Background understanding that the accounting systems of an organisation are affected by its organisational structure, its administrative systems and procedures and the nature of its business transactions

Evidence Requirements

- Competence must be demonstrated consistently, over a period of time with evidence of performance being provided of goods and services received on credit being accounted for

Sources of Evidence

These are examples of sources of evidence, but candidates and assessors may be able to identify other, appropriate sources.

- **Observed performance**, e.g.
  - Transferring entries in the primary accounts to the ledger account
  - Transferring adjustments involving creditors' accounts to the ledger account
  - Reconciling the control account in the general ledger with the total of balances in the purchases (creditors) ledger
  - Communicating with creditors

- **Work produced by candidate**, e.g.
  - Primary records
  - Analysed purchases and returns day book
  - Ledger account
  - Authorised adjustments involving creditors' accounts
  - Control account in the general ledger
  - Written communications with creditors

- **Authenticated testimonies from relevant witnesses**

- **Personal accounts of competence**, e.g.
  - Report of performance

- **Other sources of evidence to prove competence or knowledge and understanding where it is not apparent from performance**, e.g.
  - Reports
  - Performance in simulation
  - Responses to verbal questioning

Index